THE EARLIEST ENGLISH POETRY

TO
MY MOTHER AND FATHER

THE EARLIEST
ENGLISH POETRY

A CRITICAL SURVEY

of the Poetry Written before the Norman Conquest
with Illustrative Translations

BY

CHARLES W. KENNEDY

With A New Foreword

by

JAMES P. PETTEGROVE

ROWMAN AND LITTLEFIELD
TOTOWA, NEW JERSEY

METHUEN & CO. Ltd.
LONDON

FOREWORD

Since its original publication in 1943, scholars, students, and enlightened laymen have studied, quoted and admired *The Earliest English Poetry*. The clarity of Professor Charles W. Kennedy's critical prose and the sheer beauty of his illustrative translations from Old English bear witness that this book is "the precious lifeblood of a master spirit."

Meantime a new generation has matured among us, a generation in search of deeper values. Members of this new order will find much in common with the poets of the reign of King Alfred; they will, perhaps, in the author's words, receive inspiration from "the antique grace and energy of the Christian allegories." Those who are puzzled by the violence today will read with sympathy of the tribulations of England in the eighth and ninth centuries.

Grendel and the fiery Dragon, Beowulf's adversaries, were once dismissed as wild folktales belonging to the days of yore. Yet, since the advent of intercontinental missiles, it is no longer difficult to share the sense of doom that hovered over the men who heard the original recitations of *Beowulf*. One can now, perhaps, accept Professor Tolkien's argument that doom is no less literary than "hamartia."[1]

In *The Earliest English Poetry* Professor Kennedy abandons the long prevailing view that Old English literature is not art but artefact, that it is historically valuable but aesthetically insignificant. "Of this Old English poetry," the author states, "much is excellent, some is timeless and immortal."[2] As a reader of this epitome of Old English poetry one tends to grow equally enthusiastic about the elegies, the allegories, and the battle poems; Professor Kennedy's appreciation comprehends all the genres. That his tastes were not mere impulses is evidenced by the titles of some of his publications: *The Legend of Juliana* (1906), *The Poems of Cynewulf* (1910), *Beowulf* (1940), and *Early English Christian Poetry* (1952 and 1963).

FOREWORD

The late Professor Kennedy was a specialist in-depth. The universality of his critical scholarship was commensurate with his catholicity of taste. His translations, freely interspersed through this book, are patterned so closely after the original poems that they are perceived as echoes across the valley of twelve centuries.

Charles William Kennedy, Murray Professor of English Literature at Princeton University, died on July 13, 1969. The reprinting of his single greatest contribution to our literary heritage thus becomes a fitting tribute to a great American scholar.

JAMES P. PETTEGROVE
Professor of English
Montclair State College

---

1. J. R. R. Tolkien, "Beowulf: The Monsters and the Critics," *Proceedings of the British Academy,* XXII (1936), pp. 245-95. See also, F. Cordasco, "The Old English Physiologus: Its Problems," *Modern Language Quarterly,* X (1949).

2. *The Earliest English Poetry* (1943), p. 351.

PREFACE

THE present volume offers a critical survey of Old English poetry, that is, of the vernacular verse composed in England from the seventh century to the Norman Conquest. In comparatively recent years an increasing body of critical research by many distinguished scholars has clarified our understanding of this poetry, of its cultural and literary backgrounds, its sources and analogues, its conformance to established literary types and conventions. In particular, studies of Scandinavian analogues, of classical and medieval source materials, and of the liturgical and patristic literature of the medieval Church, have gone far to identify the literary influences at work in some of these poems, and to correct earlier estimates which too often treated this vernacular poetry as the primitive and naïve product of untutored bards.

The present study attempts a re-appraisal of Old English verse by the light of this modern critical scholarship. At the innumerable points at which I am indebted to other scholars I have endeavored to indicate it in text and footnote. But there is a deeper sense in which one who writes of Old English verse must owe a silent unacknowledgeable debt to all students of the period whose massed labors from the beginning to the present day have steadily advanced our knowledge and understanding of these ancient texts.

Much of the material of Chapters III and IV of the present volume, by courtesy of the Oxford University Press, and the Princeton University Press, is reprinted from the Introductions to my translations of the *Beowulf*, and the *Elegies*. Throughout the volume I have included in the discussion of the various poems translations of selected passages chosen to outline narrative, or to illustrate poetic design. Except in one instance noted, these translations, a few in prose, the rest in alliterative verse, are my own.

In the general arrangement of the volume it has seemed wise to print as an appendix the detailed discussion of the manuscripts, the Cynewulfian signatures, and the unity and classical spirit of the second and third 'Storm' *Riddles*.

I take this opportunity to record with grateful appreciation my indebtedness:

To Dr. J. Duncan Spaeth, so long an inspiring teacher of Old English at Princeton, for my vivid memories of the spirited and illuminating scholarship with which he interpreted and translated this ancient verse;

To my colleagues, Professors Albert Elsasser, Gordon H. Gerould, and Henry Savage, of Princeton, for helpful suggestions in the solution of various critical problems, over a period of many years;

Lastly, to my wife, wise counselor and kindly critic, for continuous and devoted assistance during the progress of this work.

C. W. K.

Princeton, 1943

CONTENTS

CONTENTS

I. GERMANIC TRADITION

The Settlers; *Charms;* Runes; *Runic Poem;* Heroic Verse;
Influence of Christianity; Verse Form

ENGLISH poetry of the early Middle Ages constitutes one of
the richest medieval traditions in any modern European
tongue. The period which extended from the middle of the
seventh century to the end of the tenth has left us a body of verse
unique in its variety and literary excellence. It was the product
partly of an ancient culture which had come to England with the
Germanic Settlement of the fifth and early sixth centuries, and
partly of the transforming influences of the age in which it was
written, an age of change and growth during which Germanic
strains were slowly modified by the influence of medieval learning and the Latin culture of the Christian Church.

The successive waves of the Settlement had brought to England
a wealth of Continental tradition: myth and saga, folk-tale and
chronicle, legends long known among the Germanic tribes, and
now preserved and retold in England. A race does not easily lose
memory of its past, even in the dark centuries and on foreign soil.
Tradition may grow obscure with passing years, and alien strains
engraft themselves on ancient legend in strange and puzzling ways.
But tradition survives, and the past lives on. In the songs of the
early English, and the lays that enlivened their banquets, old
memories still lingered, famous names and heroic deeds of chronicle and legend. The singer was an English *scop*, but the song was
often of the Continental past. Through the dusk of their great
halls echoed the glory of heroes long dead: Attila the Hun and
Eormanric the Goth, Theodoric and his thanes, Hildeburh of
Finnsburg, Sigemund and Signy of the Volsungs, Walther of

Aquitaine and his lady Hildegund, Beowulf of the Geats, shapes of the dead rising in repeated resurrection as the gleeman sang.

With this body of tradition came also the secret learning of the wise men and the folk wisdom of the people: runic letters of mysterious meaning and power, magic charms against ill-fortune and disease, a folk-lore of herbs and simples, and the homely wisdoms of experience set forth in proverbs and gnomic verse. The Germanic Settlers carved their crude runic inscriptions on English stone and on the utensils and weapons of early English life. In rude verse they chanted their pagan charms to defend their fields from barrenness, and their bodies from the aches and pains of rheumatic winters. In danger and doubt they appealed to the gnomic wisdom of their fathers.

The Settlement brought simple codes of conduct and grim ways of life. The worship of the Germanic gods was a rude and savage cult. The ancient religious myths symbolized a titanic warfare between the kindlier forces of nature and those hostile powers by whose ruthless strength man's life and even the might of the gods themselves were menaced. In this crude mythology was little stress upon the gentler virtues, little room for meekness and mercy in the worship of Odin and Thor. Only when from the South some slight outreach of Christian influence emerged in Balder, the White God, were there seeds of change in the ancient savage cult. Fate brooded over all, a dark, inexorable power shrouded behind numbing hardship and mortal danger. To the living of life the strong man brought heroic courage and stoic endurance. Fate would sometimes spare, if valor held out. Courage and loyalty went hand in hand. But the uncertainties and dangers of life sharpened courage to a physical edge, and loyalties were directed to men rather than to ideas or institutions.

Loyalty to leader, as a central and pivotal tie, governed the relations of men. The spirit of the Germanic *comitatus*, with its reciprocal obligations of protection and reward on the one side and loyalty and service on the other, colors the material of many a passage in Old English verse, and survives undiminished as late as *Maldon*. It followed naturally that a retainer who had lost his lord was of all men most wretched, a lonely exile who could find no solace for his loss, no substitute for the tie that had been broken. The unforgettable lament of the *Wanderer* is the classic passage for illustration of so tragic a fate.

The *Germania* of Tacitus provides a vivid estimate of the characteristics of early Germanic tribal life, out of which grew many of the qualities which entered into the Settlement of England. The stress on courage, and the love of battle, reflected in so many passages of Old English verse, seem from the beginning to have been rooted in the Germanic strain. It was the custom for young men, even of distinguished birth, to attach themselves to the person of some leader of proved valor in whose service honor could be gained in war. If a particular tribe enjoyed a long period of peace, many of its members would volunteer for service with another tribe engaged in war, because, says Tacitus, 'they hate peace and can win honor more easily among dangers, and only by force and warfare can maintain their big body of followers.' Not only, therefore, were Germanic tribesmen by temperament haters of peace, but, in an economic sense, the seeds of war were constantly present in the organized needs of the *comitatus* group. They were less inclined to plough the earth and wait for a harvest than to challenge a foe because, according to Tacitus, 'they think it feeble to win with sweat what can be won with blood.'[1]

The social life of the Germanic tribes was organized around the family or clan. Their settlements, therefore, were small towns or villages rather than cities. They disliked homes built close together and lived in scattered groups as location pleased them. A man must participate in the feuds of his clan. This was binding duty. But even at the time Tacitus wrote, it was possible for these feuds to be

1. *Germania*, 14.

composed by payment for the injury done. 'Even homicide can be atoned by a certain number of cattle and sheep.'[2] Fortunately, the wholesale reciprocal violences of these tribal feuds were gradually diminished by this recognized right of 'compensation,' and there grew up a system of *wergyld* by which payments for a man's life according to his rank, as well as for injuries of various types and to the various members of the body, were fixed in law.[3]

Personal loyalty and group loyalty, then, were central in the moral code of the Settlers: loyalty to friend, to leader, and to clan. Injury or wrong suffered by a friend must be wiped out by vengeance. 'Better,' says Beowulf, 'that a man avenge his friend than mourn over him.'[4] Injury to a member of the clan demanded strict compensation by 'feudal' vengeance or *wergyld*. Loyalty to leader must be absolute. For a member of the *comitatus* to return alive from a battle in which his lord had fallen was 'lifelong infamy and disgrace.'[5] So interwoven in the social consciousness was this central concept of loyalty that the great tragic themes of Germanic tradition were those arising from irreconcilable conflicts of loyalty, as with Hildeburh of Finnsburg or Signy of the Volsungs.

The world of nature that hedged men about was stubborn and harsh. The years were reckoned by the passing of the winters. Darkness and cold, the freezing hardships of winter on land and sea, the haunting fear of danger lurking in the shadows after the sun was gone, these are themes that set the grim mood for much of the early verse. Yet the long severity of their winter months brought by contrast a joy in returning Spring, the 'sunny and shining days that ever observe their season,'[6] the time of 'greening meadows and blossoming earth, and the music of bird-calls.'[7]

---

2. Ibid. 16 and 21.
3. See Attenborough, *The Laws of the Earliest English Kings*, Cambridge, 1922.
4. *Beowulf*, 1384–5.
5. *Germania*, 14.
6. *Beowulf*, 1135–6.
7. *Guthlac A*, 742–6.

Not a few passages of Old English verse contain brief, vivid realisms of Spring mood which make them memorable.

From of old the Settlers were at home on the sea, ranging widely in all weathers in their long, dragon-prowed Viking ships. As is true of all experienced mariners, their love of the 'salt sea-streams' was tempered by a wholesome respect for the destructive might of ocean. One of the most memorable of the elegies, the *Seafarer*, celebrates at length, and with alternating stress, this bittersweet blending of love and fear. Although this elegy is the finest single sea-poem that has survived, Old English poetry is filled with superb descriptive passages dealing with sea-voyaging by night and day, in fair weather and foul.

Much in the world of nature was of course unknown and terrifying. Superstitious imagination peopled the dark with warlocks and witches, gnomes and trolls, a malign and haunting crew of evil spirits. In their malevolent and capricious interference in the lives of men was to be found, it seemed, the secret source of misfortunes such as sickness or loss of property, and of sudden tragic disasters for which no immediate cause seemed obvious. From this same mysterious nature were culled the means to combat such evils. Folk-knowledge of herbs and simples was blended with superstition in the fashioning of magic herbal decoctions used with rituals and formulas of transfer and exorcism.

The Settlement brought to England an extensive corpus of leechdoms[8] and charms,[9] and Old English records preserve rich traces of these ancient rituals. In many instances the pagan charms were strikingly altered by the gradually transforming influence of the Christian Church, and the sutures by which the ancient pagan and later Christian elements became united are often easily discernible. The *Charm for Barren Land* provides instances in point.

8. See Cockayne, *Leechdoms, Wortcunning and Starcraft of Early England*, London, 1864-6.

9. See Felix Grendon, 'The Anglo-Saxon Charms,' *Journal of American Folk-Lore*, xxii, pp. 105-237; reprinted with introduction and critical apparatus as *Anglo-Saxon Charms*, New York, 1930.

So extensive was this body of magic that most evils of Old English life had their appropriate exorcisms, or remedial ceremonial. The charms were of distinguishable types: herbal charms; amulet, or protective charms; and charms for transfer of disease or exorcism of disease-spirits. Many were intended to protect against the loss of property or injury to private possessions: charms against thieves, against loss of cattle or bees, against pestilence among herds and flocks, against hail and rough weather. Others were addressed to the preservation of health and the remedy of particular maladies: specific exorcisms, or transfer-charms, for a long list of diseases including rheumatism, fevers, dysentery, dyspepsia, palsy, snake-bite, epilepsy, idiocy, dumbness, and many others.

Naturally, as the Christian Church became established, its uncompromising rejection of this corpus of magic art made itself felt. But, following the policies advocated by Pope Gregory, the old pagan rites were combated not so much by policies of extermination as by a gradual policy of conversion. The names of pagan divinities were excised from the charms, and heathen elements replaced by Christian. The name of Woden has survived in one charm and suggestions of the Valkyries in others, but on the whole the Christianizing of the charms was far-reaching. Just as the heathen rites of Yule-tide were replaced by Christian ceremonial commemorating the birth of Christ, the pagan charms were recast. Invocation of heathen powers was replaced by supplication of God, the Trinity, angels, and saints. Pater Nosters, the Sanctus, portions of the Litany took the place of the ancient pagan formulas.

One of the most primitive of the charms is an incantation and herbal remedy for the sudden twinges and stabbing pains, probably rheumatic, which in the absence of medical knowledge were interpreted as the piercing of invisible little arrows shot into the flesh by malign and supernatural powers, the elves, hags, and hostile gods against whom men in their need appealed to sorcery. This charm displays the conventional elements of structure which characterized a typical specimen of the form: first, the prose recipe for a herbal remedy to be administered to the patient; then, the charm verses with their so-called 'epic' introduction and exorcising incantations:

Take feverfew, and the red nettle that grows in at the door, and plantain. Boil in butter.

> Loud was their rush   as they rode o'er the hill;
> Fierce was their mood   as they flashed through the land;
> Defend thee now   and be healed of this harm.
>   Out little spear,   if herein it be!
> I seized my buckler,   my shining shield,
> When the mighty women   assembled their strength,
> Speeding the flight   of their whining spears.
> I'll give them another   as good as they gave,
> A flying arrow   full in the front.
>   Out little spear,   if herein it be!
> A smith sat forging,   a little knife shaping,
> Fiercest of irons,   wondrous fell.
>   Out little spear,   if herein it be!
> Six smiths sat,   slaughter-spears shaping.
>   Out spear!   stay not in, spear!
> If a whit of iron   be lodged herein,
> The work of witches,   it shall melt away.
> Wert thou shot in fell,   or shot in flesh,
> Or shot in blood,   or shot in bone,
> Or shot in limb,   may thy life be unscathed.
> Wert thou shot of Esa,   or shot of elves,
> Or shot of hags,   now will I help thee!
> This to heal Esa-shot;   this to heal elf-shot;
> This to heal hag-shot;   now will I help thee!
> Let her fly to the mountain   who flung the spear;
> Be thou sound of head,   and helped of the Lord!

This charm, like many others, shows interweavings of pagan and Christian material. Such survivals, to borrow Brooke's

phrase, are like 'ill-rubbed palimpsests. The old writing con-
tinually appears under the new; the new is blurred by the old,
the old by the new. The heathen superstitions have Christian
clothing, and the Christian, heathen.'[10] The reference to the smith
in line 13 is a survival from the legend of Weland the Smith. The
'mighty women' of line 8, like the 'victory women' of the charm
for the swarming of bees, are perhaps a dim reflection of the
ancient Valkyrie myth.

The charm preserves the ancient structure and pattern in unique
degree. Particularly interesting are the four strophic repetitions of
the exorcising incantation, 'out little spear,' and the indication of
a triple administration of the herbal remedy corresponding to the
triple assault of Esa-shot, elf-shot, and hag-shot. Yet the evidences
of Christian conversion are clear enough. The reduction of the
Esa, or pagan gods, into a category with witches and malign
spirits is itself an indication of Christian influence, and the final
words conclude the charm with a Christian petition.

One of the most interesting of these ancient survivals is the
charm for remedy of barren land. Obviously, we have here to
do with a ritual rooted in pagan worship of the fertility of earth.[11]
The Old English charm was a composite of ancient pagan ceremonial with Christian elements in ritual and petition. Sods were
cut from the four corners of the field and on them were laid oil,
honey, yeast, milk of every kind of cattle, twigs of every kind of
softwood tree, and bits of all known herbs. The whole was
sprinkled with holy water, and Christian formulas were repeated.
The sods were then taken into the church and over them four
masses were sung. They were then returned to their places in the
field. Before the first furrow was driven the plough was consecrated, and the turning of the furrow was accompanied by the
recitation or chanting of the following incantation:

10. Brooke, *English Literature from the Beginning to the Norman Conquest*, London, 1905,
p. 42.
11. See Grendon, op. cit. p. 220, note.

Erce, Erce, Erce,   mother of earth,
May the Almighty One,   may the Eternal One,
Grant thee acres   flourishing and fruitful,
Acres bountiful,   acres sustaining;
Birth of bright   millet harvest,
Birth of broad   barley harvest,
Birth of white   wheat harvest,
And all the harvests of earth.

There are evidences in the ritual itself that portions of the incantation were probably derived from an ancient hymn to the sun god, and invocation of the earth-spirit. But the ancient elements have been overlaid with Christian material to such a degree that the charm as it has survived to us is in much of its detail a Christian rite.

Side by side with these ancient charms, Old English records have preserved for us, with certain changes, the mysterious runic characters which were known among the Germanic peoples of the Continent. The runes are found in inscriptions carved upon stone crosses such as those of Bewcastle and Ruthwell, and upon ornaments, utensils, and weapons such as the Charnay brooch, the Franks casket, and the Thames sword. They are found also in the manuscripts. In certain of the *Riddles* runes are employed, and in four Old English poems the poet Cynewulf used runic characters for his interwoven signature.

The runic alphabet was the oldest form of Germanic writing. It was in use at least as early as the third century, since runic inscriptions have been found in southwestern Denmark on ornaments and weapons of that period. The 24 runes of the Gothic alphabet, or *futhark,* were arranged in a fixed order in 3 groups of 8 letters. Each of the runic characters had its name, the first letter of that name establishing the phonetic value of the rune. Thus, in Old English the first rune bore the name *feoh,* the first letter of which determined the phonetic value of the rune as *f.*

The fixed order of the runes in their groups made possible cryptograms based on this established runic sequence. These cryptograms sometimes involved a shift from *futhark* to *uthark,* that is, a change of *f* from the first to the final, or twenty-fourth, position in the runic sequence, thus reducing by one the position-number of every other member of the runic series. In inscriptions, the runes were sometimes written from right to left, as in the text of *Riddle 20* of the Exeter Book where the runes for *horse, man,* and *hawk* are written in reverse order. The atmosphere of mystery which surrounded the runes in the minds of the unlearned may well have been increased by such cryptographic devices.

Much remains unknown, or uncertain, concerning the origin and early history of the runes. Some of the symbols seem obviously derivative from letters of the Roman and Greek alphabets. Their angular form may possibly reflect the difficulties of carving on wood and stone. Agrell in *Runor Talmystik* suggests that the runic characters were originated by Germanic soldiers in the Roman army who had come under the influence of the Mithra cult; that the *futhark* was devised for purposes of mystery and magic; and that the accepted order of the runic symbols was a disguise, the *f*-rune coming actually not at the beginning but at the end.

Whatever their origin, the runes not only found their way to England, but there increased in number as changing phonetic requirements demanded, the Old English sequence expanding ultimately to a total of 33. The continued use of the runes in England indicated by this increase in number is born out by the Old English *Rune Poem,* which defined, in stanzas of 2, 3, or 4 verses, the meanings of 29 runes.

The manuscript text of the *Rune Poem* was destroyed with other manuscripts in the Ashburnham House fire of 1731. Fortunately Hickes had made a copy, which he published in his *Thesaurus.* The poem is a comparatively late composition, belonging probably to the eighth or ninth century. It is hardly a literary composition, but represents a kind of alphabetic descriptive verse intended to facilitate memorization of the meaning of the several runes. Its stanzas conform to a type of poetic composition illustrated in alphabetic nursery rhymes, doggerel verses which rehearse the number of days in the several months, and similar versified arrangements of material for memorization. The nature of the *Rune Poem* can be easily illustrated by the following stanzas dealing with the eight runes used in the acrostic signatures of Cynewulf. In these signatures the runic letters stood out in the manuscript, forming the poet's name; the word values of the runes were a part of the text itself.

ᚻ cēn,
(C)   TORCH on fire, blazing and bright,
           Is known to all men; it burns most often
           Where nobles and princes repose within.

ᚣ yr,
(Y)   BOW is of princes and all the brave
           A joy and honor; trim on the steed,
           A warlike weapon, firm in the field.

ᚾ nȳd,
(N)   NEED weights the heart but is help and healing
           To the children of men, if they heed it in time.

ᛗ eoh,
(E)   HORSE is for heroes a prince's joy,
           The steed proud of hoof, when warriors round
           Great ones on chargers engage in counsel;
           Tis ever a comfort to restless hearts.

ᚹ wynn,
(W)   BLISS he delights in who has little of woe,
           Little pain or sorrow, himself possessing
           The abundance of cities, blessing and joy.

ᚢ ūr,
(U)   BULL is savage, with hornéd head,
           Beast very fierce; it fights with its horns,
           A haughty moor-stepper, a headstrong brute.

ᛚ lagu

(L)   WATER seems wearisome   to the sons of men
        If they needs must venture   in plunging ships,
        When greatly the sea-waves   fill them with fear
        And the ocean-stallion   suffers no bridle.

ᚠ feoh

(F)   WEALTH is a comfort   to all mankind;
        But a man must share it   in generous mood
        If his wish is to get him   glory with God.

The runes and charms were links with an ancient Continental past that furnished material for the Old English poetry which grew up in the regions north of the Humber. The settlement of northern England broke ground for the development of a North-umbrian culture signalized in the prestige of the School of York, in the widely influential scholarship of such men as Bede and Alcuin, and in a corresponding development of Old English poetry. Although the corpus of Old English pagan and Christian verse has survived in the West Saxon dialect, the marks of its Northumbrian origin are sufficiently clear.

The Germanic Settlers were not only good sailors, hard fighters, hard drinkers, but also lovers of song. The importance of the *scop,* or poet, in Old English life is attested by familiar passages in *Beowulf, Widsith,* and *Deor's Lament;* by Bede's reference to the custom of poetic extemporizing to the accompaniment of the harp; by the less familiar picture of Aldhelm singing the old songs to entice the people into church; and by Asser's account of Alfred's love of the Saxon songs. In the hall-gatherings of the Old English, when flaming torches and the song of the *scop* drove back the menace of the dark, the minstrel stirred their spirits with lays fashioned from chronicle and saga, tales of heroes and great deeds of the past when victory was hammered out by the edge of the sword. Such hours brought their deepest satisfactions of spirit as the past lived again in song, and called forth their proud boasts of courage and vows of endurance.

From the crude harps of Old English minstrels, as they chanted these traditions of the Continental past, our earliest poetry was born. Its spirit was set by the virtues of the Germanic code: loyalty, swift vengeance for wrong, heroic courage. Its themes were derived from ancient chronicle and saga unfolded against the primitive backgrounds of a crudely vigorous race, and embellished with simple realisms of nature unsubdued by man. Elements of Scandinavian folk-tale and chronicle are welded to make the story of Beowulf; *Widsith*, the song of a wandering minstrel, gives varied reflection of Continental traditions of the fourth, fifth, and sixth centuries. Two surviving fragments of the *Waldere* are portions of an epic tale of Walther of Aquitaine. The fragment of *Finnsburg*, and a minstrel's lay in *Beowulf* dealing with the same subject, set forth a dramatic description of an ancient feudal fight at the court of Finn, a Frisian king. The *Lament* of Deor, a minstrel who has lost favor with his lord, is a series of interwoven strands of ancient legend echoing the names of Weland the Smith, Theodoric, Eormanric, and other heroic figures of Continental record. The Sigemund lay of *Beowulf* indicates a knowledge, in eighth-century England, of a body of primitive tradition from which later developed the Norse *Volsungasaga* and the Middle High German *Nibelungenlied*.

Gradually, however, as a new spirit reflected the slow spread of medieval learning and the influence of Catholic Christianity, the early themes of Old English verse were supplemented and replaced by new elements. The gradual conversion of northern England during the seventh and eighth centuries brought with it an intellectual culture rooted in classical and ecclesiastical learning, and transmitted through the ascendancy of the medieval Church.

As time passed, this ecclesiastical influence had wide expression in the native poetry. Even in the retelling of ancient Germanic themes, the Christian spirit was often present, either as an element loosely appended to the pagan material, as in *Deor's Lament*, or pervasively present as a moulding and shaping influence, as in *Beowulf*. New themes were introduced. A religious poetry grew up dealing with Biblical and Apocryphal subjects, or based upon homiletic or liturgical material.

According to tradition[12] the earliest of the religious poets was a convert named Cædmon. In the third quarter of the seventh century in the monastery of Whitby, he was suddenly and miraculously endowed with poetic skill, composing a *Hymn* which has been preserved to us, and thereafter devoting himself to the writing of religious verse. The poems of the Junius MS., the *Genesis, Exodus, Daniel,* and *Christ and Satan,* were at one time regarded as authentic compositions of Cædmon. But, as we shall see later, it has become clear that these poems are not all of the same period, and their authorship remains uncertain.

The religious element in Old English verse received its next great impulse a century later in the work of the poet Cynewulf. Aside from certain autobiographic revelations contained in his writings, little is actually known of his life. As a result of his desire for the prayers of his readers we find his signature interwoven in runic letters in the text of four poems: *Christ II, Juliana, Elene,* and the *Fates of the Apostles.* His writings reveal ecclesiastical learning and a more sophisticated skill than the so-called Cædmonian poems, cover a wider range, and reflect New Testament rather than Old Testament material.

With the poems of Cynewulf came a growth and expansion in the religious poetry. Other poets began to write in the Cynewulfian manner, producing poems of extraordinary elevation of mood and vigor of imagination, poetry such as the magnificently descriptive painting of the Last Judgment in *Christ III* or the gentle narrative of the *Death of Guthlac,* the second of two poems dealing with an English hermit saint. New poetic types

12. See Bede's *Ecclesiastical History*, IV, 24.

emerged. The dream-vision governed the structure and spirit of the *Dream of the Rood*; Christian allegory received memorable illustration in the *Phoenix,* and in the *Panther, Whale,* and *Partridge* of the Old English *Physiologus.* The unknown poet of *Andreas* took *Beowulf* as his model and endeavored to fashion a legend of St. Andrew into the pattern of the heroic epic tale. The *Judith* was shaped in the same heroic mould. Scholarly Latin riddles circulating among the monasteries furnished the patterns for a poetic series of Old English *Riddles*, including superbly wrought 'Storm Riddles' which clothed traditions of meteorology as ancient as Lucretius.

Almost all of the Old English poetry which embodies these various pagan and Christian elements is of unknown or uncertain authorship, and of somewhat uncertain date. A few of the poems can be dated with some degree of probability. Cædmon's *Hymn* can be assigned to a date not far from 670. The spelling of Cynewulf's name in his runic signatures, as we shall see later, suggests the period from 750 to 800 for *Juliana, Elene, Christ II,* and *Fates of the Apostles.* The *Genesis B*, an interpolation in the text of *Genesis,* is probably later than the middle of the ninth century if its Old Saxon original is correctly dated at 830 or 840. The *Maldon* and *Brunanburh* were presumably written not long after the dates of the battles they commemorate, that is, 937 and 991. Broadly speaking, then, Old English poetry can be assigned to three general periods. *Beowulf* and the Cædmonian verse fall in a period before 750; the poems of Cynewulf and his imitators in the period between 750 and 850; and the *Genesis B, Judith, Maldon, Brunanburh,* and certain minor poems, in the period from 850 to the end of the tenth century. Except for a few scattered poems, this corpus of Old English verse has been preserved in four manuscripts which have come to be popularly known as the *Beowulf* MS., Exeter Book, Junius MS., and Vercelli MS.[13]

13. For description of these manuscripts see Appendix A.

This Old English poetry was composed in a flexible type of four-beat, alliterative verse, used by the Germanic peoples of the Continent, and imported by the Settlers into England. The use of this alliterative measure survived into the Middle English period; though rejected by Chaucer it was employed by the authors of such outstanding poems as *Piers Ploughman* and *Sir Gawayne*. But the quality of the alliterative rhythm deteriorated after the Conquest, and the four-beat, alliterative measure, in competition with other forms, gradually lost position as the standard type of poetic line.

In the Old English period, the recitation of this alliterative verse was accompanied by chords struck on a small harp, timed to mark the stressed beats of the rhythm. It is probable that a gradual falling off in the use of the harp, in the Post-Conquest period, was an influence making for deterioration in Middle English alliterative verse. Pope, in his recent illuminating study of the rhythm of *Beowulf*,[14] has shown convincingly that so intimately was the use of the harp associated with the recitation of this alliterative verse that the omission of a stressed syllable, corresponding to a rest in a bar of music, was compensated by a chord struck on the harp, and the flow of rhythm thereby preserved unbroken.

A normal line of Old English verse was composed of two half-lines separated by a strongly marked caesural pause. A half-line had two measures, each containing a strongly stressed syllable. It was the stressed syllables which established the rhythm and carried the alliteration. The two half-lines were bound together by the convention that one of the stressed syllables (usually the first) in the second half-line must alliterate with one or both stressed syllables in the first half-line.[15] Pope's analysis of the *Beowulf* rhythm shows that in the second half-line, if a rest and a

14. Pope, *The Rhythm of Beowulf*, New Haven, 1942. See especially pp. 88–95.
15. For clarifying and suggestive discussions of Old English metre see Gummere, *Handbook of Poetics*, Ch. vii; William Ellery Leonard, *University of Wisconsin Studies in Literature and Philology*, No. 2; and J. Duncan Spaeth, *Old English Poetry*, pp. 177–88.

chord of the harp replaced the first stressed syllable, the alliteration was carried by the second.

The strongly accented, alliterative rhythm and extended caesural pause which are characteristic of Old English verse, driving home the thought as with hammer blows, may be illustrated by well-known lines from the *Battle of Maldon*:

> Híge sceal þē héardra,   héorte þē cénre,
> Mōd sceal þē māra   þē ūre mǽgen lýtlað.

> Heart must be the hardier,   courage the keener,
> Mood must be the bolder, as our band lessens.

It was usually, though by no means invariably, true that in the Old English poetic line, logical stress and poetic stress coincided. In typical instances, therefore, the result was a vigorous and strongly welded rhythmic pattern naturally and easily adapted to the accompaniment of the harp. Moreover, the danger of monotony in the use of such a poetic line throughout a long poem was successfully avoided by devices which created variation and flexibility within the standard pattern. Though the number of stressed syllables was fixed, the number of unstressed syllables in the half-line varied greatly, in *Beowulf* ranging from two to ten. There was constant variation in the relative positions of the stresses within the half-line, and a convention of subordinate stresses brought to the flow of rhythm delicate and subtle currents of adaptation and change.

The use of rhyme in Old English verse, while not unknown, was infrequent. Its occurrence here and there may reflect an influence of the rhyming Latin hymns familiar to ecclesiastical writers. When used in Old English poems, rhyme was confined within the structure of the alliterative line, and employed to unite the half-lines. In a passage of 15 lines near the end of the *Elene*,[16] Cynewulf makes use of rhyme in this manner, and a more

16. ll. 1237-51.

extended use of it is found in the 87 lines of the *Rhyme Poem* of the Exeter Book.[17] In a few other poems it is present in brief passages.

A unique characteristic of Old English verse is the conventional use of repetition, accompanied by variations of form, to add stress to an important concept. This element in Old English poetic style may in some degree reflect the fact that our early poetry was chiefly addressed to the ear through oral recitation. In such a tradition, devices of repetition and variation which, to a modern reader, suggest redundancy, were potent aids to listeners in moments of faulty hearing or misunderstanding. Of such devices of variation the most frequent and most effective is the use of the so-called *kenning*. In its less inspired use, the *kenning* is little more than a phrasal synonym for a concept already mentioned, as when a ruler is called 'prince of heroes,' or 'lord of men.' But skillfully handled, the *kenning* often took on the form of compressed, vivid statement of a highly original image, as when, for example, the ocean is referred to as the 'whale's path,' or 'gannet's bath,' or 'sea-monster's home.' Not infrequently the *kenning* represents a reduction to brief, conventional phrasing of a widely accepted poetic metaphor, as when a king is called the 'shepherd of heroes,' or the body referred to as 'life's house,' and the soul as 'life's treasure.'

This poetry of the Old English period, then, was the poetry of a new, gradually developing culture in which the Germanic tradition became fused with, and enriched by, the Christianized Latin culture of the ancient world, forming a durable amalgam which has been an element in English poetry to the present day. The completeness of this fusion is unmistakable in a poem like *Beowulf*, or a character like Alfred. They are the authentic symbols of the new cultural order, despite poems like the *Finnsburg Fragment* in which the Christian element seems quite lacking, or the

17. Fols. 94-5.

Phoenix in which conventional Christian allegory shows little influence of the Germanic strain.

A distinguishing characteristic of this Old English poetry is its prevailing mood—a sober dignity, and a melancholy recognition of the tragic seriousness of life. There was little room for the trivial or frivolous in Old English life or letters. There was little place for humor, unless we except those sudden ironic flashes, which, more often than not, increase rather than diminish the stoic gravity of tone. Here and there in certain of the *Riddles* are touches of coarse humor or leering scurrility. But they are infrequent, and not characteristic of Old English poetry as we know it elsewhere.

This poetic mood of grave dignity and melancholy is hardly to be explained, as Taine and others have attempted to do, as a result of climate or the grim severities of life. It is something deeper and more profound, firmly rooted in character and in a continuous awareness of Fact and Necessity as unescapable, shaping forces in the lives of men. In this world one does what one can, and what one must. What one can may not be enough. What one must may lead to disaster. The age, like all others, had its faults but wishful thinking was not one of them. This stoic realism of spirit reached its most poignant expressions in those tragic oppositions of conflicting loyalties which permitted no resolution, and in whose toils the individual was torn and helpless in defeat. Such was often the fate of their women who, given in marriage as inter-tribal 'peace-weavers,' had no strength to prevail against sudden and volcanic renewals of feudal violence. Such was the fate of Signy of the Volsungs and Hildeburh of the Danes. Such, Beowulf prophesied, would be the fate of Freawaru.

And yet, though ages were to pass and many changes come before Britain became 'Merrie England,' the grimness of the Old English mood has often been overstressed. Life had its varied interests, and its pleasant ceremonial. Hall-joy and the gracious strains of minstrelsy brightened many an hour. The gay advent of Spring, the 'sunny and shining days' when the note of the cuckoo sounded from the woodland, and the ocean-ways were once more safe for voyaging, of these things the poets wrote, if briefly, still with delight. Of love as the Romantic poets have sung of it we hear no word; but a lover's long years of loyal memory, and a wife's ceaseless yearning for the husband who does not return, enrich the lines of the *Husband's Message* and the *Wife's Lament*.

If the strains of courtly and scholarly verse have little to say of the domestic scene or pastoral setting, one nevertheless finds buried in the *Charms* and *Riddles* and *Crafts of Men* traces of the homespun detail that made up the common life. These poems contain material which supplements the traditional themes of the heroic and religious verse, and affords many a brief hint of the life of homestead and countryside. Here it is that we meet the numerous symbols of domestic routine, charms for the healing of live-stock and prevention of plagues, the tools and utensils of household and farm, the friendly and favorite trees whose woods served various special needs, animals and birds of mountain, meadow, and sea whose ways the Settlers noted with sharply observing eye, the discipline of weather and stubborn soil, and here and there the long roll-call of the cunning skills of men who settled a land, and fashioned a way of life, and fought to hold it.

II. CONTINENTAL BACKGROUNDS

Widsith; *Deor*; *Waldere*; *Finnsburg*; the *Sigemund lay*;
Wulf and Eadwacer

CERTAIN poems in the corpus of Old English verse furnish
evidence of the extent to which Englishmen of the seventh
and eighth centuries still preserved race memories rooted in Germanic tradition, and continued to enrich their poetry by borrowings from Continental legend and Continental annals. Not only
in the Scandinavian backgrounds of the *Beowulf* do we have testi-
mony to this surviving influence of the Continental past, but also
in other poems such as the *Widsith* and the *Deor,* the *Waldere* and
the *Finnsburg* fragment. These poems afford ample indication of
the way in which the early poetry of England continued to reflect
rich glints of the soil from which it sprang.

It is significant, moreover, that this precious material is usually
embedded in early English poetry with a brief, though pregnant,
allusiveness which suggests that the legends of the Germanic heroic
age were not only widely known in early England, but well
known. For it is frequently true that the Old English poet, in
introducing such themes, considers it unnecessary to outline an
episode or detail an allusion, a tendency that not infrequently
produces passages of tantalizing obscurity for the modern reader.
But just as a brief allusion to the cynical evil of Iago, or the filial
ingratitude of Goneril and Regan, will suggest to a modern reader
all the dark unfolding of the tragic stories of *Othello* and *King Lear,*
so in our earliest poetry these bald allusions to famous names or
tragic episodes in Continental saga undoubtedly served to quicken
in the listener's mind the historic or tragic implications of the
material upon which the poet drew. How rich was this Conti-

23

nental heritage is indicated by even the briefest glance at a glossary of the proper names found in the *Beowulf* and the *Widsith*, names suggestive of the interplay of heroic legend throughout the Continent from east to west, and from Italy to the wide north.

WIDSITH

Of the poems that reflect this Continental background undoubtedly the richest in the range and variety of its allusions is the *Widsith*,[1] a poem of 143 lines preserved in the Exeter Book.[2] A careful reading of the poem becomes a study of Continental heroic legend as reflected in an Old English poem. A detailed interpretation involves a survey of Continental chronicle and legend of the fourth, fifth and sixth centuries.[3]

The *Widsith* is the song of a wandering minstrel, a typical strolling singer of the Germanic heroic age, who fared from court to court delighting princes and nobles with his singing, and receiving the minstrel's reward of rich gifts of treasure in the hall. The most socially significant elements of the poem have to do with his travels and with the famous tribes and rulers he has known. Central in the tale of his wanderings is an account of his visit to the Gothic court of Eormanric. The poem is a carefully composed fiction, presenting an ideal portrait of the wandering *scop*. As the allusions of the poem range from the third to the sixth centuries, no actual Widsith could have known and visited all the heroic figures he mentions.

The structure of *Widsith* presents many interesting but baffling problems. The poem is certainly early in date, and seems to be in some degree a composite of old and new matter. The most careful

1. In its 143 lines, the *Widsith* passes in review some 70 Continental tribes and an equal number of heroic figures of chronicle and legend.

2. Exeter Book, fol. 84b–87a.

3. For detailed discussion and interpretation of the poem, see R. W. Chambers, *Widsith, a Study in Old English Heroic Legend*, Cambridge, 1912: and Kemp Malone, *Widsith*, London, 1936.

analysis of its structure and the most conservative view of its unity are to be found in Malone's edition.[4] Even a cursory reading of the poem will reveal indications of sectional divisions, and in some instances these divisions suggest welding of older and newer materials. The body of the poem comprises three name-lists, four sections in expansion of the name-lists, and five lyrical sections.[5]

The opening lines introduce Widsith as a much travelled minstrel of good lineage who has once visited the court of Eormanric:

> Widsith spoke,   his word-hoard unlocked,
> Who most had travelled   of men on earth
> Among many peoples,   and prospered in hall
> With splendid treasure.   His forebears sprang
> From the Myrging tribe.   In his earliest travels
> With Ealhild he went,   fair weaver of peace,
> From the East out of Angle   to Eormanric's home,
> Who was lord of the Goths,   and a loather of traitors.
> Many a tale   he told of his travels:
> 'Much have I learned   of the rulers of men!
> A prince must live   by custom and law,
> Each in succession   ruling the realm,
> If he wishes his power   to prosper and thrive.'

The poetic promise of this beginning is not immediately developed. The theme of *Widsith* is suspended in tantalizing fashion, and the poem becomes a chanted catalogue of the names of famous kings and their peoples, continuing to the mention of Offa and Alewih in line 35. Lines 18 to 35, indeed, are pure metrical catalogue, the naming of two kings and two tribes to the poetic line establishing the normal pattern of the passage.

4. Malone, *Widsith*, Introduction, pp. 1-49.
5. Introductory lines (1-13); a catalogue of kings ending with the Offa and Heorot episodes (14-49); the body of the poem, comprising the Guthhere, Ælfwine, and Eormanric material interwoven with a list of peoples visited by Widsith (50-111); a catalogue of the followers of Eormanric, including the Wulfhere and Wudga-Hama episodes (112-130); concluding lines (131-143). Cf. Malone, *Widsith*, pp. 1-2.

> Attila ruled the Huns,   Eormanric the Goths,
> Gifica the Burgundians,   Becca the Banings;
> Caesar ruled the Greeks,   Cælic the Finns,
> Hagena the Rugians,   Heoden the Glomman;
> Witta ruled the Swæfe,   Wada the Hælsings,
> Meaca the Myrgings,   Marculf the Hundings,
> Theodoric the Franks,   Thyle the Rondings,
> Breca the Brondings . . .

And so the passage continues for ten more lines in unbroken bald enumeration of peoples and kings. It would seem that we have here an example of a type of mnemonic verse familiar in epic and in folk poetry, and composed for purposes of memorization and memorial. It is to be noted that in the eighteen lines of the catalogue of kings there is no statement that Widsith visited these rulers, and this passage must be differentiated, therefore, from the later passage (57–87) in which he names the peoples among whom he sojourned in his travels.

It seems probable that the catalogue of kings is older than the *Widsith* proper and that it was caught up and incorporated in the poem, perhaps by the poet of *Widsith*, perhaps through the ingenuity or misunderstanding of a later scribe.[6] It is possible that there are other passages in the poem which represent later interpolation. Certainly the references to the Israelites, Assyrians, Hebrews, Indians, and Egyptians as peoples visited by Widsith fall strangely on the ear in this context. Chambers lists 46 lines which may perhaps be considered later interpolations.[7] Malone's more conservative view restricts the number to eight.[8]

Many names from the rich catalogues of the *Widsith* recur

6. 'The catalogue of kings is older than Widsith *proper*, yet on account of the names it contains it can hardly be earlier than the middle of the sixth century, and may be considerably later. *Widsith* seems to belong to a period later than this, but earlier than *Beowulf* . . . that is, to the seventh century.' R. W. Chambers, *Widsith* p. 178. Cf. also pp. 134–5, 150, 176.

7. Op. cit. Introduction, p. 152.

8. ll. 14–17; 82–3; 114, 118. Cf. Malone, *Widsith*, p. 7.

in other Old English heroic poems. Breca of the Brondings (l. 25) and Withergyld of the Heathobards (l. 124) are important figures in two famous episodes of the *Beowulf*. Wudga and Hama, mentioned near the end of the *Widsith* in terms of special praise, we meet again, Wudga in the *Waldere*, Hama who carried off the Brising necklace, in the *Beowulf*. An early passage in the *Widsith* (45–9) recalls the bitter feud between the Danes and Heathobards so graphically outlined in Beowulf's account of his Danish adventures.[9]

In spite of the involved structure of the poem the *Widsith* remains essentially a 'type' or 'character' portrait of the ideal Germanic wandering *scop*. The versified lists of tribes and rulers that flow from the poet's pen are something more than bare bone, and serve to suggest realistically the wide ways and ample horizons known to the traveling minstrel whose varied experience and mastery of his art brought him welcome at many a court, and in distant lands made his name familiar in the ears of men.

The ideal *scop* must have traveled long and far, singing with the poignant realism that comes from personal contact with great heroes, and from wide knowledge of saga and chronicle. As Malone has well said: 'the perfect *scop*, like Chaucer's perfect knight, must have seen the world, and wherever he went must have won praise in high quarters. Most important of all, he must tell of heroic deeds with the authority which only the eyewitness can bring to the telling.[10]

Against this suggested background of personal experience involving the many richly interwoven themes of Continental legend the lyric lines of Widsith celebrate the glory of his craft, and his pride in rich gifts from the hands of the heroic great:

> I fared through many   a foreign land
> Over spacious earth,   knowing weal and woe,

9. *Beowulf*, 2020–2069.
10. Malone, *Widsith*, p. 11.

Bereft of kinsmen   and far from my folk,
Widely wandering   over the world.
Many a song   and many a story
I can tell in the meadhall,   recounting to men
How princes and nobles   graced me with gifts . . .
I was with Eormanric;   all the while
The king of the Goths   was gracious and kind.
He gave me a ring,   the ruler of cities,
Worth six hundred sceats   counted in cost
Of shilling pieces   of smelted gold.
To Eadgils I gave it,   my gracious lord,
To requite his kindness,   when home I came;
For the lord of the Myrgings   had granted me land,
The holding and home   of my father before me.
And Ealhild gave me   another ring,
The fair folk-queen,   the daughter of Eadwine.
To many a people   her praise I published
Whenever in song   my task was to tell
Of a gold-decked queen   most kind under heaven,
Best and most gracious   in giving of gifts.
There Scilling and I   in echoing strains
Before our dear lord   lifted our songs;
Loud to the harp   the lay resounded,
And many a noble   who knew aright
Said he had never   heard better song.[11]

Here is a self-portrait of the ideal wandering minstrel, with mind filled with memories of many men and many lands, with joy in song, and pride in the precious marks of honor bestowed upon him by such royal givers as Gunther and Alboin, Ealhild and Eormanric.

Who Scilling may have been we do not know. It would be pleasant to believe, as has been suggested, that Widsith is naming his harp as warriors named their swords. For it would be difficult to find words more suggestive of the intimate, almost personal, affection of the minstrel for the harp which is the instrument of

11. *Widsith*, 50–56; 88-108.

his craft than the simple phrase, 'we two, Scilling and I'. More probably, however, we have here the name of a companion *scop* who sang with Widsith before his lord as two minstrels once sang together at the court of Attila.

The poet of the *Widsith* has left us a memorable and priceless depiction of the minstrel type and the minstrel life as known to the Germanic heroic age. And, lest his hearers misunderstand, he concludes his song with an epilogue which sums up in vivid, lyric lines the lure of the minstrel's craft and his dignity in the scheme of Continental life:

> Widely they wander   as Fate may guide,
> The strolling singers   who roam the world,
> Telling their need,   returning their thanks,
> And always finding,   or south or north,
> Some great one skilled   in knowledge of song
> Who is open-handed   in giving of gifts,
> Who seeks for honor,   and strives for fame,
> Till light and life   shall vanish together.[12]

It is easy for the modern mind to fall short in estimation of the high function and important service of the strolling minstrel in the early Germanic world. A modern age, in which news of tragedy and heroism circles the world with electric speed, in which the great legends of all lands are safely indexed upon library shelves, and in which the singing strains of instrument and voice are impressed in wax for all men to renew at will, such an age is infinite removes of distance from the dark stillness of the heroic age. The minstrels had service which cannot be paralleled today. Where they came they brought news of foreign courts and famous heroes. Their songs brought near at hand and into vividness events that were remote in distance and time. Their recitations were memorials. Their music gladdened the hall and quickened rude

12. *Widsith*, 135–42.

revels with the touch of grace. Lords and rulers were their sponsors, and the generous gifts of prince to singer were a patronage of the poetry and song which preserved this ancient material of chronicle and legend.

DEOR

It is a matter of good fortune that the *Widsith* should have preserved for us so spirited a picture of the minstrel life. But it is an equal good fortune that a companion-piece should have survived the centuries, a poem which has come to be known, from the name of the minstrel-poet, as *Deor*, or *Deor's Lament*. Its stanzas present in suggestive outline the tragic misfortune of a minstrel who has lost the favor of his lord, and has been supplanted by another.

This lyric of 42 lines, like the *Widsith*, is from the Exeter Book.[13] The lines of *Deor* are divided into six sections of varying length, each strophe concluding with the refrain: *That evil ended, so also may this*. Because of this verse form, *Deor* stands out among Old English poems with unique importance. It is equally noteworthy for its reflection of Continental legends.

We do not know who wrote *Deor*, as we do not know who wrote *Widsith*. The poet in each case has given his minstrel's name: Widsith the far-travelled, Deor the noble. But just as the *Widsith* seems obviously a poetic fiction, so it is possible that in *Deor* the poet is not rehearsing actual event, but is portraying in ideal form the pathetic fate of a minstrel surpassed in skill and supplanted in favor. The question has arisen whether both poems may be the work of the same poet, companion-pieces intentionally contrasted but affording in their combined suggestion a rounded depiction of the glory and the heartbreak of the minstrel life. Certainly the two poems resemble each other in the wide wealth of Continental legend reflected in their lines, and in a close-knit

13. Exeter Book, fol. 100a–b.

and ingenious integration of structure. But the evidence indicates that *Widsith* is earlier than *Deor*, and the treatments of the character and rule of Eormanric in the two poems seem variant and difficult to reconcile with a theory of single authorship.

The minstrel of our poem represents himself as a *scop* named Deor who was once the court-singer of the Heodenings.[14] For many years he enjoyed pleasant service under a gracious lord, but was ultimately displaced by Heorrenda, a skillful bard who took from him the 'landright' which in former days his lord had given him. Deor minimizes his ill-fortune by allusion to historic or legendary instances of misfortune and disaster familiar to those who might hear his verses. Each strophic rehearsal of ancient sorrow or wrong including the last, in which he chants his own humiliation, ends with the refrain already quoted. As Weland and Beadohild, Theodoric and the subjects of Eormanric, had conquered calamity, so also might others endure and surmount an adverse fate. The poem is not merely a lament of Deor for his own misfortune but, as Lawrence points out,[15] a '*Consolatio Philosophiae* of minstrelsy,' an exhortation to stoic courage and triumphant endurance addressed to all men everywhere who suffer under adverse fate.

> This is for all ill-treated fellows,
> Unborn, and unbegot.

The first three strophes of the poem draw their material from the legend of Weland the Smith,[16] and depend for clearness upon the reader's knowledge of the story. The opening lines refer in general terms to the afflictions Weland endured, and are followed by allusions to specific details of the legend:

14. The people of Heoden (Hethinn) mentioned by Saxo, and in the prose *Edda* of Snorri Sturleson. Cf. Chambers, *Widsith*, pp. 100 ff.
15. *Modern Philology*, ix, 23–45.
16. See Maurus, 'Die Wielandsage,' *Münchener Beiträge*, xxv, 7–57.

Weland knew fully   affliction and woe,
Hero unflinching   enduring distress;
Had for companionship   heartbreak and longing,
Wintry exile   and anguish of soul,
When Nithhad bound him,   the better man,
Grimly constrained him   with sinewy bonds.
That evil ended,   so also may this!
Nor was brother's death   to Beadohild
A sorrow as deep   as her own sad plight,
When she knew the weight   of the child in her womb,
But little could know   what her lot might be.
That evil ended,   so also may this!
Many have heard   of the rape of Hild,
Of her father's affection   and infinite love,
Whose nights were sleepless   with sorrow and grief.
That evil ended,   so also may this![17]

Obviously, to appeal to these lines as exemplifying tragic misfortune and giving point to the refrain, *That evil ended, so also
may this,* the poet must have assumed a widespread familiarity
with the legend which would make detailed narrative unnecessary. This bare skeleton of allusion takes on form and substance
from a comparison of this portion of *Deor* with the corresponding
section of the *Vølundarkviþa.* There we are told how Nithhad,
coveting the rich treasure of Weland, attacked and hamstrung the
smith and robbed him of his wealth, including a precious ring
which Nithhad gave to his daughter, Beadohild. Weland was
then compelled to labor at the king's command. An opportunity
for revenge arose when Nithhad's sons visited the smith in secret.
Weland slew them both, and of their skulls fashioned drinking
vessels for the king's table. Subsequently when Beadohild, having
broken the ring, brought it to the smith for repair, Weland over-
came her with drugged wine, and violated her. The child of this
union, a son, was the Widia, or Wudga, of the *Waldere* and *Wid-*

17. *Deor,* 1-17.

sith. The first three strophes of *Deor*, in brief outline, clearly suggest this well-known tradition of tragic wrong.[18]

The fourth strophe of *Deor* is a very brief allusion to the legend of Theodoric (Dietrich von Bern)[19], and the fifth recalls the cruel reign of Eormanric, king of the Goths.[20] Each figure, directly or indirectly, suggests the virtue of stoic fortitude to which the poet exhorts. Theodoric, because of his thirty years of exile and the loss of his knights, came to be cited as a type of endurance in the face of undeserved disaster. Under Eormanric's cruelty many men suffered and 'prayed for the overthrow of his power.'

The final strophe, in which Deor rehearses his own misfortunes, draws upon still another of the Germanic legends which had drifted to England from the Continent. The key to the allusion lies in two proper names. Deor tells us that he was once a minstrel among the Heodenings, and that he was ultimately displaced by another bard named Heorrenda. The Heoden-Hagena (Hethinn-Hogni) story is found in Saxo Grammaticus, in the prose *Edda* of Snorri Sturleson, and in various Scandinavian and Icelandic sagas. According to the version given by Snorri, King Hogni of the Hjathningar (Heodenings) had a daughter named Hild who was carried off by Hethinn, son of Hjarrandi (Heorrenda). Following

18. This revenge of Weland is carved on the front of the famous Franks Casket in the British Museum. There Weland is represented at his anvil holding in his tongs the head of one of Nithhad's sons. Directly facing the smith stands the figure of Beadohild. In the background, holding two birds by their necks, is a figure which has been identified as Egil, Weland's brother, who shot birds in order that of their feathers Weland might fashion wings with magic power of flight. An archer carved upon the top of the casket has been identified as this same Egil. See 'The Franks Casket,' A. S. Napier, *An English Miscellany*, pp. 362–81. For detailed discussion of the carvings on the casket see the articles of P. W. Souers in the following volumes of the *Harvard Studies and Notes in Philology and Literature:* 'The Top of the Franks Casket,' vol. xvii, 163–79; 'The Franks Casket: Left Side,' vol. xviii, 199–210; 'The Magi on the Franks Casket,' vol. xix, 249–54.

19. Cf. Chambers, *Widsith*, pp. 36–44. Kemp Malone (*Deor*, London, 1933, pp. 9–13) would identify Theodoric with the Wolfdietrich of German legend, the oldest son of Clovis, himself king at Rheims, 511–34.

20. Cf. Chambers, *Widsith*, pp. 15–40; 48–55.

the fleeing Hethinn as far as Norway and there learning that he had put to sea, Hogni took ship and overtook him at the island of Hoy in the Orkneys. In spite of the intercession of Hild, battle was joined and continued day after day. Each dawn, broken weapons were made whole and the dead arose to fight again. 'And it is told in songs,' remarks Snorri, 'that the Hjathningar shall so abide till Doomsday.' In this version of the story, it will be noted, Heorrenda is the father of Heoden and not a minstrel. But this same legend is the theme of the High German poem, *Kudrun*, in which occur references to the sweet singing of the minstrel Horant, a name which is obviously a variant of Hjarrandi-Heorrenda.

It would seem that there must have circulated in England some version of this legend resembling the later *Kudrun* story in establishing Heorrenda as a famous minstrel. In this setting the Old English poet has developed the tragic story of Heorrenda's displacement of Deor, a theme as old as rivalry, the theme of the bitter humiliation of the superseded.

Deor's memories of past unhappiness are still sharp but the bitterness is gone. That evil also is in some measure ended. He can tell his own disastrous story and use it to assure his hearers that no evil outlives time. His tale is for all the ill-fated, all who suffer the sharpness of outrageous fortune, that they also may learn the kindly truth that time like a poultice allays the fever and draws the pain.

> He who knows sorrows,   despoiled of joys,
> Sits heavy of mood;   to his heart it seemeth
> His measure of misery   meeteth no end.
> Yet well may he think   how oft in this world
> The wise Lord varies   his ways to men,
> Grants wealth and honor   to many an earl,
> To others awarding   a burden of woe.
> And so I can sing   of my own sad plight
> Who long stood high   as the Heodenings' bard,
> Deor my name,   dear to my lord.

Mild was my service   for many a winter,
Kindly my king   till Heorrenda came,
Skillful in song,   and usurping the land-right
Which once my gracious lord   granted to me.
That evil ended,   so also may this![21]

The story of Deor has lost nothing of its pathos with the passing of the centuries. The colors of the rich frame of ancient tradition in which it is set have dimmed, and the outlines have faded.
But even a modern reader will be aware of the skill with which
the poet has selected his material from these tales of sorrow and
bitter wrong, and reshaped it into a song of consolation and a
lyric exhortation to stoic fortitude in the presence of adverse
Fate.

WALDERE

Two other Old English poems, which have survived only in
fragmentary form, furnish startling illustration of an incalculable
loss of early poetic material. These poems, the *Waldere* and the
Finnsburg fragment, are not included in any of the famous codices
in which the bulk of Old English poetry is preserved, but have
survived in each instance through connection with a collection
of homilies.

The *Finnsburg* fragment was discovered by Hickes as part of the
binding of a manuscript of homilies in the Library of Lambeth
Palace. A transcription of it was published in his *Thesaurus* of
1705. Unfortunately, the manuscript has since been lost and the
text rests today solely on Hickes's transcription.

The two sheets of parchment which contain the fragments of
the *Waldere* were discovered by Werlauff in 1860 among loose
papers in the National Library at Copenhagen. They had at one
time served as fly leaves for a volume of little regarded sermons.
How they may have drifted to Denmark, is not known, though it

21. *Deor,* 28–42.

has been suggested that they were possibly acquired by the Danish scholar, Thorkelin, at the time he made his transcript of the *Beowulf*.

The *Finnsburg* and *Waldere* fragments are portions of poems which dealt with two of the most dramatic of Continental legends at full length, and in the heroic spirit. The *Finnsburg* must have been a lay of such spirited mood as would have endeared it to minstrel and hallmen alike. The *Waldere*, judged by the scope and design of its surviving lines, may well have been an extended narrative in the heroic manner worthy of comparison with the *Beowulf* itself. Whether these poems were heedlessly sacrificed to make fly leaves for the binding of homilies, or whether, when they had been all but wholly destroyed in other ways, their few remaining and little regarded folios were put to this use, who can say? In any case, it is impossible to read the superb lines of these fragmentary survivals without a sense of tragic loss.

The *Waldere,* like the *Widsith* and *Deor,* is an English reflection of Continental legend. Themes which we have already noted in *Deor* are here repeated in the references to Weland the Smith, and the Theodoric saga.[22] The two fragments of text are remnants of an epic narrative dealing with the story of Walther of Aquitaine. These fragments are of 32 and 31 lines respectively and, except for 4 lines of narrative, are portions of speeches in the heroic mood and of high poetic excellence. Fortunately, these 63 lines are rich in proper names, some 12 in all, and of these the names of Aetla (Attila), Guthhere (Gunther), Waldere (Walther), and Hagena (Hagen) serve immediately to identify the subject matter.

The story of Walther of Aquitaine, of which the Old English fragments are brief portions, has survived in Latin, Middle High

22. Chambers (Widsith, p. 42) cites also a reference to Theodoric in the old English *Martyrology* (ed. Herzfeld; E.E.T.S., p. 84), *þæt wæs Theodoricus se cyning þone we nemnað þeodric,* which seems to him 'conclusive evidence for the existence of vernacular tradition respecting Theodoric in England at the date when the *Martyrology* was written; that is to say the ninth century.'

German, Old Norse, and other versions. Among these, the tenth-century Latin *Waltharius,* because of its age and the scope and detail of its narrative, has a special importance.[23]

The *Waltharius* is a narrative poem of 1,456 hexameter lines, composed in the early years of the tenth century by a monk Ekkehard of the Swiss monastery of St. Gall. It is believed that the Latin poem was based on an early Germanic original dealing with the Walther and Hildegund story. However that may be, the *Waltharius* is, except for the *Waldere* fragments, the oldest of surviving versions, and accords most accurately with historic events and geographic details involved in Attila's invasion of western Europe, and the ultimate defeat of the Huns.

As set forth in the *Waltharius,* Attila in his invasion of the West had marked his conquests by exaction of noble hostages: Hagen from the Franks; Hildegund, daughter of King Hereric, from the Burgundians; and Walther, son of King Ælfhere, from the Aquitanians. For some time these three lived happily at Attila's court. Walther and Hildegund were affianced, and Walther and Hagen became comrades and captains in the army of the Huns.

When Gunther became king of the Franks and refused to continue the Frankish tribute to Attila, the position of Hagen grew difficult and he fled to join Gunther. Later Walther and Hildegund also escaped, carrying with them precious treasure taken from the Huns. When after fourteen days of weary travel they reached the river Rhine, the ferryman brought word to Gunther of the great war-horse Walther rode and the rich treasure he carried. Gunther, claiming the treasure as Frankish tribute, swore to recover it.

With twelve warriors, Hagen among them, Gunther rode out at dawn and came upon Walther and Hildegund in a rocky pass of the Vosges. Gunther refused Walther's offer of peace, and a battle began, though Hagen, caught in a conflict of loyalties, in

23. For detailed analysis and discussion of the various versions, and their inter-relationships, see M. D. Learned, 'The Saga of Walther of Aquitaine,' *PMLA,* vii, 1–208.

the beginning avoided combat against his friend. Taking his stand in a narrow defile, Walther in bitter fighting slew eleven of his foes, and Gunther and Hagen at last drew off to the wood. But among the slain was Hagen's nephew, and the bond of kinship served to bring Hagen into the battle of the following day.

At dawn Walther and Hildegund attempted to continue their journey. But before they had gone far, Gunther and Hagen broke from ambush and renewed attack. Fighting alone against them both Walther succeeded in wounding Gunther. But Walther's sword shattered, and his right hand was severed by a blow from Hagen's blade. However, with shield wedged on the bleeding stump of his right arm, and with broken sword gripped in his left hand, Walther fought on until a blow of his sword laid open Hagen's cheek from eye to jaw. With this the battle ended. Blood vows of friendship were renewed between Walther and Hagen, and each went his way. Gunther and Hagen returned to Worms; Walther and Hildegund continued on to Aquitaine. There they were wed, and there Walther, after his father's death, reigned for thirty years.

There is no difficulty in fitting the *Waldere* fragments into this frame of narrative. It is probable that the Old English poem sprang from a Germanic version of the legend similar to that on which the *Waltharius* was based.[24] The poetic development of this material in the *Waldere* must have been at much the same length as the treatment given in the tenth-century Latin poem. But there are differences of detail between the *Waldere* and *Waltharius* which suggest that the original of the *Waldere* was different from that of the Latin poem, and possibly somewhat earlier. In the Latin poem Gunther was king of the Franks while in the

---

24. 'This original was probably the Upper German (Alemannic) form, while the *Waldere* represents the Low German (Saxon) form . . . Thus we have in the *Waltharius* a tenth century adaptation of an original German version, either contemporary with that of the *Waldere*, or slightly later.' M. D. Learned, 'The Saga of Walther of Aquitaine,' op. cit. p. 181.

Waldere Guthhere (Gunther) is addressed as *wine Burgenda,* that is, 'friend,' or lord, of the Burgundians. Though the *Waldere* in this detail is at variance with the *Waltharius,* it is in accord with the *Widsith,* in which Gifica, an ancestor of Gunther, is ruler of the Burgundians. This variance, moreover, raises a second question, which cannot be answered from the Old English fragments. In the *Waltharius* Hildegund is a Burgundian princess. But in the *Waldere* if Guthhere is a Burgundian, then to what people does Hildeguth belong? Such differences in detail suggest difference in source, even though the narrative material of the two underlying originals must have been essentially similar.

The first fragment of the *Waldere* is a portion of a spirited call to combat, an exhortation to Waldere to do or die, couched in the conventional terms and vigorous phrasing of Old English heroic verse. The speaker is apparently Hildeguth, though the lines containing the name are missing. The time is the second day of the battle. Hagen has refused Waldere's offer of the famous sword and the treasure, and Hildeguth is heartening Waldere to renew the fight:

> Now the day is come
> For one or other,   O Ælfhere's son,
> To lose your life   or win lasting fame
> Among all mankind.   Not at all, my beloved,
> Can I say that ever   in play of swords
> I saw you shamefully   shun the battle,
> Or turn to the wall   to protect your life,
> Though many a hard blade   hacked at your byrny.
> But ever further   you forced the fighting
> Time beyond measure;   I feared for your fate
> Lest all too boldly   you pressed to the battle,
> The bloody encounter   in clash of war.
> Now honor your name   with deeds of note
> While God is gracious   and grants you strength.
> Fear not for the blade!   The best of weapons
> Was surely given   to save us both.

With its edge you shall beat down   Guthhere's boast
Who wickedly started   this bitter strife,
Refused the sword,   and the shining casket,
And wealth of jewels.   With never a gem
He shall leave the battle   to seek his lord,
His ancient home-land,   or here shall he sleep,
If he.[25] . . .

The opening lines of the second *Waldere* fragment are apparently from a speech of Guthhere. He refers to a famous sword, perhaps Mimming the great sword of Weland. He seems to be admitting its excellence but praising the superior quality of his own blade. As the beginning of the sentence is missing, the sense is somewhat uncertaih. The speech includes a reference to the *Theodoric* saga and reflects the Germanic tradition which represented Theodoric as slayer of giants and monsters.[26]

Of the 31 lines of this fragment 18 are from a speech of Waldere, the ending of which is missing. The lines ring with martial spirit, weary though the hero is with long fighting. His words are a lusty challenge to Guthhere to come and take, if he can, the gray corselet that Waldere had from his father, Ælfhere:

Lo! grimly you hoped,   Burgundian lord,
That the hand of Hagen   would help in the fray
And hinder my fighting;   try and take, if you dare,
Battle-worn though I be,   my good gray byrny.
Here it lies on my shoulders,   shining with gold,
Ælfhere's heirloom   of ample front,
A peerless corselet   for prince's wear
When hand guards body   and frame from the foe!
It fails me not   when the false and unfriendly
Renew their tricks,   and attack me with swords
As ye have done.[27]

25. *Waldere*, 8–32.
26. See Chambers, *Widsith*, p. 42.
27. *Waldere*, 45–56.

The *Waldere* in its entirety, we may believe, must have been an exceptionally fine eighth-century example of the Germanic heroic tale. One cannot read the broken fragments without remembering the romantic nature of the Walther legend. The narrative of the companionship of a pair of affianced lovers in the hardships of long travel, and the perils of combat, offered a type of theme which our early poetry could ill afford to lose. Old English verse has little to tell us of the way of a man with a maid. The *Husband's Message* and the *Wife's Lament* offer brief glimpses of the intimate, eternal theme. But the whole range of our early poetry offers little else in this kind. The legend of Walther and Hildegund is an essentially romantic story. The lost Old English version would be a treasure beyond price.

THE FINNSBURG FRAGMENT

We have no records by which to determine the antecedents of the *Fight at Finnsburg*. Certain of the names mentioned in the Finnsburg story we meet again in the *Widsith:* Finn himself, the son of Folcwalda, and a ruler of the Frisians; Hnæf, who ruled the Hocings; and Sæferth of the Secgan, whose name suggests the lineage of that Sigeferth, prince of the Secgan, who fought so stoutly at the door of the great hall in Finnsburg. But no Germanic lay of Finnsburg, on which the Old English versions may have been based, has survived. Yet the story is so vividly told, and the dramatic situations are so typically Germanic, that the description of the bitter hall-fight at Finnsburg reads like tribal tradition authentically grounded in tragic event.

Fortunately, in addition to the 48 lines of the *Finnsburg* fragment, defective at beginning and end, we have a supplementing, and much more extended, development of the tale in a lay sung by Hrothgar's minstrel at a feast in *Beowulf*.[28] If the two accounts of the tragedy are compared, it becomes evident that the action of

28. *Beowulf*, 1063-1159.

the *Fragment* precedes the events set forth in the *Beowulf* lay. Though there are difficulties of detail, the relation of events in the *Fragment* to events in the *lay* can be reconstructed with reasonable clearness.

Neither the *Beowulf* lay, nor the *Fragment,* throw any light on the origin of the feud between Danes and Frisians which had such tragic denouement at Finnsburg. But we find in the *Beowulf* material a not unfamiliar Germanic situation. Hildeburh, daughter of Hoc of the Half-Danes, was married to Finn, the Frisian king. It is possible that she had been wedded to Finn in order to compose a feud with the Frisians, as Hrothgar purposed to compose the Heathobard feud by the marriage of Freawaru to Ingeld. If so, the feud was of long standing, since Hildeburh had a son old enough to die in battle. If Hildeburh's office was that of 'peace-weaver' she was doomed to as tragic a failure as Beowulf prophesied for the diplomatic marriage of Freawaru.[29]

Whatever the origin and early history of the feud, at the time indicated in the *Finnsburg* fragment we find a company of Danes under their king, Hnæf, visiting the Frisian king, Finn, in his stronghold at Finnsburg. One night just before daybreak Hnæf and sixty retainers were attacked in hall by a band of Finn's men. A warrior on guard reported flashes and gleams of light outside the hall, but was uncertain of the cause. Were the gables of the hall on fire? Was it a fire-breathing dragon flying through the night? Was it the glimmer of daybreak? Hnæf recognized the light as the gleam of moonlight on weapons and armor. It is an attack on the hall! The *Fragment* begins with Hnæf's spirited call to arms:

> This is not dawn,   nor flying dragon,
> Nor fire burning   the horns of this hall,
> But men in armor!   The eagle will scream,
> The gray wolf howl,   and the war-wood whistle,
> Shield answer shaft!   Now shines the moon

29. *Beowulf,* 2020–2069.

Through scudding cloud.   Dire deeds are come
Bringing hard battle   and bitter strife.
Awake, my warriors!   Grasp your shields!
Fight like men   in the front of battle!
Be bold of mood;   be mindful of glory![30]

The Danes rushed to defend the doors, Sigeferth and Eaha guarding one door, Ordlaf, Guthlaf, and Hengest, the other. Garulf, the leader of the attacking band, shouted his challenge, asking who guarded the door. 'Sigeferth! lord of the Secgan,' was the answer; 'I have known much hardship and many bitter battles. From me you can get what you are looking for!' Then din of battle rose; bucklers broke and hall-boards resounded. Garulf was the first to fall, and many a good man lay stretched beside him. 'Swords flashed as if all Finnsburg were on fire.' 'I have never heard,' the poet says of the Danes, 'of sixty heroes who made better requital for the shining mead than his warriors made to Hnæf!' For five days they fought and not one fell, and they held the doors. Then one of Finn's men, with armor battered and broken, turned away from the battle. His lord inquired of him how the wounded men were holding out, and which of the men—and at this point the *Fragment* breaks off.

How much time elapsed between the events of the *Fragment* and the events of the *Finnsburg* lay in *Beowulf* has been a matter of discussion. When the *Fragment* breaks off Hnæf and his sixty warriors are still alive. They had held the doors for five days and not one had fallen. But more and more of Finn's men must have been drawn into the battle until losses became heavy on both sides. At last, as we learn from the *Beowulf*, Hnæf fell in the slaughter and on the Frisian side Hnæf's nephew, Hildeburh's son, was slain.

Exhausted by the indecisive struggle, with many dead on both sides, Hengest and the surviving Danes made a truce with Finn.

30. *Finnsburg*, 3–12.

Under its terms the Danes accepted the overlordship of Finn, and in turn were to receive a hall of their own and equal justice and honor with the people of Finn. If any should reproach Hengest or his men with following the slayer of their lord, or in any manner awaken the old feud, punishment by the sword would be the penalty.

There follows in the *Beowulf* lay a realistic description of the burning of the dead. A great funeral pyre was constructed and on it, side by side, were placed the bodies of Hnæf and his nephew. Beside the pyre Hildeburh lamented the fall of her kinsmen.

> The greatest of funeral fires
> Rolled with a roar to the skies at the burial barrow.
> Heads melted and gashes gaped, the mortal wounds of the body;
> Blood poured out in the flames; the fire, most greedy of spirits,
> Swallowed up all whom battle had taken of both their peoples.[31]

During the long months that followed, when 'winter locked ocean with bonds of ice,' Hengest and his men were forced to remain at Finnsburg. But the Danes were unhappy under the truce. Guthlaf and Oslaf could not bridle their restive spirits. And Hengest's thoughts 'were more of revenge than of voyaging over the wave.' When the sunny, shining days of Spring returned, a son of Hunlaf one day laid in Hengest's lap a naked battle-sword whose edge was already well known to the men of Finn, a hint that loyalty required vengeance for the death of Hnæf. Once more the feud broke out; the hall ran red with blood. Finn was killed, and Hildeburh, with much treasure, was taken back to Denmark to her own people.

Although the course of events at Finnsburg can be visualized along these general lines, it must be recognized that there are many elements of uncertainty in the tale, and questions which cannot be answered from the text. We do not know what considerations caused the visit of the Danes to Finnsburg. We do not

31. *Beowulf*, 1119–24.

know whether the attack upon the hall in the *Fragment* represents the outbreak of hostilities, or whether the peace had already been broken by the Danes themselves. We cannot be certain of all the details of the truce sworn to by Finn and Hengest. And perhaps most perplexing of all, we cannot be completely certain of the part played at Finnsburg by the Jutes. They are mentioned four times in the course of the *Beowulf* lay[32] and the various interpretations of these references represent divergent theories of elements of motivation in the stream of tragic event. The reader who desires to pursue the tempting and tantalizing vistas which the Finnsburg story opens to us should consult the enlightening studies of *Lay* and *Fragment* by Lawrence, Chambers, and Williams.[33]

The *Finnsburg* fragment presents one of the most spirited battle scenes in the entire range of Old English heroic verse. The action is vigorous and swift moving, the number of lines devoted to speech proportionally high, and devices of dialogue and verseform suggest the early Germanic lay. There is significant contrast between the more primitive style of the *Fragment* and the style of the *Beowulf* lay in which there are so many evidences of artistic reworking of the Finnsburg material to shape it for inclusion as an episode in the epic.

THE SIGEMUND LAY IN BEOWULF

The primitive Continental legends underlying the Norse *Volsungasaga,* and the Middle High German *Nibelungenlied* were evidently well known in eighth-century England. The first of the lays sung by Hrothgar's minstrel in the *Beowulf*[34] deals briefly with the heroic exploits of Sigemund and Sinfjötli, two of the heroic figures involved in the tale of the Volsung revenge.

32. ll. 1072, 1088, 1141, 1145.

33. See Lawrence, 'Beowulf and the Tragedy of Finnsburg,' *PMLA*, xxx, 372–431; and *Beowulf and Epic Tradition*, 107–28; Chambers, *Beowulf, An Introduction*, 245–89; R. A. Williams, *The Finn Episode in Beowulf*, Cambridge, 1924.

34. ll. 874–915.

In this lay we note once again the quality of allusiveness and brevity which suggests that the poet was able to assume a widespread and detailed acquaintance with this body of legend.

The account of Sigemund's heroic adventures, as given in the *Beowulf* passage, is in one respect unique. Nowhere except in the *Beowulf* do we find the theme of Sigemund's fight with a dragon. The great dragon-fight of the *Volsungasaga* is fought not by Sigemund but by Sigurd, his son. There is, moreover, no very close correspondence between the details of Sigurd's battle with Fafnir and the description of Sigemund's exploit. The victory of Sigemund in the *Beowulf* is set forth as one of a series of heroic adventures in which, in all instances but this, Sigemund and his son Sinfjötli had engaged together. 'Very many of the race of monsters they had slain with the sword.' So the poet tells us, and there follows immediately the story of Sigemund and the dragon and the statement that in this battle Sigemund was fighting alone:

> The fame spread far　after Sigemund's death
> How the keen in battle　had killed the dragon,
> The treasure-guarder.　Beneath gray rock
> The valiant hero　had ventured alone
> On the fearsome deed.　Nor was Fitela with him!
> To him it was granted　his good sword pierced
> The wondrous worm,　till it stood in the wall,
> The lordly iron;　the dragon died.
> The hero's valor　had won the treasure,
> The hoard, to enjoy　as his heart might wish!
> He loaded his sea-boat,　bore to its bosom
> The shining treasure,　the son of Wæls;
> But the surge of its fires　consumed the worm.[35]

It will be noted that while this passage dwells at some length on the theme of the dragon's hoard, it makes no reference to the curse upon the treasure. The dragon is called the 'guardian of the hoard,' and after his victory Sigemund loads his ship with a wealth

35. ll. 884-97.

of treasure. But no explanation is given, or suggested, of the origin or past history of the treasure, nor is anything said of the curse which, in the *Volsungasaga,* the dwarf Andvari lays upon the hoard. Indeed, Sigemund's dragon-fight, as given in the *Beowulf,* is too summarized to indicate to a modern reader the backgrounds and details of the legend as the poet had them in mind.

The Sigemund lay is quite as interesting for what it does not contain as for what it does. The story of the revenge of the Volsungs is not told, though Sinfjötli (Fitela), as we have seen, is mentioned and is described as the constant companion of Sigemund in his heroic adventures. In the *Volsungasaga,* Sinfjötli is the physical symbol and planned instrument of Signy's revenge, as a brief outline of the story will make clear.

According to the *Volsungasaga,* Volsung, king of the Huns, had a daughter, Signy, and ten sons, of whom Sigemund was the oldest. Signy was betrothed and married to Siggeir, king of Gautland. Angered at a supposed affront, Siggeir returned with his bride to Gautland before the marriage feast was celebrated; but invited Volsung with his sons and followers to attend a feast in Gautland three months following. When the Volsungs arrived there in acceptance of this invitation they were treacherously set upon, and all were slain except Volsung's ten sons. Placed in the stocks to die, nine of the sons were devoured by a she-wolf on nine successive nights, Sigemund alone surviving. By Signy's help Sigemund escaped, and withdrawing to the forest lived the life of an outlaw.

Signy devoted her life to avenging the treacherous wrong done her house. When her two sons by Siggeir were old enough, she sent them to Sigemund that he might test their courage and determine if they could be shaped into fit instruments to aid him in the work of vengeance. Both were found unworthy and were slain.

Convinced that only one of pure Volsung blood could be adequate to the task, Signy, in the guise of a witch, visited the stronghold of Sigemund, received shelter for the night, and nine months later brought forth a son by Sigemund, whom she named Sinfjötli. When old enough he was sent to Sigemund for testing and training and, coming to full age, proved a worthy companion in the work of revenge. Sigemund and Sinfjötli leaving their hiding-place came to the hall of Siggeir and set fire to it by night. In the conflagration all within the hall perished, and among them Signy, who, having gained her purpose, refused longer life. 'So much have I done to accomplish revenge that it is now nowise possible for me to live; I will die gladly with Siggeir the king, though I married him by compulsion.' So runs the story of the revenge of the Volsungs.

Of this theme we find no trace in the *Beowulf* lay, save in so far as Sinfjötli is the physical symbol and instrument of Signy's unwavering purpose, as the *Volsungasaga* tells the tale. The poet's omission of the revenge *motif*, if it had taken form at this early date, is not difficult to understand. We need only remember his purpose in introducing the Sigemund lay into his epic narrative. It is Sigemund, the dragon-killer, with whom the poet is primarily concerned. Beowulf's heroic achievement in the overcoming of Grendel is worthy of comparison with other great exploits of like kind. There could be no more fitting praise of his hero than the retelling of a familiar Continental tale of a similar victory of heroic courage over the malignant power of the brute and the monstrous. The legend of Sigemund, son of Wæls, lay ready at hand.

WULF AND EADWACER

It would seem that there is a relation between the *Volsungasaga* legend of Signy's revenge, or some other revenge story of very similar outline, and the 19 lines of verse now generally entitled *Wulf and Eadwacer*. These lines were long regarded as a verse riddle, the first in a series of 95 *Riddles* contained in the Exeter Book. An interpretation by Leo, long accepted, had explained the lines as a charade concealing a riddling signature of the name Cynewulf. On the basis of this 'solution,' the poet Cynewulf was hailed as the author of the poem and of the entire *Riddle* series.

In 1888, however, critical discussion of these lines assumed an entirely new aspect. In a review of Volume II of Morley's *English Writers*,[36] Bradley dwelt upon the *Riddles* at some length. Before discussing Morley's interpretation of this so-called 'First Riddle,' Bradley remarked: 'I may as well state my own view, which is that the so-called riddle is not a riddle at all, but a fragment of a dramatic soliloquy, like *Deor* and *The Wife's Complaint*, to the latter of which it bears, both in motive and in treatment, a strong resemblance.' He considered it established by grammar and syntax that the speaker is a woman, probably a captive in a foreign land, that Wulf is her lover, and Eadwacer her 'tyrant husband.' Bradley added: 'Whether the subject of the poem be drawn from history or Teutonic legend, or whether it be purely the invention of the poet, there seems to be no evidence to determine.' He then gave a proposed translation of the poem as follows:

Is to my people as though one gave them a present.
Will they give him food if he should come to want?
  It is otherwise with us!
Wulf is on an island, I on another;
The island is closely surrounded by fen.
On yonder isle are fierce and cruel men;
Will they give him food if he should come to want?
  It is otherwise with us!
I waited for my Wulf with far-wandering longings
When it was rainy weather and I sat tearful.
When the brave warrior encircled me with his arms
It was joy to me, yet was it also pain.
O Wulf! my Wulf! it was my longings after thee

36. *The Academy*, 24 March, 1888, 197.

That made me sick—it was thy seldom coming—
It was a sorrowful heart, not the want of food!
Dost thou hear, Eadwacer? The cowardly [?] whelp of us two
Shall Wulf carry off to the wood.
Easily can that be broken asunder which never was united,
The song of us two together.

Bradley's view attracted wide attention and the conviction grew that here was indeed no riddle but a fragment of a poem of lament.

In 1902 careful studies of the poem were made by Lawrence[37] and Schofield.[38] Lawrence propounded the theory that the fragment is a translation from Old Norse, deriving his evidence from the diction, faulty alliteration, and strophic structure of the poem. Lawrence's study was supplemented by Schofield's article entitled 'Signy's Lament.' Accepting Lawrence's general conclusions, Schofield went on to argue specifically that not only is the poem a translation from the Norse, but that it can be shown to be connected with the story of Sigemund and Signy from the *Volsungasaga*.

Certain it is that both the substance and the implications of the *Wulf and Eadwacer* fragment, as we spell them out, have remarkable similarity at a number of points to the narrative of Signy's revenge. Its lines of lament would be appropriate in the mouth of Signy. The term *Wulf* could be quite correctly employed in reference to Sigemund's career as an outlaw. If the *Wulf and Eadwacer* is read with the story of Signy in mind, there is poignant meaning in the lines:

When the brave warrior encircled me with his arms
It was joy to me; yet was it also pain.

Finally, the tragic conflict of loyalties in which Signy's life was caught, and all the woe of her unhappy marriage, could well be hinted in the final lines of the poem:

37. *PMLA*, xvii, 245–61.
38. Ibid. 262–95.

Easily can that be broken asunder which was never united,
The song of us two together.

There is, however, one difficulty in this interpretation of the poem which cannot be passed over lightly. In the sixteenth line is the name Eadwacer, evidently applied to the husband. There is no possible connection between Eadwacer, or Odoacer, of the *Hildebrandslied,* and Signy's husband, Siggeir. It would seem, therefore, that Schofield was hardly justified in giving to the poem the new title of 'Signy's Lament,' though Bradley[39] admitted that the imagined speaker 'is a lady whose circumstances closely resemble those of Signy.' Bradley inclined to believe that the husband of the heroine of the poem was in fact the Odoacer of the *Hildebrandslied.* Imelmann in three different studies[40] has insisted dogmatically that the *Wulf and Eadwacer, Wanderer, Seafarer, Wife's Lament,* and *Husband's Message* are interrelated portions of an original Odoacer poem, a thesis beset with many difficulties. That the *Wulf and Eadwacer* may be related to the Odoacer legend is an entirely separate matter.

The poems that reflect these Continental legends give not only outlines or fragments of the legends themselves, often blurred and confused in transmission, but suggestions of an attitude of mind and a way of life. The ancient tales reflect, on the whole, a stark world of violence and blood in which men conceived of duty largely in terms of loyalty and courage. These loyalties not infrequently came into mutual conflict from which was no issue save revenge and death, no choice but to hunt with the hounds and die with the hare. To a woman whose noble blood ordained an inter-tribal function as 'peace-weaver,' fate often brought just such tragic confrontations. The heroic death of Signy is a supreme

39. *Athenaeum,* 1902, II, 758.
40. *Die Altenglische Odoaker-Dichtung,* 1907; *Wanderer und Seefahrer im Rahmen der Altenglischen Odoaker-Dichtung,* 1908; and *Forschungen zur Altenglischen Poesie,* 1920.

symbol of the failure of the blood feud as a concept of social duty. The same recurring patterns, the same tragic situations, make memorable the names of Freawaru and Hildeburh, and the anonymous revelations of the *Wife's Lament* and *Wulf and Eadwacer*.

To the reader of the fragmentary survivals that reflect this ancient world, its tragedy and terror lie in the flinty simplicity and narrowness of its concepts. Loyalty and courage in themselves can be sterile virtues unless guided by something more than primitive rudiments of moral choice. The terror evoked by these ancient legends flows from their failure to recognize man's tragic incapacity, by his unaided strength, to save himself. Their final trust is in man's heroic strength mobilized by man's heroic will. It is the glory of these tragic tales that human will in the supreme crisis so often holds unfaltering to the end. But when human strength has reached its uttermost there is nothing beyond. To do or to die is the heroic formula.

Such a world of legend gives us a body of verse with little room for humility, and little expression of the gentleness and pathos, the tenderness and hope, of daily living. These elements, it is true, are not wholly lacking. We have brief glimpses of them in the *Elegies*, and here and there in fragments of gnomic verse. But it is not until the Christian spirit enters in to enlarge the concept and expand the scene, as in the *Beowulf*, that we find the old heroic attitudes blended with gentler themes, circled by an infinitely wider spiritual horizon, and enriched by recognition that in life's tragic struggle there are moral forces at work that reach beyond the strength of man's heroic will.

III. BEOWULF

The narrative; Scandinavian and Icelandic analogues;
historical backgrounds; Christian influence;
epic tradition; characteristic spirit

THE *Beowulf* holds unique place as the oldest epic narrative in any modern European tongue. Of unknown authorship, and dating in all probability from the early eighth century, the poem is a brilliant embodiment of the heroic tradition. Illuminating studies in comparatively recent years by Ker, Lawrence, Chambers, Klaeber, Malone, and others, have brought increasing appraisal of the extent to which Scandinavian backgrounds are reflected in its material, literary tradition in its structure, and Christian influence in its spirit.

Of the circumstances under which the *Beowulf* was composed we actually know little, though it is possible to trace with some degree of clearness the evolution of the material from which the poem is shaped. Portions of this material must have originally circulated by oral transmission. The poem itself may well have been developed from an earlier series of epic lays, though no one of these lays has survived. In any case, as Ker has pointed out, the *Beowulf*, in the form in which it has come down to us, is a single, unified poem. It is, he writes, 'an extant book, whatever the history of its composition may have been; the book of the adventures of Beowulf, written out fair by two scribes in the tenth century; an epic poem, with a prologue at the beginning and a judgment pronounced on the life of the hero at the end; a single book, considered as such by its transcribers, and making a claim to be so considered.'[1]

1. W. P. Ker, *Epic and Romance*, London, 1896, p. 158.

In the light which modern critical scholarship has focused upon the poem, it has come to be recognized that we have here a work of cultivated craftsmanship, sophisticated rather than primitive in form, and definitely influenced by literary and religious tradition. The influence of the Christian faith is marked and pervasive. There are evidences, also, which seem to support opinion that the author of the *Beowulf* was familiar with the works of Virgil, and that the structure and development of the poem were influenced by epic tradition as illustrated in the *Aeneid*.[2]

The material of which the narrative is shaped is in large measure the material not of primitive English, but of primitive Scandinavian life. In the weaving of the narrative the warp is, in part at least, fashioned from the stuff of Continental chronicle and legend. Names of early Swedish kings repeatedly mentioned in the *Beowulf* have correspondence to names of kings listed in the ninth-century *Ynglinga tal*. Names and incidents in the poem relating to the ruling house of the Danes have their analogues in the *Skjoldungasaga,* and in the *Gesta Danorum* of Saxo Grammaticus. The disastrous expedition against the Franks of 516, in which Beowulf's uncle, Hygelac, was slain, is set forth in the *History of the Franks* by Gregory of Tours, who wrote within seventy years of the events described, and in the eighth-century *Liber Historiae Francorum*.

Into this background are woven dark legends of savage feuds of the Continental tribes, feuds of the Danes and Frisians, the Danes and Heathobards, the Geats and Swedes. At Beowulf's death, the prophecy of Swedish dominion over the Geats derives its tragic foreboding from chanted memories of the bitter tribal battle at Ravenswood. The songs of the minstrel in Hrothgar's hall were fashioned from ancient Continental lays: the dragon-fight of Sigemund, the Volsung; the disastrous battle of Danes and Frisians at Finnsburg.

2. See pages 92-7.

In a setting shaped of these elements the poet has developed a narrative, the material of which is derived from Continental folk-tale. The haunting of Hrothgar's hall by the night-prowling monster, Grendel, and the troll-wife, his mother; the adventurous journey of Beowulf, the Geat, to Daneland, and his triumph over the monsters; these central themes in the narrative have their analogues in various versions of the European folk-tale of 'The Bear's Son.' Certain Scandinavian tales of the thirteenth and fourteenth centuries, the *Grettissaga,* the *Samsonssaga,* the *Hrolfssaga,* and others, include elements which show resemblance to this basic material of the *Beowulf,* and the resemblance is sufficiently unmistakable to indicate dependence of both the *Beowulf* and the sagas upon the same or similar Scandinavian sources.

The material, then, from which the story and setting of the *Beowulf* were fashioned was in its origin Continental. Of this alien and pagan material the Old English poet has shaped a poem courtly in mood, suggestive of epic tradition, and Christian in spirit. It is a mark of the poet's skill that the elements derived from these various and varied sources, from chronicle and legend, from folk-tale and lay, have been deftly integrated and fused into a new unity.[3]

This 'book of the adventures of Beowulf' is contained in a manuscript volume now lodged in the British Museum, and known as *Cotton Vitellius, A. XV.* A combination of two once separate codices, the manuscript contains nine Old English texts, four in the first codex, five in the second. The *Beowulf* (folios 129^a–198^b) belongs to the second codex, in which it is preceded by three prose texts, and followed by the *Judith.*

3. 'The whole must have succeeded admirably in creating in the minds of the poet's contemporaries the illusion of surveying a past, pagan but noble and fraught with a deep significance—a past that itself had depth and reached backward into a dark antiquity of sorrow. This impression of depth is an effect and a justification of the use of episodes and allusions to old tales, mostly darker, more pagan, and desperate than the foreground.' J. R. R. Tolkien, 'Beowulf: the monsters and the critics,' *Proceedings of the British Academy,* xxii, 270–71, 1936.

THE NARRATIVE

The narrative element in the *Beowulf* consists of two stories, of separate origin, and unified only in the sense that Beowulf is the hero of both. Of these tales, the first represents an adventure of his youth in combat with two monsters; the second, his victorious but fatal battle in old age against a dragon. A long and prosperous reign over the Geats intervenes between the two exploits. The first episode involves the first 2199 lines of the *Beowulf;* the second, the remainder of the 3182 lines of the poem.

The story begins in the land of the Danes in the glorious reign of King Hrothgar. The power and splendor of his rule were symbolized in the great hall which he built and named Heorot. The poet's statement that the light of this hall 'shone over many lands' may be taken as an index of the range and strength of Hrothgar's influence beyond his borders.

But time brought change. A horror came upon the land and the hall was haunted and ravaged by two monsters, male and female, of human shape but superhuman size, and of beastlike ferocity. The night raids upon Heorot by Grendel, the male, gradually diminished the number of Hrothgar's warriors and made the hall, as it towered up in the darkness silent and deserted, a place of dread. For twelve years a superstitious terror lay like a shadow upon the land.

News of the calamity that afflicted the Danes spread far and wide, reaching at last the land of the Geats in southern Sweden, where it came to the ears of Beowulf. Against the advice of Hygelac, his uncle and lord, the young adventurer, eager for fame, set sail for Denmark with a small band of followers to pit his courage and strength against the monsters, in the service of a friendly king.

The voyage of Beowulf to Daneland is one of the two spirited and well developed sea-pictures in the poem. The preparation and loading of the vessel, the speeding ship driving onward with its great sail filled with wind, and the landing on the Danish coast, are memorably described:

> He gave command   for a goodly vessel
> Fitted and furnished;   he fain would sail
> Over the swan-road   to seek the king
> Who suffered so sorely   for need of men.
> His bold retainers   found little to blame
> In his daring adventure,   dear though he was;
> They viewed the omens,   and urged him on.
> Brave was the band   he had gathered about him,
> Fourteen stalwarts   seasoned and bold,
> Seeking the shore   where the ship lay waiting,
> A sea-skilled mariner   sighting the landmarks.
> Came the hour of boarding;   the ship was riding
> The waves of the harbor   under the hill.
> The eager mariners   mounted the prow;
> Billows were breaking,   sea against sand.
> In the ship's hold snugly   they stowed their trappings,
> Gleaming armor   and battle gear;
> Launched the vessel,   the well-braced bark,
> Seaward bound   on a joyous journey.
> Over breaking billows,   with bellying sail
> And foamy beak,   like a flying bird
> The ship sped on,   till the next day's sun
> Showed sea-cliffs shining,   towering hills
> And stretching headlands.   The sea was crossed,
> The voyage ended,   the vessel moored.
> And the Weder people   waded ashore
> With clatter of trappings   and coats of mail;
> Gave thanks to God   that His grace had granted
> Sea-paths safe   for their ocean-journey.[4]

The coast-guard's challenge, Beowulf's assuring reply, and the march inland to Heorot[5] are set forth in swift-moving scenes,

4. *Beowulf*, 198–228.

5. The site of Heorot is somewhat generally identified by scholars with the modern village of Leire, standing about three miles from the coast on the island of Seeland; Cf. Chambers, *Beowulf, An Introduction*, 1932, pp. 16–20.

rich in color and in realistic detail. Gratefully welcomed by Hrothgar with royal entertainment in hall, Beowulf and his band were
entrusted with the task of freeing Heorot from the scourge of
Grendel. There was one jarring note in the joyous ceremonial.
Unferth, a Danish courtier, jealous and proud, alluded to a
swimming match between Beowulf and Breca, in which, he
claimed, Breca had proved himself the better man. From this he
prophesied an evil fate for Beowulf if he dared to undertake
encounter with Grendel. The reply of Beowulf and the realistic
clash of personalities underlying the scene make this episode an
outstanding passage of heightened dramatic tone.

At nightfall Beowulf and his men took over the hall, sleeping
upon the ale-benches with their weapons at hand. They had not
long to wait. Out of the mist and darkness Grendel burst in upon
them, his eyes gleaming with a 'baleful light most like to flame.'
Swiftly seizing one of the band he tore him limb from limb, gulp-
ing down the flesh in huge morsels 'even to the feet and hands.'
Beowulf, who had made a vow that he would fight Grendel without weapon, closed with the monster in a grappling struggle that
wrecked the ale-benches and the woodwork of the hall. By virtue
of his strength he was able to inflict upon Grendel a fatal wound,
wrenching his huge arm and claw clean out of the shoulder socket.
With 'bloody tracks' the monster fled to the evil pool in the fen
where he had his refuge and, plunging in, sank to the depths. And
there, says the poem, 'hell received him.'

The narrative of Grendel's attack on the hall, and the ensuing
combat, is strikingly vivid and swift-moving and is governed in
unusual degree by the realisms of severe and brutal physical
struggle:

> Storming the building   he burst the portal
> Though fastened of iron,   with fiendish strength;
> Forced open the entrance   in savage fury
> And rushed in rage   o'er the shining floor.

A baleful glare   from his eyes was gleaming
Most like to a flame.   He found in the hall
Many a warrior   sealed in slumber . . .
The demon delayed not,   but quickly clutched
A sleeping thane,   in his swift assault,
Tore him in pieces,   bit through the bones,
Gulped the blood   and gobbled the flesh,
Greedily gorged   on the lifeless corpse,
The hands and the feet.   Then the fiend stepped nearer,
Sprang on the Sea-Geat   lying outstretched,
Clasping him close   with his monstrous claw.
But Beowulf grappled   and gripped him hard,
Struggled up on his elbow;   the shepherd of sins
Soon found that never   before had he felt
In any man other   in all the earth
A mightier handgrip;   his mood was humbled,
His courage fled;   but he found no escape! . . .
There was din in Heorot.   For all the Danes,
The city-dwellers,   the stalwart Scyldings,
That was a bitter   spilling of beer!
The walls resounded,   the fight was fierce,
Savage the strife   as the warriors struggled.
The wonder was   that the lofty wine-hall
Withstood the struggle,   nor crashed to earth . . .
Continuous tumult   filled the hall;
A terror fell   on the Danish folk
As they heard through the wall   the horrible wailing,
The groans of Grendel,   the foe of God
Howling his hideous   hymn of pain,
The hell-thane shrieking   in sore defeat . . .
There Grendel suffered   a grievous hurt,
A wound in the shoulder   gaping and wide;
Sinews snapped   and bone-joints broke,
And Beowulf gained   the glory of battle.
Grendel, fated,   fled to the fens,
To his joyless dwelling,   sick unto death.
He knew in his heart   that his hours were numbered,
His days at an end. [6]

6. *Beowulf,* 721-9; 739-54; 767-73; 782-8; 815-23.

With the coming of dawn Hrothgar and the Danes gathered at the hall, rejoicing as they viewed the huge claw of Grendel, and tracing the tracks that marked his flight to the fen. As they returned from the mere to Heorot with horses proudly prancing, a minstrel extemporized a song in praise of Beowulf's heroic deed, and chanted the lay of Sigemund's victory over a dragon. The hall was decked and a great feast prepared at which Hrothgar honored Beowulf and his men with many gifts, while the minstrel sang the lay of the fight at Finnsburg:

> I never have heard   of a mightier muster
> Of proud retainers   around their prince.
> All at ease   they bent to the benches,
> Had joy of the banquet;   their kinsmen bold,
> Hrothgar and Hrothulf,   happy of heart,
> In the high-built hall   drank many a mead-cup.
> The hall of Hrothgar   was filled with friends;
> No treachery yet   had troubled the Scyldings.
> Upon Beowulf, then,   as a token of triumph,
> Hrothgar bestowed   a standard of gold,
> A banner embroidered,   a byrny and helm.
> In sight of many   a costly sword
> Before the hero   was borne on high.
> Beowulf drank   of many a bowl.
> No need for shame   in the sight of heroes
> For gifts so gracious!   I never have heard
> Of many men dealing   in friendlier fashion,
> To others on ale-bench,   richer rewards,
> Four such treasures   fretted with gold.[7]

But the coming of the night brought proof that the scourge had not been ended nor the terror laid. The female monster, avenging the death of Grendel, raided the hall. In her swift onset she slew Æschere, comrade and trusted counselor of Hrothgar, and bore off his body to the fen. Heartsick at this swift reprisal, the Danes were once more plunged in woe. But Beowulf pre-

7. ll. 1011-29.

pared again for battle, pledging Hrothgar that he would avenge the death of Æschere. 'Better for man to avenge a friend than much to mourn.'

The story of Beowulf's under-water fight against the troll-wife in a huge cave at the bottom of the pool is marked by a change in narrative mood. The poem, in this section, seems to reveal an intrusion of fabulous elements into a scene that was in origin realistic. It is possible, of course, that the poet did not fully understand his original, and interpreted as supernatural elements which the corresponding scene in the *Grettissaga* makes natural and realistic. Whatever the explanation, the reader will note in the descriptive passages of this second episode an apparent stress upon miracle and wonder.

Hrothgar's description to Beowulf of the haunted mere in which the two monsters had their watery lair is the finest 'landscape piece' of the entire poem and one of the finest in the whole range of Old English verse:

> Wild and lonely   the land they live in,
> Wind-swept ridges   and wolf-retreats,
> Dread tracts of fen   where the falling torrent
> Downward dips   into gloom and shadow,
> Under the dusk   of the darkening cliff.
> Not far in miles   lies the lonely mere
> Where trees firm-rooted   and hung with rime
> Overshroud the wave   with shadowing gloom.
> And there a portent   appears each night,
> A flame in the water;   no man so wise
> Who knows the bound   of its bottomless depth.
> The heather-stepper,   the hornéd stag,
> The antlered hart   hard driven by hounds,
> Invading that forest   in flight from afar
> Will turn at bay   and die on the brink
> Ere ever he'll plunge   in that haunted pool.
> 'Tis an eerie spot!   Its tossing spray
> Mounts dark to heaven   when high winds stir

The driving storm,   and the sky is murky,
And with foul weather   the heavens weep.[8]

The Danes and Geats together made their way to the mere. The pool was in a dismal covert of trees that overhung the gray rock and the bloodstained water beneath. On the banks and in the watery depths were snakelike monsters and strange sea-drakes. And here the grief of the Danes was made bitter by the sight of Æschere's severed head lying upon the brink:

Sudden they came   on a dismal covert
Of trees that hung   over hoary stone,
Over churning water   and bloodstained wave.
Then for the Danes   was the woe the deeper,
The sorrow sharper   for Scylding earls,
When they first caught sight,   on the rocky sea-cliff,
Of slaughtered Æschere's   severed head.
The water boiled   in a bloody swirling
With seething gore   as the spearmen gazed.
The trumpet sounded   a martial strain;
The shield-troop halted.   Their eyes beheld
The swimming forms   of strange sea-dragons,
Dim serpent shapes   in the watery depths,
Sea-beasts sunning   on headland slopes;
Snakelike monsters   that oft at sunrise
On evil errands   scour the sea.[9]

Wearing helmet and byrny and bearing his sword, Beowulf plunged into the pool. It was the space of a day before he reached bottom. As he swam down, the sea-beasts beset him sorely with their menacing tusks; the water-witch rose to meet him:

Soon she found,   who had haunted the flood,
A ravening hag,   for a hundred half-years,
Greedy and grim,   that a man was groping
In daring search   through the sea-troll's home.

8. ll. 1357–76.
9. ll. 1414–29.

Swift she grappled   and grasped the warrior
With horrid grip,   but could work no harm,
No hurt to his body;   the ring-locked byrny
Cloaked his life   from her clutching claw;
Nor could she tear   through the tempered mail
With her savage fingers.   The she-wolf bore
The ring-prince down   through the watery depths
To her den at the bottom;   nor could Beowulf draw
His blade for battle,   though brave his mood.
Many a sea-beast,   strange sea-monsters,
Tasked him hard   with their menacing tusks,
Broke his byrny   and smote him sore.[10]

He found himself at last in a great hall, free of water and
lighted with a glow as of firelight. Here he had view of the huge
water-hag. In his attack on her his sword failed him, 'would not
bite,' and he was forced to stake all on his unaided strength. The
troll-wife in a swift rush overthrew him and, kneeling upon him,
drew out her dagger. At this moment of impending defeat and
death it was by divine aid that Beowulf was enabled to regain his
feet, seize an ancient sword lying in the cave, and slay the hag:

Swift the hero   sprang to his feet;
Saw mid the war-gear   a stately sword,
An ancient war-brand   of biting edge,
Choicest of weapons,   worthy and strong,
The work of giants,   a warrior's joy,
So heavy no hand   but his own could hold it,
Bear to battle   or wield in war.
The defender of the Scyldings,   savage and grim,
Seized the ring-hilt   and swung the sword,
Struck with fury,   despairing of life,
Thrust at the throat,   broke through the bone-rings;
The stout blade stabbed   through her fated flesh.
She sank in death;   the sword was bloody;
The hero joyed   in the work of his hand.[11]

10. ll. 1497–1512.
11. ll. 1556–69.

The Danes, who held watch at the edge of the mere, seeing the waters suddenly stained with blood, believed that Beowulf had been killed, and despondently made their way back to the hall. The loyal Geats waited on. At last came Beowulf swimming up from the depths, bearing the ghastly head of Grendel and the ornamented hilt of the great sword whose blade had melted in the hag's venomous blood. Joyfully his followers gathered around him and accompanied him to Heorot. Four of them carried Grendel's head on a pikestaff, bearing it across the floor in the midst of the feasting, 'a terrible sight for lord and for lady.'

This final purging of the evil that had rested on Heorot, Hrothgar celebrated by an elaborate feast with ceremonial speech and rich giving of gifts. Wealhtheow and the youthful Freawaru, wife and daughter of the king, graced the banquet with their presence. When the night shadows deepened and the feasting came to an end, the weary Beowulf was guided by a hall-thane to a place appointed and there, with the great hall towering above him, his sleep was deep.

When the voice of the black-coated raven hailed the sunrise, and the time had come for Beowulf's return to his own country, Hrothgar bestowed upon him twelve gifts and bade him a sad farewell.

> The peerless leader,   the Scylding lord,
> Kissed the good thane   and clasped to his bosom,
> While tears welled fast   from the old man's eyes.
> Both chances he weighed   in his wise, old heart,
> But greatly doubted   if ever again
> They would meet in council,   or drinking of mead.[12]

The description of the return voyage to southern Sweden has elements of sea-realism which make the passage an appropriate parallel to the account of the earlier voyage to Denmark. Welcomed and feasted by Hygelac, Beowulf recounted his adventures

12. ll. 1870–76.

among the Danes and shared with King Hygelac and his queen, Hygd, the gifts which Hrothgar had given him. Hygelac in turn bestowed upon the hero an ancestral sword inherited from Hrethel, and honored Beowulf with a stately hall and 7,000 hides of land. So ends the first section of the narrative.

Between the slaying of the monsters and the killing of the dragon, many years intervened; more than fifty, if we take literally the poet's statement that Beowulf ruled for fifty winters.[13] In all probability, as used in this passage and a second time later in the poem,[14] the word 'fifty' is to be interpreted as a round number merely implying a long reign. No account is given, at this point in the text, of the circumstances of Beowulf's reign aside from the general statement that he ruled well. The years are spanned and the dragon *motif* is introduced in a swift passage of twelve lines.

It is the nature of dragons, so the poet tells us, to hunt out buried treasure and guard the heathen gold. The dragon in *Beowulf* conforms to this tradition, having come upon a burial treasure over which he brooded for 300 years. Only when the hoard was plundered, and a precious cup carried off by the thief, was the wrath of the dragon roused and the destructiveness of his fury unloosed upon the land.

The account of the plundering of the hoard is not completely clear, since the text at this point is quite corrupt and requires extensive reconstruction.[15] One gathers that an outcast and fugitive, perhaps guilty of a crime and fleeing from punishment, in his flight blundered into the burial barrow in which the dragon guarded his treasure. There from the hoarded riches he stole a cup which he carried back to his lord, perhaps as the price of forgiveness. Roused by the plundering of his barrow the dragon began to ravage the land with flames and fury.

13. ll. 2208-9.
14. l. 2733.
15. ll. 2221-31.

Beowulf prepared for battle against this menace to his people. Armed with his sword, Nægling, and an iron shield for defence against the fire of the monster, the king with a small band was guided by the thief to the dragon's earth-hall. Taking his stand near the stone entrance of the barrow, and the hot stream that flowed from within, Beowulf shouted his challenge. The dragon, roused by the voice of man, came forth to the attack.

The struggle so begun is described in vigorous detail; the action is divided into the three stages conventional in description of such a battle. Once more, as in his youthful adventure, the sword of Beowulf failed him; Nægling broke.

> It was not his lot   that edges of iron
> Could help him in battle;   his hand was too strong.[16]

His shoulder-companions, who at the beginning had borne no part because Beowulf had wished to undertake the battle alone, in the hour of their lord's need turned and fled to the forest to save their lives. Only the youthful Wiglaf, son of Weohstan of the Wægmundings, remained to fight under the shield of his lord. In his third rush the dragon fastened his fangs in Beowulf's throat, inflicting a deadly wound. Beowulf's rapidly ebbing strength was barely sufficient, with Wiglaf's assistance, to deal the dragon the deathblow:

> As they tell the tale,   in the king's sore need
> His shoulder-companion   showed forth his valor,
> His craft and courage,   and native strength.
> To the head of the dragon   he paid no heed,
> Though his hand was burned   as he helped his king.
> A little lower   the stalwart struck
> At the evil beast,   and his blade drove home
> Plated and gleaming.   The fire began
> To lessen and wane.   The king of the Weders
> Summoned his wits;   he drew the dagger

16. ll. 2682-4.

He wore on his corselet,   cutting and keen,
And slit asunder   the worm with the blow.
So they felled the foe   and wrought their revenge;
The kinsmen together   had killed the dragon.
So a man should be   when the need is bitter!
That was the last fight   Beowulf fought;
That was the end   of his work in the world.[17]

The king had received his death-wound, and the end was near. To Wiglaf he gave his armor and rings, and wished him well in terms which seem to imply his succession to rule over the Geats:

Heed well the needs,   the wants of my people;
My hour is come,   and my end is near . . .
You are the last   of the Wægmunding line.
All my kinsmen,   earls in their glory,
Fate has sent   to their final doom;
And I must follow.[18]

It was a lonely death. Beowulf had no son to whom he could leave the succession, and only the lad, Wiglaf, was with him when death came. Somewhere in the background hovered the traitors who had deserted their king in his hour of need. It was Wiglaf who sat at the last alone with his fallen leader in the silence of the death-watch, the living beside the dead. It was Wiglaf who pronounced the curse upon the cowards for their black disloyalty:

Wiglaf addressed them,   Weohstan's son;
Gazed sad of heart   on the hateful men:
'Lo! he may say,   who would speak the truth,
That the lord who gave you   these goodly rings,
This warlike armor   wherein you stand,
When oft on the ale-bench   he dealt to his hall-men
Helmet and byrny,   endowing his thanes
With the fairest he found   from near or from far,
That he grievously wasted   these trappings of war

17. ll. 2694–2711.
18. ll. 2800–2801; 2813–16.

When battle befell him.   The king of the folk
Had no need to boast   of his friends in the fight.
But the God of victory   granted him strength
To avenge himself   with the edge of the sword
When he needed valor.   Of little avail
The help I brought   in the bitter battle!
Yet still I strove,   though beyond my strength,
To aid my kinsman.   And ever the weaker
The savage foe   when I struck with my sword;
Ever the weaker   the welling flame!
Too few defenders   surrounded our ruler
When the hour of evil   and terror befell.
Now granting of treasure   and giving of swords,
Inherited land-right   and joy of the home,
Shall cease from your kindred.   And each of your clan
Shall fail of his birthright   when men from afar
Hear tell of your flight   and your dastardly deed.
Death is better   for every earl
Than a life besmirched   with the brand of shame.'[19]

A messenger proclaimed the news of Beowulf's fall, mingled
with dark foreboding of war and disaster now that the tribe had
lost their king. The body of the dead dragon was tumbled over
the cliff into the sea. In accordance with Beowulf's dying wish, a
funeral pyre was built upon the headland and a barrow constructed, destined to be known by sailors from distant lands as
Beowulf's Barrow. In it the dragon's treasure was once more
buried, under the earth of the headland, 'where it still remains as
useless to men as it was of yore.' On the brow of the cliff the greatest of funeral fires was kindled, and the body of Beowulf burned.
Round the pyre rode his warriors mourning their fallen lord,
chanting their dirges and proclaiming his virtue and fame. A
sense of Fate broods over these final scenes. A great and noble
king has fallen. The future looms dark and insecure.

19. ll. 2862-91.

Scandinavian and Icelandic Analogues

The supernatural forms of Grendel and Grendel's dam are obviously derivative from folk-tale, though the *Beowulf* poet in an early passage has blurred this lineage by tracing their descent from the monstrous offspring of Cain. Grendel is unusual among folk-tale monsters in bearing a name, and the name itself furnishes a hint of his primitive derivation. The word Grendel, as Lawrence points out,[20] can be associated with the Old English *grund,* i.e. ground, bottom, or watery depths, and it is significant that it is in just such depths that we find the lurking-place of Grendel and his mother. English place-names preserve records of localities known as *grendles mere* (the grendel's pool), *grindles bec* (the grendel's brook), and *gryndeles sylle* (the grendel's swamp). In these place-names the word *grendel* seems to be used as a generic term for a 'grendel,' or water-monster, and it is probable that the water-demons of the *Beowulf* have original derivation from the waterfall trolls of Scandinavian myth.

More directly, however, the male and female monsters of our poem, and the narrative of Beowulf's victories over them, are traceable to well-defined and recurring patterns in a familiar type of European folk-tale. Frederick Panzer in 1910 published the results of a careful study of over 200 folk-tales which have elements of resemblance to the Grendel story.[21] These tales with all their variations of outline have enough in common, in structure and detail, to indicate general conformance to a recurring type which has come to be known as the tale of 'The Bear's son.' The name is suggested by the bear-like attributes of the hero, who in some versions of the tale is actually the son, or the fosterling, of a bear. Vestigial traces of this element are to be noted in the *Beowulf* in the superhuman strength of the hero, and the bear-

20. *Beowulf and Epic Tradition*, p. 163.
21. F. Panzer, *Studien zur germanischen Sagengeschichte*, München, 1910.

like wrestling of his fight with Grendel and later with Dæghrefn, the slayer of Hygelac.

From the varying versions of the tale of 'The Bear's Son,' something like a central frame, or outline, can be reconstructed. An aged king builds a hall or house which is nightly haunted by a demon. The elder sons of the king are unable to overcome the invader, but the youngest son, formerly held in little esteem, wrestles with the monster and wounds him. The flight of the demon is marked by a trail of blood. An episode follows in which the hero fights in an underground lair of monsters often against a male and a female. His victory over them, sometimes by use of a magic sword, frees captive maidens who return to the upper world. But the hero is abandoned by faithless companions, and must without aid contrive means of escape from the monster's home. The tale often ends with the punishment of the traitors, and the marriage of the hero with one of the rescued maidens.

Similarities in this outline to the Grendel episodes of the *Beowulf* are, of course, general rather than precise. But it seems clear that Panzer is correct in claiming that a relationship exists, and that the *Beowulf* narrative in this respect had its earliest origin in the crude substance of folk-tale. The details of similarity suggest themselves at once: the building of the hall, the nightly invasion of the monster, the fact that the hero was little esteemed in youth,[22] the nature of the fight and the monster's wound, the trail of blood, the female monster, the fight in the cave under water, the magic sword, the desertion of the hero by comrades.[23]

Even more specific resemblance, however, exists between the *Beowulf* and certain Scandinavian sagas. The Icelandic saga of Grettir the Strong, dating from the end of the thirteenth century, has elements which resemble the *Beowulf* material and, in the account of the fight under water, throw a revealing light on uncer-

22. For traces of this *motif* in *Beowulf*, see lines 2183–8.
23. In *Beowulf*, by the Danes, ll. 1600–1602.

tainties of description in the *Beowulf* account. It is not probable that the Sandhills episode in the *Grettissaga* was based upon the *Beowulf*, but rather that both stories are independently developed from more primitive Scandinavian origins.

According to the *Grettissaga*, a hall at a place called Sandhills had for some time been ravaged by the nightly raids of a monster. The master of the house, and subsequently a housecarle, had disappeared. Hearing of these depredations, on Yule-eve Grettir the Strong undertook a watch in the hall. Toward midnight a huge troll-wife burst in. Grettir at once attacked her in a violent wrestling struggle which wrecked everything in the hall, even to the cross-paneling. The troll-wife dragged him out of the hall and down to the river bank, where Grettir succeeded in freeing his right hand, and with his short sword smote off the monster's arm at the shoulder. Thereupon she fell into the river and was washed down the force.

In the second episode Grettir led the local priest, who doubted the tale, to the scene of his victory over the hag. From the river brink they beheld a cave deep under the cliff, and the water flowing over it. Leaving the priest guarding a rope fastened to a peg, Grettir dived down under the falling torrent, and came up in a great cave in which a fire was burning. Here he fought with a giant and smote out his entrails so that the stream was colored by his blood. When the priest beheld the bloodstained water, he judged that Grettir had been killed and, leaving the rope fastened to its peg, returned home. Grettir found in the cave the bones of the two men who had disappeared. Carrying the bones in a bag, and a carved rune-staff, he made his way to the rope. Shaking it and finding the priest gone, he drew himself up through the force by main strength and returned with the bones and the rune-staff to the church porch.

One need not elaborate in this account the many details of resemblance to the *Beowulf* material. Except for the fact that the

Grettissaga reverses the order of conflict, the first struggle being
with the female, the similarity of the two accounts in important
detail is close, and clearly indicates a genetic relation between the
two narratives. In one respect there is inconsistence, and this
variance is itself suggestive. Grettir's entrance into the cave behind
the waterfall by diving through the force, and his return by pull-
ing himself up through the water by a rope, suggest for the second
episode of the Sandhills story a landscape-setting intelligible and
realistic. It is probable that in this respect the Icelandic narrative,
in spite of its later date, has more faithfully preserved primitive
realisms. The recourse to the supernatural in the corresponding
scene of the *Beowulf* would seem to represent either inability of
the Old English poet to visualize realistically the landscape
which served as a frame for the battle, or a transformation and
blurring of primitive conceptions by literary influence and epic
tradition.

Lawrence has pointed out another interesting analogue to
the under-water fight of the *Beowulf*.[24] This parallel is found in
an episode in the saga of Samson the Fair. In the account given
there of a fight between Samson and a female troll who dwelt
behind a waterfall, there are resemblances to details found in the
Grettissaga episode, and in the blurred descriptions of the corresponding scene in *Beowulf*. The fight takes place in a cave behind
a waterfall; the hero dives through the force to reach the cave;
the water of the stream is stained with the she-troll's blood; and
the waiting Gallyn decides that the hero has been killed.

Other episodes may be cited from Scandinavian saga which
seem to suggest general resemblance to the *Beowulf*, as in the
Glamr episode of the *Grettissaga,* and Orm's victories over a
female demon in cat form and a giant called Brusi in the tale of
Orm Storolfsson. But the similarities are certainly less sharp

24. 'Beowulf and the Saga of Samson the Fair,' *Studies in English Philology, A Miscellany in Honor of Frederick Klaeber,* 172–81; Also, *Beowulf and Epic Tradition,* pp. 188-91.

and conclusive than in the case of the Sandhills episode of the *Grettissaga*.

In various versions of this folk-tale material we catch hints of slow processes of reworking and reshaping, which help to explain certain forms the material has assumed in the *Beowulf*. The fact that Beowulf, after his victory over Grendel's dam, cuts off the head of the dead Grendel,[25] would seem to be a surviving trace from those stories in which the male monster is actually slain in the under-water struggle. The statement of the poem that Beowulf in youth was little esteemed[26] may well reflect the primitive tradition which made the hero of these battles against monsters a younger son, considered unworthy, who succeeded after his elder brothers had failed. The scene in the *Beowulf* in which the Danes, beholding the bloodstained water, leave the margin of the pool and return home, though Beowulf's own men remain,[27] may have taken its form from vague reminiscence of versions of the tale in which the hero is deserted by his comrades.

In one respect, the most noteworthy of Scandinavian analogues is the saga of Hrolf Kraki. In many ways this rather clumsily told tale of the fourteenth century is not as close to the *Beowulf* as is the *Grettissaga*, or even in certain respects the *Samsonssaga*. But it is significant and important that in the tale of Hrolf Kraki, as in the *Beowulf*, the theme of a land delivered by a foreign hero from the ravages of a monster is inserted into a historical pattern. In both the *Hrolfssaga* and the *Beowulf* the crude substance of folk-tale has been elevated in dignity and set in a frame of chronicle. The Hrolf of the saga is identical with the Hrothulf of the *Beowulf*. Indeed, in Scandinavian chronicle it was the reign of Hrolf (Hrothulf) rather than that of Hroar (Hrothgar) which stood out as an era of glory and splendor. The popular legend was the legend of the heroic greatness of Hrolf. It is, therefore, not altogether

25. *Beowulf*, 1588–90.
26. ll. 2183–8.
27. ll. 1600–1605.

surprising to find the tale of the slaying of the monster by Bothvarr Bjarki attached to the saga of Hrolf Kraki.

If the *Hrolfssaga* is set over against the *Beowulf,* a correspondence
is clear. The heroic service which Bothvarr Bjarki performs for
Hrolf is similar to the heroic service which Beowulf performs for
Hrothgar. And attending this chief correspondence there are, as
Klaeber points out,[28] additional similarities of detail. The name
Bjarki, like the name Beowulf, suggests the bear attributes of the
hero of the folk-tale. Bothvarr comes to Denmark from Gautland
where his brother is ruler; Beowulf from Geatland where his
uncle is king. Bothvarr's quarrel with the king's warriors when
he first comes to court suggests the Unferth episode in *Beowulf.*
There are, however, discrepancies. In the *Hrolfssaga* there is one
monster, not two, and that monster a winged creature apparently
of the dragon type, and in no way suggestive of Grendel, or Grendel's dam, of the *Beowulf.* Nevertheless, the resemblances between
the *Hrolfssaga* and the *Beowulf* in general pattern and structure
cannot be disregarded, and it seems probable that the *Hrolfssaga*
represents, in later and grotesquely transformed tradition, the same
fusion of folk-tale and chronicle that produced the Old English
epic. That there is an underlying identity of Beowulf and Bothvarr Bjarki is unmistakably suggested by the Icelandic ballads in
which Bothvarr aids Athils in battle against Ali, as Beowulf aids
Eadgils against Onela.[29]

It is not possible to trace the dragon fight of the *Beowulf* to
specific sources or analogues. There are certain details in Saxo's
account of Frotho's battle with a dragon[30] which somewhat
resemble details in the Old English poem, and those who find
these resemblances convincing explain the puzzling use of *ealond*
in the *Beowulf*[31] by its correspondence to the *island* of Saxo's narra-

28. *Beowulf,* Introd., p. xix.
29. *Beowulf,* 2391–6.
30. *Gesta,* ii, 38.
31. *Beowulf,* 2334.

tive. However, many dragons have wound their way through the pages of medieval legend, and for much of the incidental detail relating to Beowulf's dragon broad and general correspondences are to be found in various versions of the dragon myth.

It is at any rate significant that the assignment of the *Beowulf* dragon to the guarding of burial treasure is in accord with ideas of the nature and attributes of dragons as set forth in the Old English *Gnomic Verses*: 'The dragon lieth on the grave-mound, old, exultant in treasure.' It is a grave-mound and a burial treasure that has become the concern of the *Beowulf* dragon. The description of the dragon's barrow suggests somewhat precisely a type of ancient European burial mound. These mounds, constructed of earth, completely covered an inner burial chamber and entrance passage, which were built of huge slabs of stone. The opening into the passage could be closed with stone slabs, blocking entrance into the mound. In the *Beowulf* the dragon had found the mound 'standing open.' The various references in the poem to the dragon's earth-hall, or barrow,[32] are sufficiently detailed to indicate beyond doubt that it was such a burial mound the poet had in mind, and even to warrant conjecture that the description may have been based on actual observation.

Two widely differing accounts of the origin of the buried treasure are set forth in the poem: the first, in an extended elegiac passage;[33] the second, in a briefer statement near the end of the poem.[34] According to the first account a whole race of men had perished, dwindling until one solitary survivor held the accumulated wealth of the clan. Lonely of heart and grieving for the dead past, he buried the treasure in a newly-built barrow, recommitting the gold to the ground from which it came. The passage of which this is the prelude includes some of the finest elegiac verse in Old

32. ll. 2212–13, 2232, 2271, 2410, 2515, 2718 ff.
33. ll. 2231–70.
34. ll. 3051–75.

English poetry, and displays themes and imagery characteristic of such lyrics as the *Wanderer* and the *Ruin*:

> Keep thou, O Earth, what men could not keep,
> This costly treasure; it came from thee!
> Baleful slaughter has swept away,
> Death in battle, the last of my blood;
> They have lived their lives; they have left the mead-hall.
> Now I have no one to wield the sword,
> Or burnish the beaker of beaten gold,
> The precious flagon; the host is fled.
> The hard-forged helmet fretted with gold
> Shall be stripped of its inlay; the burnishers sleep
> Whose charge was to brighten the battle-masks.
> Likewise the corselet that countered in war,
> Mid clashing of bucklers, the bite of the sword—
> Corselet and warrior decay into dust;
> Mailed coat and hero are moveless and still.
> No mirth of gleewood, no music of harp,
> No good hawk swinging in flight through the hall;
> No swift steed stamps in the castle yard;
> A long line death has leveled to dust.[35]

The origin of the buried treasure, as set forth in the second passage, is quite different. In this instance the treasure had been buried in the earth by illustrious princes of old, with magic spells and a curse to protect it from invasion. As the implications of the passage are reconstructed by Lawrence, 'illustrious chieftains buried the gold with spells to protect it, pronouncing a curse upon those who should disturb it. When the hoard was plundered, the curse operated immediately; the dragon began his fearful ravages.'[36] Of these two accounts, so apparently in conflict, it seems probable that the second is the older. In such instances of variance we catch glimpses of the processes of growth and transformation by which the material of our poem has been shaped: slow accumulation of

35. ll. 2247–66.
36. *Beowulf and Epic Tradition*, p. 215.

legend, tradition upon tradition; incomplete fusion of material stratified as to age and source.

One of the most dramatic elements in the description of Beowulf's struggle with the dragon is the noteworthy depiction of *comitatus* spirit memorably personalized in the figure of Wiglaf. The youth of the lad, his heroic courage, his contempt for the cowards who have deserted their lord, and his hero-worshipping devotion to Beowulf, combine to suggest in striking terms the Germanic imperative of unconditional loyalty to overlord and king. It has been frequently noted that there are similarities between the Wiglaf scenes in the *Beowulf* and the *comitatus* episode in the *Battle of Maldon,* similarities which extend to detail, and in one instance to almost identical phrasing of the 'boast-words' of Beowulf and Leofsunu. Such parallelism can hardly be accidental. Carleton Brown, in a recent study of the relation of the *Beowulf* to the seventeenth *Blickling Homily,* inclines to the view that in the late tenth-century *Maldon,* as in the *Blickling Homily,* we have to do with passages modified and shaped by reminiscence of the *Beowulf.*[37]

The joining of the dragon fight to the Grendel material furnishes illustration of the poetic shaping that has transformed the primitive materials of folk-tale and chronicle into a finished epic tale. The story of the heroic Beowulf must be rounded out to his death. And the death must be worthy, a death in battle, but in noble battle. The material of the dragon myth lay ready at hand. Elements of the supernatural in the myth made battle with the dragon heroic and death glorious. More important, the death of Beowulf is set forth as the death not of a great king only, but of a good king. The idealism of youthful adventure had matured into the sober virtues of a ruler whose life expressed the best of his age: concern for his people, regard for his word, the preference of peace over war, the desire for fame.

37. *PMLA,* LIII, 905–16.

The artistry of a tale can be judged by its ending. The narrative of the *Beowulf* has worthy conclusion in its final scene, a 'set-piece' of outstanding excellence. The funeral of Beowulf has elements that suggest comparison with similar burial scenes of classical epic.[38] The burning of the body, the building of the barrow, the formal devotion of armor and trophies, the dirges and elegiac laments, are familiar detail of burial ceremonial reflecting the customs of the Heroic Age. It is possible that the descriptions in the *Beowulf* may reflect Gothic custom as reported by Jordanes in his account of the funeral of Attila.[39] The warriors of Beowulf who rode about his barrow chanting his virtues and mourning his death suggest the horsemen of Attila who rode 'in a circle' round his body with 'a lay of lamentation.' But it is to be noted that very much the same custom seems to be indicated in the description of the burning of the dead in the Eleventh Book of the *Aeneid*[40]: 'Thrice, girt in glittering arms, they have marched about the blazing piles, thrice compassed on horseback the sad fire of death and uttered their wail.'

HISTORICAL BACKGROUNDS

The narrative of the youthful heroism and the last battle and death of Beowulf, rooted, as we have seen, in the primitive material of folk-tale, is skilfully projected against a background of history and chronicle. The historical material in the poem is not set forth in connected sequence, but is present in passages of allusion, reminiscent or foreshadowing. Though the course of historic incident, if reconstructed from the *Beowulf* alone, is not always clear or complete, comparison with analogous material in Scandinavian and Icelandic saga and chronicle will often supplement and clarify the historical elements of the Old English epic. In general the allusions in the *Beowulf* have to do with the civil dis-

38. *Aeneid*, VI, 179–235; XI, 182–212.
39. *De Origine Actibusque Getarum*, xlix, 12.
40. *Aeneid*, XI, 182–212.

sensions, the tragic and bitter feuds, which characterize the chronicles of the Geats and the Danes. The use of this material has, of course, essential appropriateness in an epic narrative in which the two principal figures, Beowulf and Hrothgar, were respectively of Geatish and Danish blood.

The *Beowulf*, then, suggests in somewhat shadowy outline the fateful history of two dynasties, the glories of great kings, and their tragedies of violence and blood. The opening verses of the poem stress the splendor of the Danish line. As the story begins, Hrothgar, son of Healfdene and fifth in the line of Scylding succession, held the throne. The fame of his rule was widespread and the light of Heorot, his great council hall, 'shone over many lands.' His queen, Wealhtheow, lady of the Helmings, holds no minor position in the poem, but plays her part with dignity and grace in the established ceremonial of the court.

But seeds of dissension had been sown, and foreshadowing of tragic events now and again darkens the lines of the poem. The succession from Healfdene should have descended through Heorogar, the eldest son, to Heorogar's son, Heoroweard. But Heoroweard had been passed over and Hrothgar, his uncle, had succeeded to power. The reasons that had led to this apparent usurpation are not made clear. Some dim light, perhaps, is thrown upon the matter by Hrothgar's gift to Beowulf of Heorogar's armor.[41] Such alienation of his father's war-gear should normally have been considered a disgrace to Heoroweard. But Hrothgar intimates that it had been Heorogar's own wish that his armor should not descend to his son. Whatever of justice, or injustice, may lie hidden behind this extraordinary incident, the slighted and neglected Heoroweard is a figure of the tragic background biding his time, and in the end winning a short-lived revenge.

It is Heoroweard's cousin, Hrothulf, son of Halga, who throughout the poem holds a place of honor at court, living on

41. *Beowulf*, 2155–62.

apparently friendly terms with Hrothgar and the king's sons,
Hrethric and Hrothmund. But there are passages in the poem
which seem to imply uneasiness on the part of the king and queen
about the fate which might befall their sons when Hrothgar's
death should leave them vulnerable. Wealhtheow, it is true,
expresses her confidence that Hrothulf will favor and protect
Hrethric and Hrothmund,

> if he bears in mind
> The many honors   and marks of love
> We bestowed upon him   when he still was a boy.[42]

But the very qualification of the remark seems to intimate suspicion and fear, and this may explain the earnestness of Wealhtheow's request that Beowulf befriend her sons with counsel and
help. It may have been a similar uneasiness in Hrothgar's mind
that led to his adoption of Beowulf as foster son,[43] and to Beowulf's assurance that, should Hrethric ever have reason to come to
the Geatish court, he would find there a multitude of friends.[44]

Whatever the degree of foreshadowing in such passages, the
Scandinavian analogues make it clear that after Hrothgar's death
Hrothulf took arms against Hrethric, slew him, and seized the
throne.[45] But his treachery was not to go unavenged. The long-
brooding, slighted Heoroweard struck at last. With a small following of Danes augmented by a Swedish force, he attacked and
killed Hrothulf and set fire to the hall. But in the very moment of
triumph, and in the act of receiving the oath of homage, Heoroweard was stabbed to death by a surviving follower of Hrothulf,

---

42. ll. 1185-7.
43. ll. 946-50.
44. ll. 1836-9.
45. Kemp Malone ('Hrethric,' *PMLA*, xlii, 268-313) suggests an ingenious outline
of Hrothulf-Hrethric relations. Malone brings evidence from Scandinavian sources into
relation with the *Beowulf* to indicate that Hrethric for a time actually held the Danish
throne, having driven Hrothulf out of power only in turn to be overthrown again by
Hrothulf.

and amid the smoke of the burning hall the Scylding dynasty came to its end.

Side by side with the allusions in the *Beowulf* to this chain of dissension and treachery, there is more extended reference to the bitter and bloody feud which the Danes waged with their neighbors, the Heathobards. The origin of the feud apparently dated from the reign of Healfdene, who was slain by Froda, king of the Heathobards. The Danes in turn avenged Healfdene's fall, killing Froda and burning his hall. It was at this stage that Hrothgar proposed to compose the feud by the betrothal of his daughter Freawaru to Froda's son Ingeld.

The betrothal of Freawaru permits the poet to develop one of the most dramatic themes inherent in this historical material. A passage in Beowulf's narrative of his Danish adventures[46] expresses his foreboding that, in spite of Hrothgar's diplomacy, the feud is certain to flare up with renewed bitterness. Beowulf foresees that when Ingeld shall lead his lady into hall she will be attended by a Dane wearing sword and armor which had been taken as spoil in battle with the Heathobards. The son of the slain and despoiled Heathobard, angered by this affront, is incited to revenge by an older warrior, who used the opportunity to awaken the ancient feud:

> Do you see, my lord,   the sword of your father,
> The blade he bore   to the last of his fights,
> The pride of his heart,   as under his helmet
> The Scyldings slew him,   the savage Danes,
> When Withergyld fell,   and after the slaughter,
> The fall of heroes,   they held the field?
> And now a son   of those bloody butchers,
> Proud in his trappings,   tramps into hall
> And boasts of the killing,   clothed with the treasure
> That is yours by your birthright   to have and to hold?[47]

46. ll. 2024-69.
47. ll. 2047-56.

Heathobard resentment, thus fanned into flame, brought bitter renewal of the feud, and in the end Ingeld led an invading force which stormed Heorot and attacked Hrothgar. The Old English *Widsith*[48] gives a brief record of the defeat and slaughter of the Heathobards in this battle: 'For a long time,' we are told, 'Hrothwulf and Hrothgar, nephew and uncle, kept peace with one another after they had driven off the Viking race, crushing the attack of Ingeld and hacking down in Heorot the Heathobard host.' Ingeld apparently died in the battle, and of the youthful Freawaru, so woefully enmeshed in this web of tragic fate, we hear no more.

There are few passages in the *Beowulf* which strike a more dramatic note than this story of the aged warrior, whose repeated incitement inflames to vengeance the humiliated son and pours out in renewed bloodshed all the rancors of the ancient feud. It is dramatic narrative done with relish and vigor, and may well have its kinship to those songs of Ingeld for love of which Alcuin once rebuked the Northumbrian monks in his famous letter to Bishop Hygbald of Lindisfarne.[49]

A somewhat detached figure, a certain King Heremod, whose position in the Danish line is by no means clear, is twice[50] prominently mentioned in the *Beowulf* in terms which indicate that legends of his life and rule afforded familiar material for poetic use. The *Anglo-Saxon Chronicle* lists Heremod as the father of Scyld, the founder of the Scylding line. In spite of suggestions of myth, the story of Heremod has obvious elements of realism, and it is a matter of interest that his name has the *H* alliteration characteristic of the Scylding dynasty. Whatever his position in the line of succession, he seems to have been widely known for his deeds of violence, and for lack of that generosity which the *comitatus* ideal required of a noble lord and leader.

48. *Widsith*, 45–9.
49. 'Quid Hinieldus cum Christo? Angusta est domus; utrosque tenere non poterit.'
50. *Beowulf*, 901, 1709.

References in Saxo to the father of Scyld, there called Lotherus, seem to throw light upon the story of Heremod. It would appear that it was after an elder brother had proved incompetent that Heremod seized the throne, and ruled the Danes. But his vices speedily disclosed themselves. He was guilty of slaying comrades in drunken rage, and of lack of generosity toward loyal followers. Driven from power in the end, he seems to have furnished a stock *exemplum* of unworthy rule, and Hrothgar's homiletic speech[51], shortly before Beowulf's departure, urges him to avoid Heremod's vices and to learn from Heremod's fate.

Those passages in the *Beowulf* which deal with the chronicles of the Geats and their constant wars with the Swedes are somewhat less clear than the poet's treatment of the Scylding dynasty and, except for the fine passage on the battle of Ravenswood[52] and the elegiac lines suggested by the death of Herebeald,[53] less dramatic. Beowulf is portrayed in his later years, and as king of the Geats; indeed, he is represented in the poem as the great king of that dynasty. But it is notable that his name does not alliterate with *H* as is characteristic of the names of the kings who preceded him, Hrethel, Hæthcyn, Hygelac, and Heardred. Evidently, as the material of the poem took shape, he was inserted into the Geat succession and, in this respect, was drafted from folk-tale into chronicle. Lawrence finds him less convincing as a figure of chronicle than as a hero of folk-tale. 'Beowulf constantly betrays his origin as a folk-tale hero. A certain unreality surrounds him as king; he is more at his ease as a slayer of monsters.'[54]

Within the range of our poem, the royal line of the Geats may be said to have begun with Hrethel. His reign was darkened, and his old age embittered, by one of those tragedies which from time to time gave such dramatic pathos to legends and chronicles of

51. ll. 1700–1784.
52. ll. 2922–99.
53. ll. 2444–62.
54. *Beowulf and Epic Tradition*, p. 87.

Germanic life. Hrethel had three sons, Herebeald, Hæthcyn, and Hygelac. Herebeald died before his father, accidentally killed by an arrow from Hæthcyn's bow. Such a death created for Hrethel the most tragic situation that could grow from the customs of the Germanic feud, involving, as it did, an irreconcilable conflict of loyalties. It was his duty to avenge Herebeald's death. But duty and loyalty alike withheld him from taking vengeance upon his own son.

A fine elegiac passage in the *Beowulf* springs directly from this incident. The poet, in his treatment of the theme, describes an aged father who, like Hrethel, mourned for a son killed under circumstances which precluded revenge:

> In the house of his son   he gazes in sorrow
> On wine-hall deserted   and swept by the wind,
> Empty of joy.   The horsemen and heroes
> Sleep in the grave.   No sound of the harp,
> No welcoming revels   as often of old!
> He goes to his bed   with his burden of grief;
> To his spirit it seems   that dwelling and land
> Are empty and lonely,   lacking his son.[55]

It was in this mood that Hrethel mourned for Herebeald. His days and nights were shadowed by this tragic sorrow, and in the end he died of a broken heart.

The bitter wars between the Geats and the Swedes seem to have begun in the reign of Hæthcyn as a result of attacks on the Geats made by Onela and Ohthere, sons of Ongentheow, the Swedish king. In revenge Hæthcyn led an invading force against the Swedes, captured Ongentheow's queen, and fought a pitched battle with the Swedish force near the forest of Ravenswood. This battle is mentioned near the end of the *Beowulf*, where the description has marked dramatic relevancy, occurring, as it does, in a speech which prophesies renewal of the Swedish feud as a result of Beowulf's death.

55. *Beowulf*, 2455–62.

In the battle of Ravenswood, as described in the *Beowulf*,[56] Ongentheow slew Hæthcyn and rescued the Swedish queen. He drove the wearied forces of the Geats into the forest where he held them through the night hemmed in and helpless:

> All the long hours of the night   he thundered his threats
> That some on the morrow he would slay   with the edge of
>   the sword,
> And some should swing on the gallows   as food for the fowls.[57]

But hope returned with dawn when the hard-pressed Geats heard the horn of Hygelac and the trumpets of the troops he brought to their aid. The stronghold to which Ongentheow withdrew was stormed and taken by the Geats, and in the struggle Ongentheow was killed by two brothers, Wulf and Eofor. Eofor's heroism was rewarded by marriage with the only daughter of Hygelac.

During the lull in the Swedish wars which followed, Hygelac embarked upon the famous expedition against the Franks in which he lost his life. This raid, probably to be dated about 516, is described in Gregory's *Historia Francorum*, and in the *Liber Historiae Francorum*, and is repeatedly mentioned in the *Beowulf*.[58] Hygelac was successful in the initial attack, devastating the land, taking prisoners, and loading his ships with spoil. But before he could embark he was attacked by Theodoric's son, Theodobert, and killed. His fleet of ships was defeated in a naval battle and the captured booty recovered by the Franks. Certain lines of the *Beowulf*[59] reflect, even in this material of chronicle, the fabulous nature of legends that clustered around Beowulf's name. After slaying Dæghrefn who had killed his uncle, he made his way to the shore with thirty suits of armor on his back, and escaped by swimming the sea-stretches from Friesland to southern Sweden.

56. ll. 2922–99.
57. ll. 2937–41.
58. ll. 1202–14; 2354–68; 2501–8; 2913–21.
59. ll. 2354–68.

After Hygelac's death, his queen, Hygd, offered the rule to Beowulf, having no hope, as we learn from the poem,[60] that her young son Heardred could defend the land against foreign foes. Beowulf refused the offer, but undertook to serve as protector until the youthful Heardred should come of age.

During Heardred's reign war with the Swedes once more broke out.[61] The cause of the renewal is not altogether clear. Apparently, in some manner, the nephews of the Swedish king Onela, his brother Ohthere's sons Eanmund and Eadgils, had become involved in a conspiracy against Onela. The conspiracy had failed, and they had taken refuge among the Geats under the protection of Heardred. In revenge Onela attacked the Geats. Eanmund was slain, Eadgils fled, and Heardred lost his life in defending the exiled Swedish princes.

With Heardred's death the rule passed to Beowulf, and there seems to have been an interval of peace. But later, the poem tells us,[62] Eadgils made a second attempt on the Swedish throne in a war in which he had strong support from Beowulf, and in which he was successful. Thereafter, during Beowulf's long reign, there is no hint of further trouble between the Geats and the Swedes. But as the poem comes to its close, with Beowulf dead and his power ended, the minds of the Geats are filled with dark forebodings of a renewal of this ancient inter-tribal feud.

These are the themes of tribal tradition, the tragic legends of violence and fate, borrowings from which are interwoven with transcript of folkway, and epic invention, to shape a frame for the fabulous tales of Beowulf's triumph over monster and dragon. The interweaving of these strains of chronicle, legend, and folktale must have been a process of gradual fusion through long years of tradition. But the poet's skill in control of this traditional

60. ll. 2369-72.
61. ll. 2379-90.
62. ll. 2391-6.

material is displayed throughout the poem. The allusions are sufficiently central and sharp to suggest the historic background and, where the nature of the material has invited more extended poetic development, the poem has been enriched by deft and artful use of these themes. The story of Ingeld, the lines on Heremod, the elegiac portrait of Hrethel mourning for his son, and the dramatic description of the fight at Ravenswood, all serve to provide background and perspective. The material of tribal history and tribal legend is employed to heighten action, and to adorn the telling of an epic tale.

CHRISTIAN INFLUENCE

We have seen that the primitive material of the *Beowulf* was derived from pagan folk-tale, chronicle, and legend, and slowly welded into new unities. It remained for the Old English poet to complete this process of fusion by the conversion, or transmutation, of this material from pagan to Christian. The epic emerges at last as a Christian poem. This mutation, moreover, is not merely a matter of altered phrases, or of interpolated references to the Christian faith, but is a deeply pervasive infusion of Christian spirit coloring thought and judgment, governing motive and action, a continuous and active agent in the process of transformation.

This mutation of material could not in the nature of things be absolute or complete. There are pagan elements in the poem which resist change, or which are only partially subdued by the influence of the Christian spirit. The presence in the poem of references to the curse upon the dragon's hoard, and the survival of this *motif* side by side with another and quite different account of the origin of the treasure, is one example among many of the persistence of pagan tradition in a Christian poem. Other examples of this incomplete fusion of pagan and Christian will be found in a parallelism of reference to the blind and inexorable power of *Wyrd*, or Fate, and to the omnipotence of a divine Ruler who governs all things well. But even in survivals of pagan material the modifying influence of Christian thought is often evident. In both instances in which there is reference to the curse upon the dragon's treasure[63] the poet specifically excludes from the operation of the curse one who has God's favor. Elsewhere in the poem *God* and *Wyrd* are brought into juxtaposition in such manner as to imply control of Fate by the superior power of Christian divinity. The original derivation of Grendel and his dam from the Scandinavian waterfall troll is submerged and lost in the poet's identification of the monsters with the fiends of Christian mythology, incarnations of evil and adversaries of God. Though Beowulf has a remote prototype in the laggard younger son of folk-tale, and has been accorded a place in the succession of Geatish kings, his character has been recast and developed in the spirit of the Christian tradition. Throughout the poem, divine guidance is invoked, and acknowledged, as the assisting force by which the heroic deeds of Beowulf are accomplished. After his death his fame is celebrated not only, and not most, for valor and venturous deeds, but for the gentler qualities of Christian virtue. And it is precisely this presence in the poem of pagan derivatives modified by Christian influence which points, in Chambers' opinion, to the Age of Bede rather than a later date, as the period in which the *Beowulf* was written.[64]

The Christian influence in the *Beowulf* is a matter of transforming spirit, rather than of reference to dogma or doctrine. And it is, in the main, an influence reflecting the Old Testament rather than the New. The poem contains specific references to Cain's murder of Abel, and to the stories of the Creation, the giants, and the Flood. But we find no such allusions to New Testament themes as characterize, for example, the *Christ* of Cynewulf. Indeed, considering the nature of the material with which the poet is working, we should hardly expect such references.

63. ll. 3052, 3069.
64. Chambers, *Beowulf, An Introduction*, p. 488.

Some critics have believed that the *Beowulf* was composed not by a Christian but by a pagan poet, and that the presence of the Christian material is to be explained by subsequent excision of pagan, and interpolation of Christian, passages. Others have argued that the Christian elements represent the work of a poet with only vague and general knowledge of the new faith, or merely nominal adherence to it. The weight of evidence does not support such opinion. The Christian spirit is too deeply ingrained in the poem to permit the hypothesis of original composition by a pagan poet. A just appraisal of the pervasive nature of these Christian elements supports Chambers' opinion that the *Beowulf* cannot be regarded as 'the work of a man whose adherence to Christianity is merely nominal.'[65]

It is not unnatural, therefore, that the essentially Christian genius of the poem is most clearly perceived not so much in details of Biblical theme and phrasing, as in those passages in which Christian ethics are central in shaping speech and influencing conduct. We find such a passage in the homiletic speech of Hrothgar in which the Danish king paints for Beowulf a warning portrait of the man betrayed by worldly prosperity into pride, and by pride into sin:

> He lives in luxury,   knowing not want,
> Knowing no shadow   of sickness or age;
> No haunting sorrow   darkens his spirit,
> No hatred or discord   deepens to war;
> The world is sweet,   to his every desire,
> And evil assails not,   until in his heart
> Pride overpowering   gathers and grows!
> The warden slumbers,   the guard of his spirit;
> Too sound is that sleep,   too sluggish the weight
> Of worldly affairs,   too pressing the Foe,
> The Archer who looses   the arrows of sin.[66]

65. Op. cit. p. 126.
66. *Beowulf*, 1735-44.

The substance and import of the *exemplum* are clearly in the tradition of the medieval Christian moralist. The treatment of the material affords an unusually interesting illustration of the manner in which the Christian spirit is at work in the poem, transforming and supplementing the stuff of pagan tradition. The similarity of this passage to the material and spirit of certain passages in Cynewulf's *Christ* and *Juliana* has often been noted. But the 85 lines of Hrothgar's speech[67] have seemed to some critics an inartistic interruption of the narrative, tediously homiletic in substance. Such a judgment seems to overlook, or underestimate, the process by which a cruder system of pagan morals is being reshaped in these lines by the criteria of Christian ethics.

It must be recognized that Hrothgar's warning against the sin of pride, and its corroding effect in character, is by no means an unnatural intrusion into the narrative. To understand fully the spirit of his advice to the young Beowulf, we must remember the closeness of the tie that had grown up between them. It is not only a natural gratitude that motivated Hrothgar's words, but also a warm personal affection. He has already adopted Beowulf as a foster son,[68] and at their final parting there are tears in the old king's eyes, and grief in his foreboding that they may never meet again.[69] It is, therefore, not unnatural that in these last hours he should muster, from ripe old age and experience, words of kindly counsel to the youth whose heroic career is now in its brilliant dawn. And it is not unnatural that the Christian poet should give the turn to the passage which he does give.

The warning example which Hrothgar uses is the career of Heremod. The wrongs for which the name of Heremod was execrated were the evils of violence and greed in his relations with his *comitatus*, and with his people. He slew his followers in fits of

67. ll. 1700–1784.
68. ll. 946–9.
69. ll. 1871–6.

drunken rage, and failed in the generous bestowal of rewards which the *comitatus* relation required from lord to retainer. He was unfaithful to the two outstanding obligations imposed by the *comitatus* bond, the duties to protect, and to reward, his followers. These obligations were rooted in a pagan code. Censure and warning in this passage, therefore, could have been grounded on purely pagan convention.

But the Christian poet, in his homily on pride, derives from the story of Heremod ethical judgments that go beyond the pagan code. He traces the sins of violence and greed backward to roots in pride, and forward to punishment here and hereafter. The concepts of a pagan morality are expanded into Christian ethics in a formal passage suggestive of the moralizing allegories of virtue and vice so characteristic of later medieval literature.

When all is said, the fact remains, since the *Beowulf* is not a religious but a secular poem, that its Christian elements are more general and diffused than is characteristic of distinctively religious Old English poetry. The old heroic themes furnish stubborn material, and retain some portion of their native strength even in the hands of a Christian poet. The nature and degree of the Christian influence is best understood when one estimates the poem as a composite of traditional themes of pagan heroism retold by a Christian poet. The resulting fusion of pagan and Christian is what could naturally be expected under such circumstances. The material affords no opportunity for reflections of the intimate and personal responses of the individual soul to the Christian drama of the New Testament. We need not look for mystical adoration, as in the *Dream of the Rood*; or for echoes of the liturgy, as in *Christ I*; or for reflections of theological dogma, as in *Christ II*. The *Beowulf* is a tale of the pagan past in which the endurance, the loyalty, the courage, and the strength, of the heroic age are tempered by union with Christian virtues, graced with courtly manners, and elevated in presentment to levels of epic dignity.

THE INFLUENCE OF CLASSICAL EPIC

It is difficult to estimate precisely the degree of influence exerted by classical epic, particularly the *Aeneid*, upon the shaping of the *Beowulf*. But it is certainly not unnatural that we find reflections of the Virgilian epic in the form and spirit of the Old English poem. The *Aeneid* was well known in the early Middle Ages. We have record that Bede, Aldhelm, and Alcuin were lovers of Virgil, and it would seem unlikely that an educated poet of the Age of Bede could have shaped the epic tale of *Beowulf* without having had in mind the model of the classical epic. Careful study of the two poems has shown that there are many lines in the *Beowulf* which read like echoes of Virgilian phrase, and elements of structure which suggest parallels in the *Aeneid*. Klaeber, in an article entitled 'Aeneis und Beowulf,'[70] and Haber, in his comparative study of the *Beowulf* and the *Aeneid*,[71] have compiled exhaustive lists of parallelisms in phrase, theme, and situation.

It seems unlikely that additional parallelisms between the *Beowulf* and the *Aeneid* remain to be discovered. But there is an influence of the *Aeneid* upon a passage in the Old English poem which has not hitherto been pointed out. A description in the *Beowulf* of Grendel's mere, a finely wrought passage of twenty lines (1357–76), lingers in the mind of many a reader as perhaps the finest 'set-piece' of the poem. The descriptive suggestiveness of this picture of the forbidding landscape of Grendel's pool affords evidence of a sensitively poetic mind at work. The passage is a familiar one and has received extended consideration by many critics. As long ago as 1912, in a study entitled 'The Haunted Mere in *Beowulf*,'[72] Lawrence gave us an admirable analysis of this passage and an illuminating comparison with corresponding material in the *Grettissaga*.

70. *Archiv für das Studium der neueren Sprachen und Literaturen*, CXXVI, 40-48; 339-59.
71. *A Comparative Study of the Beowulf and the Aeneid*, Princeton, 1931.
72. *PMLA*, XXVII, 208-45.

Parallels in this *Beowulf* passage to seemingly correspondent, or at least suggestive, passages in the *Aeneid* have been noted.[73] In each of three instances the *Beowulf* text has several suggested parallels in the *Aeneid,* and, perhaps for this reason, it has not been emphasized that *one* possible parallel for *each* of the three passages in the *Beowulf* is found within a scope of 92 lines (479–571) in the Seventh Book of the *Aeneid*. If the Old English poet, then, had recently been reading the Seventh Book he might from this reading have had lodged in memory three elements which have been unified in his description of Grendel's mere: the hart pursued by hounds, the stormy waves that rise to the sky, the gloomy landscape of the mountain torrent. This fact is significant and suggestive, presenting, as it does, the possibility that fused reminiscence of elements from a comparatively short passage of Virgil influenced the development of Hrothgar's famous description of Grendel's pool.

The possibility of such fused reminiscence in these lines of the *Beowulf* seems no less likely for the fact that in the Virgilian passage[74] the three elements cited are not unified, as they are in the *Beowulf*, as elements in a single passage of description. The reference to the stormy waves rising to the sky occurs in the *Aeneid* as the material of a Virgilian simile. The episode of the haunted stag is introduced as a motivation in the design of the Fury, Allecto, to stir up war between the Latins and the Trojans. The painting of a forbidding landscape occurs in a description of the Vale of Amsanctus, a hell-mouth into which, her purpose fulfilled, Allecto sank and 'relieved earth and heaven of her hateful presence.'

The parallelism I have cited deserves special consideration, both

73. *Beowulf*, 1357–67 to *Aeneid*, vi, 136–9; 237–8; 295–7; 369; 438; vii, 565–71; xi, 522–5.

  Beowulf, 1368–72 to *Aeneid*, iv, 69–73; vii, 479–504; xii, 749–55.

  Beowulf, 1373–5 to *Aeneid*, i, 133–4; iii, 422–3; v, 790–91; vii, 529–30; xii, 204–5.

74. *Aeneid*, vii, 479–571.

because of the triple nature of the resemblance involved, and because of the bearing of the Virgilian passage upon a statement in Hrothgar's description, the appropriateness of which in its context is at least dubious. If we think of the poet as shaping his inherited material with realism, and uninfluenced by literary reminiscence, lines 1373–6 of the *Beowulf* seem inappropriate in a description of an inland lake, or pool, or swamp. If it is an inland mere that we are dealing with, and the weight of evidence seems to indicate that it is inland water and not an arm of the sea, then it is difficult for the reader to accept even a poetic statement that 'from it the tossing waves rise dark to the sky, when the wind stirs up foul weather.' Such a statement is surely far more applicable to the high waves on a storm-tossed ocean, and this is undoubtedly the reference in Virgil's simile.[75] But if we postulate that the Old English poet, dealing with a landscape not wholly understood, is composing description less realistic than literary, and with a vivid sea simile of the *Aeneid* in memory, the possibility of Virgilian coloring in these lines of the *Beowulf* becomes clearer.

The possibility that Virgil's description of the Vale of Amsanctus[76] is reflected in lines 1359–64 of Hrothgar's description seems also worth close attention. In the Virgilian landscape a swift torrent in swirling eddies pours down over rocks, shut in between wooded ridges dark with foliage. There is also a 'ghastly pool,' a 'breathing-hole of the grim lord of hell, and vast chasm breaking into Acheron.' Through this hell-mouth the Fury, Allecto, returns to the underworld. Even the briefest comparison of the two passages will indicate the similarities in the two descriptions: the mountain torrents, the ridges or cliffs in the gloom of which these streams pour down, the trees that overshadow, the dismal and gloomy nature of the landscape.

It is interesting to remember in this connection the assertion of

75. Ibid. 528–30.
76. Ibid. 563–71.

the *Beowulf* poet,[77] when the wounded and fleeing Grendel
plunged into the mere, that there 'hell received him.' It may be
that we have in this line merely a natural implication of the tradition by which, throughout the poem, Grendel is repeatedly
identified as a demon and an enemy of God. The statement may
represent foreshadowing of his death, and the return of his spirit
to hell. But it can also represent a more literal statement, and it is
significant that in Virgil's lines the Fury, Allecto, returns to the
underworld through the hell-mouth of Amsanctus.

Virgil's wounded stag of the Seventh Book[78] has no such role
as the *Beowulf* poet assigns his antlered hart in suggesting the
eerie nature of the mere by willingness to die upon the bank
rather than enter the water. But again it is significant that Virgil's
stag is upon the bank of a stream, and turns away from it when
wounded, and pursued by hounds. The reasons in the two
instances are quite different, but the situations are the same in this
respect, that in each poem we have a stag wounded, pursued by
hounds, and at the water's edge, and in each instance the stag turns
away from the water to die.

The attempt to appraise the influence of one work upon another
is properly approached with caution. Critics most convinced of
the influence of the *Aeneid* upon the *Beowulf* may be least convinced of the validity of particular parallels. And we must not
forget that the Old English poet had inherited a scenery original
with his folk-tale material, however it may have been modified in
tradition. But it would in no way be unnatural if his reshaping of
this inherited material had been influenced by details from Virgil
which could so easily fuse with the scenic elements of his original.
If any single passage of the *Beowulf* tempts one to believe that the
Old English poet was composing with pen guided by reminiscence of the *Aeneid,* it is, I think, this description of Grendel's

77. *Beowulf*, 852.
78. *Aeneid*, vii, 483–6, 493–5.

mere and the hints of Virgil's Seventh Book that seem latent in it.

In any attempt to isolate and appraise an influence of the *Aeneid* upon the *Beowulf* we meet with difficulties. The manners and customs of the Age of Troy were in many ways like the manners and customs of the Germanic Heroic Age, representing similar cultural levels, and similar folkways. Parallels between the two poems, then, may arise from similar methods in the reflection of similar conventions. It could hardly be considered surprising if the descriptions in the two poems of social ceremonial, of war and council, feast and funeral, should follow very similar patterns. Lists of parallels, therefore, however imposing, have not produced unqualified conviction that the *Beowulf* reveals borrowing from the *Aeneid*. Lawrence expresses the cautious opinion that 'while the influence of Vergil may be regarded as entirely possible, it cannot be conclusively established.'[79]

Judgment regarding a direct borrowing from the *Aeneid* does not, however, completely dispose of the question of Virgilian influence in the *Beowulf*. Even if it were granted that in all the parallelisms that exist between the two poems there is no conclusive evidence that the English poet borrowed from the Latin epic, there still remains a question of indirect and diffused influence of the form and spirit of classical epic upon the shaping of the Old English poem. Chambers' remark on this point is important and suggestive. 'But the influence may have been none the less effective for being indirect: nor is it quite certain that the author, had he known his Virgil, would necessarily have left traces of direct borrowing. For the deep Christian feeling, which has given to *Beowulf* its almost prudish propriety and its edifying tone, is manifested by no direct and dogmatic reference to Christian personages or doctrines.'[80] It is notable that the *Beowulf* in general

79. *Beowulf and Epic Tradition*, p. 285.
80. *Beowulf, An Introduction*, pp. 330-31.

form and movement displays a literary quality of richly developed theme, and an epic dignity of speech and action. And it is precisely this general element in the poem which could easily and naturally have come from the influence of Virgil's epic, in years in which the *Aeneid* was well known among the scholars of England.

THE SPIRIT OF THE POEM

To what extent is the *Beowulf* an old tale retold merely for the joy of the telling? To what extent is it developed as an exemplification of noble kinghood and the Christian ideal? An epic tale lends itself gracefully to purposes of doctrine, as the tradition of the epic so richly shows. A well-known letter of Edmund Spenser, outlining the design and structure of the *Faerie Queene*, sets forth in clear terms the underlying purpose with which the author had shaped the allegory of his immortal poem: 'The generall end therefore of all the booke, is to fashion a gentleman or noble person in vertuous and gentle discipline.'

It is never a simple matter to separate in a work of art didactic purpose from the aesthetic aims of creation. And in the case of the *Beowulf* we have no such statement of purpose as Spenser's to throw light upon the poem, and no knowledge of the poet's identity, or way of life, by which to guide interpretation of his underlying intent. Many would define his purpose quite simply, as the desire to tell an old tale of heroism in verse, and to tell it well.

Yet many passages in the poem suggest that the author had more in mind than the mere retelling, however well, of a heroic tale. There is a difference between tales of heroism and a narrative of a heroic life, and in the story of *Beowulf* the reader is made to feel that the author is conscious of this difference. The Old English Christian poet, as we have seen, had his moralizing strain and, like his Renaissance successor, may have felt that a narrative of a heroic king, elevated to epic dignity and illumined by the

Christian ideal, could well serve for the fashioning of men to magnanimous and noble living.

Certain it is that under the pen of the *Beowulf* poet the stubborn stuff of Scandinavian legend is tempered and refined, and there emerges the figure of a noble and Christian king. The poem reflects the spirit, not of Scandinavia, but of English life of the seventh and eighth centuries, presenting a blending of old folkways with new, a welding of pagan heroism with Christian virtue. The miracle of the *Beowulf* is the artistry of its refashioning. However widely the poem may range through the tribal lands of Scandinavia, the mood and spirit are the mood and spirit of England; the poetic ideal is the Christian ideal. The pagan backgrounds of the poem sink into shadow. The old dark tales of men and lands beyond the sea echo as from a vast distance. The story of Beowulf becomes an English poem. It becomes a poem suited to a Christian court, and fitted for the shaping of men in 'vertuous and gentle discipline.' Even an ancient tale of pagan heroism, transformed by Christian spirit, could become an element in the stream of influence that flowed from the Christian Church. Lives of saints and martyrs formed a literature for the stirring of men's souls to faith and virtue and, side by side with such spiritual heroisms, the ancient tale of Beowulf's struggle with monster and dragon may well have lent itself to the uses of Christian allegory.

The unmistakable English strain in the *Beowulf* is perhaps clearest in the elegiac tone and moral temper of the poem. The elegiac element, which twice wells up with a poignancy suggestive of the lyric sadness of the *Wanderer* and the *Ruin*, is the poetic symbol of early English life amid the scattered and ruined reminders of the Roman settlement. And in the moral temper of the poem there is clear reflection of the birth and shaping, largely through the dawning influence of the Christian faith, of nobler concepts of human relations and political duty. Feud and treachery, murder of kindred and usurpation, have illustration in the poem, it is true, as they had illustration in contemporary English annals. But a new order of life is symbolized in the condemnation and repudiation which, in the poem, are unfailingly directed against such manifestations of violence and crime.

The youthful Beowulf of the beginning and the aged king of the final scenes alike illustrate the chivalry of spirit that ennobles heroism. The Beowulf of the Grendel adventure was in essentials a knight-errant of his age. It was no call of duty which urged him across the sea to stake his life against monsters. Indeed, though his personal followers urged him on, Hygelac had endeavored to dissuade him from the undertaking. So we learn from his uncle's words at the banquet after Beowulf's return:

> I had no faith   in this far sea-venture
> For one so beloved.   Long I implored
> That you go not against   the murderous monster,
> But let the South-Danes   settle the feud
> Themselves with Grendel.[81]

Such were the words of expediency! It can be granted that the poet portrays a youthful hero fired with love of adventure. But there is more than love of adventure that urges Beowulf on; there are demons to kill, and a curse to be lifted. More than once his words to Hrothgar reflect the sober spirit of one who strives with the powers of evil: 'I will fight to the death, foe against foe; then let the one whom death takes put his trust in the Judgment of God.' In all the young lad does and says, there is courage. But, more important, there is also magnanimity.

The tradition of doom in the dragon fight is a survival from the pagan world. But it has taken on new depth of implication. The tragic glory of the conflict is its illustration of man's heroic war with powers of darkness and evil beyond his strength. The tragic glory of Beowulf's death is its illustration of that fated

81. *Beowulf*, 1992–7.

courage which fights to the utmost, knowing the utmost will not avail, and fighting on.

It is in the exercise of the powers and responsibilities of kingship that the poet stresses most Beowulf's magnanimity, and the Christian ideal. In his early manhood, refusing power for himself, Beowulf served as Protector of the young king Heardred. Becoming king at Heardred's death he had for fifty years ruled wisely and well. At the end, as he lay dying, his thoughts were of the needs of his people. For himself, as he looked back upon his life, he rejoiced that after death the Lord of mankind could not charge against him the killing of kinsmen. His reign had been a reign of peace and justice. Abiding by his appointed lot he had sworn no unrighteous oaths, had kept his own well, had courted no quarrels. As the smoke of his funeral pyre rose to the sky, his people lamented the passing of the kindest of earthly kings, the mildest and most gentle.

The *Beowulf* is a priceless heritage from the earliest age of English poetry. Forgotten for centuries, and rediscovered, it has at last by the devotion of many scholars come into its own, unfolding before us its ancient excellence. Across the centuries from the Age of Bede it proclaims the ideal of gentleness united to strength, and valor ennobled by virtue. It speaks to the modern world in moving accents of honor, of courage, and of faith. It is a tale of a vanishing age retold in the dawn of a new day. The pagan gods were fading into the darkness; new light was upon the world. The flash and thunder of Thor were not wholly forgotten; but the bolt was spent and the echoes dying. The old legends of violence and blood formed shadowy background for a tale of Christian courage and virtue. Twice in a heroic lifetime mortal valor was pitted in crucial conflict with the ravening forces of evil. Twice a hero turned back the invading dark. In his youth he conquered and lived; in age he conquered and died. To live or to die was as fate might ordain. To conquer was all.

IV. THE ELEGIES

Wanderer; *Seafarer*; *Ruin*; *Wife's Lament*; *Husband's Message*; Elegiac elements in *Beowulf*

INCLUDED among the poems of the Exeter Book is a group of lyrics which, from their mood of sadness and lament, are usually described as elegies. These poems are the *Wanderer*, *Seafarer*, *Ruin*, *Wife's Lament*, and *Husband's Message*. Various critics have suggested that there is a genetic tie by which certain of these poems, together with the *Wulf and Eadwacer* lament, are related as fragments of a lost poem dealing with the subject matter of some heroic legend. Grein[1] believed that the *Wife's Lament* and *Husband's Message* are broken fragments of a single poem. Trautmann[2] and Brandl[3] set forth similar opinion. Imelmann[4] insists dogmatically that the *Eadwacer* fragment, the *Wanderer*, *Seafarer*, *Wife's Lament*, and *Husband's Message* are interrelated portions of a lost *Eadwacer* poem. Miss Rickert[5] would link the *Wife's Lament* to an Old English *Offa* saga. Such is the variation of critical opinion.

It must be recognized that any attempt to link the *Elegies* to the material of *heldensage* must take into account a wide difference in the nature of the *Elegies* themselves, in accordance with which they fall into two groups. In the *Wanderer*, *Seafarer*, and *Ruin* we have poems of simple theme and structure in which there is no evidence of dependence upon heroic legend. On the other hand, as Lawrence[6] points out, in the *Wife's Lament*, the *Husband's*

1. *Kurzgefasste Angelsächsische Grammatik*, p. 10.
2. *Anglia*, XVI, 222 ff.
3. *Geschichte der Altenglischen Literatur*, p. 977.
4. *Die Altenglische Odoaker-Dichtung*, 1907; *Wanderer und Seefahrer im Rahmen der Altenglischen Odoaker-Dichtung*, 1908; *Forschungen zur Altenglischen Poesie*, 1930.
5. *Modern Philology*, II, 321–76.
6. 'The Banished Wife's Lament,' *Modern Philology*, V, 387–405, p. 399.

Message, and the *Wulf and Eadwacer* lament, 'the very backbone of the dramatic structure is in all probability a well known heroic tale.' To date, however, no one of the various attempts to isolate and identify this underlying heroic material has been completely convincing.

In spite of the centuries which lie between the present and the age reflected in this body of verse, the spirit and in many instances the details of the *Elegies* have that timeless quality which marks the simple treatment of themes universal in significance, and independent of changing civilizations. The *Seafarer*, for example, is one of the finest sea-poems in our tongue. English poetry has given us a large body of verse which reflects emotionally the impact of the sea upon the lives of men, and the varied moods and images arising from contemplation of sea life have contributed to the realisms and symbolisms of our literature from the age of the Saxon raiders to the days of Swinburne and Masefield. Yet not many poems in this long line of tradition have excelled the *Seafarer* in fashioning into lyric rhythms an authentic depiction of the hardship, the danger, the lure of ocean life for men who go down to the sea in ships.

Another lyric in this group, the *Wanderer*, still today endures comparison with any poem of our literature which clothes with primitive realism love of land and leader, or elevates to stoic fortitude the ache of loneliness and exile. Indeed, such have been the changes in the forms of civilization, the tragic symbol of a 'man without a country' can hardly be as bitterly vivid to the modern mind as was the fate of his Germanic prototype to our early English ancestors.

This stress upon the grief and loneliness of the lordless and friendless exile is a Germanic note which recurs frequently in Old English verse. It has been suggested[7] that the *Wanderer* and *Sea-*

7. Helga Reuschel, 'Ovid und Die Angelsächsischen Elegien,' *Beiträge zur Geschichte der Deutschen Sprache und Literatur*, LXII, 132–142.

farer reflect a knowledge of the *Tristia* and *Epistolae ex Ponto* of Ovid, and in some degree owe to these sources their artistic inter-weaving of themes of exile, wintry weather, and elegiac sadness. Such as influence is, of course, conceivable, but there is no conclusive evidence of it. Ovid's sophisticated epistles, lamenting the imperial edict which exiled him to Tomis and contrasting the genial Italian climate to the bitter winters of the Black Sea coast, have little in common with the *Wanderer* and *Seafarer* in substance or shaping. The mood of these elegies is a familiar Old English mood, and the tragic sadness of the *Wanderer* grows from the bitter implications of the broken ties of the *comitatus* bond.

Two of the *Elegies* are love poems—stirring in their emotional appeal. *The Wife's Lament*, voicing the grief of a wife separated from her husband, subjected to the faithless cruelty of his kin, and ignorant of the fate of her beloved, is tragedy elevated and ele-mental. *The Husband's Message*, rehearsed by a wooden tablet carved with runes, which passed in lieu of letter from lover to mistress, summons her to renew old vows and join her lover in a land beyond the sea.

The quality of timelessness and universality in this group of lyrics is reinforced by an elegiac strain, of exceptional poignancy, which characterizes portions of the *Wanderer* and *Seafarer*, and is of the very form and substance of the *Ruin*. With these poems from the Exeter Book may be included two passages occurring near the end of *Beowulf*,[8] which stand out from the framework of that poem with a narrower integrity of spirit and design conferred by the informing presence of this strain of elegy.

These Old English elegies differ markedly in mood and pattern from the personal elegy. They do not bewail the death, or eulo-gize the life, of an individual. They have little in common with modern elegies of the type of *Lycidas* and *Adonais*. In detail and design they owe no debt to the pastoral idyll. Their range of

8. *Beowulf*, 2231-70; 2444-62.

interest is universal, deriving from a moving sense of the tragedy of life itself—*sunt lacrimae rerum*—a consciousness of the transience of earthly joy, and the fleeting glory of earthly strength. Their rhythm is tuned to the ceaseless flow of time and change. Their pathos springs from knowledge that all life moves with frail feet and fragile wings. Their dignity clothes a recognition that man's years of breath are first a hope and brief struggle, then silence, memory, and the ruin of time.

The mood of the Old English elegies is the mood of undaunted reflection upon the universal lot of mankind, the inexorable limitation of man's existence by the mutable and mortal. Written, in all probability, in the eighth or early ninth century, these lyrics must have been responsive to dominant elements in the life of that troubled era. The turbulent wars of Northumbrian and Mercian kings, with their attendant destruction of records and ruin of monuments, must have sharpened in sensitive minds a sense of the unsubstantial nature of worldly power and achievement. The influence of spreading Christianity, with its emphasis upon the transience of earthly, and the permanence of spiritual, values, furnished a background of thought fitted to exhibit and interpret the elegiac mood.

But it is not necessary to emphasize external literary or social influence for the development of popular elegy. Elegiac themes are native to the thoughts of sensitive minds, and the appeal of these themes, clothed with the dignity of universal application to human fortune, is amply illustrated in English poetry by the popularity of so characteristic an expression of the genre as Gray's *Elegy Written in a Country Churchyard*. The contemporary spirit of the Old English elegies is itself a reflection in poetic style of the poignancy of emotion with which each generation must recognize the weakness of human strength, the fleeting breath of earthly beauty, the hovering mystery of death.

Not the least characteristic quality of these elegies is the temper of stoic endurance whereby their emotional intensity never weakens to sentimentalism, nor their meditations on mortal fate to self-pity or despair. Their genius blends a sensitive perception of human woe with an acceptance of a mortal destiny in whose grip man's virtue is less to struggle than to bear.

THE WANDERER

It is a mark of the literary excellence of the *Wanderer*[9] that its sustained intensity of poetic emotion and its realisms of detail and atmosphere banish all thought of the centuries which have passed since its composition. The opening theme of the lyric, bewailing the bitterness of exile and the hopeless drifting of a life cut off from ties of loyalty to clan or leader, has a relative validity for any age, but in the *Wanderer* derives a special significance from the Old English social background against which the poem is projected.

The social unit in Germanic and early Anglo-Saxon life was the clan, and in this unit originated primitive conceptions of social duty and political loyalty. Indeed, it may be said that in the organization of family, clan, and *comitatus* lay the primitive germ of all subsequent social and political systems of Germanic life.

The place of the individual in such a society ranged between two polar limits. At one extreme stood the head of a powerful clan clothed with an individualism symbolic of the utmost in authority and splendor; at the other extreme, the clanless man, the lordless wanderer, who had no 'gold friend or protector.' In a society which had not yet achieved the concepts of nationalism and citizenship, such a man could have little protection of law, or focus of loyalty. Loosed from ties to clan or leader he became in a very special sense a man adrift. The misery attending such a fate is a frequently recurring note in Old English poetry, but nowhere has it received such vivid, extended, and emotional presentment as in the *Wanderer*.

9. Exeter Book, fol. 76b—fol. 78a.

One root of the modernity of atmosphere which characterizes this poem is its faithful depiction of nature. This realism, though selective in detail, derives not from literary convention but from first-hand and observant contact with the external world. An evidence of the actuality of experience which underlies the treatment of nature in the *Wanderer*, and in other poems of this group, is found in the recurring portrayal of details of climate. In few poems of our tongue may we find more continuous stress upon the interrelationship of elements of weather with the lives of men.

Both the *Wanderer* and the *Seafarer*, in the weather described and the scenery portrayed, are so touched with the chill of winter hardship that it has been somewhat generally, and perhaps too easily, assumed that these poems reflect the climate of the Northumbrian coast, and are of Northumbrian origin. It is a view, however, that cannot be taken for granted. In 1939, Miss Hotchner, in an informative and penetrating study,[10] assembled a considerable weight of evidence in support of her suggestion that certain poems in the Exeter Book, notably the *Wanderer, Seafarer, Ruin, Riddles,* and Exeter *Gnomes,* are to be regarded as West-Saxon productions.

Whatever its provenance, the lines of the *Wanderer* are stormy with the breath of winter: the breaking crests of icy combers on wintry seas; gray stretches of tossing ocean empty save for the wings of gull and gannet; snow and hail driven by the blast of the gale against ruined walls, the mouldering memorials of a vanished age; frost and cold and the dark terror of night.

Such are the details which create the atmosphere of lines in which the Wanderer recalls the days of his happy youth when in the service of a beloved lord he had known the 'joys of the hall,' the feasting and revelry, the bestowal of treasure. But his days of happiness had ended with the death of his leader and, when the dark earth had closed the grave, nothing remained but to take

10. Cecilia A. Hotchner, *Wessex and Old English Poetry, with special consideration of the Ruin*, New York, 1939.

ship with sorrowful heart over wintry seas, seeking a new gold-lord, a new friend and protector.

In the years of his exile the Wanderer finds no lord who can take the place of the lost leader of his youth, and the poem contains a suggestive intimation of the lingering ache of that early loss in a vivid description of the memories which haunt his dreams:

> And, dreaming, he clasps   his dear lord again,
> Head on knee, hand on knee,   loyally laying,
> Pledging his liege   as in days long past.
> Then from his slumber   he starts lonely-hearted
> Beholding gray stretches   of tossing sea,
> Sea-birds bathing   with wings outspread,
> While hail-storms darken,   and driving snow.
> Bitterer then   is the bane of his wretchedness,
> The longing for loved one: his grief is renewed.[11]

A host of associated recollections steal in upon his loneliness. In the fog that shrouds gray leagues of sea he beholds the faces of former friends and comrades. But they are illusions of the mist bringing no comfort, speaking no word of friendship. They melt into air, and the actualities of loneliness and exile once more close in about him.

This note of separation and bereavement characterizes the first half of the poem, and forms an appropriate introduction to the elegiac mood of the remainder. The transition is a natural one. As in the individual life youth and friendship fail, and old age is stripped of the strength and joy of former days, so is it with the centuries, so with the race. All mortal things decay, and vanish in the night of the past.

> Where now is the warrior?   where is the war-horse?
> Bestowal of treasure   and sharing of feast?
> Alas! the bright ale-cup,   the byrny-clad warrior,
> The prince in his splendor!   Those days are long sped.[12]

11. *Wanderer*, 40-50.
12. ll. 92-5.

Only shattered walls, the ruin of former strength, remain as a memorial of a splendor which once stood supreme.

> No wonder, therefore, in all this world
> If a shadow darkens upon my spirit
> When I reflect on the fates of men —
> How one by one proud warriors vanish
> From the halls that knew them, and day by day
> All this earth ages and droops unto death.[13]

It is this theme which introduces the definitely Christian ending of the *Wanderer*. The poem concludes, as it began, with a reference to the mercy of God. It has been suggested that the Christian element is not an integral portion of the original poem. Critics have explained its presence by the assumption that portions of two distinct poems have by error been joined to form the existing text, or that the Christian passages represent later additions to an earlier poem. Similar views have been urged as to the Christian element in the *Seafarer*. These suggestions seem to imply that there is inconsistency between the religious and secular passages in these poems which needs explanation. But this is not a necessary assumption.[14] Indeed, in each poem it is possible to regard the Christian passages as following with complete literary consistency from the elegiac passages. The transition is not unnatural, but is governed by a contrast in the poet's mind between the mutable and transient nature of earthly life and the changeless and eternal life of a celestial kingdom where joy is without end, and where the soul finds an everlasting stronghold. So interpreted the *Wanderer* is noteworthy for its rendering of elevated themes in lyric form, its unity of design, and its liveliness of mood and image. It affords an example of high excellence in its genre.

13. ll. 58-63.

14. Cf. Lawrence's conclusions as to the *Wanderer* in his penetrating article, 'The Wanderer and the Seafarer,' *Journal of Germanic Philology*, IV, 460-80.

The Seafarer

The lyric qualities which we have noted in the *Wanderer* are exemplified in almost equal degree in the *Seafarer*.[15] Its lines reflect the actualities of ocean life and seamanship with such faithful directness that, save for the idiom, the poetic rendering is as expressive of the emotions and attitudes of the nineteenth century as of the ninth. The sailor's intimate struggle with elemental forces of ocean and air; the rigor, loneliness, and danger of wintry voyages in uncharted seas; the lure and fascination that intertwine even with knowledge of peril, and strip it of repelling force; these attributes of the sailor's life and mood are set forth in the *Seafarer* with sensitive faithfulness.

A song I sing   of my sea-adventure,
The strain of peril,   the stress of toil,
Which oft I endured   in anguish of spirit
Through weary hours   of aching woe.
My bark was swept   by the breaking billows;
Bitter the watch   from the bow by night
As my ship drove on   within sound of the rocks.
My feet were numb   with the nipping cold,
Hunger sapped   a sea-weary spirit,
And care weighed heavy   upon my heart.
Little the land-lubber,   safe on shore,
Knows what I've suffered   in icy seas
Wretched and worn   by the winter storms,
Hung with icicles,   stung by hail,
Lonely and friendless   and far from home.
In my ears no sound   but the roar of the sea,
The icy combers,   the cry of the swan;
In place of the mead-hall   and laughter of men
My only singing   the sea-mew's call,
The scream of the gannet,   the shriek of the gull;
Through the wail of the wild gale   beating the bluffs

15. Exeter Book, fol. 81b—fol. 83a.

The piercing cry   of the ice-coated petrel,
The storm-drenched eagle's   echoing scream . . .
Yet still, even now,   my spirit within me
Drives me seaward   to sail the deep,
To ride the long swell   of the salt sea-wave.
Never a day   but my heart's desire
Would launch me forth   on the long sea-path,
Fain of far harbors   and foreign shores.[16]

Strangely enough, this very fusion in the sailor's mind of fear and fascination—surely a sufficiently familiar psychological phenomenon—has led more than one critic to interpret the poem as a dialogue between an aged seaman, weary of toil and hazard, and a youth whose longing for adventure lures him to the sea.[17] There is little ground in the poem itself to support such a division into dialogue, and the case of those who propound this theory is not strengthened by the fact that they have been unable to agree as to points of division. Indeed, the theory that the sea passages represent a dialogue goes far to destroy the subtlety and psychological realism of the author's conception. Those who have written intimately of the sea have not infrequently measured her hold upon the hearts of men precisely by the fact that it is a spell which cannot be permanently weakened by hardship or peril, but continues to draw the sailor to the sea in spite of his recognition of its cruelty and strength. It is this thought which fashions the salty appeal of certain of the sea passages in this poem.

To a greater degree than is true of the *Wanderer*, the *Seafarer* is Christian in spirit. The religious element, concentrated in the second half, has caused extended debate concerning the unity of the poem, and many scholars have accepted the view that, in the

---

16. ll. 1–25; 33–38.

17. Rieger in 1869, *Zeitschrift für deutsche Philologie*, i, 330 ff., suggested division of the poem into dialogue assigning to the aged mariner ll. 1–33; 39–47; 53–7; 72 to the end; to the young sailor 34–8; 48–52; 58–71. Kluge, *Englishe Studien*, vi, 322 ff., Boer, *Zeitschrift für deutsche Philologie*, xxxv, 1–28, and others, have accepted the theory of dialogue, but vary in their divisions.

form in which it has come down to us, the *Seafarer* cannot be considered the work of one poet. Those who hold this opinion regard the original poem as ending at line 64, and an added Christian section as beginning at that point with the lines,

> But fairer indeed   are the joys God has fashioned
> Than the mortal and mutable   life of this world.

It is questionable whether critical scholarship has not, in more than one instance, gone to unjustified lengths in the dissection of Old English poems to divorce passages considered pagan and original from Christian passages regarded as added or interpolated. It could hardly be considered unnatural if a poet of the early centuries of Northumbrian Christianity, experiencing conversion to the new faith and devoting his talents to its service, produced verse which blends, in unusual degree, realistic elements from secular experience with the accepted conventions of Christian literary tradition. It is noteworthy and suggestive that the two halves of the *Seafarer* present just such a contrast.

An interesting interpretation of the *Seafarer* as religious allegory was proposed in 1909 by Ehrismann.[18] He accepts the poem as a unit in the sense that it is the work of one author, though much of the material was traditional both in content and form, and the whole, in that sense, a reworked composite. Ehrismann regards the *Seafarer* as an allegorical rendering of the transient joy and pain of earth in sea imagery, with this presentment set in contrast to the everlasting bliss of a heavenly kingdom. The contrasting sections are linked into unity by the implications of the elegiac passages and their emphasis on the mutability and mortality of earthly life.

The principal doubt as to this interpretation arises from the style of the first section of the poem, where sharply subjective

18. 'Das Gedicht vom Seefahrer,' *Beiträge zur Geschichte der deutschen Sprache und Literatur*, xxxv, 213–18.

mood and realism of detail are so obtrusive as to seem incompatible with the theory that a general idea is there clothed in the conventions of allegory.

The use of sea imagery in an allegorical contrast of earthly existence and the Christian vision of life after death is not without parallel in Old English poetry. An instance particularly in point is to be found in a passage of 17 lines with which Cynewulf concludes the second division of the *Christ*. The thought of the passage was suggested by a sentence in Gregory's homily upon the Ascension[19] in which the turmoil of earthly life is viewed as a tossing upon stormy seas, and the voyager admonished to 'fix the anchor of hope upon an eternal fatherland.' From this brief, but definite, suggestion, Cynewulf has developed an extended simile, detail by detail in Virgilian manner:

> Now it is as if we sail in ships on ocean floods over chill waters, voyaging in our barks, our ocean-stallions, over the spacious sea. Perilous the flood, turbulent the surges, whereon we toss throughout this changeful world; windy the waves upon the deep sea-path! Bitter our way of life until we came to land over the ocean's ridge. Then came help when God's Spirit-Son guided us into the harbor of salvation and granted us grace, that we may know, even from the vessel's side where, fast at anchor, to tether our ocean-stallions, our old sea-steeds. Therefore, let us set our hope upon that haven which heaven's Lord, in holiness on high, has opened unto us by His Ascension.[20]

Even a cursory comparison of this artistic use of allegory with the specific realisms of the first half of the *Seafarer* is likely to strengthen a conviction that an interpretation of the *Seafarer* as didactic allegory is definitely challenged by the style of the poem itself.

19. Gregory, *Homiliarum in Evangelia*, II, 29, 11.
20. *Christ*, 850-66.

It seems much more likely that we have here to do with a poem which, though a unit, divides somewhat definitely into two contrasting sections generally corresponding to two types of experience in the life of the unknown author. Conversion to the Christian faith may well have separated adventurous, sea-faring years from a later period of religious devotion. The first half of the *Seafarer*, then, may reflect sharp memories of the hardships and adventurous joys of earlier secular life; the second half, with its Christian stress upon the hereafter, may represent in verse the fruit of later years of religious meditation and study.

Like the *Wanderer*, the *Seafarer* is a poem of northern atmosphere. Frost and cold, snow and hail, sea-mist and rain, wild gales that sweep the coast and carry the eerie cry of gull and gannet over stormy waves, these details set the stage for days and nights of numbing hardship and perilous adventure. The sailor who has been put to it to beat off a lee shore in the teeth of a gale will best estimate the actuality of the poet's recollections in such lines as,

> My bark was swept   by the breaking billows;
> Bitter the watch   in the bow by night
> As my ship drove on   within sound of the rocks.

The sea is portrayed as a capricious mistress, exacting and cruel, seductive and fatal. Her days are toil and hardship; her nights are weariness and peril. And yet there runs through the lines of the *Seafarer* a minor melody, a counterpoint of pride in the age-old struggle with ocean, a grim, affectionate loyalty to the ancient, implacable foe. Wind and salt spray and the circle of the distant sea-line have worked their sorcery in the mariner's heart and, even in the tumult of the gale and the dangers of the night watch, we catch the note of his scorn for the land-lubber 'safe on shore, whose town life pleasantly passes in feasting and joy, sheltered from peril.'

Details of past experience, vividly remembered and sharply

reproduced, set the tone of the poem and lead naturally to the elegiac and Christian passages. For it is the adventurer, the man of action striving upon the thin edge of peril and hazard, who most clearly recognizes the impermanence of earthly things. In the end strength fails, or fate betrays, and violence, or sickness, or old age breaks the thread of life. Only in a spiritual kingdom beyond death is there permanence and peace.

The expression of these themes in a vocabulary of unusual richness and variety, and the sustained mood of strong and tender feeling, suggest that the work of this unknown author was the product of a cultured and poetic mind composing in the spirit of established literary tradition.

THE RUIN

The *Ruin*[21] is an elegiac fragment of some 33 lines following immediately in the Exeter Book after the *Husband's Message*. An injury to the MS. as a result of fire, or the corrosion of damp, has worked such serious damage to the text of the *Ruin* that at two points, at line 9 and at line 33, occur passages which do not permit of reconstruction.

The theme of the poem consists of a poet's musings upon a mass of stone ruins which stand before him. His reflections are touched into vividness by a retrospective imagination which brings sharply to his thoughts the vanished splendor of these ruined structures, and the grandeur and glory of the men who built and occupied them. Such architectural hints as the text affords seem to imply that the ruins described are the varied and extensive remains of a Roman city. The broken walls and towers of stone, the shattered roofs of tile, mark the site where once stood splendid banqueting halls and Roman baths.

The descriptive material of the poem is general rather than specific. Such evidence as it affords for positive identification of

21. Exeter Book, fol. 123b—fol. 124b.

the ruins pictured is to be found in details which suggest the Roman character of these ruins, and in the allusions to hot baths or hot springs. The wording of the text[22] indicates clearly that the reference can hardly be to a system of baths artificially heated, like the Roman hypocausts, but must be to actual hot springs.

Because of the Roman details and the allusions to hot springs, Leo[23] in 1865 and Earle[24] in 1872 independently concluded that the Old English poem describes the ancient Roman ruins of the city of Bath, the Roman Aquae Sulis. Except for Herben's quite unconvincing suggestion that the description can be more appropriately applied to ruined sections of Hadrian's Wall,[25] the identification of the poem with Bath has been generally accepted. How strong is the evidence which supports this theory is clearly shown by Miss Hotchner in her monograph of 1939.[26] By a comparative study of the warm springs of England, together with a judicious assessment of archaeological and architectural evidence, she goes far toward establishing the identification with Bath beyond question.

It is the implication that the poem has to do with a definite place which differentiates the *Ruin* from a similar passage descriptive of ancient ruins in the second part of the *Wanderer*. In the latter the author is thinking not so much of a particular ruin as of the general extent to which, throughout the world 'in various places,' time and change bring destruction to the works of man. In both poems the depictions of the shattered walls fuse naturally with the elegiac material, and by specific illustration deepen and intensify the elegiac note.

The *ubi sunt* formula, employed so frequently in elegy, and

22. Strēam hāte wearp wīdan wylme.

23. *Carmen Anglo-Saxonicum in Codice Exoniensi servatum quod vulgo inscribitur Ruinae*, Halle, 1865.

24. *Proceedings Bath Natural History and Antiquarian Field Club*, II, 3,259-70.

25. 'The Ruin,' *Modern Language Notes*, LIV, 37-9 (Jan. 1939).

26. *Wessex and Old English Poetry, with special consideration of the Ruin*, New York, 1939, pp. 9-59.

exemplified in the lines of the *Wanderer* beginning, 'Where is the warrior, where is the war horse?', is not used in the *Ruin*. The more lyric interrogative is here replaced by gnomic rehearsal. The skill of the builders, the splendor of the palaces and baths, the glory and stately pride of the warlike race which inhabited them, these details are graphically set forth and touched with the elegiac mood:

> Many a mead-hall   rang with their revelry,
> Many a court   with the clangor of arms
> Till Fate, the all-leveling,   laid them low.
> A pestilence rose,   and corpses were rife,
> And death laid hold   on the warrior host.
> Then their bulwarks were broken,   their fortresses fell,
> The hands to restore them   were helpless and still.
> Desolate now   are the courts, and the dome
> With arches discolored   is stripped of its tiles.
> Where of old once the warrior   walked in his pride,
> Gleaming with gold   and wanton with wine,
> Splendidly shining   in glittering mail,
> The structure lies fallen   and scattered in ruin.[27]

Fragmentary and mutilated as is the text, the *Ruin* calls up in the reader's mind an emotional recognition of the contrast between the ruin of the present and the vanished glory of the past. In their brief and swift suggestiveness the lines invest the authentic spirit of Old English elegy, a recognition of earthly mutability, mortality, and overshadowing fate.

THE WIFE'S LAMENT

The *Wife's Lament*,[28] because of the obscurity of certain passages, presents more problems of interpretation than any of the poems we have been considering. The speaker of this poignantly dramatic monologue is a woman. The essential outlines of the unhappy fate she rehearses are clear enough. Her husband has gone

27. *The Ruin*, 23–34.
28. Exeter Book, fol. 115 a–b.

beyond the sea, and in his absence his kinsmen have plotted to alienate husband and wife. They have apparently succeeded, for at his command the wife has been condemned to take up her dwelling in a solitary cave under an oak tree, a punishment appropriate in Germanic legend either to marital unfaithfulness or to witchcraft. In this abode, shaken by uncertainty as to the fate of her lord, and wrung by love of him which her lot has in no way diminished, she gives expression to her wretchedness and longing. In their emotional energy the lines attain a note of passion which is heightened by the unusual dramatic situation in which the protagonist is a woman:

> A song I sing   of sorrow unceasing,
> The tale of my trouble,   the weight of my woe,
> Woe of the present,   and woe of the past,
> Woe never-ending   of exile and grief,
> But never since girlhood   greater than now.
> First, the pang   when my lord departed,
> Far from his people,   beyond the sea;
> Bitter the heartache   at break of dawn,
> The longing for rumor   in what far land
> So weary a time   my loved one tarried.
> Far I wandered, then,   friendless and homeless,
> Seeking for help   in my heavy need.
> With secret plotting   his kinsmen purposed
> To wedge us apart,   wide worlds between,
> And bitter hate.   I was sick at heart.
> Harshly my lord   bade lodge me here.
> In all this land   I had few to love me,
> Few that were loyal,   few that were friends . . .
> Lovers there are   who may live their love,
> Joyously keeping   the couch of bliss,
> While I in my earth-cave   under the oak
> Pace to and fro   in the lonely dawn.
> Here must I sit   through the summer-long day,
> Here must I weep   in affliction and woe.[29]

29. *The Wife's Lament*, 1–17; 33–9.

It is not altogether clear whether the *Wife's Lament* can be regarded as an independent *giedd*, or lay, or whether it is a fragment of a longer poem belonging to some cycle of legend. A decided stumbling-block to the theory that the theme of the *Wife's Lament* reflects material from any one of the various cycles of heroic legend which have been suggested is the absence in the text of a single proper name which would serve as identifying evidence. This same situation exists in the case of the *Husband's Message*, unless one is willing to accept Imelmann's reading[30] of the runes at the end of that poem as spelling out the name Eadwacer. And yet the frame of each poem is sufficiently extended, and the dramatic situation sufficiently crucial, to make the complete absence of proper names extraordinary if these lyrics are in fact fragments of a longer poem, or poems, dealing with traditional material of popular legend.

It is unfortunate that the meaning of the *Wife's Lament* has been obscured rather than clarified by interpretations for which the text of the poem affords little justification. Lawrence has shown clearly[31] the weaknesses of Schücking's attempt[32] to prove that the *Lament* is not uttered by a woman at all. It is equally difficult to take seriously Roeder's hypothesis[33] conjuring out of lines 42–8 the shadowy figure of a young man who has come between husband and wife and caused their separation. Roeder interprets the subjunctive form *sy* of lines 45 and 46 as a subjunctive of imprecation, and renders the passage as a series of maledictions which the lady calls down upon the author of her misfortunes.

A natural and unforced translation of the text gives a very different meaning. The passage runs as follows:

30. *Forschungen zur Altenglischen Poesie*, 163–79.
31. W. W. Lawrence, 'The Banished Wife's Lament,' *Modern Philology*, v, 387 ff.
32. *Zeitschrift für deutsches Alterthum*, xlviii, 436 ff.
33. See 'Die Familie bei den Angelsachsen,' *Studien zur Englischen Philologie*, iv, 112–19.

Ever must a young man   have sorrow of spirit,
Bitter musings of the mind;   he must likewise maintain,
In misery and crowding woes,   a cheerful demeanor
Whether all the joys   of the world be his portion,
Or whether it be   that, hunted and harried,
In a far country   under rocky cliffs
My friend sits smitten   with winter storms,[34] etc.

So translated these lines give no support to a theory which would introduce a third person into the pattern of this domestic tragedy. The statement with which the passage begins is a conventional gnomic utterance asserting that man's life is subject to hardship and sorrow which he must endure with cheerfulness.[35] The universality of this gnomic reflection is particularized in the mind of the wife by her thought of her absent husband on whom in his exile rests this same stoic imperative. Wherever he may be, he must still remember the happy years before their separation. The fate which has parted them is only one illustration of the woe by which human life is conditioned: man's years are always subject to sorrow, and the thoughts of his mind to sadness; yet he must maintain a cheerful demeanor, even when care oppresses the heart.

One other passage in the *Lament* has caused difficulty. Lines 17–21 are sometimes cited as evidence for a theory that the absent husband, hiding his feelings and assuming a friendly demeanor, is planning murder. But the word *morþor* of line 20 does not, of necessity, mean 'murder' or 'death.' Not infrequently it has the more general meaning of 'evil' or 'wrong.' Since the poem contains nowhere else any hint of murderous intention, lines 17–25 should probably be translated:

34. *The Wife's Lament*, 42–8.
35. Of these lines Miss Williams says in her study of the gnomic element in Old English poetry: 'I cannot here admit other than a general interpretation. The signs are significant—the *A scyle* formula, with its consequent material, is the same as that found in *Beowulf*, and the *Edda*, where universal truths are uttered, suggested by the immediate circumstance, but unquestionably free from it.' Blanche C. Williams, *Gnomic Poetry in Anglo-Saxon*, New York, 1914, pp. 49–51.

Therefore my heart   is heavy with sorrow
At finding the man   most suited to me
Unhappy in fortune,   despondent of heart,
Masking his mood   and planning a wrong.
With blithe hearts often   of old we boasted
That naught else should part us   save death alone.
All that has failed   and our former love
Is now as if   it had never been.[36]

It seems obvious, not merely from the sense of the passage itself, but from its relation to lines which immediately precede and immediately follow, that the lady of the *Lament* is bewailing her husband's altered mood and growing hostility not toward another, but toward herself. The helplessness of her position is in the fact that his kinsmen have so poisoned her husband's mind that her innocence has no defense against his suspicion. Apparently, some harder fate, some more bitter affliction, hangs over her. Perhaps her imprisonment in her cave-dwelling is to be ended by the penalty of death. Perhaps a temporary confinement is to be made permanent. Whatever the nature of the purposed wrong which she ascribes to her husband, it seems clear that it is a wrong against herself.

We have then, in the *Wife's Lament,* a self-contained lyric, nameless and timeless in its rehearsal of tragic fate, realistically recalling or assuming dramatic episode and situation, and evoking sincere emotion and the lyric mood. Whether the theme be a borrowing from ancient legend, or personal experience, or pure shaping of imagination, the *Wife's Lament* is a dramatic monologue of a high order of merit. Its obscurities are largely dissolved by a close reading of the Old English text; the most cursory reading is sufficient to prove its sincerity and passion.

The poem is unusual among Old English heathen poems in viewing tragedy through a woman's eyes. In the Christian poetry women naturally emerge to positions of prominence. In the Old

36. *The Wife's Lament,* 17-25.

Testament poems, for example, the eminence of Eve, and of Judith, is developed quite in accord with their respective traditions. In the saints' legends, such feminine figures as Juliana and Elene are protagonists set forth at full length with detailed stress upon motive and action. Even in *Beowulf*, Hrothgar's queen holds a position of graceful eminence in the ceremonial of court life. But in no other poem do we find, as in the *Wife's Lament*, an interpretation of tragic fate solely from the feminine point of view, or a definition of tragic catastrophe in the familiar modern terms of frustrated love.

THE HUSBAND'S MESSAGE

The *Husband's Message*, in its generally accepted form, is found on folio 123a–b of the Exeter Book. But there has been dispute as to the precise point in the MS. at which the poem begins. Folios 122b, and 123a–b contain four consecutive sections of verse, each beginning in the MS. with a large initial letter, and each followed by the conventional mark to denote a conclusion.[37] In spite of the implication of these scribal devices, the third and fourth sections are unmistakably joined by unity of theme. It is clear, moreover, that section A is not in any way to be connected with the following three sections. It is, in fact, a second version of the thirtieth riddle, which is found earlier in the Exeter Book on folio 108.

The case of section B is less certain, and the opinion has been advanced that these lines also form a riddle.[38] But a review of all available evidence seems to favor a judgment[39] that sections B, C, and D, instead of being separate and distinct units, are in fact constituent portions of a single poem. Indeed, the nature of the subject

37. For convenience of reference these sections may be lettered, according to their order in the MS. as A, B, C, and D.

38. Tupper (*The Riddles of the Exeter Book*, pp. 198–9) believes that a relationship exists between section B and the 'Reed' riddle of Symphosius.

39. Cf. Blackburn's article, *Journal of Germanic Philology*, III, 1–13.

matter of the three sections suggests a unity of design joining them in one coherent whole.[40]

The speaker, perhaps in all three sections, certainly in B and C, is a tablet of wood upon which has been carved in runic letters a message from an exiled husband to his wife. Section B rehearses how the wood once grew as a sapling in the sand of a seashore near a cliff. Few eyes beheld its lonely dwelling, but each dawn the dark wave played round it in flowing embrace. Little did the solitary dweller expect to have power of speech, or to hold discourse over the mead. But knife-edge and man's skill had fashioned it to bring the lady a secret message which no other person might understand.

Though the injury to the MS. has rendered somewhat doubtful the opening lines of section C, they seem to refer unmistakably to the growth of the sapling, thus linking the two sections. The carved tablet rehearses, for the lady's ear only, how it had grown and flourished until, fashioned to the service of her lord, it traversed wide seas to visit distant lands. Now, at the end of its voyaging, it brought the wife her husband's message proclaiming his loyal faith and enduring love.

It has been suggested that in section D the runic tablet is no longer conceived as the speaker, and that the words are to be credited to a human envoy who bears the carved wood as his credentials.[41] The speaker calls upon the lady to remember vows plighted in former days before the violence of a tribal feud had driven her lover from his native land. It recites the hardships he

40. The question of the interrelationship of the three sections in question is not made easier by an injury to the leaves of the MS. with resultant mutilation of portions of the text of C and D.

41. This view would seem to have some support in the use in the first line of section D of the phrase, *sē pisne bēam agrōf*, 'he who carved *this* wood,' suggesting by the word 'this' a lack of identity between the speaker and the carved wood. It may, however, be maintained that the text permits an interpretation which would make the *runic letters of the message*, by the phrase *pisne bēam*, refer to the wood upon which they were carved.

had undergone, and his happy issue from these afflictions. In a far country he has prospered until he now dwells in plenty, possessing wealth and a lordly estate. One lack remains—reunion with the 'prince's daughter' to whom he had pledged the faith and plighted the vows of his youth. Her lover now urges that, when she shall hear the cuckoo plaintively calling from the wooded hill-slope, she take ship for the south to join him, letting no living man delay the voyage or stay her journey.

> Lady ring-laden,   he bade me implore thee,
> Who carved this wood,   that thou call to mind
> The pledges ye plighted   before ye were parted,
> While still in the same land   together ye shared
> A lordly home   and the rapture of love
> Before a feud   drove him far from his folk.
> He it is bids me   eagerly urge
> When from the hill-slope,   out of the wood,
> Thou hearest the cuckoo   plaintively calling,
> Haste thee to ship   on the tossing sea.
> Let no living man, then,   delay thee in sailing,
> Stay thee in leaving   or stop thee in flight.
> Spread thy sail   on the home of the sea-mew,
> Take seat in thy galley   and steer away south
> To where o'er the sea-lane   thy lover awaits.[42]

The poem ends with a weaving into the text of runic letters: first *S* and *R*, then *EA* and *W*, and finally *D*. Whether these runes are used as letters forming a name, or with the separate word values of the runes themselves, or as symbols for names beginning with these rune letters, is by no means certain. All three theories have been proposed, but it must be admitted that no conclusively satisfactory interpretation of the passage has yet been suggested. One thing is clear, that the runes are intended to lend strength to the husband's oath renewing his former vows.

Of the various interpretations of the runes which have been

42. *The Husband's Message*, 30-46.

proposed, that of Trautmann[43] seems, on the whole, the most tenable. The construction of the passage, he believes, shows conclusively that the runes stand for proper names, in this instance names of men nominated by the exiled husband as sureties, or guarantors of his faith in the reaffirmation of a former oath. It is impossible, of course, to establish definitely the proper names symbolized by the runes, since variant forms would answer all requirements of runic usage.[44] Believing that the *Husband's Message* is a fragment of a longer poem, and perhaps related to the *Wife's Lament*, Trautmann suggests that, had we the entire text, we might well have the key to the names suggested by the runes.

It is a matter of interest that in line 11 of section D of the *Husband's Message*, as also in line 53 of the *Seafarer*, we have a reference to the song of the cuckoo occurring in connection with thought of a sea voyage. Kershaw[45] interprets the reference as being in general agreement with the treatment of the cuckoo in Irish poetry as the herald of Spring, and as suggesting the tendency of Old English and Scandinavian sailors to avoid winter voyaging whenever possible.

It may be, however, that these two references to the cuckoo's song contain a more definite implication of date than a merely general reference to the coming of Spring. In the two passages referred to, the same adjective is applied in each instance to the cuckoo's call, namely *gēomor*, sad, sorrowful, mournful. This particular adjective seems ill-chosen to characterize the cuckoo's note since rather generally in medieval and modern English verse the song of this bird is regarded not as mournful or plaintive, but as jocund and joyous.[46]

43. 'Zur Botschaft des Gemahls,' *Anglia*, XVI, 219–22.

44. As examples of possible renderings of runic *S* and *R*, Trautmann suggests S(ige) R(ēd), or S(ige)R(īc), or S(ǣ)R(ēd); for *EA* and *W*, EA(d)W(ine), or EA(rd) W(ulf), or EA(ld)W(ine); for *M*, M(on) or M(onna).

45. Cf. note to line 53 of the *Seafarer* in his *Anglo-Saxon and Norse Poems*, p. 169.

46. Cf., for example, the 'murie sing cuccu' of the thirteenth-century Cuckoo song, *Oxford Book of English Verse*; 'The merry cuckoo, messenger of Spring,' *Sonnet*, Spenser; 'O blithe newcomer,' *To the Cuckoo*, Wordsworth.

Light is thrown upon the use of the adjective in the passages under discussion by the fact that the cuckoo's call undergoes a change in late May or early June.[47] The cuckoo comes to England in April. Thorburn, writing of its habits, says: 'The males, travelling in advance of the females, soon announce their presence by the well-known call which, continuing through the month of May, becomes *broken and hoarse* before ceasing in June.'[48] There is also reference to this harsh and unpleasant change of note in one of the epigrams of John Heywood:

> In April the cuckoo can sing her song by rote;
> In June, out of tune, she cannot sing a note;
> At first, cuckoo, cuckoo, sing still can she do,
> At last, cuck, cuck, cuck,— six cucks to one coo.[49]

Old English poets usually employed adjectives of form, color, and sound with a realistic accuracy which reflected careful observation. It may well be, therefore, that the application in these passages of the adjective *mournful* to the cuckoo's song had reference to this unpleasing change of note in late May or early June, and that the reference was intentionally employed to suggest a sailing date, not in early Spring when seas might still be rough, but in June when the ocean would normally be safe and calm for pleasant voyaging.

In spite of all its uncertainties of interpretation the *Husband's Message* is one of the most charming of Old English poems. Like the *Wife's Lament* it reflects a prevailing mood of emotional intimacy. It is marked by the convincing realism with which it sets forth the fortunes of a nameless hero unconventionalized by any setting of martial or courtly splendor. Its substance and spirit are essentially romantic.

47. My attention was called to this point by my colleague, Professor Henry Savage, of Princeton.

48. A. Thorburn, *British Birds*, 11, 53.

49. Epigram 95 of the sixth hundred, *The Proverbs, Epigrams, and Miscellanies of John Heywood*, ed. John S. Farmer, London, 1906.

In this poem, as in the *Wife's Lament*, the severing shadow of adverse fate has parted lover from lover. In each poem the words of one of the divided pair become the expressive symbol of pangs of separation which only reunion may assuage. In the *Husband's Message* the love and loyalty of the man are projected against a background of active life and successful achievement in distant lands. In the *Wife's Lament* the spell of emotion is more absorbing, more subtly enveloping. Both poems exhibit a mood of unusual lyric passion, and in their lines the lovers, nameless and unknown, are vivid and vital still with the haunting breath of the anonymous.

BEOWULF (2231-70), (2444-62)

Two passages from the third, or dragon, episode of the *Beowulf* afford additional illustration of the elegiac mood. The first (2231-70) constitutes in itself a small but complete unit easily detached from the frame of surrounding text, and strikingly setting forth the substance and the spirit of Old English elegy. The elegiac strain in this passage is so poignant in its phrasing that, as Lawrence remarks,[50] it 'suggests vividly the tone of the so-called "Northumbrian lyrics," ' and brings immediately to mind the corresponding strains of the *Wanderer*.

The lines in question have to do with the treasure of the dragon's hoard. To a student of *Beowulf* the passage presents certain difficulties since the poem contains, at a later point in the narrative,[51] a second and, in some details, conflicting account of the origin of the treasure. The questions thus raised need not, however, detain us, since the first of the two passages, which particularly concerns us here, is unified and consistent in itself, and the second account is lacking in those elegiac elements which give lines 2231-70 their elegiac mood.

After Beowulf had slain the night-prowling monsters, Grendel

50. *Beowulf and Epic Tradition*, p. 219.
51. ll. 3047-75.

and Grendel's dam, thus purging Hrothgar's hall of the evil which for twelve years had cursed it, there occurs an interval in the narrative. During this period Beowulf, having returned to his own country, ultimately succeeds Hygelac, his uncle, in power and for fifty years rules his people well. It is in the hero's old age, then, that a dragon, angered by the plundering of the treasure hoard he guards, begins to ravage the realm. Beowulf's hall is burned by flames kindled by the dragon's fiery breath, and once more it is necessary for him to take up arms against a scourge of the people.

The two accounts of the genesis of the dragon's hoard are widely variant. The version given in lines 3047-75, as reconstructed by Lawrence, is that centuries earlier 'illustrious chieftains buried the gold, with spells to protect it, pronouncing a curse upon those who should disturb it. When the hoard was plundered, the curse operated immediately; the dragon began his fearful ravages.[52]

In the earlier version the details are quite different. A mighty race has dwindled to one solitary survivor. He has inherited the wealth of his clan. But his days are numbered, and for a little time only may he hope to enjoy the treasure. In this version no curse is placed upon the hoard. Its final owner lodges it in a barrow beside a sea headland, and there guards the store of gold and precious plate until the coming of death,

> Lonely and sad   survivor of all,
> Restless by day   and wretched by night
> Till the clutch of death   caught at his heart.[53]

After his death the hoard is discovered by the dragon, and since, as the poet declares, it is the nature of dragons to seek out buried treasure and guard the heathen gold, the monster broods for three hundred winters over the barrow and the treasure trove. At last, a fugitive from justice, seeking means to expiate by gift or pay-

52. *Beowulf and Epic Tradition*, p. 215.
53. *Beowulf*, 2267-70.

ment a wrong he has committed, steals from the hoard a precious
cup. The anger of the dragon thus kindled leads to the ravaging
of the land, the burning of the hall, and to Beowulf's last fight
and death.

The elegiac elements in this passage are found chiefly in the
formal speech with which the treasure is committed to the barrow
by its last, solitary owner. His words begin with an address to
earth itself:

> Keep thou, O Earth,   what man could not keep,
> This costly treasure;   it came from thee![54]

The lines that follow contain the conventional material of the
Old English elegy in its lament for the vanished glory of the past.
A race has perished; they have lived their lives, they have left the
mead-hall. Not one remains to polish the flagon, or burnish the
battle-mask and sword. Warrior and armor alike are mouldering
in earth.

> No mirth of gleewood,   no music of harp,
> No good hawk swinging   in flight through the hall;
> No swift steed stamps   in the castle yard,
> A long line death   has levelled in dust.[55]

So passes the glory of earth! Of the proud host one only remains for a little time of wretchedness, a few hours of loneliness
before the coming of death. Of former wealth and magnificence
only this tarnishing heap of golden treasure survives, and that too
in the end returns to the earth from which it was digged. The rest
is silence, the stillness of ruin and death, and the soft, enveloping,
ceaseless flow of time.

An even briefer passage in the *Beowulf*[56] affords a particularly
interesting and significant illustration of the elegiac mood. To a

54. ll. 2247-9.
55. ll. 2262-6.
56. ll. 2444-62.

degree not found elsewhere, these lines suggest how readily the characteristic images of elegiac invention hardened into a conventional pattern. The evidence is found in the fact that in this passage certain of these characteristic elegiac images are employed in circumstances in which there is no grounding of realism to suggest them.

At this point in the *Beowulf* the poet is comparing the sorrow of the old king Hrethel, whose son Herebeald, was killed by his brother, to the grief of a father whose son has been executed upon the gallows. The underlying similarity and ground of comparison in the two instances lies, of course, in the fact that under the conventions of the feud neither father could avenge the death of his son, in the case of Hrethel because he could avenge one son only by slaying another; in the second instance, because legal execution for crime did not permit of vengeance.[57]

The five-line passage with which we are concerned sets forth the hopeless sorrow of the aged father whose son has met death under such circumstances. There is no room for action, no opportunity for vengeance. The son's dwelling, empty and silent, is a daily symbol of unassuaged bereavement:

> In the house of his son   he gazes in sorrow
> On wine-hall   deserted   and swept by the wind,
> Empty of joy.   The horsemen and heroes
> Sleep in the grave.   No sound of the harp,
> No welcoming revels   as often of old.[58]

In these lines certain details of imagery lack appropriateness. The son, indeed, is dead. But who are the horsemen and heroes who sleep in the grave? Obviously, they can only be those conventional figures of a vanished past whose shadowy shapes are conjured back to pathetic remembrance in the scenes of such

57. See D. Whitelock, 'Beowulf 2444-71,' *Medium Aevum*, VIII, No. 3, 198-204, October 1939.

58. *Beowulf*, 2455-9.

elegies as the *Wanderer* and the *Ruin*. In the *Beowulf* passage it is convention, not realism, that calls them to mind.

Such are the themes, and the spirit, of these Old English elegies. They are, in our literature, a first welling up of that clear lyric strain which through the centuries has continued to pour its melody and passion into the full stream of English verse. A thousand years have not staled their freshness, nor changed convention made them strange. Their substance is familiar to all who have felt deeply the moving pathos of human fate; their decorative background to all whose daily lives have known unsheltered contact with the world of nature. Time itself bears witness for them that, in the poetry of our tongue, they have their place with all forms which are a shaping into beauty of the timeless and universal.

V. THE RIDDLES AND GNOMIC VERSE

The Exeter *Riddles;* Exeter *Gnomes;* Cotton *Gnomes;*
Gifts of Men; Fates of Men

THERE are two groups of Old English poems which are examples of poetic composition in highly conventionalized and widely prevalent genres. The first group is a collection of vernacular *Riddles* found in the Exeter Book; the second, the *Gnomic Verses* of the Cotton and Exeter manuscripts. Both these poetic types have illustration in many literatures, and the Old English examples have particular significance in revealing the influence of formal genres in our early verse, and in illustrating the work of Old English poets in these traditional patterns.

The Old English *Riddles*[1] are preserved in the Exeter Book in three groups.[2] Unfortunately, the third group occupies the final pages of the manuscript, the centers of which, from the effect of some corrosive agent, have been seriously damaged. As a result of this injury to the manuscript, 19 *Riddles*[3] have suffered serious impairment of text. *Riddles* 20 and 40 are incomplete, in all probability as a result of missing folios. We must omit from the *Riddle* series the so-called 'First Riddle,' which the studies of Bradley, Lawrence, Schofield, and others have shown to be not a riddle at all, but a fragment of dramatic monologue, now somewhat generally known as *Wulf and Eadwacer*.[4] *Riddles* 2 and 3, moreover, are almost certainly not two riddles, but one.[5]

1. In references to the *Riddles* by number, I have followed the numbering in Krapp and Dobbie's edition of the Exeter Book.
2. *Riddles* 1–60 on folios 101a–115a; *Riddle* 60, and a second version of *Riddle* 30 on folios 122b–123a; *Riddles* 61–95 on folios 124b–130b.
3. 30b, 63, 67, 71, 72, 73, 77, 78, 81, 82, 83, 84, 85, 87, 88, 89, 92, 93, 94.
4. See pages 48–51.
5. See Appendix C.

The *Riddles*, as they have come down to us, raise many questions beside those for which they were framed. Do they all date from the same period? Are they the work of a single poet? To what extent are they based upon Latin originals?

As is true of so much of our earliest poetry nothing is known about their authorship. The early ascription of them to Cynewulf, based upon Leo's[6] fantastic interpretation of the so-called 'First Riddle,' never had substantial merit and fell to the ground when this so-called 'riddle' was identified as a dramatic monologue and rejected from the *Riddle* series.[7] It is far from certain that the *Riddles* can be regarded as the work of one author, though Tupper inclines to look upon them, with the exception of *Riddles* 40 and 66, as the work of a single poet of the early eighth century.[8]

Comparative studies have shown that relations exist between the vernacular *Riddles* of the Exeter Book and various collections of Latin riddles which were current in England in the eighth century.[9] Symphosius, Aldhelm, Tatwine, and Eusebius were all composers of Latin riddles which must have circulated somewhat widely among scholars, and to which in some degree the Old English *Riddles* seem to have been indebted.

Symphosius, an obscure poet possibly of the late fifth or early sixth century, composed 100 Latin riddles, each compressed into three hexameter lines. Some of his subjects were later borrowed by Aldhelm, who acknowledged a general indebtedness to Symphosius in the *Epistola ad Acircium,* which served as a prose preface for Aldhelm's riddles.[10] Tatwine, consecrated Archbishop of Canterbury in 731, was the author of 40 Latin riddles, many of which reflect his theological interests. They are preserved in manuscripts

---

6. *Quae de se ipso Cynewulfus tradiderit*, Halle, 1857.

7. Bradley, *The Academy*, 24 March, 1888, 197.

8. Frederic Tupper, Jr., *The Riddles of the Exeter Book*, 1910, Introd. p. lxxix.

9. See Ebert, *Die Rätsel des Exeterbuches*, 1877, and Tupper, op. cit., Introd., pp. xxxvii-li.

10. Tupper, op. cit., Introd., p. xxxi.

at Cambridge and in the British Museum, and are supplemented in each manuscript by an additional group of 60 riddles composed by a certain Eusebius, possibly the friend of Bede[11] who became Abbott of Wearmouth in 716.

We would naturally expect to find some influence of these Latin collections upon the Old English *Riddles*. And here and there throughout the series an influence of the work of Symphosius and Aldhelm is discernible. Although Wyatt regards it as 'improbable that Tatwine or Eusebius exercised any influence on the writers of the Exeter Book enigmas,'[12] he believes that details and hints borrowed from Aldhelm and Symphosius appear in a number of the Old English *Riddles*. Tupper finds 12 riddles in the Exeter series which, in his opinion, 'employ motives of Symphosius and Aldhelm in such fashion as to suggest direct borrowing from the Latin enigmas.'[13] Even by the most conservative estimate of this Latin influence, it is pretty well established that *Riddles* 35 and 40[14] of the Old English series are reworkings of the *lorica* and *creatura* riddles of Aldhelm, that 47 and 60 are indebted to the *tinea* and *harundo* enigmas of Symphosius, and that 84 is a variant handling of Aldelm's *aqua* riddle.

In the Old English *Riddles* no use is made of acrostic, or of other such suggestive devices of form. There are, however, in the Exeter series four *Riddles*[15] in which Old English runes occur, and one *Riddle*[16] in which a secret script[17] is employed in writing the Latin words *homo, mulier,* and *equus,* which furnish the solution of the riddle.

11. See Bede, *Ecclesiastical History*, v, 23, 24.

12. *Old English Riddles*, Introd., p. xx.

13. Tupper, op. cit., Introd., pp. xli–xlii.

14. A free reshaping of a portion of *Riddle* 40 appears as *Riddle* 66 in the Exeter Book series.

15. *Riddles* 19, 24, 64, 75.

16. *Riddle* 36.

17. The substitution, for every vowel, of the letter immediately following in the alphabet.

The Old English *Riddles* compose a brilliant series of thumb-nail sketches of the daily realisms of Old English life. Their wide-ranging themes in some measure combine to form a picture of simple folkways framed in by nature. They constitute a mosaic of the actualities of daily experience: a record of man's observing companionship with bird and beast, a listing of the things of which his daily life was woven, the food and drink that assuaged his hunger and thirst, the tools with which he toiled, his instruments of music, and the weapons and armor with which he fought. In the range and vivacity with which the *Riddles* set forth these sketches they richly supplement the depictions of Old English culture which we derive from the narrative and lyric poems.

The range of subjects drawn from Old English life is notable. Among familiar birds we find the cuckoo, hawk, jay, nightingale, owl, swallow, and swan. The animals of country life are repre-sented by the bullock, cock and hen, dog, hedge-hog, ox, sow, badger, wolf. The list of implements and utensils of rustic life is especially wide-ranging, including the bucket, churn, flail, lock and key, loom, millstone, plow, poker, wine-cask, and wagon. Various food stuffs are mentioned, as are also ale, beer, mead, and wine. Fishery and the sea are represented by the anchor, boat, fish, oyster, a storm at sea, the wake of a ship. The ever-present threat of violence and war is reflected in the many descriptions of weapons and items of armor: the bow, dagger, helmet, lance, coat of mail, scabbard, shield, sword, and swordrack.

The mood and method of presentment vary somewhat through-out the series. In certain of the *Riddles* description is expanded and elaborated beyond the needs of enigma. In such instances it is clear that the poet has forgotten the riddle pattern, and has lost himself for the moment in the artistic completion of a descriptive sketch. The riddler has yielded the pen to the descriptive poet. In such instances the lines are frequently invested with a vividness of metaphor and personification that etches the riddle with cameolike sharpness. This dramatic intensity is well illustrated in *Riddle* 5, the unmistakable and memorable riddle of the *shield*:

> A lonely wanderer,   wounded with iron,
> I am smitten with war-blades,   sated with strife,
> Worn with the sword-edge;   I have seen many battles,
> Much hazardous fighting,   oft without hope
> Of comfort or help   in the carnage of war
> Ere I perish and fall   in the fighting of men.
> The leavings of hammers,   the handwork of smiths,
> Batter and bite me,   hard-edged and sharp;
> The brunt of battle   I am doomed to endure.
> In all the folk-stead   no leech could I find
> With wort or simple   to heal my wounds;
> But day and night   with the deadly blows
> The marks of the war-blades   double and deepen.

In other instances the poet's method is less direct, less dramatically realistic. The enigma is more deeply buried, and is set forth with more ingenious invention and with a shrewd relish in the anomalous relation of elements confronting one another in the structure of the riddle. Composition in this mood produces greater subtlety of implication, and employs devices of irony and wit. It should be noted, however, that this employment of wit in the shaping and clothing of a concept is, in the Old English *Riddles*, wholly compatible with simplicity of design. This fact is well illustrated in the ten lines of *Riddle* 16 on the *anchor*. In this instance the subtlety of an otherwise simple description lies in the witty and at first glance paradoxical truth that the power of the anchor is linked with stillness, and its weakness with movement:

> Oft I must strive   with wind and with wave,
> Battle them both   when under the sea
> I feel out the bottom — a foreign land.
> In lying still   I am strong in the strife;
> If I fail in that   they are stronger than I,
> And, wrenching me loose,   soon put me to rout.

> They wish to capture   what I must keep.
> I can master them both   if my grip holds out,
> If the rocks bring succor   and lend support,
> Strength in the struggle.   Ask me my name!

Many of the *Riddles* are marked by primitive realisms of style. In certain of them, a quality of lewd suggestiveness sometimes descends into indecent *double entente*, and develops a coarseness of flavor more appropriate to the folk riddle than to its literary cousin, and more suggestive of crude rusticity than of literary wit. Aside from this group there are riddles which combine realistic naturalism with hints of humor, achieving a style which borders upon irony, a quality not uncharacteristic elsewhere in Old English verse. *Riddle* 27, for example, sets forth with homely and ironic candor the intoxicating effect of the mead which the early English fermented from honey:

> I am valued by men,   fetched from afar,
> Gleaned on the hill-slopes,   gathered in groves,
> In dale and on down.   All day through the air
> Wings bore me aloft,   and brought me with cunning
> Safe under roof.   Men steeped me in vats.
> Now I have power   to pummel and bind,
> To cast men to earth,   the old man and young.
> Soon he shall find   who reaches to seize me,
> Pits force against force,   that he's flat on the ground,
> Stripped of his strength   if he cease not his folly,
> Loud in his speech,   but of power despoiled
> To manage his mind,   his hands or his feet.
> Now ask me my name,   who can bind men on earth
> And lay fools low   in the light of day.

Many of the familiar implements and utensils of Old English daily life are well portrayed in the *Riddles*. Among these, one of the best for its continuous spirit of personification, and its ingenious interweaving of clues, is the Fifteenth *Riddle*, on the *horn*. Because of its origin, and the wide variety of uses to which the horn was put, the subject provided the shaper of the *Riddle* with an abundance of significant detail which he has used to great advantage. The poetic whole suggests a sophisticated skill in image-making:

> Time was when I   was weapon and warrior;
> Now the young hero   hoods me with gold,
> And twisted silver.   At times men kiss me.
> At times I speak   and summon to battle
> Loyal companions.   At times a courser
> Bears me o'er marchland.   At times a ship
> Bears me o'er billows,   brightly adorned.
> At times a fair maiden   fills me with breath;
> At times hard and headless   I lie on the board,
> Bereft of beauty.   At times I hang
> Winsome on wall,   richly embellished,
> Where revellers drink.   At times a warrior
> Bears me on horse,   a battle-adornment,
> And I swallow, bright-shining,   the breath from his bosom.
> At times with my strains   I summon the heroes
> Proudly to wine.   At times I win back
> Spoil from the spoiler,   with sounding voice
> Put foemen to flight.   Now ask what I'm called!

Some of the most interesting riddles in the Old English series have to do with birds. Certain of these riddles embody close observation of characteristic features of bird life; others deal with ancient and well-known traditions, or superstitions, associated in literature and folk-lore with certain birds. Of the first type are the Fifty-Seventh *Riddle*, which describes a flock of swallows, and the Eighth, which describes a song bird sometimes identified as the nightingale, but more recently, and more probably, identified as the English song-thrush. To the second type belong the Ninth *Riddle*, on the cuckoo, and the Seventh, which deals with the swan.

The cuckoo *Riddle* is developed from the familiar legend of the cuckoo's ingratitude, a theme as old as Aristotle, and widely known in folk-lore and literary tradition. Here and there the poet may have borrowed a detail from a Latin riddle of Symphosius. But the debt, if any, is slight, as the two riddles differ greatly in treatment of the theme. Symphosius stresses the desertion of the cuckoo by its parents, and its adoption by a foster parent. But he does not extend the theme to include the ungrateful conduct of the adopted bird when grown to its full strength. In the Old English *Riddle*, on the other hand, it is this detail which is stressed, the poet's ironic treatment of it in the final lines indicating that he regarded this element as centrally significant in the cuckoo legend. This *Riddle* is among the best of the bird enigmas in its compressed structure and ingenious use of the conventional clues:

> In former days   my father and mother
> Abandoned me a dead thing   lacking breath,
> Or life or being.   Then one began,
> A kinswoman kind,   to care for, and love me;
> Covered me with her clothing,   wrapped me in her raiment,
> With the same affection   she felt for her own;
> Until, by the law   of my life's shaping,
> Under an alien bosom   I quickened with breath.
> My foster mother   fed me thereafter
> Until I grew sturdy   and strengthened for flight.
> Then of her dear ones,   of daughters and sons,
> She had the fewer   for what she did.

The swan *Riddle*[18] has no analogues among the Latin enigmas. The Old English *Riddle* is based on a folk tradition, mentioned also in line 137 of the *Phoenix*, that when the swan is in flight its feathers make music. This particular legend has no relation to the more widely known superstition as to the death-song of the dying swan.

The origin of the belief that a swan's feathers make melody as it flies is lost in antiquity. There is nothing in the characteristic behavior of the common swan that throws light on this curious bit

18. No. 7 in the Exeter series.

of folk-lore. It is possible, however, that the whistling sound made
in flight by the wild swan, or 'whistling swan,' may underlie the
tradition. In any case the belief was widespread, and the Exeter
riddler chose it as the subject matter of his enigma:

> My attire is noiseless   when I tread the earth,
> Rest in its dwellings,   or ride its waters.
> At times my pinions,   and the lofty air,
> Lift me high   o'er the homes of men,
> And the strength of the clouds   carries me far
> High over the folk.   My feathers gay
> Sound and make music,   singing shrill,
> When no longer I linger   by field or flood,
> But soar in air,   a wandering spirit.

Perhaps the most poetic, certainly the most sophisticated in
phrasing, of all the bird *riddles* is the Eighth, which has to do with
a bird whose song is lovely in its changing notes, and modula-
tions of melody. Its evening harmonies are welcome to the hearts
of men. At the sound of its voice men sit silent in their dwellings,
listening to the clear strains of its minstrelsy:

> I carol my song   in many a cadence,
> With modulation   and change of note.
> Clearly I call,   keeping the melody,
> An old evening-singer   unceasing in song.
> To earls in their houses   I bring great bliss;
> When I chant my carols   in varying strains,
> Men sit in their dwellings   silent and still.
> Say what I'm called   who mimic so clearly
> The songs of a jester,   and sing to the world
> Many a melody   welcome to men.

Many solutions have been proposed for this *Riddle*, including
nightingale, wood-pigeon, and jay. Any solution must meet four
conditions clearly set forth in the Old English text: the bird must
be a song-bird whose strains are characterized by a running variation of note and modulation of theme; it must at times sing near

the dwellings of men; it must be an evening-singer; and it must be a mimic. No one of the hitherto favored interpretations meets all these demands. But a solution recently proposed by Jean Young[19] seems to do so. She suggests, as the subject of *Riddle* 8, the English song-thrush. The suggestion is a happy one, for the Saunders-Clarke *Manual of British Birds*, describes the song-thrush (Turdus Philomelos Clarkei) as a bird of much admired song that some-times sings in town-gardens, frequently utters its song 'on fine nights,' and 'readily adopts the notes of other birds.'[20]

One of the chief literary merits of the *Riddle* series lies in the fact that it preserves to us, in the so-called 'Storm' *Riddles*, over a hundred lines of the most realistic and spirited nature description to be found anywhere in Old English verse. It has been customary to regard these superb lines as constituting three *Riddles* (1, 2, and 3), though Trautmann[21] and Erlemann[22] have suggested that this material comprises in reality a single *Riddle* dealing with a storm, and describing its various aspects.

The fact is, I think, that the 'Storm' material comprises neither three *Riddles*, nor one *Riddle*, but two. *Riddle* 1 seems to be a unit, and *Riddles* 2 and 3 are certainly a unit.[23] *Riddle* 1 has been usually interpreted as a vivid depiction of a thunderstorm and its violent effects in uprooted trees and burning buildings. But the second *Riddle*, that is 2 and 3 combined, deals with the *wind*, and it is quite possible that *Riddle* 1 is a development of the same theme.

In these 'Storm' *Riddles* the imagery of natural phenomena is so dramatically conceived, so vigorous and sustained, that the poems are unique in Old English poetry of nature. Usually in Old

19. 'Riddle 8 of the Exeter Book,' *The Review of English Studies*, July 1942, pp. 308–12.

20. H. Saunders, *Manual of British Birds*, third edition revised and enlarged by W. E. Clarke, London, 1927, p. 242.

21. *Anglia*, Beiblatt, v, 46.

22. *Archiv für das Studium der neueren Sprachen und Literaturen*, cxi, 49–59.

23. See Appendix C.

English verse the nature passages are relatively brief, falling in one or other of two definitely marked types: passages realistically reflecting daily experience and observation and composed in obedience to perceptions of eye and ear, or brief recurring passages of highly stereotyped and conventional phrasing. But in the natural imagery of the 'Storm' *Riddles* the sweep of imagination and sustained elaboration of design suggest the stimulus and control of some tradition of meteorology. It was the study by Edmund Erlemann that first recognized adequately the presence of this element in the 'Storm' *Riddles*, and suggested a relationship in subject matter to Bede's *De Natura Rerum* and passages in the similar work of Isidore of Seville.

Whatever the degree of the Old English poet's indebtedness to Bede, it seems clear that the 'Storm' *Riddles* at many points set forth classical explanation of atmospheric phenomena. To what extent the *De Rerum Natura* of Lucretius was known to Old English writers is uncertain. He is quoted once by Aldhelm in *De Metris*,[24] and once faultily by Bede, if indeed the work is his, in the *De Variis Computi Regulis*.[25] In each case the line quoted may have been adopted at second hand from one of the grammarians. But it seems probable that the various medieval works *de natura rerum* were in a stream of tradition that reached back to Lucretius. Bede's writings in this field definitely echo passages in the *De Natura Rerum* of Isidore of Seville. And Isidore, it is significant, begins his thirty-sixth section treating the nature and influence of the winds by citation of Lucretius and quotation of line 685 of the Sixth Book as authority for the definition of wind with which he begins his discussion.

It is certain, moreover, that portions of the *Natural History* of the Elder Pliny were well known at the time of Bede. Laistner[26]

24. Line 661 of *De Rerum Natura*, II.
25. Line 652 of *De Rerum Natura*, v.
26. 'Bede as a Classical and Patristic Scholar,' *Transactions of the Royal Historical Society*, 4th series, xvi, 69–94.

finds extensive use of the second book of the *Natural History* in the scientific writings of Bede, and believes that he was also familiar with books 4, 5, 6, 13, and 16.

It is significant, then, that in the sixth book of Lucretius and the second book of Pliny, the force of the wind is set forth as the cause of various kinds of storms and violent disturbances in nature.[27] More than 400 lines of the sixth book of Lucretius (96-508) are devoted to discussion of the causes of natural phenomena such as lightning, thunder, rain, water-spouts, tornadoes, and earthquakes. In each instance the wind is represented as a causational agent. The Lucretian exposition covers, as is true of the second Old English 'Storm' *Riddle*, the influence of wind under earth, in the sea, above sea and earth, and in the upper air.

It is this classical tradition of meteorology which underlies the sustained power and dramatic imagery of the 'Storm' *Riddles*. Nowhere else in Old English verse do we find a treatment of natural phenomena comparable in length, realism, or descriptive skill. The unique literary quality of this 'Storm' poetry is most readily illustrated by the second *Riddle*:

> At times I resort,   beyond man's discerning,
> Under surging billows   to seek the bottom,
> The ocean depths.   Then the sea is shaken,
> Convulsed with foam,   and the whale-flood rages
> In giant uproar.   The ocean streams
> Beat on the shore   and batter the slopes
> With rock and sand,   with seaweed and wave.
> As I struggle and strain   in the ocean depths
> I shake the land   and the vast sea-bottom.
> From my watery covering   I cannot forth
> Till He grant me freedom   who guides my way
> On every journey.   O wise of wit,
> Tell who can draw me   from ocean depths
> When the seas grow still   and the waves are calm
> Which formerly covered   and cloaked me over.

27. See Appendix C.

Closely at times   my master confines me,
Forces me under   the fruitful plain,
The earth's broad bosom,   and holds me at bay,
Pens my strength   in prison and darkness
Where the earth sits heavy   and hard on my back!
Out of that bondage   escape is barred,
But I wrench and rock   the dwellings of men.
The halls horn-gabled   totter and topple
And over the households   the high walls shake;
The air seems still,   and the sea is silent,
Until from bondage   I burst my way
As He may guide   who in the beginning
Laid fetters upon me   and bitter bonds;
I may not ever   escape from His power
Who governs my going.   At times from above
I must rouse the waters   and stir the waves
And dash on its beaches   the flint-gray flood.
The foaming breakers   fight with the sea-wall;
Hills of water   heave dark on the deep;
Each follows other   in dusky track,
Churning combers   that batter the cliffs
At the edge of the land.   On ships is uproar,
Shouting of sailors.   The steep stone cliffs
Await the sea-war,   the crashing of waves,
As the dashing billows   buffet the headlands.
On ship is dread   of the perilous strife
Lest the ocean bear it   with its burden of souls
To the dreadful hour   when foaming it drives,
Bereft of rudder,   and stripped of sailors,
On the shouldering surges.   Then a terror shall come
In stormy might   on the sons of men,
Which is stronger than I.   Whose power shall still it?
At times I rush   through the clouds that ride me,
Black vessels of rain,   and scatter them far;
At times I join   and gather them in.
The greatest of tumults   resounds over cities,
The loudest of thunders,   when cloud meets cloud,
Edge against edge.   Then swift over men

The swart shapes sweat   bright fire and flame,
And dark o'er the hosts   with the greatest of dins
The thunder breaks.   Then the battling hosts
From their bosoms shed   dark showers of rain,
Water from the womb.   They fight their way on,
Dread troop on troop,   and the terror grows,
Dismay of men   and fear in the cities,
When the stalking spectres   shoot forth their fire.
The fool then fears not   the deadly arrows,
But he perishes surely   if God in sooth
Out of the rain   and the roar of the whirlwind
Looses against him   a flying bolt.
But few survive   whom the swift foe strikes,
Reaches with weapon.   I rouse this strife
When I rush in might   with a meeting of clouds
O'er the breast of torrents;   then burst with a roar
The cloud-troops on high.   Then low under heaven
I bow to earth   and load on my back,
At the word of my lord,   the burden I carry.
And so at times,   a powerful slave,
I work under earth;   at times I descend
Under surges of ocean;   at times from above
I rouse the sea-streams;   at times I mount up
And whirl the cloud-drift.   Widely I fare
Strong and swift!   Say what I'm called;
Who it is rouses me   when I may not rest;
Who it is stays me   when again I'm still.

Such an extended description as the foregoing, in its sustained
and stormy violence, unless carefully handled might easily have
aroused in a reader's mind an impression of repetition and over-
elaboration. The poet himself apparently recognized this danger,
and endeavored to minimize it by indicating clearly a fourfold
division of his *Riddle*, corresponding to the four provinces in
which the wind's influence asserted itself. To mark the ending of
each of these four sections of the poem he has inserted a reference
to the divine power that rules the wind. One other device of

structure is noteworthy. The tumult of the sea produced by a submarine force of wind is differentiated from the storm that sweeps the ocean's surface by the poet's insertion in the latter passage of a dramatic description of a wrecked and storm-driven ship—the one detailed shipwreck in Old English verse.

A notable characteristic of this *Riddle* [28] is its blending of classical tradition and Christian spirit. The Christian element is sharply evident at more than one point in the text. Lines 13, 28-31, 47-50, 68-72, and 88-9 are strongly suggestive of Biblical passages which set forth the power over wind and storm of the Old Testament Jehovah, and the New Testament Christ. Line 50 is quite naturally interpreted as briefly suggestive of Christ's stilling of the waves in Matthew viii. 24-7. The general conception of God as Almighty Ruler of wind and storm has firm rooting in such a passage as occurs in slightly variant forms in Psalms cxxxv. 7 and Jeremiah x. 13: 'When He uttereth His voice there is a multitude of waters in the heavens, and He causeth the vapors to ascend from the ends of the earth; He maketh lightnings with rain, and bringeth forth wind out of His treasure.'

In their variety of theme and their descriptive realisms, the Exeter Book *Riddles* are among the most interesting survivals of Old English verse. Their wide diversities in quality and form suggest that they are a collection rather than the product of a single pen. Nor is there anything unnatural in the inclusion of these poetic riddles in the Exeter Book. It would not have been difficult for such riddle collections to pass from monastery to monastery. Riddles, acrostics, charades, and similar forms have always had their appeal for the scholar in his playful moods, and such intellectual diversions undoubtedly engaged and enlivened odd moments of time for monks of witty and ingenious mind. Even the lewd enigmas of the Exeter Book could have won a sly suffrage from those who, like Chaucer's Friar, were of 'wanton and

28. *Riddles* 2 and 3, so-called, combined.

merry' disposition. It is in the 'Storm' *Riddles* only that the Exeter collection is unique. For there we rise high above the levels of scholarly wit and ingenuity, hearing the strains of a poetry of nature indebted to classical tradition, and touched with a dramatic imagination and a creative energy which transcend the riddle form, using it not for itself, but as a convenient convention.

Gnomic Verse

The gnomic strain runs like a clearly marked thread through the entire body of Old English poetry. It is found in concentrated form in the *Gnomic Verses* of the Exeter Book and the Cotton MS.,[29] the two sections together making up 272 lines, 206 in the Exeter Book, 66 in the Cotton MS. But quite apart from these specific representations of the genre, many passages in Old English lyric and epic verse, both pagan and Christian, reveal the gnomic mood, and in structure and substance bear the impress of its formative influence.

This body of gnomic verse has its analogues in other literatures. In Hebrew, the Proverbs of the Old Testament furnish outstanding illustration. And so definite was this strain in Greek poetry that the term 'gnomist' was applied to a school of sententious poets beginning with Hesiod and Theognis. Miss Williams, in her discerning study of Old English gnomic verse,[30] has shown that this element in our early poetry is paralleled in the North Germanic tradition, and that many themes of Old English gnomic poetry are duplicated in the Norse gnomes. Both literatures furnish illustration of gnomic stress on the glory of courage, the shame of cowardice, the virtue of discretion, the wisdom of the aged, the woes of human fortune, and the inexorable power of Fate.

The gnome may be defined as a maxim, or proverb, or brief,

29. Exeter Book, 88b–92b; Cotton MS. Tiberius, B, 1, 115 a–b.
30. B. C. Williams, *Gnomic Poetry in Anglo-Saxon*, pp. 18–29.

pithy, sententious saying. In Old English poems gnomes are employed, sometimes to set forth proverbial or folk wisdom, sometimes in more elaborate form to affirm a moral, or define a virtue or vice. Their concise brevity, framed in the alliterative pattern of Old English verse, endows them with the aphoristic and trenchant memorability which is an outstanding quality of the type. A knowledge of the more characteristic gnomes was evidently a portion of the literary and folk heritage of an Old English poet, providing him with a fund of moral aphorisms upon which he drew from time to time as particular episodes in a poem could be enlightened, and their significance enforced, by the sententious assertion of a widely accepted truth. The Exeter and Cotton collections seem to be gatherings of gnomic sayings familiar in Old English ears and presenting a ranging variety in subject matter and spirit. Indeed, these collections have little central unity and, not infrequently, where discordant gnomes have been grafted into the alliterative pattern, the sutures are clearly marked. The gnomes that make up these collections vary in length from brief half-lines to more extended passages of ten to a dozen lines. They vary also in spirit and in substance. Some are older than others, showing no influence of Christianity and obviously surviving from a primitive culture. Others are of later origin, more sophisticated in spirit, and either rooted in the Christian tradition or definitely modified and moulded by it.

Of the obviously older gnomes, some are related to the physical world, compressing into few words primitive knowledge of nature, realistic observation of characteristics of animals, and details of weather. In some instances it is clear that gnomes which in these respects, must be of early origin have been subsequently amended to bring them into harmony with the Christian mood and tradition. The seven lines beginning at B. 72 of the Exeter gnomes constitute such a passage:

> Frost shall freeze; fire melt wood;
> Earth shall blossom; ice shall bridge,
> Shall roof the waters, wondrously lock
> Earth's budding growth. But One shall unbind
> The fetters of frost, the Almighty God.
> Winter shall pass, fair weather return,
> The sun-hot summer, the restless sea.

In these lines it seems certain that the second half-line of B. 72, 'fire melt wood,' has survived from an early stichometric arrangement of nature gnomes in which the freezing of frost and ravage of fire were brought into contrast in a single line by the *f* alliteration. This surviving allusion to fire was ignored by the poet, whose Christian development of the passing of winter and return of summer originated wholly in the initiating suggestion of the first half-line, 'frost shall freeze.'

A passage from the Cotton collection reveals this same re-moulding of old gnomes under the influence of the Christian faith. And once again the dovetailing of old and new leaves visible marks of the joining:

> Wyrd is mightiest; winter is coldest;
> Spring is frostiest, lingering cold;
> Summer sun-fairest, sunshine the hottest;
> Autumn most glorious, giving to men
> The fruits of the year which God has granted.

Here the reference to Wyrd, or Fate, like the reference to fire in the former passage, has little direct relation to the theme developed. The cyclic procession of the year is once more the subject of the poet's lines, in this instance set forth with illustration from the four seasons, in place of the more primitive contrast of winter and summer. Obviously it was the *W* alliteration which originally brought into superficial unity the unrelated elements of winter and Wyrd, and again it was one of those elements only which later received expanded treatment.

Some of the gnomes in these two collections are clearly related to the ancient folkways of primitive Germanic life, briefly but sharply reflecting the Heroic Age in spirit and custom. Such are the four lines (203-6) which conclude the Exeter gnomes. The heroic spirit is as unmistakable, the reflection of the *comitatus* as sharp, as in any passage of battle poem or pagan epic:

> Shield shall be ready,   barb on shaft,
> Edge on sword,   and point on spear;
> Stout heart for hero,   helm for the brave,
> And ever for faint-heart   scantest of hoards.

Another passage in the Exeter collection bears the mark of derivation from old Germanic custom and rite. Lines 81-92 constitute a unit setting forth the qualities requisite for worthy rule by king and queen. The passage begins with an allusion to the custom of marriage by purchase, and reference is made to the virtues of war-might and generosity in a king; but thereafter the passage is developed wholly as a portrait of the ideal queen. The high position of woman in Germanic society is indicated throughout, and the reference to the function of the queen as cup-bearer suggests the Germanic ritual in accordance with which at the banquet in *Beowulf* it is the queen, Wealhtheow, who offers the hall-cup first to Hrothgar and then, one by one, to his guests:

> A king with wealth   shall purchase his queen,
> With beakers and bracelets;   both, from the first,
> Shall be gracious in giving.   The lord shall grow
> In courage and war-might;   the lady shall thrive
> Beloved of her people,   a keeper of counsel,
> Happy-hearted,   and open-handed
> With horses and treasure;   at drinking of mead
> Before the host   she shall first give greeting
> To the leader of warriors,   to hand of her lord
> First tendering cup;   knowing wise counsel
> To the good of both,   house-owners together.

A particularly interesting insert in the Exeter gnomes is the famous 'Frisian woman' passage, which follows close on the passage just quoted. The opening lines (94-9) are obviously lyric, rather than gnomic, in spirit. It has been suggested that these lines present a snatch of sailors' song, and Stopford Brooke calls attention in this connection to the tradition of a small Frisian settlement north of the Tweed.[31] Line 100 marks resumption of the gnomic mood, and succeeding lines reveal characteristic devices of gnomic form. The passage seems to offer one more illustration in these gnomic collections of the welding of materials varying in age and subject matter:

> Welcome her lover   to Frisian wife
> When the ship is at anchor,   the sailor home,
> Her own food-giver;   she welcomes him in,
> Washes his garments   stained by the wave,
> Gives him clean raiment.   Sweet is the shore
> For one whose spirit   love constrains.
> A wife should ever   keep faith with her man;
> But often she shames him   with evil ways.
> Many are steadfast;   many are fickle,
> Wooing strange men   when their lords are away.
> Often the sailor   is long at sea;
> But one must look   for the loved one's coming
> Awaiting the union   one cannot speed,
> When the time shall come   that he turns again home,
> Alive and well,   unless ocean trammel,
> Or deep sea hold him   with clutching hand.

The earlier Old English gnomes tend to be constrained in form into somewhat stereotyped patterns, and even in later, and Christian, examples of gnomic spirit traces of the older formulas often survive. It is hardly possible, of course, to make a completely inclusive classification according to form, but Old English gnomes can be somewhat readily divided into three or four clearly distinguishable groups.

31. *A History of Early English Literature*, 1,233.

One of the simplest and oldest of these types is marked by the *sceal* formula, a type in which the verb is employed to assert a necessity inherent in the nature and attributes of the object described. Such gnomes, for example, are the *frost sceal frēosan, fȳr wudu meltan* already cited. The central meaning of these gnomes lies in their implication that the action asserted, or attribute described, is of the essential nature and quality of the object contemplated. Such gnomes are simple and brief in form, and usually descriptive.

Closely associated with this type of gnome is a similar group distinguished in form by the briefly descriptive *byð* formula: *Wyrd byð swīðost, winter byð cealdost;* 'Fate is mightiest, winter is coldest.' Such gnomes are often confined within the half-line and, as in the case of the *sceal* group, usually imply tested observation of the physical qualities of natural phenomena, or authoritative report of social rite.

When the subject under discussion lies beyond the simple boundaries of unquestioned physical fact or social folkway, and the gnomc offers increased opportunity for moral judgment and didactic stress, the formulas are varied. The variation not infrequently involves addition of the adverbs *often* or *always* to the *sceal* and *byð* formulas, and we have the resultant and recognized types of *ā sceal, ā maeg,* and of gnomes distinguished by the adverb *oft.* In such gnomes, by implication, folk experience is analyzed and moralized into assertions of norms of social experience, and standards of social behavior.

A third type of gnomic passage is characterized by the *swā sceal* formula. As would be expected from the nature of the formula itself, such passages are more usually found as constituent elements in longer poems, where the gnomic reflection is suggested to the poet by details of character or action developed in the course of the poem, and inviting moralizing generalization. The preceding materials of incident or characterization assume the nature of *exempla* which the poet rounds out to gnomic completion by the use of the *swā sceal* formula. In such passages the moral and didactic implications are strong. The 'swā sceal geong guma' and 'swā sceal man dōn' passages of *Beowulf*[32] are excellent examples of this type.

A fourth group, marked out by the *sum* formula and best illustrated in the *Gifts of Men* and *Fates of Men*, is found also in brief passages scattered through the narrative and lyric poems, as, for example, *Christ II*, 664-81, and *Wanderer*, 80-84. Its stereotyped rhetorical structure can be illustrated by the following lines from the *Christ*:

> Sum mæg godcunde
> Reccan ryhte æ.   Sum mæg ryne tungla
> Secgan, sīde gesceaft.   Sum mæg searolīce
> Wordcwide wrītan.[33]

This particular type of gnomic verse lent itself readily to a stress on the scope of human experience, the variety of men's powers and the diversity of their fortunes, and in the hands of the Christian poets was aptly employed for the glorification of God, whose wise providence and power includes all. Miss Williams has called attention to similar balanced patterns in Ecclesiastes iii. 2-8, and in Matthew v. 3-11. The *Iliad*[34] and *Odyssey*[35] furnish even closer analogues.

A gnomic poem, essentially Christian in spirit, is the *Gifts of Men*. It falls naturally into three sections: an introduction (1-29); a discussion of the diversity of God's gifts to men (30-97); and the conclusion (98-113). The Christian elements are most marked in the introductory and concluding sections. The list of gifts set forth is an extensive one, running to some forty enumerated aptitudes both secular and religious. In the religious field, for

32. *Beowulf* , 20 ff. and 1534 ff.
33. *Christ*, 670-73.
34. *Iliad* XIII, 726-34.
35. *Odyssey* VIII, 167-77.

example, men are differentiated according to the nature of their work: one piously concerned with his own soul's need; one skilled in ecclesiastical office; one fearlessly engaged in strife with the Devil, and battle against sin. The list of secular aptitudes is more extensive, including references to the skills of the armorer, smith, hunter, fowler, trainer of horses, sailor, carpenter, minstrel, scholar, scribe, warrior, and worker in gems.

The Fates of Men is a far better poem than the Gifts. In outline it conforms to the same structural pattern: an introduction (1-9); a description in the body of the poem of the varied fortunes of men (10-92); and a strongly Christian conclusion stressing the wise and merciful providence of God (93-8). In the nine lines of introduction the poet sketches in rapid, graphic strokes the common human ritual of the begetting, birth, and rearing of offspring, contrasting it to the diversity of fortune that comes with the years. It should be noted that, in the otherwise firm structure of the body of the poem, one feels toward the end a slight blurring of the theme brought about by the poet's references to the crafts of man in lines in which the central stress is upon varieties of human fortune. The unit passages in the Fates are somewhat longer and more fully organized than in the Gifts of Men. The descriptive sketches are developed with more realistic detail. The material is more sharply reminiscent of the ancient folkways. The stress on the hardships and wretchedness of life, on hunger, war, and exile, is the ancient Germanic stress. Lines 48-57 give us a realistic sketch of a drunken brawl among the members of a comitatus flushed with drink and excited to quarreling and strife:

> From one on the mead-bench,   a wine-flushed warrior,
> A quarrelsome drunkard,   the sharp-edged sword
> Shall wrest away life;   his words were too rash.
> One at the beer-feast,   maddened with mead,
> With no mind longer   to curb his mouth,
> Shall lose his life   in a wretched brawl,

Suffering misery,   stripped of joy;
And men shall call him   a self-slain man,
Telling abroad   the drinker's debauch.

Of all passages in the poem the grimmest in its quality of stark realism, and judged by this criterion one of the most graphic in Old English poetry, is the picture of the body of an executed criminal swinging lifeless from the gallows. It is a passage which illustrates the elements of Old English poetic realism at its best: the economy of phrase, the precision and pregnancy of detail, the emotionless objectivity. In such passages the descriptive elements display a stark faithfulness to fact free of literary emotionalism:

One shall swing   on the stretching gallows
Dangling in death   till the body breaks,
The bloody frame,   and the black-coated raven
Picks at the eyeballs,   plucks at the corpse.
Against the outrage   his hands are helpless;
They may not defend   from the winged foe.
Life is vanished,   all feeling fled;
Stark and pallid   he swings on the gallows,
Shrouded in death-mist   enduring his fate;
His name is accursed.[36]

Such a passage suggests the harsh severities necessary to the replacement of ancient violence and crime by established order and law. Many such a grim object lesson was to be necessary before it could be boasted that a woman with her babe could walk in safety from end to end of England. The crossroads and marches made loathsome by the dangling bodies of criminals and the circling wings of the scavengers were brutal but prophetic symbols of the passing of outlaw and 'wulf.'

The gnomic tradition exerts a constant and subtle influence upon Old English verse not to be interpreted solely in terms of the gnomes of the Exeter and Cotton collections, or such character-

36. *Fates of Men,* 33-42.

istically gnomic poems as the *Gifts of Men* and *Fates of Men*. The gnomic spirit is present in passage after passage of Old English lyric and narrative verse, and it is often in just such passages that the gnomic mood attains its greatest flexibility of form and richness of content. In the *Beowulf*, for example, 23 passages varying in length from one half-line to five lines in length have been classified as unmistakably gnomic in spirit.[37] These bring to the development of incident and character a continuous enrichment of moral interpretation. It was the presence of this gnomic commentary running through the structure of the poem which led Earle and Brandl to regard the *Beowulf* as in some degree addressed to a courtly audience as a mirror for princes.

Of the gnomic passages in *Beowulf* the majority are secular, though about a fifth of the number are unmistakably Christian in substance and spirit.[38] Many of the secular gnomes reflect the ancient backgrounds of Germanic life, stressing as they do the *comitatus* imperatives of loyalty and generosity, the bond of kinship and duty of revenge, the shame of cowardice and the glory of courage, the inexorable decrees of Fate.

Even in the religious poetry the gnomic element persists. The older gnomic formulas could not, in all cases, be harmonized with Christian ethics, and the extensive didactic and moralizing elements in Christian poetry, often following doctrinal patterns, offered fewer opportunities for the use of stereotyped maxims. Some of the older gnomes, however, permitted a reworking and adaptation that fitted them for the Christian contexts of the Cynewulfian and Cædmonian verse. In such instances there is usually a loss of the brevity and directness of the older forms.

This loss of brevity can be well illustrated by a passage from the *Seafarer*. Lines 72-80 of that poem appear to be an expansion of a familiar gnome used in lines 1384-9 of *Beowulf*, where the hero,

37. B. C. Williams, *Gnomic Poetry in Anglo-Saxon*, p. 29.
38. *Beowulf*, 183b–8; 440b–41; 930b–31; 1663b–4a; 2291–3a.

having vowed vengeance for the slaying of Æschere, exclaims: 'Each of us must abide the end of life in this world; let him who may, win glory, before death. That is best for a man when life is over.' In the *Seafarer* the gnome has undergone an extensive Christian expansion:

> Of memorials the noblest   for man is the praise
> Of men who survive him,   who speak of his deeds,
> That striving on earth   ere the hour of death
> He carry on boldly   the battle with Satan
> And put to confusion   the malice of fiends.
> So, in ages long after,   men still shall exalt
> His fame; and his glory   eternally gleam
> Among angels forever,   a splendor unending,
> A joy with the heavenly   hosts on high.[39]

It will be noted that in this passage the winning of glory before death is defined in terms of a victory over Satan, and that the simple concept of *Beowulf*, 'when life is over,' is expanded in definitely Christian terms. The brevity and forcefulness of the gnome have been lost in the literary elaboration.

In the *Wanderer* also, as in the *Beowulf*, we find rich veins of embedded gnomic material. The amount, in proportion to the length of the poem, is considerable and the interwoven passages, as in *Beowulf*, are reminiscent of the older gnomes in subject matter and in trenchant brevity:

> Woe of heart
> Withstandeth not Fate;   a failing spirit
> Earneth no help![40]

> Who bears it knows   what a bitter companion,
> Shoulder to shoulder,   sorrow can be![41]

39. *Seafarer*, 72–80
40. *Wanderer*, 15–16.
41. Ibid. 29–31.

Such lines stamp themselves indelibly on the mind. It is in this close union of moral and didactic strains with narrative and lyric material that the gnomic element brings most artful enrichment to Old English verse. In narrative it serves to create from folk-way a moral frame within which character is defined and action assessed. In the lyric it lends itself gracefully to union with the elegiac and the reflective. Wherever present, it is the voice of old experience and the ancient wisdoms men have learned by living.

VI. THE CÆDMONIAN POEMS

Cædmon; the *Hymn; Genesis A; Genesis B;*
Exodus; Daniel; Christ and Satan

THE establishment of the Christian faith in England, with its attendant enrichment of the national spirit through the influence of the Roman church, modified in varied ways the spirit and subject matter of Old English poetry. The Christian spirit not only reworked and transformed the ancient materials of Continental tradition, but also enlarged the scope of Old English verse by the provision of themes derived from the rich culture of Catholic Christianity. The parallel presence in Old English codices of Continental and Biblical themes indicates the overlapping of Christian and pagan elements in the Old English culture of the seventh and eighth centuries. A wise tolerance in the early church avoided too peremptory endeavor to crush out surviving traditions of pagan backgrounds. Memorials of Germanic legend and folklore, and pious versification of Biblical story, were fostered side by side and preserved together.

The conversion of England to the new faith was marked in many ways by a readiness on the part of early Christian teachers to modify and adapt the older pagan forms to the use and spirit of the new religion. Details of pagan ritual and pagan myth, transformed in spirit, were absorbed into the literature and ceremonial of the Christian faith. Such blendings of ancient and new are clearly illustrated in the absorption of elements from the pagan New Year festival of Yule into the ceremonial of the Christian Christmas; in the union of pagan and Christian detail in the *Charm for Barren Land*; in the traces of the Balder myth present in lines of *Christ III*; and in other instances, not a few, in which similar unions or absorptions are perhaps less easily traced, but equally unmistakable. Such partial adaptation of the older culture to the use of the new was wholly in keeping with the spirit of Gregory's advice to Augustine that the pagan temples of the English should not be destroyed but, purified by holy water and consecrated by Christian altars, should be converted from the worship of demons to the worship of the true God. It was natural, then, that Old English poetry should reveal this blending of pagan and Christian culture. The pagan legend of *Beowulf* was reshaped into an unmistakably Christian poem. Conversely, Christian themes were versified and adorned in the spirit, and with the detail, of the pagan heroic lay.

The simplest, and perhaps the earliest, of the essentially religious Old English poems took the form of versification of themes culled from Old Testament books: the stories of the Creation, the Flood, the Tower of Babel, the destruction of Sodom and Gomorrah, the Offering of Isaac, the Jewish Exodus from Egypt, the Crossing of the Red Sea, the reign of Nebuchadnezzar, and other episodes from the books of Genesis, Exodus, and Daniel. From such simple beginnings grew a rich and varied body of religious verse rendering into the vernacular not only materials of the Old and New Testaments and the Apocrypha, but also Saints' legends, religious allegory, portions of the liturgy, doctrinal and devotional themes, and homiletic exposition derived from the writings of the Church fathers. To an extent that is sometimes understressed, Old English religious poetry reflected the rich culture of the Christian Church with all its varied treasures of learning and discipline.

It is the name of a monk, Cædmon, that is for all time associated with the beginnings of religious poetry in England. In a beautiful legend in the *Ecclesiastical History* Bede describes how this lay brother, under the rule of the abbess Hilda at Whitby,[1] was magically blessed with the gift of song, and thereafter composed the

1. i.e. between 658 and 680.

first religious poems of our language with a sweetness and inspiration that kindled men with 'contempt of the world and desire of the heavenly life.' According to Bede's account, Cædmon had lived a secular life until advanced years, and had never learned the art of versification. For this reason, often at feasts when improvisation to the accompaniment of the harp was the order of entertainment, Cædmon would slip away from the banquet in humiliation as he saw the harp approaching him.

> Once having done so, and having gone out of the house where the banquet was held to the stable where he had the care of the cattle that night, he there at the proper time composed himself to rest. Thereupon one stood by him in his sleep and, saluting him, called him by name and said, 'Cædmon, sing me something.' But he answered 'I cannot sing, and for this reason I left the banquet and retired hither, because I could not sing.' Then he who spoke with him replied 'Nevertheless, you can sing to me.' 'What shall I sing?' he asked. 'Sing the beginning of Creation' said the other. Having received this answer he straightway began to sing to the praise of God, the Creator, verses which he had never heard, the purport of which was after this manner.[2]

There follows in Bede a version of this *Hymn* of Cædmon, and an extended list of the religious subjects which he subsequently versified. Marks of the miracle legend in Bede's account need not lead us to doubt the essential veracity of his story. We may reasonably believe that an individual named Cædmon lived at Whitby while Hilda was abbess, and composed religious poems on the subjects mentioned by Bede; that he was a layman without literary education until he was received into the church; that his poetic powers were first kindled by a religious impulse, and that shortly thereafter he turned monk.

It was not, however, until the beginning of the second quarter

2. Bede, *Ecclesiastical History*, IV, 24.

of the seventeenth century that any known poems, other than the *Hymn*, were associated with Cædmon's name. About 1630 an Old English manuscript containing the text of *Genesis, Exodus, Daniel,* and *Christ and Satan*, was given by Archbishop Ussher of Armagh to a Francis Dujon of Leyden, librarian to Lord Arundel and known in literature as Junius. This manuscript, with others, was subsequently presented by Junius to the Bodleian Library, where it is catalogued as MS. Junius XI.[3] Because of a slight correspondence between the opening lines of Cædmon's *Hymn* and the opening lines of the *Genesis*, and because also of a partial correspondence between the subjects of Cædmon's poems as listed by Bede and the Biblical themes of the Junius text, the poetry of this manuscript came to be accredited to Cædmon, and the whole known as Cædmon's 'Paraphrase.'[4]

Since the ascription of these poems to Cædmon many problems have arisen, as scholars have sought definitive tests of the validity of the attribution.[5] There is little positive evidence to support the assignment of the Junius text to Cædmon, or indeed to any one poet, since the results of critical study suggest that these poems should probably be assigned to somewhat widely separated dates, and to more than one author. In the process of destructive criticism the *Hymn* alone has endured challenge as authentic composition of Cædmon. One would like to be able to believe that *Genesis A* may be a fragmentary and imperfectly transmitted work of Cædmon. But there is little or no positive evidence to support this theory.

GENESIS

The *Genesis,* a poem of 2935 lines, comprises the first 41 sections of the Junius manuscript. Certain linguistic, metrical, and structural characteristics mark out verses 235-851 from the preceding

3. See Appendix A.
4. An edition of the 'Paraphrase' was printed by Junius in Amsterdam in 1655.
5. See Wülker's *Grundriss*, pp. 111-46.

and following portions of the poem, as an obvious interpolation. These two divisions of the poem have come conveniently to be known as *Genesis A* (vv. 1-234 and 852-end) and *Genesis B* (vv. 235-851).

In 1875 Sievers[6] made the brilliant suggestion regarding *Genesis B* which was later so remarkably confirmed. Calling attention to the fact that in places the vocabulary, syntax, and alliterative structure of *Genesis B* are Old Saxon rather than Old English, Sievers suggested that these interpolated lines were a translation of an Old Saxon paraphrase of the Old Testament. Portions of this conjectured original were later discovered in the Vatican Library, and the dependence of *Genesis B* upon the Old Saxon version definitely established.[7]

Genesis A, on the other hand, is an Old English poem describing in its first 234 lines the fall of the angels and portions of the Creation. At that point a considerable portion of the poem has been lost. The narrative is resumed at line 852, and continues in free and expanded paraphrase of the Book of Genesis through the Offering of Isaac. Into the break in *Genesis A* at line 234 is inserted *Genesis B*. In its 617 lines *Genesis B* contains a second account of the fall of the angels and the entire story of the temptation and fall of man. The joining of the two fragments probably resulted from the desire of a scribe to piece together an unbroken narrative. *Genesis A* is certainly older than *Genesis B*, which is usually dated about the middle of the tenth century. Gerould[8] proposes a date some 25 years later, and suggests that the Old Saxon original may have been brought to England by the same foreigner who later, about the year 1000, wrote a life of St. Dunstan.

Of all the themes of *Genesis* that which receives most extended

---

6. *Der Heliand und die angelsächsische Genesis*, Halle, 1875.

7. See Karl F. W. Zangemeister and Theodore W. Braune, *Bruchstücke der Altenglischen Bibeldichtung*, Heidelberg, 1894, for an account of the discovery, a text of the Old Saxon fragments, and a consideration of their relation to *Genesis B*.

8. *Modern Language Notes*, xxvi, 129-33.

treatment and is most notably reshaped by the creative imagination of the poet is the account in *Genesis B* of the temptation and fall of man. It can fairly be said that this section of the *Genesis* constitutes in primitive form an Old English 'Paradise Lost,' and it is an interesting question whether there exists any direct relation between *Paradise Lost* and *Genesis B*, whether Milton ever saw the Junius manuscript, whether his knowledge of Old English was sufficient to permit his use of the Old English text, or, if not, whether the Cædmonian account of the fall of the angels and the temptation of man may have been made available to him in translation.[9]

Masson,[10] in the well-known biography of Milton, notes 'striking coincidences between notions and phrases in Satan's soliloquy in hell in the Cædmonian *Genesis*, and notions and phrases in the description of Satan's rousing himself and his fellows in the first book of *Paradise Lost*.' Since the manuscript of the Old English poems had been given to Junius about 1651 before Milton became blind, and since Junius was residing in London at the time, Masson considers it just possible that Milton had become acquainted with the Old English text. 'If he heard of it,' Masson adds, 'he was not likely to remain ignorant of its nature or contents.'

There are undoubtedly similarities of detail between *Paradise Lost* and *Genesis B*. But such resemblances as exist are not necessarily evidence that Milton drew upon the Old English poem. The really important tie that links *Genesis B* and *Paradise Lost* is to be found in the fact that both poems reflect and in some measure form a part of a stream of literary tradition incorporated in the so-called Hexaemeral writings, that is, the tradition which had its origin in commentaries on the Book of Genesis, and exegetical

---

9. See Wülker, *Anglia* iv, 402 ff.; Brandl, *Geschichte der altenglischen Literatur*, p. 1090; and Stephanie V. Gajsek, 'Milton und Cædmon,' *Wiener Beiträge*, 35.

10. *Life of Milton*, vi, 557, note.

writings of the Church Fathers dealing with the six days of Creation.[11] The Hexaemeron of Basil (Bishop of Caesarea 370-79), was the earliest Christian work devoted exclusively to the Creation,[12] and from this work until the Renaissance the body of Hexaemeral writings increased in volume and scope. The basic theme continued to be the six days of Creation but there came to be associated with this material (a) the Revolt and Fall of the angels, and (b) the Temptation and Fall of man. The union of the three themes in literary form took on the nature of a great celestial trilogy. Though Old English poetry has detailed illustration of these themes only in *Genesis B* and a portion of *Christ and Satan*, Middle English literature furnishes many and varied reflections of the tradition in poetry and drama.

Genesis B opens with God's injunction that the newly created Adam and Eve may eat freely of all fruits in Paradise save only the fruit of the tree of death. The vivid description in the Old English poem of the two trees of life and death, a set piece of marked excellence, furnishes outstanding contrast to Milton's use of the single tree of knowledge. The pronouncement of the ban is followed by a dramatic account of the revolt of the angels, repeating in somewhat extended outline an earlier and briefer reference in *Genesis A*. In accord with tradition, it is pride that motivates the uprising of Satan and leads to his overthrow. He plans to build a stronger and higher seat in heaven, an empire in the north and west. He is no longer willing to be subject to God. It is the revolt of a great vassal against his king:

> Why must I slave? What need (quoth he)
> To serve a master? Strong are my hands
> To work many wonders. I have power to shape
> A goodlier seat, a higher in heaven.
> Why must I yield, or fawn for His favor,

11. See McColley, *Paradise Lost, An Account of its Growth and Major Origins*, Introduction: The Hexaemeral Tradition.

12. Robbins, *The Hexaemeral Literature*, 1912, pp. 42 ff.

Or bow in submission?   I may be God
As well as He!   Stout comrades support me,
Warriors unyielding,   who will not weaken in strife.[13]

Enraged at this presumption, the Almighty hurls Satan from
his lofty seat and chains him down upon the floor of hell. There
in blazing fire, and bitter frost,[14] in darkness and gloom, the fallen
angels experience a measureless woe 'because they had broken
allegiance to God.' But the heart of Satan, even in hell, remains
untamed and untamable. His arrogant will invests his speeches
with a contemptuous and unbending defiance:

>Unlike indeed   is this narrow place
>To that other home   that once we held
>In heaven's high realm,   though we could not keep
>What my Lord bestowed,   nor rule our kingdom,
>Against God's will.   He has done us wrong
>In hurling us to the depths   of this fiery hell,
>Depriving us of heaven.   He has marked it out
>For mankind to settle.   'Tis my greatest sorrow
>That Adam, fashioned   and shaped of earth,
>Should hold my high seat   and abide in bliss
>While we suffer this torment,   this torture in hell.
>Woe! Alas!   if I only had power
>To use my hands,   have my freedom one hour,
>One winter hour,   then with this host
>I would—   But fetters of iron
>Lie heavy upon me,   the bondage of my chains.[15]

In the midst of his torment he devises a plot for revenge and the
ruin of man. Being himself bound and helpless to carry out his
plan, like some great Germanic prince in the midst of his *comitatus*

13. *Genesis*, 278–85.

14. In the main, the depiction of hell in *Genesis B* reflects conceptions usual in the
writings of the Church Fathers. Alternation of heat and cold was a form of torture in
the Buddhist hells, and occurs in the Book of Enoch, through which this detail may
have found its way into the Christian *Visions*.

15. *Genesis*, 356–72.

he reminds his shoulder-companions of the rich gifts he has heaped
upon them in the past, calling for a volunteer who will requite
his favors and undertake the temptation of man.

> If ever to any thane   in days of old,
> When we dwelt in that good kingdom   and happily held our
>   thrones,
> I dealt out princely treasure,   at no dearer time
> Could he make me requital,   repayment for gifts,
> If some thane would be my helper   and out from hence
> Break through these bolted gates   with strength to wing,
> Cleaving the sky,   to where, new-shaped on earth,
> Adam and Eve abide   in the midst of abundance
> While we are cast out hither   to the depths of hell . . .
> Take thought how you may ensnare them.   More softly then
> Shall I lie in these chains   if they lose the heavenly kingdom.
> Whoever shall bring that to pass   shall have share forever
> In all we may win of advantage   amid these flames.
> I will let him sit next me.[16]

In response to this appeal of Satan one of his followers under-
takes to carry out the work of revenge. Skilled in crooked word
and crafty speech he darts upward through the doors of hell and
wings his way to earth. There he comes upon Adam and the
woman with him. Near them stand two trees laden with fruit,
the sweet and pleasant tree of life, and the tree of death, dark,
sunless, and full of shadows.

In the temptation scene of *Genesis B* there is inconsistency in
one important detail, namely, the form in which the tempter
appears to Adam and Eve. In one passage[17] the fiend enters the
body of the serpent and, winding himself about the tree of death,
plucks the fruit. But elsewhere he apparently wears angelic form,
since he represents himself as a messenger sent by God to revoke
the ban upon the forbidden fruit. Adam is now to eat of it as

16. ll. 409–21; 432–8.
17. ll. 491–3a.

freely as of all the other fruits of the Garden. The whole development of the temptation scene is based upon Eve's acceptance of the tempter as an angelic messenger bringing a new command, an acceptance impossible had the tempter worn the serpent's form.[18] The drawings of the Junius MS. reveal the same inconsistency, two drawings showing the serpent, while others portray the tempter in angelic form. This inconsistency probably reflects a contamination of apocryphal legend with the conventional detail of the Biblical Genesis.[19]

In contrast to the Miltonic version, the demon of *Genesis B* first approaches Adam, representing himself as come from afar in God's service:

> Not long ago   I sat by His side;
> On this errand He sent me,   bade you eat of this fruit,
> Said your powers would be greater,   your strength and spirit,
> Your body more radiant,   your form more fair.[20]

The characterization of Adam in this episode is free of all complexity. He is superbly consistent in faithful adherence to a former command, and in blunt and obstinate rejection of the new:

> Though you come with lies   and with cunning wiles
> I do not know   that you come from God,
> A messenger from heaven.   I can make out naught
> Of your words or ways,   your errand or sayings.
> But well I know   what our Lord decreed
> When last I saw Him: to observe His word,
> Follow His teaching   and perform it well.
> You are not like   to any of His angels
> That ever I saw.[21]

18. Such assumption of angelic appearance by a demon is, of course, not unique in this scene. It is found, as a device of craft, in the temptation scenes of many saints' legends, and in Old English poetry occurs again in Cynewulf's *Juliana* (244b), where it is one of many details borrowed directly from the Latin *Vita*.

19. For a discussion of the problem see F. N. Robinson, 'A Note on the Sources of the Old Saxon Genesis,' *Modern Philology*, iv, 389-96.

20. *Genesis*, 498-503.

21. ll. 531-9.

It is only after the temptation of Adam has failed that the fiend turns to Eve and labors to persuade her that he is indeed God's messenger, that Adam has defiantly rejected God's most recent command, and that only if she eat of the fruit and persuade Adam to eat can the wrath of the Almighty be averted. With tricks and lies, so runs the account, he tempted the woman to sin until his counsel began to work within her—for God had fashioned her spirit the weaker—and her heart yielded to his persuasion. Transgressing the command of God she accepted and ate the fatal fruit of the tree of death.

By the deceptive craft of the tempter, Eve was led to believe that the eating of the fruit had brought her increase of faculty so that she seemed to have sight of God himself in heavenly splendor and 'unnumbered myriads of angels clothed in beauty circling in winged flight about His throne.' Trusting in this deceptive vision she urges Adam also to eat of the fatal apples, citing this amplitude of faculty as proof of the benefits of the fruit:

> Who else could bestow   such power of understanding
> If it came not straight   from the heavenly King?
> Far can I hear,   far can I see
> Over all the world   and the wide creation.
> I can hear the hymns   of rapture in heaven;
> My heart is illumined   without and within,
> Since I ate of the fruit.[22]

All day long she pleads, urging him to the dark deed. All this, the poet tells us, she did with good intent and had no knowledge that so many evils, such grim afflictions, would come upon mankind. At last Adam, yielding to her persuasion, eats:

> When the apple within him   touched at his heart
> Then laughed aloud   the fierce-hearted fiend,
> Capered about,   gave thanks to his lord
> That both were undone.[23]

22. ll. 671–7.
23. ll. 723–6.

The denouement is swift. The fiend dives downward to the flames of hell; the false vision fades from the eyes of Eve; and wretched in heart Eve and Adam know that they have sinned. Adam's words are heavy with reproach. What is to become of them? How, in their nakedness, are they to withstand hunger and thirst and weather, scorching sun and winter's cold, wind and frost, rain and hail? They have no shelter nor store of food. And God is angered. 'Well may I repent to all eternity,' Adam cries to Eve, 'that ever I laid eyes upon you'![24] They turn away weeping into the green wood where they make themselves clothing of leaves, and each morning bow in prayer beseeching God's mercy and instruction. So ends *Genesis B*.

Genesis A resumes with line 852. In contrast to the sharp break at the beginning of *Genesis B*, the transition here to the resumed narrative of *A* shows few, if any, marks of joining. The subsequent narrative follows the Biblical Genesis somewhat closely, replacing the dramatic tone and poetic invention of *Genesis B* with a simple and little-expanded paraphrase of Genesis iii. 8-24.

The narrative deals in sequence with the appearance of the Almighty in the Garden 'after the mid-day'; the hiding of Adam and Eve in nakedness and shame; God's demand whether they have eaten of the fruit of the forbidden tree; Adam's confession and blame of the woman; Eve's confession and blame of the serpent. The penalties imposed follow closely the Biblical text. The serpent is to go upon his belly forever and live in enmity with man; the woman is subjected to man's dominion and condemned to conception and childbirth in pain and tears. Adam, after their expulsion from the Garden, is to win their sustenance from a stubborn earth in toil and sweat, and in the end death, first tasted in the apple, shall lay them low. 'Lo now,' exclaims the

24. The Vatican Library fragment of the Old Saxon original of *Genesis B* sets forth this speech of Adam (*Genesis*, 791-820) lacking the concluding three-and-a-half lines.

poet, 'we know how our afflictions came upon us, and our mortal misery.'

The primitive motivation of *Genesis B* lies centuries removed from the richly woven philosophic pattern of the Miltonic version of the Fall. The Old Saxon poet has left us a simple and appealing narrative graced by energetic episode and sensitive characterization. But the story of the Temptation and Fall in *Genesis B* is not shaped to any depth or range of philosophic commentary. The Old English text makes little attempt to 'justify the ways of God to men.' Indeed, after the fall of Eve, the poet can only marvel that the Almighty has permitted this evil to come to pass. 'Never was worse deed wrought for men! Great is the wonder that Eternal God would let so many of his thanes be tricked with lies by one who brought such counsel.'[25] The ancient legend becomes in *Genesis B* a tragic example of puzzled loyalties, a tragic defeat of willing obedience vastly torn between observance of the ban and acceptance of its announced repeal. Virtue, tested in 'worlds not realized' is deceived, but not seduced.

Immediately after the Temptation and Fall there follows the story of Cain and Abel. The narrative in its main outlines follows the Book of Genesis, but is expanded beyond the Biblical text to include elements derived from Hebrew tradition and exegetical Christian writings. Early commentary on the story of Cain was motivated, as Emerson puts it,[26] by the belief that 'something more than human depravity was necessary to account for such an extraordinary crime as murder in the comparative innocence of the early world.' Rabbinical lore, therefore, made Cain the son, not of Adam, but of the devil. Other traditions explained the evil of his nature as a taint resulting from the time of his birth, namely, after the sin, but before the repentance, of Adam and Eve. The

25. *Genesis*, 594–8.
26. Cf. 'Legends of Cain, especially in Old and Middle English,' *PMLA*, xxi, 831–929.

mark or sign placed upon Cain to set him apart from men was also variously defined.[27] But there is uniform stress in the legends on the central idea that the curse of Cain is an everlasting curse, not only visited upon Cain himself, but illustrated in the evil nature of his offspring.

As the Cain legend grew, more and more stress was placed upon the monstrous nature of Cain's issue. In the *Beowulf*, for example, specific reference is twice made to the descendants of Cain[28] in terms which divide them into two general groups: (1) monsters and demons, and (2) giants[29] that 'strove against God a long time.' In a later passage of *Beowulf*[30] there is an allusion to the Flood and, though the name of Cain in this instance is not mentioned, there is again reference to the 'giant race' who had become estranged from God by their evil, and upon whom God poured His vengeance.

This tradition of a 'sinful giant race' long busied in evil is reflected in *Genesis A*.[31] The Old English text develops hints derived from Genesis vi. 7 in identifying the giants as offspring of intermarriage between the sons of Seth and the daughters of Cain. To this intermarriage was traced the spread of evil upon earth, and in this detail the story of Cain became the motivating link between the Fall of man and the Deluge which purged earth of sin.

The description of the Flood given in *Genesis A*[32] follows somewhat closely the Biblical text. The theme is presented in smoothly flowing narrative. But there is no such magnificent nature poetry as we have in the 'Storm' *Riddles*, and no such powerful and creative force of imagination applied to natural phenomena. The

27. In the Middle English prose version of *Adam and Eve*, the mark is a spasmodic trembling of the head; in the Cornish play of the *Creation*, a pair of horns.

28. *Beowulf*, 111–14, 1266–7.

29. Cf. Genesis vi. 4.

30. *Beowulf*, 1688–93.

31. *Genesis*, 1265–9.

32. ll. 1290–1500.

story of the Flood furnished a theme capable of great poetic extension. But the Old English poet nowhere quite rises to the magnitude of his theme. One looks in vain for anything comparable to the sustained surge of descriptive energy of which the poet of the 'Storm' *Riddles* was at all times master. A relatively brief but central passage will illustrate the quality of the narrative:

> Then the Lord unloosed   the rains from the heavens,
> Let the roaring torrents   and rushing streams
> From every channel   overflow the world.
> Over the barrier of the shore   the seas surged up.
> Strong and stern was He   who ruled the waters!
> The dark flood covered   the children of evil,
> Laid waste their homes   and their native land.
> God avenged their sins   on the sons of men!
> For forty days   and for forty nights
> The sea laid hold   on that fated folk.
> Dire was the disaster   and deadly to men.
> The stormy surges   of the King of glory
> Banished life from the bodies   of those wicked men.
> The fierce flood,   heaving beneath the heavens,
> Covered the high hills   throughout the wide world,
> Lifted the ark   from the earth, on its bosom,
> And all living things   which the Lord had blessed
> When our Savior fastened   the door of the ship.
> Then over the deep,   under the heavens,
> That best of dwellings   and the burden it bore
> Were driven afar.   No watery terrors
> Could touch those sailors;   but holy God
> Saved them and ferried them.   Fifteen ells deep
> Over the hills   lay the rolling flood.
> 'Twas a fearful fate![33]

In versifying the story the poet has not infrequently translated the material of Biblical narrative into the familiar terms of Old English life. The ark tossed on the waters of the Flood is described with imagery appropriate to a sea-voyage. It is not swept away

33. ll. 1371-99.

by a Deluge but drives through stormy surges flinging spray from its bows. 'Foaming the ship fared on.'[34] The poet refers to Noah and his family as 'wave-farers,' and 'sea-farers' longing for 'rest from their sea-journeying.' In such passages the poet has adopted for the decoration of his narrative the conventional poetic imagery associated with ocean voyages, precisely as elsewhere he borrows the conventional imagery of Old English battle poetry.

In one instance the use of this conventional decorative detail has notably vivified the poet's treatment of his original. The Biblical Genesis (viii. 7) describes how, when the Flood abated, Noah sent forth from the ark a raven, of which we are told merely that it 'went forth to and fro until the waters were dried up from off the earth.' As the Old English poet treats the scene, the picture takes on an infusion of the conventional associations which surround the raven as a bird of battle, a feaster on corpses:

> Then after long days   the son of Lamech
> Let fly from the ark   a black-feathered raven
> Over the steep flood.   Noah counted it sure,
> If in its flight   it should find no land,
> The raven would return   unto the ark
> Over the wide waters.   But Noah's hope failed him!
> The raven rejoicing   lighted and perched
> On the floating corpses.   The dusky-feathered
> Would not return.[35]

The story of the Flood is followed by a versified genealogy of Noah's descendents. Thereafter, the narrative deals in succession with the Tower of Babel and confusion of tongues, the wanderings of Abraham and Lot, Abraham's settlement in Canaan, the coming of famine and the flight into Egypt, Pharaoh's love of Abraham's wife Sarah, the return of Abraham to Canaan, and Lot's settlement in the city of Sodom.

34. ll. 1417.
35. ll. 1441–8.

The chronicle of the war of the Elamites against Sodom and Gomorrah, and their defeat at the hand of Abraham, is one of the more extended episodes of the latter part of *Genesis A.* This bit of narrative contains some passages of really spirited verse. In the martial episodes the poet has adorned his lines with the customary imagery of the Old English battle scene:

> Onward advanced   the slaughtering armies.
> (Loud sang the javelins.)   Amid the spears
> The dark bird croaked,   the dewy-feathered,
> In hope of carrion.   Heroes hastened
> In mighty squadrons,   stalwart of mood,
> Till from north and south,   from near and far,
> The hosts were gathered,   heroes in helmets.
> Then was hard hand-play,   hurling of death-darts,
> Crashing of weapons,   tumult of war.
> From sheaths men snatched   their ring-decked swords,
> Doughty of edge;   full easily then
> An earl might find there   his fill of fighting,
> Whoso was not yet   sated with war.[36]

Genesis A continues with a brief treatment of the story of Hagar and Ishmael, following which the paraphrase expands into a more elaborated passage dealing with the destruction of Sodom and Gomorrah. Though the depiction of the 'brimstone and black fire' that fell from heaven upon the doomed city lacks the energy and extension that make the fire-paintings of *Christ III* so unforgettable, the rendering of the theme has vividness:

> All that was green   in the golden cities
> The flame devoured,   and no small deal
> Of the wide land round   was ravaged and wasted
> With fire and terror.   Flourishing groves
> And fruits of the earth   turned ember and ash
> As the vengeance swept   over stretching lands.
> A ravaging fire,   a roaring flame,
> Swallowed up all   of spacious and high

36. ll. 1982–95.

That men held dear   in Gomorrah and Sodom.
God laid all waste,   and the folk as well.[37]

The remainder of *Genesis A* is devoted to the story of Abraham's service under Abimelech, the king's love for Sarah parallel-
ing the former Egyptian episode, the birth of Isaac, the exile of
Hagar and Ishmael, and the final episode of the Offering of Isaac.
In this last scene the poet has caught well the elevation of mood
that marks the original. In its austerity and avoidance of the
sentimental, the narrative of the Offering of Isaac suggests well the
spirit of heroic sacrifice.

Considered as a whole, the *Genesis* is uneven in quality. The
section in which the poetic narrative attains to highest excellence
in action and characterization is, as we have seen, an inset which
reflects the merits of an Old Saxon original. The remainder of
Genesis includes a few passages of really spirited verse. But, with
the exception of *Genesis B*, the poem must be rated as somewhat
elaborated paraphrase rather than poetic creation.

EXODUS

Following *Genesis* in the Junius MS. is the *Exodus*, a poem of
589 lines comprising sections 42-9 of the manuscript. The text
has many errors of transmission, including careless omission and
repetition of words. In some passages the textual obscurities are
of a nature to suggest that the scribe was writing from dictation.

The style of *Exodus* lacks the narrative simplicity of many parts
of *Genesis*, and would seem to indicate different authorship. The
poem has somewhat generally been regarded as older than *Genesis
A* and *Daniel*,[38] this judgment being based largely on the use of
the article and weak adjective, with some corroboration from the
results of metrical tests.

Exodus is a versified narrative of the flight of the Israelites from

37. ll. 2550–62.
38. See Brandl, *Geschichte der altenglischen Literatur*, Strassburg, 1908, p. 1028.

Egypt and the crossing of the Red Sea. In its introductory passages the poem treats of Moses and his laws, the plagues of Egypt, and the release of the Israelites. It then describes in its principal episodes the march of the Israelites to the Red Sea, the pursuit by Pharaoh's army, the division of the waters and crossing of the Israelites, the destruction of the pursuing Egyptians, the hymn of Moses, the rejoicing of his people, and the plundering of the Egyptian dead.

Napier has pointed out[39] that in the description of the march to the Red Sea the narrative is confused because, he believes, of a displacement of two passages. As the text stands, a description of the pillar of cloud is followed by: (1) a description of the third encampment of the Israelites; (2) a reference to *both* the pillar of cloud and the pillar of fire, as if the latter had already been described; (3) a resumption of the march to the Red Sea; and finally (4) a description of the pillar of fire. Napier explains this confusion by the theory that passages 86-107 and 108-24 have been reversed by 'the wrong folding of a couple of leaves in the MS. from which Junius xi was copied, or at any rate descended.' His suggested transposition of the two passages would give the following arrangement of text: lines 63-7, second encampment; 68-85, description of the pillar of cloud; 108-24, description of the pillar of fire; 86-107 and 125-9, third encampment and march to the Red Sea; 129-34, fourth encampment.

Another passage in *Exodus* constitutes such an extended interruption of the narrative that it has been suggested that these lines may have been interpolated into the text by a later author or scribe. The passage in question (362-446) injects into the poem, after the description of the crossing of the Red Sea, fifteen lines dealing with Noah's Flood followed by an extended narrative of the Offering of Isaac. It can hardly be denied that these lines constitute a definite interruption of sequence and deal with material whose relation to the narrative seems extremely remote.

39. 'The Old English Exodus, 63-134,' *Modern Language Review*, vi, 165-8.

Nevertheless, as early as 1882 Ebert[40] protested against the prevailing rejection of this passage, and suggested an explanation of it essentially in agreement with the theory later developed by Bright[41] in an important study of the relations of *Exodus* to the liturgy.

The lines under consideration raise fundamental questions concerning the structure of *Exodus*. The main episodes of the poem contain material drawn chiefly from Exodus xiii. 17-xiv. 31 and Exodus xv. 1-21. Because of this partial nature of its dependence on the Vulgate it is clear that the Old English poem cannot reasonably be regarded as a poetic paraphrase of Exodus. To what extent, then, did the author make use of other sources and other material? To what extent, if at all, was he indebted to the well-known medieval poem on the Passage of the Red Sea, the *De Transitu Maris Rubri* of Avitus?

It has been suggested that *Exodus* shows an influence of Avitus,[42] but the admirably thorough analysis of the structure of *Exodus* by Samuel Moore goes far toward rendering this opinion untenable.[43] Moore shows conclusively that in passages in which the phrasing is somewhat suggestive of Avitus, the poet of *Exodus* was drawing from other sources, or was making a natural development of the material in hand.

It was in the following year that Bright's illuminating and important study of the poem established the probability that a design and method quite different from paraphrase or simple narrative governed the composition of *Exodus*. Bright set forth the opinion that the poem is 'definitely related to the liturgy; that it is specifically ecclesiastic, having been composed in the church, so to

40. *Anglia*, v, 409-10.

41. 'The Relation of the Cædmonian *Exodus* to the Liturgy,' *Modern Language Notes*, xxvii, 97-103.

42. Cf. Groth, *Composition und Alter der altenglischen Exodus*, Berlin, 1883, p. 17; and Mürkens, *Untersuchungen über die altenglische Exodus*, Bonn, 1898.

43. 'On the Sources of the Old English *Exodus*,' *Modern Philology*, ix, 83-108.

speak, as an echo of the service of one of the most elaborate solemnities of the Christian year.' The service referred to is that of Holy Saturday, the Saturday before Easter Sunday, and it is Bright's opinion that themes from twelve 'prophecies,' or selections from Scripture, appointed to be read at that service, were interwoven by the poet to produce the structural and symbolic unity of the poem.

These services of Holy Saturday were devoted in the medieval church to the baptism of the catechumens. Symbolically associated with the death and resurrection of Christ the baptismal service was a solemn rite of supreme importance. The ceremonial was intended to impress the catechumens with the central meaning of the new dispensation, and to stress the significance of baptism as a spiritual rebirth. The twelve selections from Scripture appointed for reading included, with other material, the story of the Passage of the Red Sea, a theme which had become for the Church a conventional symbol of baptism and God's saving grace.

The service began with the lighting of the Paschal candle, typifying Christ's resurrection and serving also as a symbolic representation of the pillar of fire. The twelve 'prophecies' from the Old Testament, each followed by a prayer, were then read to the catechumens, the 'prophecies' instructing them in the 'effects and fruits' of baptism, the petitions imploring for them all its benefits. The reading was followed by a procession to the baptistry led by the Paschal candle as typifying 'the pillar of fire that guided the Israelites by night to the Red Sea in whose waters they found salvation.' The font was then blessed, the priest several times dividing the waters with his hands, and the catechumens baptized.

It was the rich symbolisms inherent in this service, both in ceremonial detail and in the appointed readings and prayers, which governed the structure of *Exodus*. The Old English poem must be considered, in some sense, a *carmen paschale* growing out of one of the most significant ceremonials of the Christian year.

Included among the lections for this service were the stories of the Deluge and the Offering of Isaac. Since these themes occur as essential elements in the liturgy for the baptismal service, it may well be that the references in *Exodus* 362-466 to the Deluge and the Offering of Isaac reflect a direct influence of the liturgy. These themes have an essential relation to the central structure of the poem as it developed in the poet's mind under the influence of the baptismal service. He is stressing the heroic virtue of Noah and Abraham, the two figures most significant in relation to God's covenant with Israel. It was a covenant begun with Noah and strengthened by the trial of Abraham. As Bright puts it: 'Abraham became the father of the nation (*him waes ān faeder,* 353) and to him were made the promises that sustained the national mind. The faith of Abraham, and the destiny of his seed, govern the plan of the poem.'

Such symbolic association of Scriptural themes has frequent parallel in ecclesiastical writings. It can be illustrated in the structure of certain medieval Latin hymns. A well-known Easter hymn of St. John of Damascus exemplifies the manner in which medieval Christianity associated the miraculous passage of the Red Sea with the Resurrection as images of God's deliverance of His people from physical and spiritual bondage.

Bright's study, establishing this strong probability of liturgical influence in the composition of *Exodus*, has thrown a flood of light upon the poem. The derivation of theme from a liturgical source has especial significance, since it was this same influence that governed the composition of portions of the *Christ*. The Advent hymns of *Christ I* are poetic expansions of medieval antiphons appropriate to the services of Advent. The structure of *Christ II* is governed by portions of a sermon on the Ascension by Gregory the Great. *Christ III* owes much to an alphabetic

Latin hymn dealing with the Day of Judgment, and quoted by
Bede in the *De Arte Metrica*. In the *Christ* alone, then, we have
three separate illustrations of the influence exerted on a religious
poem by the rich symbolisms of the medieval liturgy. If *Exodus*
can be added to the *Christ* as owing the very unity of its structure
to this same relationship, it may well be, as Bright suggests, that
Old English poetry 'stands in closer relation to the liturgy than
has been assumed hitherto,' and that our early lyric and reflective
poetry is under a debt to the same influence that was later to play
so important a part in our early drama. Indeed, the more closely
this early verse is studied, the more apparent it becomes that Old
English religious poetry had its roots not only in the Scriptures,
but in the services of the medieval Church, its canticles and hymns,
the exegetical writings of the Christian Fathers, Christian allegory,
great collections of saints' lives and chronicles of the martyrs, and
all the wealth of ecclesiastical lore which interpreted and enriched
the Christian faith.

The style of *Exodus*, like its structure, is highly sophisticated in
a conscious striving for effect. Details of description are massed
and elaborated; there are many images, some vigorous and unusual, others derived from tradition and cliché. At times indeed
the author, in his desire for effect, expands his descriptions beyond
the limits of realism. For example, the narrative of the march to
the Red Sea and the Egyptian pursuit contains a passage in which
the poet is obviously borrowing the conventional imagery of the
Old English battle scene. In this passage the reference to the birds
of battle circling above corpses has no realistic appropriateness,
since there has been no conflict, and no field of slaughter:

> Then the hearts of the earls   were hopeless within them
> When they saw advancing   on the southern roads
> The forces of Pharaoh,   a glittering host
> With waving banners,   bearing their spears
> On the border-paths.   Their pikes were in array,

The battle-line rolled on,   bucklers gleamed,
Trumpets sang.   Over corpses circling
The war-birds clamored,   dark carrion-lovers,
Dewy-feathered,   greedy for battle.
In hope of food,   the wolves fierce-hearted,
Grim beasts of slaughter,   on the heels of the host
Chanted their night-dirge,   foretelling the fall
Of the great folk-troop.   In the midnight hour
The march-wardens howled;   fated souls fled,
The host was hemmed in.[44]

In other passages also there occurs a straining and exaggeration
of imagery. When the Egyptian army perishes, the violent image
of blood spreading through the waves can hardly be considered
appropriate to a description of drowning. In both passages the
poet's desire for dramatic heightening seems to have seduced him
beyond the limits of the factual and the realistic.

This same striving for vividness of imagery, aided perhaps by
an ecclesiastical stress on the miraculous, is found in the poet's
description of the manner in which a path is opened for the Israelites
through the Red Sea. The poet does not visualize an ebbing with-
drawal of the sea from sandy shallows to provide a dry crossing,
but a piling up of the waters into rampart-walls reaching to the
sky, between which as through a roofless tunnel the marching
tribes escaped:

The waves rise up;   the waters form a rampart,
The sea is thrust aside,   the ways are dry,
Gray army-roads,   ancient foundations
Which never man before   set foot upon,
Shining plains,   imprisoned deep sea-bottoms
Which from of old the waters   covered with waves . . .
God has raised up   the red streams to a rampart.
The walls are well reared   to the roof of clouds,
A wondrous sea-passage.[45]

44. *Exodus*, 154–69.
45. *Exodus*, 282–9; 295–8.

It is possible that one or two passages of *Exodus* show an influence of the *Beowulf*, particularly of the scene in which Beowulf struggles under water with Grendel's dam. This portion of *Beowulf* must have been well known to the *Exodus* poet, since line 58 of *Exodus*, *enge ānpaþas, uncūþ gelād*, is borrowed verbatim from a passage of *Beowulf*[46] in which it is employed to describe the wild and rugged country through which Hrothgar and Beowulf made their way to Grendel's pool. This borrowing from the *Beowulf* suggests the possibility that the inappropriate image of blood spreading through the waves in *Exodus* 449-50 and 463 could have been taken from this same section of *Beowulf*. It is the waters of Grendel's pool which become stained with blood as the Danes and Weders on the brink awaited the outcome of Beowulf's struggle in the depths.[47]

The poet of *Exodus* has a flair for dramatic detail, whether borrowed or the product of his own imagination. All that his mind pictures it pictures vividly. When the waters of the Red Sea are thrust back, the sight of ocean-bottoms never before uncovered since the world began has for his imagination the wonder and the freshness of a new creation. The psychology of crisis, by which trivialities of experience are permanently associated in memory with momentous event, has illustration in the poet's reference to the flash of sunlight on shields as the sea broke over the Egyptian host: 'War-shields flashed; the wall of water, the mighty sea-stream, rushed over the heroes.'

It is nevertheless true that the emotional stress of *Exodus* is not to be found in its vivid reflection of external realisms, or in its dramatic rendering of action, but chiefly in the religious earnestness with which the poet blends the rich symbolisms of his chosen theme. The deeply underlying *motif* of *Exodus*, as of all the Junius group, is the power and the glory of a God, who puts down the

46. *Beowulf*, 1410.
47. ll. 1593-4.

mighty from their seats and shows mercy upon His elect. Over and over in the Junius poems, as an epilogue to themes of swift and tragic catastrophe, is heard, as here, the refrain of the poet: 'They had striven against God.'

DANIEL

Immediately following *Exodus* in the Junius MS. are the 765 lines of *Daniel*. The narrative is incomplete, the story of Belshazzar's Feast being cut short by a defect in the manuscript. The chief episodes of the poem are based on the Vulgate, following somewhat closely the material of the first five chapters of the Book of Daniel. There is little addition of extraneous material. In this respect the *Daniel* differs widely from *Exodus*. The introductory lines of the poem are not derived from the Vulgate Daniel, and the reference in these lines to the departure of the Israelites from Egypt suggests a possibility that this opening passage was not part of the original text, but was composed by the compiler of the Junius MS. as a transitional link between *Exodus* and *Daniel*. Bright,[48] indeed, was inclined to see an even closer relationship between the two poems. In the baptismal office of Holy Saturday, which, we have seen, influenced so markedly the structure of *Exodus*, the twelfth 'prophecy' consisted of the first 24 verses of chapter iii of the Book of Daniel. This passage set forth the story of the three youths and the fiery furnace. Since the *Daniel* follows immediately after *Exodus* in the Junius MS. and includes this subject matter, Bright was tempted to assume that *Daniel* like *Exodus* was written under the influence of the baptismal services of Holy Saturday, and that both poems are by the same author.

It is possible, of course, that this versifying of material from the Book of Daniel was suggested to the poet's mind by the passage appointed to be read on Holy Saturday. But this theory is hardly justified by the slight evidence at hand; it leaves great differences

---

48. *Modern Language Notes*, xxvii, 97–103.

of style between the Old English *Exodus* and *Daniel* still to be accounted for, and apparently disregards all evidence of difference in date of composition.

Two passages in *Daniel* have close correspondence to two independent lyrics. *Daniel* 279-332 is a rendering of the prayer of Azarias, a variant version of which is included in the Exeter Book. *Daniel* 362-408 depends on a canticle preserved among the Vespasian hymns, the *cantus trium puerorum*. The interest of the *Daniel* poet in this Vespasian hymn may well have sprung from its liturgical use as a canticle.

Daniel opens with a somewhat extended introductory passage rehearsing the expansion of the Hebrew power after the Exodus until in their prosperity the Hebrews forgot God's covenant with Abraham, and in arrogance and pride turned away from their ancient worship. God's punishment is visited upon the sin of Israel by the Babylonian captivity. The lords of Israel had prospered as long as the Lord permitted. Gathering a host of savage legions, Nebuchadnezzar marches westward against Jerusalem. The city is sacked, Solomon's temple despoiled, and Israel carried off to captivity in Babylon.

Then to Nebuchadnezzar there came in slumber a terrible dream prophesying a bitter end to his reign and to all the joys of earth. When the wolf-hearted prince awoke he was shaken with terror, though the dream itself he could not remember. Sending for his wise men he demanded that they reveal what he could not recall. No one of them could do so until Daniel came at dawn to the king and rehearsed the dream and expounded its meaning. Thereafter Daniel had great honor at the hands of the king.

The second episode of *Daniel* rehearses the story of the golden image which Nebuchadnezzar set up in the plain of Dura, commanding all men to worship. Three men of Israel, Ananias, Azarias, and Misael, refused to obey the decree. In his wrath Nebuchadnezzar ordered a fiery furnace to be prepared and the

young men burned to death. When the three were thrust into the
furnace, the flames took no hold on them, but turned against their
heathen persecutors. The king beheld the three youths unharmed
in the furnace and a fourth with them, an angel of God. 'No whit
of harm had come upon them, but within the furnace it was most
like when in the summer season the sun shines, and the dew-
fall comes at dawn scattered by the wind.'

Then follows the hymn of Azarias. The passage seems obviously
an interpolation not too neatly fitted into its frame. Lines immediately following the hymn describe the coming of an angel
as if in response to the words of Azarias, and as if there had been
no previous mention of angelic aid. The passage contains, moreover, a second simile comparing the temperature in the furnace
to mild and pleasant summer weather. 'Then in the furnace, when
the angel came, the air was cool and pleasant, most like the
weather in the summer season when rain falls during the day and
warm showers from the clouds.'[49] The substance of these lines is
sufficiently like the simile[50] already quoted to suggest that the
second simile is a variant of the first.

The third episode rehearses a second dream of Nebuchadnezzar
and its interpretation by Daniel. The dream was of a great tree
which overshadowed the world, giving shelter and food to bird
and beast. By God's command the tree was to be cut down and
cast away, but its roots were to remain in the earth that new shoots
might grow:

> Then to Nebuchadnezzar   there came in his sleep
> A troubling dream.   Him seemed that a tree
> To others unlike   flourished on earth
> Firm-rooted and fair,   shining with fruit.
> It towered high   to the heavenly stars,
> With branches and boughs   overspreading the world,
> The regions of earth,   to the shores of ocean.

49. *Daniel*, 345–9.
50. ll. 273–7.

As he gazed he saw   that the tree gave shelter
To beasts of the field;   the fruit of the tree
To fowls of the air   gave store of food.
In his dream an angel   came down from heaven
With clear voice speaking;   bade fell the tree;
Bade birds of air   and wild beasts flee
When its fall should come;   bade sever its fruit,
Its boughs and branches,   leaving its roots
As a token firm   fastened in earth
Till once again,   by the grace of God,
Green shoots should grow.   Then he gave command
To bind the great tree   with bands of iron,
With fetters of brass,   and cast it forth
To ruin and death   that its pride might know
A greater than it   has power to punish.[51]

When the king awoke, the fear of the dream was still upon him. Again he summoned his wise men and again no one of them could expound the dream until Daniel was called. He perceived that the vision was an allegory of the king's evil reign and the divine punishment to follow. And he so interpreted it to the king:

As the tree grew high unto heaven so art thou lord and ruler over all the dwellers of earth and there is none to withstand thee save God alone.   He shall cut thee off from thy kingdom and drive thee into exile without friends. Thy heart shall be changed so that there shall be no thought in thy heart of worldly joys, nor any reason in thy mind save the ways of the wild beasts, but thou shalt live a long time in the forest ranging with the deer. Thou shalt have no food save the grass of the field, nor any fixed abiding-place, but the showers of rain shall drench thee and harass thee even as the wild beasts, until after seven years thou shalt believe there is one God for all mankind.[52]

51. ll. 495–522.
52. ll. 562–79.

As the roots of the great tree were to remain in earth until new shoots grew, so should the kingdom stand until Nebuchadnezzar returned to his throne. But the king refused to heed the words of Daniel, boasting of the glory of Babylon and the strength of his kingdom.

Then God's wrath fell upon Nebuchadnezzar and he was driven forth from his kingdom into the waste where 'he trod the bitterest road of God's vengeance that ever living man trod.' For seven years he suffered a desert-life with beasts. When the seven years were fulfilled, he was recovered from his madness. Seated again upon his throne, with 'a better heart and a clearer faith,' Nebuchadnezzar prospered until death, and his descendants after him.

The last and incomplete episode of *Daniel* treats of the ending of the Chaldean dynasty and the passing of the Babylonian kingdom to the Medes and Persians. The narrative rehearses the insolence and pride which brought the loss of Belshazzar's kingdom. At a great feast Belshazzar ordered the gold and silver treasure of Israel brought into the hall and, boasting that his gods were mightier, drank to them in the holy vessels of the Jewish sacrifice. Then appeared an angel's hand, writing upon the wall mysterious words in letters of scarlet. Once again the Chaldean magicians are unable to interpret the portent, and once again it is Daniel who explains its meaning. He upbraids Belshazzar for using the holy vessels of Israel to drink to devils, and for denying 'the living God.' At the 22nd line of Daniel's speech the poem breaks off.

The *Daniel*, in certain of its episodes, is a somewhat better narrative than is sometimes assumed. It is true, the introductory sections and the broken fragment of Belshazzar's Feast afford no great evidence of poetic skill. But portions of the narrative of the fiery furnace are well done, and the dream of the tree and the metamorphosis of Nebuchadnezzar are clearly conceived, and developed with power and pathos. The poet lacks the skill in imagery and in integrated structural design which marks the poetic endowment of the author of *Exodus*. But, at its best, *Daniel* presents passages of restrained and simple poetic narrative fairly comparable in quality and style to the episodes of *Genesis A*.

CHRIST AND SATAN

The 733 lines of verse which follow *Daniel* and constitute the second part of the Junius MS. have come to be known as *Christ and Satan*. Whether in these lines we have one, two, or three poems is a question which cannot be answered with complete certainty. The 733 lines fall into three definite sections dealing with easily distinguishable, though not unrelated, subject matter. In lines 1-365 we have a *Lament* of the fallen angels; in 366-664 a *Harrowing of Hell*; and in 665-733 a broken fragment on the theme of Satan's temptation of Christ.

Critical opinion has been divided concerning the unity of this section of the Junius manuscript. Early critics[53] regarded the three sections as three separate poems. Later criticism, however, has tended to the opinion that there is in these 733 lines an underlying unity. It has been suggested,[54] for example, that the poem has been imperfectly transmitted and that the *Christ and Satan*, as we have it, is composed of fragments of a longer original which a later scribe attempted to restore to unity by poetic links of his own invention. There is, however, no evidence that such a longer original ever existed and, in the absence of such evidence, this particular opinion regarding the structure of *Christ and Satan* remains highly conjectural.

Another and quite different theory[55] of the development and structure of the poem regards the 733 lines of *Christ and Satan* as being unified in the sense that they constitute a genetic whole.

53. See ten Brink, *Early English Literature*, I, 86-8, 375-6; Sievers, *Beiträge zur Geschichte der deutschen Sprache und Literatur*, x, 195-9; Wülker, *Grundriss*, 111-46.

54. Groschopp, *Das angelsächsische Gedicht 'Crist und Satan,'* Halle, 1883.

55. Abbetmeyer, *Old English Poetical Motives derived from the Doctrine of Sin*, Minneapolis, 1903.

The first 365 lines of the poem represent, it is suggested, a gradual evolution of a cycle of plaints, or laments, of Lucifer originating in the material of early portions of *Genesis*, and later shaped and extended by addition of the Harrowing of Hell, and other homiletic material. According to this theory, the Temptation fragment was added not because it dealt with Christ, but 'because it described some of the sufferings of Satan, for these form the real subject of the poems.'

A still more recent study[56] likewise interprets the poem as an evolution, but finds its germinal element in the second section rather than in the first. The poet's original intention, according to this theory, was to 'compose a narrative poem on the events in the history of Christ after his crucifixion, similar in general to the synthetic works exemplified in the seventh Blickling homily.' Stirred by the story of the Harrowing of Hell, a favorite medieval theme, the poet developed and dramatized his material by adding the dialogue between Christ and Eve, and the speech of Christ to the liberated patriarchs, two elements without counterpart in conventional accounts of the Harrowing. For an introduction to the Harrowing of Hell the author drew upon another sort of material.

> 'The terror of the devils in anticipation of Christ's assault upon their realm was expressed in speeches of moderate length, both in the *Gospel of Nicodemus* and in the Blickling homily. But the poet thought he could work in the story of the fall of the evil angels, and introduce certain laments of theirs which would show the contrast between their original glory and their present (and impending greater) degradation—such laments as he was familiar with in another poem or (possibly) collection of poems.'[57]

The total design, so runs the theory, proved somewhat beyond the author's powers. His interest in the laments, and in didactic

56. M. D. Clubb, 'Christ and Satan,' *Yale Studies in English*, lxx, 1925.
57. Clubb, op. cit. p. liv.

material suggested by the laments, brought an expansion of this material into what is almost an independent poem and the union of this material with the Harrowing of Hell is far from skillful. 'Moreover, the relation between the characters Christ and Satan had so taken hold of his imagination that he could not refrain from returning to it again in the third part, in spite of the necessity, under which this laid him, of committing a gross anachronism.[58]

Clubb's analysis of the evolution and structure of *Christ and Satan* affords in many ways the most reasonable interpretation of the various problems involved in these 733 lines. There is nothing unlikely in the theory that an Old English poet concerned with a versification of the Harrowing of Hell attempted 'to work in the story of the fall of the evil angels.' As we have already seen, the example of the *Genesis* suggests the likelihood that the stream of Hexaemeral tradition exerted more influence upon Old English poets and homilists than has been generally assumed. It is not improbable that the laments of the first section of *Christ and Satan* may owe a debt to this body of tradition. The resulting lack, or apparent lack, of unity need not be too greatly stressed, for it cannot be forgotten that there is constantly recurring evidence in Old English religious poetry that in many instances the central unity of these religious poems develops from theological, rather than from literary, roots.

Certain apparent relationships between the *Christ and Satan* and other writings are interesting and puzzling. As was pointed out by Abbetmeyer, there is striking similarity between the first section of *Christ and Satan* (1-365) and *Guthlac A*, 529-656. The speeches of the demons who threaten St. Guthlac, and the saint's replies to these threats, contain elements which are strongly suggestive of thoughts and expressions in the *Lament* of *Christ and Satan*. These resemblances are of such a nature as to indicate either that the author of *Guthlac A* has borrowed from the *Christ and*

58. Clubb, op. cit. p. lv.

Satan, or that both poems are dependent on a common original. No such original is known, but that one may have existed is not unlikely. Traces are not lacking of an earlier literary interest in the state of mind of the fallen Lucifer. Gregory the Great, for example, displayed such an interest in the 34th of his homilies upon the Gospels. Avitus of Vienne, in the *De Originali Peccato*, ascribes to Lucifer a lament for his lost glory, and Aldhelm concerns himself with the lost pre-eminence and degradation of Lucifer in the *De Octo Principalibus Vitiis,* and in three lines of his *Lucifer* riddle.

This first section of *Christ and Satan*, the *Lament* of the fallen angels, represents Satan and his fellows as bemoaning their sin in hell and dreading God's further vengeance. The description of hell itself is even more vigorously wrought than that set forth in *Genesis B*, including as it does certain dramatically descriptive details which do not appear in *Genesis B*. Hell is pictured as a vast and windy hall in the lowest abyss; its floor flames with fire and venom; its gates are guarded by dragons. Through its wide and dreary spaces resound the woe and anguish of fallen and accursed spirits. 'They have no hope but only frost and fire, torture and pain and swarming serpents, dragons and adders, and a home of darkness. He who stood within twelve miles of hell might hear a gnashing of teeth, loud and full of woe.'[59]

In this grim hall of torture Satan confesses his former sin and laments his departed glory. It is no longer the defiant voice of *Genesis B*. Realization of sin, and the punishment of sin, colors these speeches of Satan. Though his words 'fly forth like sparks' this is not the unyielding and unrepentant spirit which in *Genesis B*, even in the bondage of hell, hurls that broken threat of vengeance against God: 'Alas! Could I but use my hands and have my freedom for an hour, one winter hour, then with this host I would —'

It is of the essence of Satan's punishment that unendingly he

59. *Christ and Satan*, 334-9.

must rehearse his sin, and the glory of the heavenly life which through that sin has passed from him forever. The mood of Satan reflects that ultimate poignancy of spiritual torture which Marlowe centuries later phrased in the unforgettable words of Mephistopheles:

> Thinkest thou that I who saw the face of God
> And tasted the eternal joys of heaven,
> Am not tormented with ten thousand hells,
> In being deprived of everlasting bliss?

Gone, too, are Satan's power and dominion over the fallen angels. The Satan of *Genesis B* still retained his sovereignty. But in this poem he is scorned by those who shared his fall; to his laments their bitter and contemptuous taunts are an unending antiphonal. This change in the attitude of his former followers toward Satan himself constitutes one of the major differences between the hell scenes of *Genesis B* and those of the first section of *Christ and Satan*. The relation between Satan and his followers in *Genesis B* reflects, as we have seen, the unswerving loyalty, even in disaster, of the Germanic *comitatus*. Satan's appeal in that poem for a volunteer to go forth from hell and carry out upon earth the vengeful designs against God and man which Satan's bondage prevents his undertaking, is couched in the language of a Germanic leader who reminds his followers of his many acts of generosity, and appeals to their loyalty. Nowhere in *Genesis B* is there suggestion that there has been any weakening in the bonds of that loyalty. But in *Christ and Satan* the dominant mood of the fallen angels is one of bitter awareness, not only of the horror of the life that has become their portion, but of the folly, pride, and false leadership of Satan which has brought them to their present state:

> Lamenting their torment
> The foul fiends answered,   sinful and black:
> 'With your lies you taught us   not to serve the Savior.
> To you it seemed   you had power of all,

Of heaven and earth;   that you were Holy God,
The Creator himself.   Now you are one of the accursed,
Fettered fast   in bondage of flame.
In your splendor you weened,   and we angels with you,
That you owned the world   and the power of all things.
Loathsome your face!   For your lying words
We suffer the more sorely.   You told us as truth
That your son was Shaper   of all mankind.
Now is your torment   and torture the worse.'[60]

The depictions of hell and hell torment are more extended, more detailed, and more terrifying than those of *Genesis B*. Once more we find the conventional stress upon fire and darkness, heat and cold. But there are additional elements not found in *Genesis B*. The conception of hell as a windy hall is unusual. Its floor burns with fire and venom. Its gates are guarded by dragons. A hissing of adders fills the air. Most loathsome of all, if in lines 135b-136a we accept Thorpe's emendation of *winnað* to *windað*, we have the horrid image of hell serpents twining themselves about the bodies of naked sufferers. Suggestions of the snake-pit mould the image. Indeed, far more than in the case of *Genesis B* the descriptions of hell are elaborated with a kind of sadistic stress upon horror which is suggestive of certain types of medieval painting. But in spite of the fascination these themes hold for the poet, the laments of the first part of *Christ and Satan* attain greatest poignancy of phrasing from contrasts which owe as much to vivid conceptions of lost glory as to such sadistic delineation of present horror:

                              Here is no glory of the blessed,
   No wine-hall of the proud,   no joy of the world,
No angel throngs,   no heritage of heaven.
This horrid home is aflame!   I am God's foe!
Ever at hell's doors   dragons are on watch
Inflamed and furious.   Hope not for help from them!
This terrible home   is filled with torment;
   We have nowhere to hide our heads   in the gloom of hell,

60. ll. 51-64.

Nor cover ourselves in the depths   with shades of darkness.
Here is the adder's hiss!   Here serpents dwell!
Firmly the bonds of pain   are fastened upon us.
Fierce are the fiends of hell,   swarthy and black.
Day never lightens this dark,   nor the glory of God . . .

So large am I of limb   I may not lie hid
In this wide hall,   wounded with my sins.
At times heat and cold   in hell are mingled;
At times I can hear   the hell-slaves howl,
A wretched race   bemoaning this realm of pain
Deep under the nesses   where round about naked men
Serpents entwine.   All this windy hall
Is filled with horror.   Never shall I know
A happier home,   city or stronghold,
Nor ever look with eye   on the gleaming world again . . .

Farewell to the glory of God!   Farewell to the Helm of hosts!
Farewell to the might of God!   Farewell to the world!
Farewell to the light of day   and the bliss of God!
Farewell to the angel hosts!   Farewell to heaven!
Alas!   that I have lost   eternal joy!
Alas!   that I may not reach with my hands   to the heavens above,
Nor thither lift up mine eyes,   nor hear with my ears
The pealing trumpet sound,   because from His seat
I would have driven God's Son,   and seized for myself
Dominion of glory and bliss.   Worse fate befell
Than I could foresee!   From the shining host I am severed,
Cast out from light   into this loathsome home.[61]

The second part of *Christ and Satan*, which has come to be known
as the *Harrowing of Hell*, treats material far more extensive than
such a title suggests. This section of the poem must be recognized
as belonging to a type of synthetic poetry the unity of which in-
heres more in theological than in literary elements. The theme of
the Passion and Descent into Hell is followed in the poem by a
number of shorter sections dealing with the Resurrection, Ascen-

61. ll. 92–105; 129–39; 163–77.

sion, and Last Judgment, and elaborated with additions of homiletic material. The lines on the Harrowing of Hell may be said to have as their ultimate source the Apocryphal *Gospel of Nicodemus*. This fourth-century story of the Descent, widely known throughout the Middle Ages, has survived in three Old English prose versions. Its characteristic themes are reflected not only in *Christ and Satan*, but also in the *Harrowing of Hell* of the Exeter Book, and in lines 558-85 of Part II of the *Christ*. There is no evidence, however, that the poet of *Christ and Satan* drew directly from the Apocryphal Gospel, and it is possible that this section of the poem derives, as Ten Brink suggested, from some lost homily for Easter Sunday generally similar in form to the seventh Blickling homily.

An interesting and important feature of this second part of *Christ and Satan* is the pervasive resemblance to passages in the Cynewulfian poetry, especially the *Christ, Phoenix* and *Guthlac*. A reference to Clubb's tables[62] will disclose repeated similarities or identities of phrasing. Moreover, as Clubb points out, these similarities of phrasing do not adequately indicate the degree of resemblance to the Cynewulfian verse. 'Wherever, in the latter, there occur extended exhortations, or passages describing the bliss of heaven or the torments of hell (often in connection with the Judgment Day) one is sure to recognize an affinity in conception and tone between these passages and those in *Christ and Satan* which treat the same themes.'[63]

The first 13 lines of this second section form a brief resumptive link which treats the revolt of Satan and his banishment, and serves as an introduction to the Harrowing of Hell. Terror comes upon all the accursed at the coming of their Judge. 'Before Him goes a fairer light than ever our eyes beheld save when we were with the angels.' There is thunder and din in the dawn. God himself has come to overthrow the powers of hell and redeem the souls of the

62. Clubb, op. cit., pp. xxxi-ii; xxxvii-xl.
63. Clubb, op. cit., pp. xl-xli.

chosen. Eve's voice is heard in hell retelling the sin of Eden, and beseeching mercy for Mary's sake, daughter of Eve. The Eternal Lord thrusts the accursed 'deeper into that deep darkness,' and leads the blessed to their eternal home.

The third division of *Christ and Satan*, the anachronistic *Temptation* is a broken fragment of some 67 lines, noteworthy only in one passage, but in that preserving one of the finest bits of verse in the Junius MS. This is the passage in which Christ spurns Satan, and sends him back to measure the boundless width and depth of hell that he may realize it is God against whom he strives. The lines have at least a suggestion of the majestic phrasing that characterizes great passages of the Book of Job. No original for the lines has been found. Clubb suggests a brief passage from the Blickling homily for the first Sunday in Lent. But the resemblance is slight and, in the absence of further evidence, the lines stand as an original passage of great strength:

> Depart, accursed,   to the place of pain,
> The torture appointed,   not the kingdom of God!
> My power is highest;   you shall never in hell
> Bring hope to hell-dwellers.   Tell them your woe,
> That you met the Maker   of all mankind,
> The King of all creatures.   Get behind me, accursed!
> Know how broad and boundless,   how bitter is hell.
> Measure it with your hands;   take hold on its bottom;
> Explore till you know   its limitless expanse.
> Measure it from above   even to the abyss;
> Measure how broad   the black mist stretches!
> When your hands have measured   the depth and height
> Of the compass of hell,   the grave-house grim,
> Then shall you know   that you strive against God.[64]

So ends the Junius manuscript. A sharp and realistic personalization of the forces of good and evil, as protagonists in a universal drama, engenders the dignity and strength of these Junian poems.

64. *Christ and Satan*, 690–707.

They portray a warfare, expressed in terms of Christian faith, between the powers of light and the powers of darkness, beginning with the Titanic struggle between God and Lucifer which results in the temptation and fall of man, and ending with the conquest of the hosts of evil in the Harrowing of hell.

An abiding sense of God's covenant with His chosen people binds into unity these tales of His sure guidance or stern correction. Through all the shifting struggle of good and evil, interwoven as an unbroken thread, runs the divine Providence. It is the portrayal of this divine Providence which is the central theme of the Junian poems, and the elevation and dignity with which this theme is presented in *Genesis*, and in parts of *Christ and Satan*, make them in this respect incommensurable with other Old English religious poems.

VII. THE SIGNED POEMS OF CYNEWULF

The poet; Juliana; Elene; Christ II, Fates of the Apostles

CYNEWULF has distinction as the one Old English poet whose authorship of certain specific poems·is definitely established. His signature in runic letters is woven into the text of four poems, the *Juliana, Elene, Christ II,* and *Fates of the Apostles.*[1]

The fact that Cynewulf's name has survived to us in these signatures is not the result of a poet's pride of authorship, but derives from his desire that those who read, and have pleasure in, his poems may utter a prayer for his soul. In the *Juliana* Cynewulf specifically requests his readers to pray for him *by name*[2] that God may be merciful in the Day of Judgment. The same request is repeated in the *Fates of the Apostles.*[3]

Of no other Old English poet do we know at once so little and so much. Evidence of dialect suggests that he was certainly an Anglian, though whether a Mercian or a Northumbrian is uncertain. He probably lived in the second half of the eighth century. But, apart from academic surmise, our actual knowledge of his life and circumstances is slight. He is the shadow of a name reproduced in eight Old English runes. Conjecture has variously portrayed him as a wandering minstrel, and as a priest or bishop of the Christian Church. So far as external evidence is concerned we are ignorant of nearly all that made his life.

Yet of the man himself we know much. In the four poems signed with his name the runic sections are enclosed in passages of self-revelation which give us insight into his character, and suggestive glimpses of his inner life. Apparently there came at some

1. For description of the runic signatures see Appendix B.
2. *Juliana*, 720b.
3. ll. 88–91.

period of Cynewulf's career a sharp and decisive change. Touched by the influence of the Christian faith, the current of his life was turned. A sense of sin and a dread of final judgment, blended with faith in the goodness and justice of God, give an intimate note to these striking passages of personal revelation which have outlasted all record of his way of life.

A close study of the four signed poems indicates that the religious spirit and substance of Cynewulf's poetry can hardly be regarded as the work of a layman. Whatever his position in the Church, whether monk, priest, or bishop, the evidence is unmistakable that Cynewulf was a professional ecclesiastic. His knowledge of the liturgy and of ecclesiastical literature, of scripture and exegesis, of homilies and saints' lives, of dogma and doctrine, is so clearly reflected in the signed poems that it is impossible to think of him as a layman.

The theory that Cynewulf was in youth a wandering minstrel was, as we have already seen, based on a now discarded interpretation of certain Old English riddles. Leo[4] regarded the *Riddles* of the Exeter Book as the work of Cynewulf, believing that the 'First Riddle' could be interpreted as forming his name, and the last as meaning *a wandering minstrel*. Connecting these interpretations with the allusion in the signature passage of *Elene* to the receipt of treasure and appled gold in the mead-hall,[5] Leo argued that the three passages taken together definitely identified Cynewulf as a wandering minstrel. This quite unfounded identification unfortunately persisted for many years in spite of the fact that in 1888 Bradley's analysis of the so-called 'First Riddle'[6] established conclusively that the poem is not a riddle at all, but a fragment of a poem of lament. As for the *Elene* passage, a careful reading of the unemended text makes it quite clear that the allusion to the receipt

4. *Quae de se Cynewulfus tradiderit*, Halle, 1857.
5. *Elene*, 1259–60.
6. *Academy*, 24 March, 1888.

of treasure in the mead-hall is a reference to social custom, not to personal experience, and has no autobiographic significance whatever.[7]

The identity of Cynewulf remains undetermined to the present day. It is possible that a clue to an approximate dating of his work is to be found in the spelling of his name in the runic signatures. In the *Juliana* and *Elene* the name is spelled with an *e*, Cynewulf. In *Christ II* and the *Fates of the Apostles* the *e* is omitted and the name appears as Cynwulf. Sievers pointed out[8] that, in general use, the name underwent two changes in spelling, the original form being Cyniwulf, a shift from *i* to *e* coming about the middle of the eighth century, and a tendency of the *e* to disappear[9] asserting itself near the end of the eighth, or the beginning of the ninth, century.

By this test it would seem unlikely that the *Juliana* and *Elene* were written before 750, or the *Fates of the Apostles* and *Christ II* before 800. It is not safe, however, to lean too heavily on this type of evidence. Such transition periods of linguistic change cannot be too definitely dated, and the evidence of charters and other legal records seems to indicate that, in general use, various spellings of names overlapped in time. Moreover, the attempt to apply this test to the Cynewulf signatures shows its uncertain value since the *Elene*, according to the spelling of the signature, should be one of the earlier poems, whereas it is in this signature that the poet specifically dwells upon his age and describes himself as near to death.[10] The value of Sievers' test, as applied to the signed poems, is its indication that we are probably safe in assigning Cynewulf's work to a period in or near the last quarter of the eighth century.

The religious nature of Cynewulf's poetry and the many evi-

7. See Carleton Brown, *Englische Studien*, xxxviii, 207, 212, 218.
8. *Anglia*, xiii, 11-15.
9. *e* disappearing before h, l, r, w, and s.
10. *Elene*, 1237.

dences of his ecclesiastical learning argue a connection with the Church, and attempts have been made to identify him definitely with one or other of three known ecclesiastics of the same or similar name, two of whom lived in or near the conjectured period in which the signed poems were written. These are: Cenwulf, abbot of Peterborough and Bishop of Winchester, who died in 1006; Cynewulf, Bishop of Lindisfarne, who died about 783; and Cynulf, one of four priests in the company of Tidfrith, Bishop of Dunwich, who at the Council of Clovesho, 12 October 803, signed his name after that of the Bishop to a decree forbidding laymen to be elected to the lordship of monasteries.

The early identification with Cenwulf of Winchester, first suggested by Kemble,[11] may be dismissed as no longer deserving serious consideration. The name Cenwulf is a separate and distinct form, not a variant of the name Cynewulf,[12] and the date is much too late.

The theory which would identify Cynewulf with Cynulf, the priest who accompanied the Bishop of Dunwich, at the Council of Clovesho, was first proposed by Cook.[13] It is true that the date fits well with the conjectured dates of the signed poems, and that the form of signature employed by the Dunwich priest is substantially that used by the poet in *Christ II* and the *Fates of the Apostles*. But it must still be recognized that, if there is little against this theory, there is no conclusive evidence to support it. It is an interesting possibility, but it still remains for it to be proved anything more than that.

The theory which, in many ways, is most tempting identifies the poet as Cynewulf, the Bishop of Lindisfarne. To accept this identification one must date all the signed poems earlier than 783, since the Bishop of Lindisfarne left his charge in 779 or 780 and died some three years later.

11. *Archaeologia*, xxviii, 362.
12. Sievers, *Anglia*, xiii, 20.
13. *The Christ of Cynewulf*, Introd., pp. lxxii–lxxvi.

This identification was opposed by Cook,[14] on the ground that the *Elene* must have been written later than 800. He based this opinion on his belief that lines 1277-1321 of *Elene* reflect ideas contained in Alcuin's *De Fide Sanctae et Individuae Trinitatis,* III, 21.[15] But Carleton Brown[16] has shown that these ideas concerning the fires of Judgment Day, which Cook regarded as peculiar to Alcuin and Cynewulf, were current in the writings of the earlier Church Fathers and therefore easily available to the Bishop of Lindisfarne.

Positive identification of the poet Cynewulf with the Bishop of Lindisfarne is not possible. Much depends on the question whether the linguistic evidence of Sievers closes the door to a date earlier than 783 for the *Christ II* and *Fates of the Apostles.* If the dates of composition of all the signed poems could be shown to be earlier than 783, the internal evidence in these poems would in many ways make identification of the poet with the Bishop entirely plausible. The theological learning of the poet of the signed poems, the evidences of training in the arts of rhetoric and poetry, and the constant stress on Christian doctrine, would be natural qualities of his verse if the poet were the Bishop of Lindisfarne.

The most definite information which we have about Cynewulf is from his own lips and is set forth in twenty lines of the *Elene,*[17] the poem in which he tells the story of the finding of the true cross by St. Helena. In other poems he speaks of his conviction of sin, his dread of Judgment, his desire for the prayers of readers and friends, and his need of the intercession of the saints. But in the *Elene* he tells us somewhat more than this. The passage states in balanced and rhetorical phrases, interwoven with assonance and rhyme, that he is aged and near to death; that his younger years were years of sin and sorrow until there came the gift of God's

14. *Anglia,* xv, 7-20.
15. *Patrologia Latina,* Migne, ci, 53.
16. 'Cynewulf and Alcuin,' *PMLA,* xviii, 308-34.
17. *Elene,* 1237-57.

grace, knowledge to console old age, and an awakened poetic
skill which he has since then happily employed; that he had no
true knowledge of the Cross until his conversion; that he had
pored over the story of the Cross as he found it in books; and that
he had arranged his material and versified it in the weary watches
of the night. The picture is that of a convert whose subsequent
years were devoted to monastic learning, who had discovered and
used to God's glory a skill in verse, and who had now arrived at
old age.

This self-portrait is one which fits well with evidence implicit
in the signed poems. Both in form and substance Cynewulf's
work suggests the influence of medieval scholarship. His writings
indicate that he was both a devout scholar and a sensitive poet,
widely versed in ecclesiastical lore, with professional knowledge
of Church ritual and doctrine, and with a poet's interest in the
rhetorical and metrical arts. Where this learning was acquired he
nowhere intimates. The natural supposition is that some considerable portion of his life must have been spent at one of the
northern Cathedral schools which were centers of medieval
scholarship. Cook, as we have seen, suggests Dunwich and mentions the tradition which stresses the influence of Dunwich in the
founding of the University of Cambridge. But the most widely
known and influential center of learning in the north was the
Cathedral School of York and, if Cynewulf was a Northumbrian,
this would have been for him a natural affiliation. York at this
period was celebrated as the finest Monastic School in Europe. At
the end of the eighth century its library was second only to that
at Rome. Alcuin's catalogue of its contents includes the names of
many authors whose writings were fundamental to the literary
and theological scholarship of the Middle Ages: Ambrose, Aristotle, Augustine, Bede, Boethius, Cassiodorus, Cicero, Gregory,
Lucan, Lactantius, Orosius, Pliny, Statius, Virgil, and others,
among them Alcuin himself.

Theology, of course, received important stress in the scholarship of the period. But the learning of the great Schools was not exclusively theological. Portions, at least, of the works of Aristotle, Cicero, Lucretius, Pliny, and Virgil were known and read. There are characteristics of Cynewulf's verse which suggest that he must have devoted himself in some measure to studies of rhetoric and poetic. He may well have been familiar with such treatises on rhetoric as the *Institutiones Grammaticae* of Priscian, a late fifth-century grammarian,[18] the *Ars Major* of Donatus,[19] and the metrical studies of Bede in the *De schematis et tropis Sacrae Scripturae* and the *De Arte Metrica*.

The poetry of Cynewulf displays in many passages a conscious striving after rhetorical effects. Illustrations of these conscious patterns of composition are found in his use of assonance and rhyme in *Elene* 1237-51, in passages of extended antithesis as in *Christ* 589-98, and in finely wrought and extended metaphor and simile such as those of *Christ* 696-703 and 850-66. An especially fine figure is that of lines 397-409 of *Juliana*, in which Cynewulf is metaphorically describing the overthrow of spiritual resistance to sin in terms of a military image of the siege of a walled city. When the tempter has spied out how the heart is fortified within and its resistance strengthened, then through temptation he batters down the gate in the wall; once the tower is pierced and a breach made, he looses through that entrance the arrow-flights of sinful thoughts. Such a figure is an excellent example of those conscious devices of structure which demonstrate the importance of the Latin influence upon Cynewulf's work. These are not the qualities of the older Germanic tradition, but of a metrical art definitely influenced by medieval rhetoric.

Undoubtedly, in some instances rhetorical effects apparent in Cynewulf's poetry were suggested by the form of his originals.

18. Mentioned by Alcuin in his inventory of the York library.
19. Also mentioned by Alcuin.

Not infrequently in Old English religious verse borrowings from patristic originals reflected both form and content. In *Christ III*, for example, the rhetorical arrangement of contrasts in lines 1652-60 represents a direct reproduction of the form, as well as the material, of the Gregorian text from which the poet drew. Cynewulf's fine simile devoted to the wind in *Elene* 1272-7 seems clearly an imitation of Virgil's description of Aeolus and the winds in the first book of the *Aeneid*.[20] On the other hand, that in many instances the poet's stylistic effects were the product of his own rhetorical and metrical skill, and not of his originals, is suggested by such a passage as *Christ II*, 850-66, in which a brief hint in the text of Gregory has been developed into a lengthy and finely wrought simile in the Virgilian manner.

The evidences of Cynewulf's theological training are equally clear. Pervasive throughout his verse is a stress upon Christian doctrine as accepted by the Western Church. The signed poems contain repeated reference to the Trinity, and in *Christ II* and *Juliana* Trinitarian doctrine becomes explicit in the mention of a Trinity of three Persons in one God.[21] Christ, the Son, is coeternal with the Father.[22] The themes of the Incarnation, Crucifixion, Harrowing of Hell, Resurrection, and Ascension are repeatedly interwoven in the signed poems with devout and reverent stress upon their spiritual significance as elements in the cosmic drama of man's redemption. Of this the Cross is the symbol, and the *Elene*, which tells the story of its recovery, enjoins a pious commemoration of the event.[23] The risen and ascended Christ sits at the right hand of the Father,[24] whence he shall come to judge the world.[25] Man is to be judged according to

20. *Aeneid*, 1, 50-63.
21. *Juliana*, 726; *Christ*, 773.
22. *Christ*, 465.
23. *Elene*, 1229-36.
24. *Christ*, 531-2.
25. *Elene*, 726; *Christ*, 791.

deeds done in the body,[26] and, in accordance with his record of word and deed, will be assigned to heaven, to purgatorial fire,[27] or to hell.

In subject matter, the authentic poetry of Cynewulf consists of versifications of the Latin prose *Vitae* of two saints, St. Juliana and St. Helena; a versification of a Latin prose homily of Gregory dealing with the Ascension; and a versified martyrology setting forth the mission and manner of death of each of the twelve Apostles. The miracle of Cynewulf's work is that these poems, with the exception of the *Fates of the Apostles*, are so much more than mere versified translations of their Latin prose originals. They are in large measure new creation, faithful to their sources, but rising above them to the level of spontaneous poetry.

The chief and pervasive addition which the poet makes to the material of his originals is the intimate reflection of his own sensitive and lovable personality. This is most easily seen in those personal passages which precede and follow the runic signatures. But it is by no means confined to those passages. Throughout his verse one feels a realistic intensity which grows from the play of his imagination upon the text before him. The briefest references in his originals to war and the sea, to images of earth and sky, to forces of fire and flood evoke those imaginative expansions which are the vitalizing energy of his verse. Such passages have been frequently misinterpreted as reflections of the poet's past to prove that Cynewulf was once minstrel, or mariner, or warrior, as if a poet's work were of recollection only all compact, as if Homer could not have written of the Trojan War unless he had been a soldier, or Milton justified God's ways to men unless he had been a professional ecclesiastic and theologian.

The dominant characteristic of Cynewulf's poetry is its fusion of the sensitive and highly personalized faith of the churchman with the shaping and vitalizing imagination and emotion of the

26. *Christ*, 782-5.
27. *Elene*, 1295-1316.

poet. From this fusion spring those tender, moving, unforgettable passages clothing a religious faith which had become the inmost expression of the heart. The strictness of this faith is not concealed by the quietude, nor its integrity by the variety, of its expression. The poetic fusion is complete, all-embracing, and energized.

If the life of Cynewulf was in any measure a cloistered one, his poetry, at least, is marked by no aloofness from the world. He was a lover of the human scene with a sense of its fugitive loveliness. He had kindly understanding of the human heart. In the religious exhortations of *Christ II* there is no harsh denunciation, no fanatical zeal. Yet Christian charity is never sentimentalized. His theology taught him to expect stern judgment for men hereafter according to their earthly record, and his life was lived, and his poetry written, with a recognition of the reality of that Judgment in mind. He craves the prayers of his readers and the intercession of the saints. With all his faith he has also a sense of the mystery of life, and the loneliness of the human soul. 'How great a need have I,' he writes in the *Fates of the Apostles*, 'of kindly friends upon that journey when I seek out alone my long home, that unknown dwelling-place . . . For I shall fare far hence alone unto an alien land, set out upon a journey out of this world, I myself know not whither.'[28]

Above all, the spirit of Cynewulf had not been moved to ascetic repudiations of life, or the world's beauty. The love of the sea runs through his verse, issuing in such vigorous and joyous scenes as the sea-voyages of *Elene*. His spirit reaches out to the stir and movement of congregations of men, the embarkations in *Elene*, the procession that bore Juliana's body to the grave. He has the sensibility of the poet to scenes of cruelty and bloodshed. His imagination quickens in portrayal of scenes of battle, the crash and drive of armed force, the destruction and carnage. He employs these symbols to suggest the nature of evil. He joys in all

28. *Fates of the Apostles*, 91–3; 109–12.

high aspirations of the human spirit, and in the crowning courage of martyrdom. He has recognition of the kindly interdependences of men and their need of one another. He cherishes a love of learning as the means by which men may avoid darkness and find true light. And, in all he writes, a vital sense of the potential goodness of life is interfused with a spirit of worship and adoration of that divine Creator, who is also Redeemer, of the world.

It is altogether fitting that the writings of the one Old English poet of whose work we have some certainty should come from the religious life. In the turbulent centuries of early England it was within the arms of the Church that peace, and some measure of safety, could be found. Even before the Danish wars, life on English soil was unquiet. The struggles of Mercia and Wessex in the eighth and ninth centuries were a disturbance of life even beyond those kingdoms. Only in the Church, amid these distractions of the civil life, could art and letters flourish, and men and women find quietude of spirit.

JULIANA

The *Juliana*, a poem of 731 lines with Cynewulf's signature interwoven between lines 704 and 708, is found in the Exeter Book. There are two breaks in the manuscript at lines 288 and 558, in all probability caused by missing leaves. The *Juliana* is perhaps the earliest of the signed poems. There are various straws of evidence which suggest early composition. The narrative style lacks something of the fluent vivacity of the *Elene*. There is less evidence of the love of nature which produces many of the vividly descriptive passages of *Elene* and *Christ II*. The personal passage in *Juliana* gives no such allusion to the poet's age as is expressed in the signature of the *Elene*, and suggested by the signature of the *Fates of the Apostles*.

Mention of St. Juliana is found in the *Martyrologium Vetustissimum*, ascribed to St. Jerome (d. 420), and the *Martyrologium*

Romanum Vetustius, which dates perhaps from the end of the seventh century. Both these references are brief. Bede in his Martyrology[29] gives her story at greater length. Two prose lives of St. Juliana are found in the Bollandist collection of the *Acta Sanctorum* under date of 16 February. One of these, edited from eleven manuscripts, presents a text which, if not the actual source on which Cynewulf drew, must have been closely similar to it.

The story of St. Juliana, as set forth in the prose of the *Acta Sanctorum*, may be given in a few words: In the reign of Maximian (308-14), Juliana, a maiden of Nicomedia, daughter of Africanus, a persecutor of Christians, was wooed by Eleusius, a Roman prefect. Rejecting his suit because he refused to embrace the Christian faith, she suffered persecution at the hands of her suitor by scourging, imprisonment, fire, breaking on the wheel, and immersion in molten lead. So great was her fortitude and faith that she was enabled by divine aid to endure these sufferings, and to convert many bystanders who witnessed her tortures. Her martyrdom was finally consummated by decollation, and her body taken by a certain Sephonia to Puteoli, where a tomb was built for her one mile from the sea. Eleusius, setting sail soon thereafter for his suburban villa, was caught in a great tempest and drowned with twenty-four of his men.

Between the legend of the *Acta Sanctorum* and the poem of Cynewulf a number of discrepancies exist. It may be that the text before the poet was not that of the *Acta,* but a version somewhat similar, and suggestive of these variations. No such version, however, is known. Of extant texts that of the *Acta* is the closest to the Cynewulfian version, and from that text the Old English poem could easily have developed. There is nothing in *Juliana* so alien to the Latin of the *Acta* as to indicate that the poet *must* have been using a different text. Cynewulf would naturally have used his source material with a poet's freedom. The *Juliana* was not in-

29. *Patrologia Latina,* Migne, xciv, 843.

tended to be a translation in the strict sense of that term, but a versified rehandling of material that would bring into poetic fusion selected themes from the legend of the saint and her martyrdom. Indeed, a close comparison of the poem with the Latin text discovers not a few evidences of a conscious craftsmanship employed for the shaping of the source material into new poetic design.

The divergences of *Juliana* from the Latin text are of two general types: omissions or modifications of material, and expansions or additions. In many instances the omissions can be explained on ecclesiastical grounds, that is, by the desire of the poet to exalt the character of the saint, to purge the text of oaths, to suppress references to pagan worship, and to eliminate the names of pagan gods.

At the very beginning of the Latin *Vita*, Juliana is convicted of something approximating deceit. Being unwilling to marry Eleusius she grounds her refusal on ambitious desire of power and position, stating that unless her suitor held the dignity of a prefecture she could not marry him. Eleusius takes appropriate measures to accomplish her wish. The Latin naively tells us that 'he gave a gift to the Emperor Maximian and succeeded the other prefect who was then ruling.' When Juliana learns that her demand has been fulfilled, and when Eleusius once more presses for her hand, she is obliged to change her ground. This time she gives her real reason and demands his conversion to the Christian faith as a prerequisite to marriage. Cynewulf, undoubtedly finding a blemish of characterization in this duplicity, and in subordination of a prenuptial proviso so important in the eyes of the Church, omits all reference to the prefecture and makes belief in the true God Juliana's one demand of her suitor.

It is in passages of expansion and addition that we most clearly see the poet shaping his borrowed material to new poetic patterns. In the opening lines of *Juliana*, for example, Cynewulf describes the persecutions endured by the early Christians in the reign of the Roman emperor, Maximian. Material which the *Vita* passes over with 'persecutoris Christianae religionis' is expanded in the Old English poem into a detailed picture of the sufferings of the faithful under religious persecution.

Judged for craftsmanship, the most firmly conceived and delicately wrought passage of the poem is undoubtedly that in which Cynewulf elaborates the concept of the invasive power of evil in terms of a military storming of a stronghold. In this passage the eternal conflict between good and evil is set forth in a metaphor which may have been suggested to the poet by the well-known description of the armor of righteousness in verses 11-17 of the sixth chapter of *Ephesians*. The Cynewulfian metaphor, however, not only parallels the Biblical picture of the righteous man clad in the whole armor of God, but from that initiating suggestion passes on to a briefly but firmly unified image of an attack on a fortified city. The passage, a portion of the Devil's confession of his evil wiles, runs as follows:

> When I meet a brave man,   bold in the battle,
> A champion of God   unflinching in the fray,
> Who, heedful of heart,   lifts up against me
> His spiritual armor,   buckler and shield;
> Who deserts not God   but standing at bay
> In prayer is faithful;   then must I flee
> Abased and humbled,   with joyless heart
> In the grip of gledes   bewailing my sorrow
> That I could not conquer   by strength in the strife.
> Then must I sadly   seek out a weaker one,
> Less bold under banner,   whom I may ensnare,
> Entice with temptation   and hinder in battle.
> Even though in beginning   he purpose some good,
> I am quick to spy out   his secretest thought,
> How his heart is strengthened,   his resistance wrought.
> Through corruption I weaken   the gate in the wall;
> When the tower is pierced   and an entrance opened,

Then into his soul   in a storm of darts
I loose the arrows   of evil thought.[30]

There is another passage, a portion of the final prayer of Juliana, in which, in somewhat similar fashion, the poet is expanding and uniting suggestions found in familiar lines of the new Testament. The image of the house built on solid ground in contrast to the house built upon sand, and the destinctive theological metaphor of a Church founded upon living rock, are fused in these final lines. In the development of the image, Cynewulf has also blended phrasings from Scriptural passages stressing prayer and vigil, and the composite whole expresses a sincerity of mood which elevates the passage above its context. Once again the poet's love of martial imagery to express the Christian attitude toward evil is evident. The vigil of the faithful is a watch and ward against the embattled powers of evil that may bar the way to the city of God:

Wherefore, beloved,   fulfilling the law,
Have heed to my teaching,   make firm your house
Lest with sudden blasts   the winds overblow it.
The strong wall then   shall more stoutly withstand
The stormy gales,   the suggestions of sin.
In love of peace,   with faith serene,
Fix your foundations   on the Living Stone.
Toward one another   cherish good will,
Holiness and peace,   in your hearts' desires.
Then the Father Almighty   will grant you mercy,
And after your wretchedness   comfort shall come
From the God of might   in your greatest need.
And because ye know not   your going hence,
Nor the wane of life,   wary it seemeth
To keep watch and ward   against sudden foemen
Lest, battling against you,   they bar your way
To the City of Glory.[31]

30. *Juliana*, 382–405.
31. ll. 647–65.

It is in such occasional passages of *Juliana* that Cynewulf is at his best. The poem, estimated as a whole, is not distinguished composition. This is particularly felt in the long debate between Juliana and the fiend, the subject matter of which is more likely to evoke the interest of a theologian than of a poet. The first and final sections of the poem, because of the nature of their material, are freer from the wearisome repetitions of pattern which characterize the central section.

The depictions of Old English life are less frequent, less expanded, and less vivid than in the *Elene* and *Christ II*. A few brief passages are scattered through the poem. As a prelude to their conference, Africanus and Eleusius, according to Old English custom, lean their spears together, as Beowulf's men stacked their weapons before entering Heorot. Near the end of the poem we find a conventional and quite unexpanded reference to beer-drinking and treasure-giving in the mead-hall, and a brief and undeveloped mention of the sea-voyage of Eleusius. As in many of the religious poems, in depictions of the eternal conflict between good and evil, the conventional terminology of Old English battle scenes is employed. God is the 'Protector of warriors'; Satan the 'Accursed Foe.' Their followers are their 'thanes.' The temptations of Satan are developed in terms of military attack.

Judged as early work, which it seems to be, *Juliana* gives repeated evidence of the poetic powers of its author. But these powers are not yet matured. The narrative tension fluctuates and the style affords few marks of the rhetorical and metrical skills which the *Elene* and *Christ II* display. On the other hand, all those elements of Cynewulf's style which have their roots in personality are present in this poem, as in all he signed: the evidences of ecclesiastical learning, the simple piety and serene faith, the dread of coming judgment, the craving for the intercession of the saints and prayers of the righteous.

ELENE

The *Elene*, a poem of 1321 lines with Cynewulf's signature interwoven between lines 1258 and 1270, is found in the Vercelli MS., folios 121a to 133b. This versified tale of the Invention of the Cross must be regarded as a late, perhaps the latest, poem of Cynewulf. This opinion is supported by the unmistakable evidence of the personal passage in its specific reference to the poet's age, and by the technique and style of the poem, which bespeak maturity of craftsmanship. In no other signed poem do we find the religious theme embellished with so many reflections of the stir and color of Old English life. In the poet's narrative of Elene's embarkation and sea-voyage, and in the account of Constantine's battle against the heathen, we have Cynewulf's descriptive power at its matured best. Both passages are flavored by the racy realisms conventional to the Old English depiction of such scenes. Both descriptions are developed with the firm touch of a poet composing with easy spontaneity.

As a treatment of the substance of saint's legend, the *Elene* differs notably from the *Juliana*. In the *Elene* the poet is obviously attempting to shape his material in the form of a religious heroic tale. The endeavor to imitate the structure and decorative devices of the heroic poem can be easily traced, even though the material has not always lent itself happily to the attempt. In the general shaping of the story, in the elaborate treatment of battle scene and ocean voyage, and in the heroic stress upon Elene's struggle with the Jews, we see evidences of a type of creative design which sets the *Elene* in contrast to the *Juliana*. Recognition of this design is furthered by comparison of the *Elene* with other heroic tales fashioned from religious material, such as the *Andreas* and the *Judith*.

The source of the *Elene* is usually given as the *Vita Quiriaci*, a text included in the *Acta Sanctorum* under date of 4 May. The

Vita gives an account of St. Helena's journey to Jerusalem, and her discovery there of the cross and the nails used in the Crucifixion.

This story is told by Cynewulf in great detail. The narrative begins in the sixth year of the reign of the Roman Emperor Constantine. His empire is threatened by invading hordes of Huns and Goths. The Roman armies are mustered for defense, but with little hope of holding the kingdom against forces vastly superior in numbers.

One night in a dream Constantine sees an image of the Cross adorned with jewels and gold, and enwreathed with the words: 'By this sign you shall overcome the foe.' Moved by the vision, the Emperor has a replica of the Cross made and carried before him into the battle. The conflict is bitter, but under the Christian standard the Romans defeat the Huns and scatter them along the rugged shores of the Danube. But few of them ever return again to their homes. The most striking quality of this battle scene is the sustained energy that enlivens the entire description:

> Then Constantine at dawn,   at the coming of day,
> Bade muster the warriors;   in the weapon-storm
> Lift up the banners   and carry the Cross
> Into battle before them;   against the foe
> Advance God's standard.   War-trumpets sang
> Loud o'er the legions.   The raven rejoiced,
> The dewy-feathered eagle   looked down on the fight
> The battle of heroes.   The wolf raised his howl,
> Comrade of the forest.   War-terror came.
> Then was hard hand-swing   and breaking of bucklers,
> Crash of fighters   and fall of heroes,
> When first they endured   the storm of darts.
> With fingers strong,   on the fated folk
> Savage warriors   shot their shafts,
> Their battle-adders,   among the bold,
> Storms of arrows   over yellow shield.
> Grim of purpose   forward they pressed

Shattered the shield-wall,   sank home the sword.
The stout-hearted stormed;   standards were lifted,
Banners over brave men   shouting in triumph.
Golden helmets   and war-spears glittered
On the field of battle.   The heathen fell;
Knowing no quarter   they died the death.
Then took to flight   the host of Huns
As the King of the Romans   raised up the Cross,
Urged on the fight.   Their forces were scattered.
Some battle took;   some in the struggle
With terrible striving   got away safe;
Some half dead   fled to a fastness,
In the stone-cliffs' shelter   saving their lives,
Finding asylum   on the Danube's shores.
Some were swept away   in the surging stream
At an end of life.[32]

Stirred by this miraculous turning of the tide of war, Constantine summoned his counselors and demanded to know of what God the Cross was the emblem. By the wisest of them he was instructed concerning the Incarnation, Crucifixion, and Ascension of Christ. 'And the prince received baptism at their hands, and from that time forth walked in the will of the Lord through the days of his life.'

Learning through study of the Scriptures the details of the Savior's life and His crucifixion at the hands of the Jews, Constantine sent his mother, Helena, to Jerusalem to recover the Cross. The narrative at this point is enlivened by a fine description of the embarkation and voyage of Elene, which in its length, vivacity of phrasing, and realism of image is one of the best sea scenes in Old English poetry:

Ships stood ready   on the shore of ocean,
Fettered sea-stallions   floating on the sound;
Wide-known of men   was the lady's leaving
As she sought the surges   with all her train.

32. *Elene*, 105-37.

To Wendel shore   came many a proud one,
Over the march-paths,   troop after troop.
They loaded their barks   with battle-corselets,
With men in byrnies,   with buckler and spear,
With man and maid.   Their tall ships, foaming,
Set their sails   for the open sea.
In the welter of waves   the breaking billows
Hammered them hard.   The sea resounded.
Never did I learn   early or late
Of lady attended   with fairer band,
On the paths of ocean.   Who saw that sailing
Saw scudding ships   drive over the deep
Under swelling sails;   saw wave-ships wallow,
And sea-wood skim.   Blithe were the warriors,
Keen-hearted heroes.   The queen rejoiced.
When they sailed their ring-stemmed   ships into harbor
Over ocean lanes   in the land of the Greeks,
They left at the shore,   much battered of billows,
Swinging at anchor,   their old sea-homes
To wait on the wave   the fate of the heroes
When the queen with her convoy   should come again
Over Eastern roads.[33]

Arrived in Judea Helena summoned the Jews to council, de-
manding that they select their wisest for questioning concerning
the Christ whom they had put to death. Three thousand were
selected, but Helena's questioning was of no avail. Winnowed to
one thousand, and finally to five hundred, the Jewish wise men
still maintained that, though learned in the Hebrew law, they
knew of no offense that the Jews had committed. Helena in
anger threatened all with death if they persisted in concealment
of the truth.

In the end, a certain Judas after repeated questioning, chains,
hunger, and imprisonment, broke down and agreed to reveal the
truth. Leading the way to the hill of the Crucifixion, but having

33. ll. 226-55.

no knowledge of the spot where the Cross had been buried, he prayed for a sign. Guided by a vapor miraculously rising from the earth, Judas dug and laid bare three crosses twenty feet under ground. Not knowing upon which cross the Son of God had been crucified, Judas bade the multitude await a revelation. At the ninth hour came a company bearing the body of a dead man on a bier. Judas ordered the body laid upon the ground and the crosses lifted up above it. At the raising of the first two, the body remained lifeless and inert. But when the third cross was lifted up, life returned to the body of the dead man and he arose, whereupon all the company together praised God for the miracle. A church was built on the spot where the Cross was found, and the Cross, adorned with jewels and gold and enclosed in a silver box, was lodged there.

Subsequently, by a second miracle, the nails used in the Crucifixion were also found. In answer to a prayer of Judas there gleamed forth from earth a light by which men saw the nails deep in the ground shining like stars or gems. Quickly recovered, the nails were inwrought in a bridle for the war-horse of Constantine. Thereafter, whoever used that bridle had valiant heart and glory in war.

Judas, having received baptism, was renamed Cyriacus and consecrated Bishop of Jerusalem. And there came to him, often and from afar, lepers and blind men, the lame and halt, the wretched and sorrowful, and found healing at the Bishop's hands, and eternal salvation. Helena, before returning home, bade the faithful keep well a holy festival of the day on which the Cross was found. Cynewulf concludes the narrative with a prayer for all those who 'observe the most lovely feast of the Cross.' The last 85 lines of the poem comprise the personal passage, the runic signature, and a fine description of the Last Judgment.

The legend of Constantine's vision and the discovery of the Cross by St. Helena is one section of a vast body of legendary

literature connected with the Cross which sprang up in the early
Christian centuries and flourished throughout the Middle Ages.
Most of these traditions are concerned either with the history of
the wood from which the Cross was made, or with the fate of the
Cross itself after the Crucifixion.[34]

The legend of the discovery of the Cross arose within a century
after the event. Eusebius was the first to tell of the Emperor's
vision.[35] The sequel to the vision, Helena's journey to Jerusalem
and the finding of the Cross and nails, is added in the ecclesiastical
histories of Socrates and Sozomen. In Sozomen's account, the
information which leads to the discovery is obtained from one of
the Hebrews, who had it by tradition from his forefathers. This
detail is reproduced in the *Vita Quiriaci*, and in *Elene*.

In spite of the evidence that the *Elene* is a late work of Cynewulf it must be granted that as poetic composition it is uneven in
quality. There is wearisome repetition in the narrative of Helena's
struggle against the unbelief, and stubbornness of spirit, of the
Jewish leaders. This section of the *Elene* calls to mind the equally
plodding narrative of Juliana's debate with the demon. In such
passages, it is the Churchman, rather than the poet, who wields
the pen.

For the lover of Cynewulf the greatest interest of the poem
undoubtedly lies in his choice of subject, and in the personal
passage in which he tells of the long and patient reading by which
he had lovingly traced the history of the Cross. It is Cynewulf's
reverent adoration of this central token of the Christian faith
which animates the poem, and finds expression in the prayer of
the poet for all who observe and celebrate the feast of that dearest
of symbols. The *Elene* is the poem of a lover of the Cross, as is
also in marked degree the *Dream of the Rood*, a poem so clearly
in Cynewulf's manner that it must be either his, or the work of a

34. See Morris, *Legends of the Holy Rood*, E.E.T.S., 46.
35. *Life of Constantine*, chap. 28.

singularly faithful imitator. Taken together, these two poems are a precious survival of that medieval spirit which, in adoration of the Cross, blended the intellectualism of the theologian, the mysticism of the poet, the aspiration and hope of the Christian penitent.

The poem ends, as does *Juliana* and *Christ II*, with a reference to the Last Judgment following closely on the runic signature. The *Elene* resembles the *Christ* in setting forth an extended description of the fire of Judgment Day. But it stands alone among the signed poems in a unique reflection of early patristic doctrine. In *Christ II* the depiction of the Judgment fire is confined to its function as destroyer of the world and all earthly possessions. In *Elene*, however, the Judgment precedes the fire, and the function of the flame is particularized as the purger and punisher of sin. All souls must suffer in the flame, but in three groups. The righteous, uppermost in fire, suffer little since for them the flame is assigned as may be mildest and most endurable. Transgressors, in the midst of the fire, undergo purgation. Both groups shall see God. They shall be purged of sin like pure gold that is cleansed of every blemish. They shall enjoy peace and lasting blessedness. The third group, destroyed by sin, shall be lowest in the flame. They shall be cast out from that battlewave of fire into the pit of hell. Never again shall they come to the remembrance of God.

CHRIST II

The first 1664 lines of the Exeter Book have by many critics been treated as a single poem, which has come to be known as the *Christ*. But it is more than doubtful whether these lines do in fact constitute a unit. Because of fundamental differences in subject matter, structure, and style, the lines in question fall into three distinct sections or divisions: *Christ I*, 1-439; *Christ II*, 440-866; *Christ III*, 867-1664. The runic signature of Cynewulf is interwoven near the end of *Christ II*.[36]

36. ll. 797-807.

The history of the highly controversial discussions of the unity of these lines can be easily consulted in the Introduction to Cook's edition of the poem.[37] After careful consideration of the problems involved, Cook supports the opinion that we have here a single poem, and that this poem in its entirety is the work of Cynewulf.

By any conservative interpretation of the evidence this opinion can hardly be accepted. The problem, as Cook indicates, is two-fold. Do the three sections constitute a single poem? Was Cynewulf the author of all three sections? With respect to the first question it must be stated at once that, if these 1664 lines are to be considered a single poem, that poem, in its lack of unity in structure and subject matter, differs completely from normal types of unified poetic composition. A brief analysis of the material and style of the three divisions will establish the point.

Christ I (1-439) is chiefly lyric in nature. Its 439 lines comprise 9 lyric elaborations of antiphons appointed for use in the Advent season; a unique passage of dramatic dialogue between Joseph and Mary;[38] and 2 lyrics[39] based upon antiphons for Trinity Sunday and on themes inherent in the Feast of Trinity. Whatever unity of design might be supposed to govern the poetic elaborations of Advent and Trinity antiphons is certainly broken by the presence of the passage of dramatic dialogue referred to.

Christ II (440-866) differs markedly from *Christ I* both in subject matter and in structure. It is in large measure homiletic, being for the most part based on the text of a homily on the Ascension by Gregory the Great.[40] The development of the source material is a free poetic expansion rather than close paraphrase. But the dependence of the Old English poem on the Latin original is sufficiently close to suggest that the poet must have had the Gregorian homily before him as he composed. It is this section

37. A. S. Cook, *The Christ of Cynewulf*, pp. xiii–xxv.
38. ll. 164–213.
39. ll. 378–415, and 416–39.
40. Number 29 of his *Homilies on the Gospels* (Migne, lxxvi, 1218–19).

which is definitely marked by the runic signature as the work of Cynewulf.

Christ III (867-1664) is a dramatic description and exposition of the Last Judgment, done in detail and with an energy of design which clothes the imaginative concepts with great realism of imagery. A chief guiding source of this section is an alphabetic hymn upon the Last Judgment, the 'Apparebit repentina dies magna Domini' cited by Bede in *De Arte Metrica*. Some of the finest verse in Old English religious poetry is found in *Christ III*.

It may fairly be asked how a body of verse marked by such diversity of material, and difference in structure and style, could ever have been seriously considered a single poem. The explanation lies perhaps in the realm of theology rather than of poetics. It was Dietrich[41] who first stressed the interrelationship of the Advent, Ascension, and Last Judgment as organically unified elements in the Christian drama of man's redemption, and suggested that in these 1664 lines of the Exeter Book we have a single poem on the threefold 'Coming' of Christ: the Coming to earth, or Incarnation; the Coming into glory, or Ascension; the Second Coming, or Last Judgment. The suggestion is more ingenious than convincing. One may grant the theologically organic interrelationship of the three bodies of subject matter, without holding the opinion that we are dealing with a poetic unity. Dietrich's suggestion passes over much too lightly the diversities of structure and style which contradict the theory that the three divisions are one poem.

The question whether Cynewulf wrote all three sections has likewise been much debated. From the other signed poems we know that it was the poet's practice to interweave his signature, as one would expect, at the end of his poems. In each instance, when he has completed the subject matter of the poem, there follows a passage of intimate personal reference and the inter-

41. *Zeitschrift für deutsches Alterthum*, ix, 193-214.

woven runic signature. In the case of the *Christ* the signature occurs near the end of the second section, and according to the poet's normal practice could hardly apply to the text of the third section. Nor is there any convincing reason for believing that the signature covered the preceding text of the Advent lyrics.

Conservative interpretation of all the evidence, therefore, compels belief that in the 1664 lines generally referred to as the *Christ* we have not one poem but several. These lines in fact include a collection of lyrics interpretative of Advent and Trinity (*Christ I*), and two longer poems, the *Ascension* and the *Last Judgment* (*Christ II* and *Christ III*). Of these only the *Ascension* can be definitely included in the Cynewulfian canon.

Reserving the Advent and Trinity lyrics and the *Last Judgment* for discussion with other poems which cannot be definitely assigned to Cynewulf but which are certainly in the Cynewulfian manner, we turn to a consideration of his *Ascension*. In this poem, to a greater degree than in any other work of Cynewulf, we have evidence of matured control of material and design in the re-fashioning of Gregory's homiletic prose into Cynewulf's most studied poetic composition. The *Ascension* is in many ways a superb mosaic of fragments borrowed from the Gregorian homily and other sources, and shaped and fitted into poetic design. But it is a mosaic controlled by a very definite intellectual pattern, and shaped with rhetorical and poetic skill.

In addition to the Gregorian homily, Cynewulf drew, though much less extensively, from subsidiary sources. A Hymn on the Ascension ascribed to Bede beginning 'Hymnum canamus gloriae,' if not an actual source, is certainly an important analogue to the Cynewulfian poem, and another homily of Gregory, the Homily on Ezekiel,[42] apparently furnished Cynewulf material for lines 683-5.

The *Ascension*, in its opening lines, presents one of the most

42. Migne, lxxvi, 899.

tantalizing questions in Old English poetry, for the answering of which information is unfortunately lacking. Cynewulf began the poem with an admonition directed to some unknown 'illustrious man' to meditate, and strive earnestly to understand, a point of Scriptural exegesis. 'Why was it,' he asks, 'that at the Nativity the angels were not robed in white, whereas in the description of the Ascension the white robes of the angels are specifically mentioned?' If only we had information by which to identify the 'illustrious man' for whom this question is posed, what a flood of light might well be thrown upon the circumstances of Cynewulf's life! Was his unknown friend Mercian or Northumbrian, layman or cleric, noble patron or youthful protégé? We do not know. That he could have been a high church dignitary, or distinguished scholar, seems unlikely, since the question he is asked to ponder should present little difficulty to one trained in Scriptural exegesis. Beyond that we have no hint.

The question posed is no exegetical triviality, but is fundamental to Gregory's discussion of the Ascension. Gregory, having raised the question, settles it at once. In the Incarnation, divinity, taking on human form, was thereby humbled and humiliated. White robes, the garb of jubilation, were therefore inappropriate. In the Ascension, when divinity in human form rose to glory, humanity was exalted and the white robes of rejoicing were appropriate.

There is a more extended stress on the cosmic significance of the Ascension in the homiletic passages of Gregory than in Cynewulf's poetic description of the actual scene. But the simplicity with which that scene is outlined produces the same kind of instantaneous conviction implicit in the canvases of some of the primitive Italian paintings of religious themes. Nor is there any ultimate loss, since the entire poem in structure and detail is an elaborate setting-forth of the significance of the event.

Then sudden in air   came a rush of sound,
A host of heaven's angels,   a beauteous, bright band,
Messengers of glory,   in gathering throngs.
Our King rose up   through the temple's roof,
Where the gazing throng   of His chosen thanes
Remained on earth   in their place of meeting.
They saw their Lord   ascend on high,
Their God from the ground.   Their souls were sad,
Their spirits burning   within their breasts;
They mourned in heart   that they might not longer
See their Beloved   beneath the sky.
Then sang their songs   the heavenly angels,
Adored the Prince,   and praised life's Lord,
Rejoiced in the light   that shone from the Savior.[43]

There is included in the Ascension scene an elaborate lyric
chant of angels robed in shining raiment. Their words are directed
to the disciples who stand gazing in sadness after their ascended
Lord. The lyric is in two divisions: 510-26 and 558-85. Both sections are by the same speakers and addressed to the same hearers.
It may be that the latter section is misplaced in the manuscript, and
should follow immediately after line 526. The second section of
this lyric chant includes lines on the Harrowing of Hell in which,
in characteristic Cynewulfian manner, the conflict of good with
evil is developed in the imagery of warfare and battle which the
poet employs so naturally and with such success.

There follows a passage (586-99) in which Cynewulf exalts the
importance of the Ascension as the means by which man has been
set free to live by choice, devoted either to good or evil. In an
extended series of contrasts, pointed by internal rhyme, the poet
stresses man's freedom to choose either 'the shame of hell or the
splendor of heaven, the gleaming light or the loathsome night,
the spell of glory or the misery of darkness, joy with the Lord or
tumult with devils, torment with fiends or bliss with angels, or
life or death as may be dearer to him.'

43. *Christ*, 491-505.

Lines 613-32 have central importance. They are based on a brief statement in which Gregory interprets the Ascension as an annulment of the judgment of man's corruption and the decree of his doom. That mortal nature of which it had been pronounced, 'Dust thou art, and unto dust shalt thou return,' had in the Ascension risen to the heavens. Cynewulf's use of this passage is particularly felicitous. The material of Gregory is artistically set as the climax of an extended list of gracious gifts for which mankind should praise the Lord. God has bestowed upon men food and abundance of possessions, prosperity in wide-stretching lands, and kindly weather under sheltering skies. The sun and moon, candles of heaven, shine for all men on earth. Dew falls and rain, bringing forth rich bounty for the sustenance of men. For all these things mankind should give thanks to God, but especially for the gift of salvation granted in His Ascension.

One of the most interesting and significant symbolisms of the poem[44] Cynewulf borrows directly from Gregory. The image of a bird's flight is used to typify the Incarnation and Ascension, the bird at one time descending to earth, at another rising into the heavens.[45] Gregory based the image upon a suggestion in Job xxviii. 7. A chief interest of the passage is the degree to which the poet goes beyond his original in expansion of the borrowed image. The greater part of the Cynewulfian passage is devoted to a poetic elaboration of the dipping and soaring course of the bird, and the mystery of its flight in the heavens, unknown to foes on earth. Only in the last five lines of the passage does Cynewulf stress the bird's flight as a symbol of the Ascension's annulment of man's ancient doom.

Lines 659-90 of the *Ascension* set forth an interesting treatment of God's gifts to men. These lines are based upon a brief passage in Gregory: 'He gave gifts to mankind, by the Spirit sent from

44. *Christ*, 633-58.
45. ll. 646-50.

above, allotting to some the word of wisdom and to others the word of knowledge, to some the power of strength and to others that of healing, to some divers kinds of tongues and to others the interpretation of tongues. Thus gave He gifts to men.'

The Latin text is greatly expanded and reworked in the corresponding Cynewulfian lines. The poet increases the list of God's gifts, adding to it skills and talents which the Old English world prized highly in its own particular culture — skill in harp-playing, knowledge of the stars, prowess in war, skill in armory, and seamanship. Cynewulf's list has interesting parallels in the *Gifts of Men* and *Fates of Men*. The central theme of the variety of the gifts with which men are endowed by divine grace is of course a traditional one, having Scriptural roots in 1 Corinthians xii. 8-11, and even more ancient analogues in the Homeric epics.[46]

Cynewulf's expansions of the Latin text at this point add concreteness to the more generalized phrasing of Gregory. The specialized intellectual aptitudes which the poet adds to Gregory's list have particular interest. It is perhaps not fanciful to find in Cynewulf's references to skill in oratory, music, theology, astronomy, and possibly rhetoric, a reflection of studies that held important place in the medieval curriculum.

In justifying the ways of God in this varied distribution of gifts, Cynewulf apparently goes beyond the immediate homily with which he was engaged, and draws material from a brief passage on pride in another homily of Gregory, that on Ezekiel: 'For all things are not given to one man lest he fall, puffed up in his pride. But to this man is given that which is not given to you, and to you is given that which is denied to him.' It would seem that this passage, and closely similar statements from Gregory's *Commentary on Job*, furnished the originals upon which Cynewulf based his explanation of the partial nature of man's endowment.[47]

46. *Iliad*, iv, 320-25; xiii, 726-34; *Odyssey*, i, 347-9; viii, 167-77.
47. *Christ*, 683-5.

The most unusual image in the *Ascension* is reproduced directly from the Latin in elaborated form, the curious image in terms of which the various important phases of Christ's mission are represented by Gregory as 'leaps.' A Scriptural suggestion for the image is found in the Song of Solomon ii. 8: 'Behold He cometh leaping upon the mountains, skipping upon the hills.' Gregory comments upon this statement as follows: 'Certainly, in coming for our Redemption He gave, so to speak, certain leaps. Do you wish, dearest brethren, to know those leaps of His? From heaven He came into the womb, from the womb He came to the manger, from the manger He came to the Cross, from the Cross He came to the sepulchre, and from the sepulchre He returned to heaven.' The five leaps of Gregory represent, therefore, the Incarnation, Nativity, Crucifixion, Deposition and Burial, and Resurrection and Ascension.

This mystical rendering of the mission of Christ as a series of 'leaps' is found also in the writings of other Church Fathers. The ultimate source of the image was traced by Cook to two passages in Ambrose. The 'leap' is also found in the writings of Cassiodorus and Alcuin.[48] In Ambrose and Cassiodorus, Christ's baptism in the Jordan is also rendered as a 'leap,' the third in the series, though in Gregory, Alcuin, and Cynewulf, this 'leap' is omitted. On the other hand, in the *Ascension* we find the Harrowing of Hell represented as the fifth in Cynewulf's series.

As the *Ascension* draws to its close we find once more appearing, as already noted in *Juliana*, and in *Christ* 558-70, Cynewulf's love of the imagery of warfare to describe the temptations of Satan and the conflict of evil with good. The development of the image lacks the rounded completeness and finish of the *Juliana* miniature of a beleaguered stronghold, but the poet makes extended use of arrow-storm and poisoned dart, piercing weapon and livid wound,

48. See Cook, *The Christ of Cynewulf*, pp. 143-4.

to give pictorial force in his references to the corrupting power of
evil.

> From heaven the Holy One   sends His angels,
> Who shield us from spoilers   and their deadly darts,
> Lest the fiends work wounds   when the Author of evil
> Against God's people   shoots bitter shafts
> From His bended bow.   Wherefore fast and firm
> We must warily watch   against sudden onslaught
> Lest poisoned arrow,   or pitiless dart,
> Or the foe's swift cunning   should pierce our frame.
> Grievous that hurt,   most ghastly of wounds![49]

There follows immediately on this passage an extended description of the Last Judgment, into which is woven the runic signature
of the poet. In the lines introductory to the Judgment scene Cynewulf contrasts sharply the first and second Coming of Christ. He
who once meekly humbled Himself to a Virgin's womb shall
come at the Last Day to a stern and righteous Judgment. This
contrast appears twice in the Judgment section, in lines 785-90
and 820-25.

The depiction of the fires of Judgment is vividly done. In this
instance, however, all reference is omitted to their purgatorial
cleansing of men's souls, 'as pure gold is purged of every blemish,'
which characterized the description in *Elene*. The swift, red flame
is pictured as the destroyer of the world, and the fire-bath of the
damned.

The poem ends with a simile, developed detail by detail in the
Virgilian manner, in which Cynewulf expands a brief suggestion of
Gregory into one of the most finished poetic images in Old English religious verse. Gregory's homily, using one of the conventional modes of allegory, compares life to a voyage. The turmoil
of earthly existence is a stormy tossing on perilous seas. Man's
only salvation lies in 'fixing the anchor of hope upon an eternal
fatherland.' From this hint the poet develops the beautiful sea-

49. *Christ*, 759-71.

image with which the *Ascension* ends. Nowhere do we have clearer evidence of Cynewulf's matured skill in the control of original materials which he shapes into poetic designs of strength and beauty.

In these concluding sections of the *Ascension* we hear once more the accents of the living poet. Theological exegesis and patristic symbolisms drop away to be replaced by the simple phrases of Christian penitence and aspiration. Still after centuries the poem brings Cynewulf's kindly admonition to all storm-tossed hearts 'to set our hope upon that haven which the Lord of heaven has opened to us by His Ascension.'

THE FATES OF THE APOSTLES

The *Fates of the Apostles*, a poem of 122 lines containing the runic signature of Cynewulf in lines 98-104, follows the *Andreas* in the Vercelli MS.[50] In the early editions of the manuscript, the *Fates* was printed as an unsigned poem ending at line 95. But in 1888 Napier noted that the 27 lines of verse on the following page of the manuscript (54a) were a continuation of the poem, and included the runic signature of Cynewulf. The discovery increased the number of the poet's signed poems to four.

The *Fates* is a versified martyrology setting forth briefly the mission and manner of death of each of the twelve apostles. The material is too diversified, and the structure too compressed, to give great opportunity for poetic imagery or design, save in the personal passage which includes the familiar Cynewulfian reflections on death, and appeals for sympathy and prayer. No direct source for the poem has been found, but Krapp points out[51] that, though the poem differs somewhat from the *Martyrology* of Bede and the *Breviarium Apostolorum*, it may well have been compiled from such Latin lists as these were based on.

---

50. Fol. 52b-54a.

51. Krapp, *Andreas and the Fates of the Apostles*, Introd., pp. xxx–xxxii.

Examination of the paging, sectioning, capitalization, and punctuation of the manuscript corroborates Napier's opinion that the 27 lines of folio 54a, and therefore the runic signature, are an integral part of the *Fates*. But in spite of this evidence of the manuscript and internal evidence in the poem itself, the unity of the two sections has been frequently disputed on curiously mistaken ground. It is claimed that the joining of the two bodies of material produces what has been called an inartistic 'second' ending of the poem unworthy a poet of Cynewulf's skill. But a careful reading of the text itself shows clearly that no such 'second' ending exists.

The structure of the poem, at this point, is as follows: The opening lines of the personal passage contain a reference to the 'long journey,' and a request for the prayers of his readers. Then follow the Cynewulfian runes in the order F W U L C Y N. Immediately after the signature the personal passage is resumed with a second reference to the 'long journey,' and a second request for the prayers of his readers.

It is odd that Sievers,[52] Trautmann,[53] Krapp,[54] and others, should have assumed without question that this repetition of material must be considered an inartistic ending of the poem. The reasons for the repetition become quite obvious if we compare the signature of the *Fates* with the signature of the *Juliana*, which is in phrasing the closest to the *Fates* of all the runic passages. We know from the *Juliana* that Cynewulf's purpose in signing his poems was in order that his readers, knowing his name, might pray for him *by name*.[55] The *Juliana* contains but one request for the prayers of readers (718-29) because in that poem the runic signature precedes the request. A shrewd reader has already spelled

52. *Anglia*, xiii, 21-5.
53. *Anglia Beiblatt*, vi, 21.
54. Op. cit. Introd. p. xlv.
55. *Juliana*, 720, *bī noman mīnum*.

out the poet's name in the runic letters, and Cynewulf is in position to ask that the reader pray for him by name.

In the *Fates* the situation is reversed. The familiar material of the Cynewulfian personal passage begins in lines 88-95:

> And now I pray the man who has pleasure in the course of this lay to entreat that holy band for me in my sorrow, for help and peace and protection. How great a need have I of gentle friends upon my journey when I seek out alone my long home, that unknown habitation, and leave behind this body, this bit of earth, to be a spoil and feast for worms.

This first request for the prayers of readers is made before Cynewulf has disclosed his name. Realizing this, in the next sentence he begins the runic passage with the introductory statement: 'Now may a shrewd man, who has pleasure in song, learn who composed this lay.' He then supplies the runes that form his name and adds the assurance: 'Now you may know who, in these words, was unknown to men.' Immediately, and quite naturally, he renews his request for their prayers: 'May the man who has pleasure in the course of this lay be mindful to ask for me aid and comfort. For I must go elsewhere far hence alone, set out on a journey out of this world to a habitation I myself know not where. Unknown are those dwellings, that habitation and home.' This repetition of the request for intercession and of the reference to the 'long journey' is in no structural sense inartistic. It is not a 'second' ending of the poem, but a resumptive device rhetorically not ineffective.

There can be little doubt, then, that the 122 lines of the *Fates of the Apostles* constitute a unit made up of 88 lines of versified martyrology followed by 27 lines containing the characteristic material of the Cynewulfian runic signature.

But, from quite another point of view, the *Fates* has continued to be the subject of discussion and debate. It has been suggested

that, since the *Fates* follows immediately after the *Andreas* in the
manuscript, it may have been composed as a kind of epilogue to
the longer poem, the runic signature applying therefore not
merely to the *Fates*, but to the preceding *Andreas* as well.[56]

There is little to support the theory that the *Fates* was intended
as an epilogue. The manuscript throws no clear light upon the
matter, but such evidence as can be drawn from the two poems
themselves points against the theory. The results of word tests
and metrical tests set the *Andreas* quite apart from the signed writings of our poet. In its borrowing from the heroic verse, and its
straining after the heroic style and diction, the *Andreas* is nearer
to *Beowulf* than to Cynewulf. Moreover, a uniting of the *Andreas*
and the *Fates*, even in the relation of poem and epilogue, produces
unfortunate repetition in the cases of Andrew and Matthew, since
they are treated at length in the *Andreas*, and once again with the
other apostles in the *Fates*.

One bit of evidence which indicates that the *Fates* was not
designed as an epilogue is found in the opening lines of the poem
itself: 'Lo! travel worn, with weary heart, I fashioned this lay,
gleaning far and wide the record how those princely men,
honored and renowned, showed their heroism. Twelve were
they, famous for their deeds, chosen of the Lord.' It is significant
that in this formal opening of the *Fates* the statement of theme
includes no summary of material treated in the *Andreas*, but is a
definitely proleptic reference to material which is to constitute
the subject matter of the *Fates* itself.

The *Fates of the Apostles*, then, is one of the four signed poems
of Cynewulf, a brief and compressed and versified martyrology.
There is no conclusive reason for believing it an epilogue to
another poem. Belonging to a type of composition familiar in

56. The 'epilogue' theory has been supported chiefly by Sarrazin, Gollancz, and
Trautmann. A second theory, advanced by Skeat, that the *Fates* is a necessary and
integral part of the *Andreas*, runs counter to all the evidence supplied by the two poems
themselves.

church literature, it presents no anomaly in its brevity and lack of poetic extension. Nor need we wonder that the poet should mark so brief a composition with his runic signature. The personal passages of *Juliana* and the *Fates* alike set forth the poet's reason for his signature. Not pride of authorship, but devout desire that the prayers of his readers may be offered for him by name is the motive. A saint's life, a versified homily, a versified record of the fates of the twelve Apostles, all these alike offer opportunity to beseech the intercession of the faithful. Time has dealt kindly with the record, and all the turmoil of eleven centuries has not drowned out that gently repeated request of an humble and a contrite heart.

Such is the record of the signed poems of the poet Cynewulf, and from these signed poems only can evidence be fairly drawn as to the poet's personality and poetic talent. Fanciful ascription of unsigned poems affords little that is trustworthy in interpretation of his life and work. Cynewulf, the wandering minstrel; Cynewulf, the warrior and mariner; Cynewulf, the youthful noble and courtier; these are portraits painted in mist. What survives unchallenged is the record of a gentle churchman and theologian, a Christian penitent, versed in the Scriptures, acquainted with patristic learning, skilled in rhetoric and poetics, a lover of the faithful. His poetic powers were devoted to the service of his religion under the banner of the Cross which he revered and adored.

VIII. POETRY IN THE CYNEWULFIAN MANNER

Christ I; Christ III; Guthlac A; Guthlac B; Dream of the Rood

IN ADDITION to the signed poems, there is a group of poems which cannot be definitely attributed to Cynewulf on the evidence available, but which possess characteristics of theme, style, and diction which suggest that, if not his work, they are the work of collaborators or imitators. To this group belong the Advent and Trinity hymns of *Christ I*; the descriptive poem on the Last Judgment known as *Christ III*; the lyric *Dream of the Rood*; *Guthlac A* and *B*, and the *Phoenix*.[1] In three of these poems occur passages sufficiently similar in style and phrasing to the personal passages of the signed poems to make it possible that we have in them authentic, if unsigned, work of Cynewulf. These are the *Dream of the Rood, Guthlac B*, and the *Phoenix*.

CHRIST I

The short poems or hymns which make up *Christ I* are, as remarked above, lyric elaborations of antiphons, or anthems, borrowed from the liturgy of the medieval church. The antiphons underlying the greater portion of *Christ I* were appointed to be sung at the services of Lauds, Vespers, and other Hours, during the Advent season. In the medieval liturgy these Advent antiphons were interpretive of various aspects of the manifold significance of Christ's coming. Preceding and following the psalms and songs of the season, they served to call attention to their special significance, and to emphasize those portions which deserved particular stress in the services of the day. Among them were seven so-called 'greater' antiphons, appointed for use in the services of

1. For discussion of the *Phoenix* see chapter on Christian Allegory, pp. 290-300.

the seven days immediately preceding the Vigil of Christmas. Listed by their opening phrases they were the following: O Eternal Wisdom; O Lord and Ruler of the House of David; O Root of Jesse; O Key of David; O Rising Brightness; O King and Desire of All Nations; O Emmanuel. To these the Advent liturgy at times added others selected from a group of 'lesser' antiphons, which included: O Virgin of Virgins, O Mistress of the World, O King of Peace, and O Jerusalem. It was this combined group of greater and lesser antiphons which furnished the germinal phrasings from which the poet elaborated his Advent lyrics.[2]

These Advent antiphons, however, were not the only sources of *Christ I*, since antiphons for Trinity Sunday, and for Epiphany, and the Feast of the Circumcision, quite clearly furnish material for certain lyrics in the group. Lines 378-415 of *Christ I* are based upon two Trinity antiphons used as one: 'O beata, et benedicta, et gloriosa Trinitas,' and 'Te jure laudant.' The final lines of the poem, 416-39, show an influence of the 'O Wondrous Intercourse' used at the Feast of the Circumcision and at the Vigil of the Epiphany.

These various antiphons account for almost all the material of *Christ I* with the exception of a remarkable passage of dialogue between Joseph and Mary in lines 164-214. It has been suggested that in these lines we have the earliest dramatic scene in English literature, and that the passage in this sense constitutes a precursor of the medieval miracle plays. Conybeare[3] remarks of this section:

> It is in fact a dialogue between the Virgin Mary and
> Joseph, imitated probably from some of those apocryphal
> writings current in the Middle Ages under the title of the

2. The correspondences of material between the antiphons and the various sections of *Christ I* are as follows: *Christ* 1-17, O King and Desire of All Nations; *Christ* 18-49, O Key of David; *Christ* 50-70, O Jerusalem; *Christ* 71-103, O Virgin of Virgins; *Christ* 104-29, O Rising Brightness; *Christ* 130-63, O Emmanuel; *Christ* 214-74, O King of Peace; *Christ* 275-347, O Mistress of the World; *Christ* 348-77, O Root of Jesse and O Eternal Wisdom.

3. *Illustrations*, p. 201.

Life, or the Gospel, of the Virgin. The dialogue com-
mences with an address of the Virgin to Joseph ex-
pressing her fears lest she should be subjected by the
rigor of the Jewish law to the punishment of an adulteress;
and the answer of Joseph is occupied partly by the
assurance of his steady belief in her purity, and other expressions calculated to remove her distress; and partly by
prayer and thanksgiving to the power which had so
signally favored himself and his lineage.

The presence of this bit of dialogue embedded among the
lyrics of *Christ I* has given rise to much discussion as to the possible
liturgical use of the entire Advent group. It has been suggested[4]
that the whole series may have been composed to be sung in
appropriate Advent services, and that, in this section, Joseph and
Mary may actually have been introduced before the eyes of the
congregation. This theory is perhaps in some degree motivated
by a tempting desire to establish, at this early date in English
literature, the germ of the later medieval mystery play. Both
Wülker and Brooke advance the idea of dramatic representation
quite tentatively, however, though both are inclined to hold fast
to a belief that the Advent hymns were intended for singing in
parts, or by half-choirs, in appropriate festival services.

A matter of interest in the Advent lyrics is the poet's use of his
source material. Cook[5] has pointed out that, brief as the Latin
antiphons are, they are organized in triadic form with elements
of invocation, recital, and petition. These elements are repeated
in the Old English lyrics. But they are repeated in expanded form,
and these expanded and elaborated borrowings from the antiphons
are colored by the poet's 'reflections upon their rich devotional
and doctrinal contents,' and blended with cognate material drawn
directly from Scriptural sources.

The poet's method may be most easily made clear by an exam-

4. Wülker, *Grundriss*, 385; Brooke, *History*, 392–4.
5. *The Christ of Cynewulf*, Introd., xli–xliii.

ination of his use of certain of the separate antiphons. The antiphon which underlies the first seventeen lines of the poem reads: 'O King and Desire of all nations, and chief Cornerstone, you who make two to be one: come now and save man whom you shaped of clay.' From this wording the poet selects and stresses the image of the cornerstone and its special service in binding into firm union the walls of the building. He extends the image of the building to symbolize not only the Christian Church, but the individual Christian as well, and sets forth the world's need that the Craftsman come to repair this structure which now lies decayed under its roof. For it was He who shaped the body and limbs of clay, and it is He who will rescue the wretched from affliction and fear.

The second of the Advent hymns is based on the antiphon: 'O Key of David and Sceptre of the house of Israel, you who open and none shuts, who shut and none opens: come and lead forth from the house of bondage the captive who sits in darkness and the shadow of death.' The image of a leading-forth from bondage is entirely eliminated in the Old English elaboration, and in place of it the just Ruler who holds the keys of life is petitioned to 'show forth His light' upon those who sit sorrowing in prison. In the second half of the lyric the image of the key leads the poet to the theme of the Virgin birth as the means whereby spiritual grace is to spread throughout the world, and life come to those who dwell in darkness.

There is in the entire group no finer example of the poet's effective handling of his liturgical source material than the third of these Advent hymns. It is based on the antiphon: 'O Jerusalem, city of the great God: lift up your eyes and behold your Lord, for He comes to loose you from your chains.' The poet's treatment of this material is a somewhat closer paraphrase than is employed in the two preceding instances. Each important element in the antiphon is included in the Old English lyric, but in greatly expanded form. 'Jerusalem, city of the great God,' is extended to a descriptive passage of nine lines, and the phrase, 'lift up your eyes and behold your Lord,' expands into a detailed portrayal of the coming of Christ in fulfilment of prophecy. The concepts symbolized by the 'holy Jerusalem' fluctuate throughout the lyric, the term suggesting sometimes the heavenly Jerusalem, sometimes the earthly city, sometimes the Virgin Mary. The lyric is poetically one of the finest in the series:

> O holy Jerusalem,   Vision of Peace,
> Choicest of kingly seats,   city of Christ,
> Homeland of angels,   in thee alone
> Rest forever   the souls of the righteous,
> In glory exulting.   No token of sin
> In that city-dwelling   shall ever be seen,
> But from thee all transgression   shall flee afar,
> All trouble and toil.   Thou art wondrously filled
> With holy hope,   as thy name is named.
> Lift up thine eyes   on the wide creation,
> The dome of heaven,   on every hand;
> Behold His coming;   the King of glory
> Himself approaches   to seek thee out,
> Takes abode in thee   as the blessed prophets
> In their books foretold   the birth of the Christ,
> To thy comfort spoke,   thou fairest of cities!
> Now is the Child come,   born to demolish
> The works of the Hebrews.   He brings thee bliss,
> Looses thy bondage,   draws nigh unto men,
> For He only knows   their harrowing need,
> How man in his wretchedness   waits upon mercy.[6]

A fourth antiphon, which the poet elaborates in lines 71-103, is a dialogue between the daughters of Jerusalem and the Virgin: 'O Virgin of virgins, how is this come to pass? Ye daughters of Jerusalem, why look ye wondering at me? What ye behold is a divine mystery.' This brief question and answer is greatly expanded

6. *Christ*, 50-70.

by the poet into a detailed discussion of the mystery of the Virgin birth. Mary's answer becomes a doctrinal statement of the significance of Christ's coming. The sin of Eve is done away, the curse revoked, the lowlier sex exalted. New hope is come for man and maid.

Lines 275-347 are a lyric hymn to the Virgin based upon the antiphon: 'O Mistress of the world, sprung of royal seed; from thy womb did Christ go forth as a bridegroom from his chamber; here in a manger lies He who rules the stars.' The praise of Mary goes far beyond the wording of the antiphon, including the fine image of the prophecy of Isaiah by which the Virgin is identified with the 'princely portal, the lofty door with firm-fixed bolts,' through which the Savior came to earth. The opening lines of the hymn illustrate the mood of lyric invocation which characterizes the whole:

> Hail, Thou most worthy   in all the world!
> Thou purest maiden   that ever on earth
> Through the long ages   lived among men!
> All mortals rightly   with happy hearts
> Name thee blessed   and hail thee Bride
> Of the King of glory.   The thanes of Christ,
> In heaven the highest,   carol and sing,
> Proclaiming thee lady   of the heavenly legions,
> Of earthly orders,   and the hosts of hell.[7]

Near the close of these Advent hymns (378-415) are 38 lines based on two Trinity antiphons. United these antiphons read: 'O holy, blessed, and glorious Trinity, Father, Son, and Holy Spirit; Thee all creatures rightly praise, adore, and glorify, O blessed Trinity.' From this suggestion the poet has developed a hymn in praise of the Trinity placed in the mouths of the 'righteous order of Seraphim,' whose state of glory he has already described. This passage has been compared by Burgert[8] to the

7. ll. 275–86.
8. *The Dependence of Part I of Cynewulf's Christ upon the Antiphonary,* p. 18.

Doxology used to terminate Church hymns, and used by him as evidence that the poet attempted to bind these Advent hymns into a structural unity. Aside from other uncertainties in Burgert's theory, it should be noted that these lines do not actually terminate the Advent hymns, since they are followed by concluding lines (416-39), which recapitulate and complete the general theme of the lyrics, namely, the mystery and wonder of the Advent. This final passage is based, in part at least, on the antiphon: 'O Wondrous intercourse: the Creator of the race of men has stooped to be born of a Virgin; assuming mortal flesh and appearing without seed as a man, He has bestowed His divinity upon us.' From this recapitulation the poet turns to his concluding exhortation: 'wherefore we should exalt Him by deed and word in full devotion' that every man may 'come to the joy of the land of the living where thenceforth we may dwell forever in bliss.'

Even a first acquaintance with the Advent hymns reveals their unusual quality. The poet's versatility in poetic elaboration is outstanding. His expansions of material vary throughout the series both in method and degree. In some instances, as in the 'O Jerusalem,' the expansion is simple in nature, consisting chiefly in the enlargement, by synonym and detail, of elements existent in the antiphon. But in other instances the method is far more complex. In the lyric based upon the 'O King of Peace,' certain phrases of the antiphon are elaborated into definitely doctrinal statement, and others are illustrated or symbolized by new and striking images not contained or implied in the original. Elsewhere, as in the Trinity lyric, the process rises from paraphrase and elaboration to creative improvisation in the spirit of the original, as when the 'Te jure laudant' phrase is developed into a hymn in praise of the Trinity sung by the Seraphim. Perhaps the most characteristic feature of this body of religious verse is its blending of the poet's lyric gift, sensitive and sustained, with the churchman's doctrinal concern in the central mysteries of the Advent season.

CHRIST III

The third part of the *Christ* (867-1664) is a superb descriptive unit reflecting a variety of sources. The organization of the poem is chiefly governed by an alphabetic Latin hymn on the Last Judgment quoted by Bede in his *De Arte Metrica*, chapter 2, the *Apparebit repentina dies magna Domini*.[9] Though the poet has omitted material contained in certain couplets (B, L, P, Y, Z), and has greatly amplified the brief suggestions of other portions of the hymn, the descriptive order of *Christ III* is the order of the hymn, and there are many verbal correspondences between the Latin and the Old English texts. In addition to this principal source, occasional sections of the poem quite clearly are in varying degree dependent on passages in the writings of Ephraem Syrus, Augustine, Caesarius of Arles, and Gregory. Even this list of sources, or analogues, does not account for all the material of the Old English poem; a considerable portion must be credited to the poet's own creative invention, or to an undiscovered source or sources.

The *Christ III* reveals descriptive power of a high order of excellence. As in *Genesis B*, there is unusually frequent occurrence of the long six-stress line, and the vocabulary employed seems here and there to suggest Old Saxon influence. These facts led Binz[10] to believe that the *Christ III*, like the *Genesis B*, is a translation of an Old Saxon original.

The Old English poem is an extraordinarily dramatic and emotional vision of the Last Judgment in which the cosmic fury of the fires of Doomsday and the hope and terror with which the souls of men are brought to Judgment are superbly set forth. Many of the descriptive details which give dramatic intensity to the scene

9. See Cook, 'Cynewulf's Principal Source for the Third Part of Christ,' *Modern Language Notes*, IV, 340–51; also Cook's edition of the *Christ*, pp. 171–7.

10. G. Binz, *Untersuchungen zum altenglischen sogennanten Christ*, Basel, 1907.

are found not merely in the text of the alphabetic hymn which underlies the poem, but in well-known passages of Scripture. Such features of Doomsday as the darkening of sun and moon,[11] the falling of the stars,[12] the earthquake[13] and fires of judgment,[14] the gathering of mankind from the four quarters of the world,[15] and the coming of the Son of man with power and great glory,[16] all have their familiar Scriptural analogues.

The poem from its opening lines has an intensity of mood and a dramatic vividness of detail which make it descriptive painting of unusual excellence. The great day of the Lord shall come suddenly, as a crafty thief steals upon sleeping men. With this keynote of suddenness and surprise the description of Doomsday is begun:

> Then from the four quarters   of this fair world,
> From the uttermost corners   of the kingdom of earth,
> In unison sounding   all-shining angels
> Shall blow their trumpets   in one great blast;
> Middle-earth shall tremble,   the ground under men.
> Loud shall resound   the strains of the trumpets
> Swelling clear   to the course of the stars.
> They shall peal and sing   from south and north,
> From east and west   over all creation.
> They shall waken from death   the sons of warriors,
> The race of men   from the ancient earth,
> In terror of Judgment.   They shall bid them stand,
> Starting up straightway   from their deep sleep.
> Then shall one behold   a sorrowing host,
> Sad in spirit and sore distressed,
> In woe lamenting   the deeds of life,
> Trembling in terror . . .
> Then sudden on Mount Sion   from the south and east
> Shall come from the Creator   a radiance of the sun

11. Isaiah xiii.10; Ezek. xxxii.7; Joel ii.10; iii.15; Mark xiii.24.
12. Mark xiii.25; Rev. vi.13.
13. Rev. vi.12.
14. Ps. l.3; xcvii.3; Hav. iii.5; 2 Thess. i.8.
15. Mark xiii.27.
16. Mark xiii.26.

Beaming more brightly   than men may imagine,
Shining in splendor,   when the Son of God
Through the arching heavens   appears to man.
Then cometh the wondrous   presence of Christ,
The glory of the Great King,   from the eastern skies,
Sweet of spirit   to His chosen people,
Stern to the sinful.[17]

At the appearance of the Great Judge there need be no fear for
Christ's beloved, who have pleased Him well in words and works.
They shall behold with great joy a gracious and gentle friend. But
to sinful men the sight shall be a terror. There follows a brief
homiletic passage in which the poet points out how great a blessing
for men of wisdom is this knowledge of Judgment to come. By
this warning they shall be so moved to virtue that in the Last Day
they shall have no need to fear when the Lord of all creation
appears in glory to judge the hosts of men.

There follows a vivid portrayal of the raging wind and fire of
Judgment, whose combined fury consumes the universe. Amid
the ravening flame and crashing of the storm ring out the strains
of the heavenly trumpets. The earth withers in the whirlwind;
the heavens crash; the stars fall from their stations:

There is din through the deep Creation.   Before the Lord
The greatest of raging fires   goes flaming over earth.
The hot blaze surges;   the heavens shall crash,
The steadfast light   of the stars shall fail.
The sun shall be darkened   to the hue of blood,
Which shone so brightly   for the sons of men
Over the ancient earth.   The moon herself
That by night illumined   mankind with her light
Shall sink from her station;   so also the stars,
Swept by the whirlwind   through the storm-beat air,
Shall vanish from the heavens . . .
Loud shall resound   over the spacious earth
The peal of heaven's trumpets;   on seven sides

17. *Christ*, 878–92; 899–908.

The winds shall rage,   raving in uproar.
They shall wake and wither   the world with their storm;
They shall fill with fear   all creatures of earth.
Then shall be heard   the heaviest of crashes,
Mighty and deafening,   a measureless blast,
The greatest of tumults,   terrible to men.[18]

For the most striking image of *Christ III* the Latin hymn offers no original. As the Old English poet paints the scene of Judgment, when the physical universe sinks in ruin and light dies out from sun, moon, and stars, the Cross shall shine resplendent over all creation in the place of the sun. As it towers in the heavens, drenched with the Savior's blood, its radiance illumines the universe. In its rays all shadows are dispelled. It is the shining symbol of the hope of the righteous and the terror of transgressors.

It is not possible to point with certainty to a specific source for this magnificent passage, though the image itself is contained in Matthew xxiv. 30. A respond from the liturgy of the Feasts of the Invention of the Cross, and Exaltation of the Cross, and certain passages from the writings of Ephraem Syrus could have furnished the poet with many of the details which he employs.[19] The respond reads: 'The sign of the Cross shall appear in the heavens when the Lord comes to Judgment; then shall be manifest all the secrets of the heart.' A passage from Ephraem Syrus furnishes an even closer analogue:[20] 'On the last day when the second coming of our Lord shall have dawned, the holy Rood in great glory, with a host of angel choirs, shall appear in the heavens, bringing terror to transgressors but joy and light to the faithful, announcing the coming of the great King.'[21]

18. *Christ III*, 930–40; 947–55.
19. See Cook, *The Christ of Cynewulf*, pp. 189–93.
20. *Opera*, v, 212.
21. Neither of these source passages, it will be noted, represents the Cross as still moist with the Savior's blood. It is interesting that this detail occurs not only in *Christ III* but also in the *Dream of the Rood*, where the poet has vision of the Cross alternately drenched with the sacred blood, and gleaming with jewels and gold.

Amid these scenes of tumult and terror all the race of men
shall rise to Judgment:

> Then straightway all   of Adam's kin
> Shall be clothed with flesh,   shall come to an end
> Of rest in earth;   and all mankind
> Shall rise to life,   put on body and limbs,
> Made young again   at the coming of Christ.
> Each shall have on him,   of evil or good,
> All his soul gathered   in the years gone-by,
> Shall have both together,   body and soul.
> Then the manner of his works,   and the memory of his words,
> The hidden musings   and thoughts of his heart,
> Shall come to light   before the heavenly King.[22]

In repentant terror mankind shall realize too late that it was the
Lord of all creation who suffered upon the Cross. Even the dumb
creation had wondrously recognized the divinity of Christ. But
sinful man had failed in perception. There follows a catalogue of
evidences of nature's sympathy with the Passion of our Lord. The
heavens had put forth a radiant herald of His Nativity. The sea
had rendered itself firm to His footing. At the Crucifixion the sun
darkened; the earth quaked and gave up her dead; trees ran with
bloody sap.

In these lines the poet may have been following portions of a
homily of Gregory.[23] There are many correspondences of detail
between the homily and the Old English text: the star of the
Nativity (1151), the earthquake (1143), the darkening of the sun
(1132), the splitting of walls and rocks (1141-2), the giving up of
the dead (1161). But there is also a marked difference in the two
accounts in the order in which these phenomena are set forth.
The *Christ III* passage, moreover, contains illustrations of nature's
sympathy which are not found in Gregory. If the homily of
Gregory is in fact the original of the Old English lines, the poet

22. *Christ III*, 1027-38.
23. *Hom. in Evang.*, 1, 10.

used his original quite freely, perhaps from memory, and added details from other sources, or of his own invention. One such detail, the bloody sap of trees, occurs in the Apocryphal 2 Esdras v 5: 'et de ligno sanguis stillabit.' There, however, the bloody sap is a detail of apocalyptic vision, whereas in *Christ III* it is referred to the Crucifixion.

One of the most dramatic sections of the Old English poem is a long indictment of man's ingratitude, spoken from the throne of Judgment and rehearsing man's creation, the blessings of paradise which he had lost through sin, God's pity shown in the Incarnation and Passion, and sinful man's rejection of divine mercy: 'Heavier for me the Cross of your sins whereon I am unwillingly hung, than that other Cross whereon I mounted up of Mine own free will ... Poor was I in the world that you might have wealth in heaven; wretched was I in your kingdom that you might have bliss in Mine. Yet for all this you knew no thanks in your heart to your Savior.' Analogues to this passage are to be found in the *De Judicio et Compunctione* of Ephraem Syrus,[24] and in a sermon of Caesarius of Arles.[25] Portions of the *Christ III* passage are almost literal translation from this latter work.

The final lines of the poem[26] are outstanding in felicity of imagery and rhythm. They are based on a portion of a commentary of Gregory,[27] and from this original take over both idea and phrasing. The passage is a conventional picture of the heavenly life set forth in transcendent fullness of light and love, peace and blessedness. Form and phrasing are governed by an extended antithesis, in which these heavenly joys are set in contrast to the inherent imperfections by which the ideal is inevitably conditioned in this earthly existence. In Gregory this antithesis is em-

24. *Opera*, v, 51.
25. *Sermo* 249, Migne, xxxix, 2207.
26. 1634–64.
27. *In Septem Psalm. Poenit. Expositio*, Migne, lxxix, 657–8.

bodied in a massed series of brief, parallel phrases, e.g. 'light without darkness, gladness without grief, health without blemish, life without death.' In the Old English elaboration of the material this continuous massing is broken, the antithetic phrases being distributed, and assigned in the Old English verse structure only to second half-lines. An extended use of balanced elements becomes a controlling feature of the poetic structure. The passage thus affords an excellent example of the shaping skill of the poet's technique in transformation of the Latin prose original into new rhetorical and rhythmic patterns. The recreated whole forms a fitting epilogue to a poem in which conventional conceptions of the Judgment scene are rendered with doctrinal sincerity and poetic vigor. In the body of Old English religious verse *Christ III* ranks high for the energy of imagination, felicity of diction, fluency of rhythm, and wealth of rhetorical adornment by which a borrowed and conventional subject matter is shaped into new patterns of dignity and grace:

> There is song of angels   and bliss of the saints,
> The Savior's dear presence   shining more bright
> On all His beloved   than light of the sun.
> There is love of dear ones;   life without death;
> A joyous company;   youth without age;
> A host of heaven's multitudes;   health without pain;
> For the souls of the righteous   rest without toil.
> There is splendor of the blessed;   day without darkness
> Shining and glorious;   bliss without sorrow;
> Peace among friends   forever without dissension
> For the happy in heaven;   love without envy
> In that holy throng.   No hunger there nor thirst,
> Nor sleep nor sickness,   nor burning sun,
> Nor cold nor care.   But the band of the blessed,
> Most shining of legions,   shall delight forever
> In the grace of the King,   and glory with God.[28]

28. *Christ III*, 1649-64.

GUTHLAC

Following *Christ III* in the Exeter Book[29] is a versified saint's legend. The subject matter is derived from a Latin chronicle of an English hermit-saint, Guthlac of the Fens, and is set forth in two sections, *Guthlac A* and *Guthlac B*. These two sections are in fact separate poems, apparently written at different dates, and perhaps by different poets. *Guthlac A*, or *Guthlac the Hermit*, runs to line 818;[30] *Guthlac B*, or *Guthlac's Death*, from 818 to the end. Both sections draw material from the Latin life of the saint written by a certain Felix of the Abbey of Croyland.[31]

Guthlac A is a narrative of the assaults and temptations brought against Guthlac by demons who haunted the countryside in which he had made his hermitage. Their attempts to shake the Christian faith of the saint are described in detail, and Guthlac's final triumph over the powers of evil is celebrated in spirited verse. *Guthlac B* contains a brief résumé of portions of this material, but is chiefly devoted to an account of the saint's last illness and death.

The problem of the relationship between the two poems brings up puzzling questions which cannot be dogmatically answered. But in some matters of importance we have reasonable certainty. It is clear that both poems are in some degree dependent on the Latin *Vita*; that *Guthlac A* was apparently of earlier date, and known to the poet of *Guthlac B*; and that *Guthlac B* has many characteristics of Cynewulfian mood and idiom. These close resemblances in style have led to the conjecture[32] that *Guthlac B*

29. Fols. 33b–52b.

30. Line numbering in this discussion of *Guthlac* is based on the text of Krapp and Dobbie, in their edition of the Exeter Book.

31. It has been generally admitted that *Guthlac B* depends upon the Latin *Vita*, (*Acta Sanctorum*, Vol. II, April, 37ff.) but there has been difference of opinion regarding *Guthlac A*. Gerould's detailed analysis, however (*Mod. Lang. Notes.* XXXII, 77–86), indicates clearly that material in *Guthlac A* also is drawn from the Latin of Felix.

32. Cf. Charitius, *Anglia*, II, 265–308.

may have been written by Cynewulf, and it has been suggested[33] that the missing ending of the poem may have included the characteristic runic signature.

GUTHLAC A

It is not quite clear at what point in the manuscript *Guthlac A* does in fact begin. A passage of 29 lines immediately following line 1664 of the *Christ* has been variously regarded as the ending of *Christ III*, as the beginning of *Guthlac A*, and as a fragment of an independent poem. The row of capitals with which the passage begins in the manuscript indicates the judgment of the scribe that a new poem is beginning. There is, moreover, no scribal indication of any break after line 29. The evidence of the manuscript, therefore, favors the opinion that these 29 lines are the opening lines of *Guthlac A*. The nature of the subject matter, on the other hand, has led many to regard the passage as an independent fragment.

The temptation of St. Guthlac took place, so the poet tells us, 'within the times of men who still remember and revere him.' But it would be a mistake to assume from this statement, or from others in the poem similar to it,[34] that *Guthlac A* is a rendering of material which came to the poet chiefly by oral tradition. Gerould has clearly shown that in not a few sections of *A* the author was working, more closely or less closely, with subject matter which he must have derived from the Latin text.[35]

But there are evidences in the poem that the poet's shaping of his material was affected in important ways by the influence of literary and ecclesiastical tradition. In the prologue[36] is a passage not found in Felix, which begins, 'Many are the orders in this world which ascend to be numbered among the saints.' Here the

33. Wülker, *Grundriss*, 183.
34. Cf. ll. 108–10; 401–2; 752–4.
35. *Mod. Lang. Notes*, xxxii, 77–86.
36. *Guthlac*, 30–62.

poet is clearly writing, as Gerould points out, in the tradition exemplified in the 'Multi variique sunt gradus per quos ad coelorum regna conscenditur,' of Gregory of Tours,[37] and in Lactantius' employment of the same figure in the *De ira dei*.[38]

There is a close literary relationship between a portion of *Guthlac A*[39] and the first 365 lines of *Christ and Satan*. Clubb in 1925 pointed out that in those lines of the poem which are devoted to the threats of the demons and Guthlac's replies, 'the phraseology throughout is strongly reminiscent of the "laments" in *Christ and Satan*, and in some lines necessitates the assumption either of direct borrowing of one poem from the other, or of indebtedness on the part of both to some common source.'[40] Clubb's tables of correspondence[41] show the frequency of these parallels. Since the phrases common to the two poems 'have much more point in their setting in *Christ and Satan* than in *Guthlac*,' Clubb concludes that either the poet of *Guthlac A* borrowed from *Christ and Satan*, or both poems were dependent on a common source as yet undiscovered.

The narrative material in *Guthlac A*, the strife of the saint with the demons, is derived from the *Vita* of Felix. Guthlac's youth had been wayward. In later years, an angel and a demon, after the fashion of later morality plays, did battle for his soul. In the end God decreed the defeat of the devil.

With a guardian angel in constant attendance, St. Guthlac established a hermitage in the wilds. A host of demons, who had formerly haunted the lonely borderlands where Guthlac settled, make repeated assaults upon the saint, filling the air with unhallowed tumult and threatening him with death by fire. But the evil shapes which gather against him so fiercely in the murky

37. Migne, *Pat. Lat.*, lxxi, 1055.
38. *De ira dei*, 2, Brandt, 1893, p. 69.
39. *Guthlac*, 530–684.
40. 'Christ and Satan,' *Yale Studies in English*, lxx, p. xxvii.
41. Op. cit. pp. xxviii–xxix.

night find the saint constant in piety and virtue. He defies the
fiends to do their worst against the body, rejoicing that they may
not lay hand upon the soul:

> Although fierce-hearted   you harry my flesh
> With surge of fire   and greedy flame,
> Yet shall you never   turn my resolve,
> While my wit holds out.   Though you punish the body,
> You may not with evil   pierce to the soul;
> You shall bring it to better things.   Therefore I bide
> What my Lord allots me,   dreading not death.
> Though my blood and bone   shall both together
> Be for earth's increase,   the spirit that lives
> Shall journey forth   unto fairer joys,
> And there delight   in a lovelier dwelling.[42]

From this point the trials of Guthlac are set forth in spiritual
rather than in physical terms. The cruder horrors of the earlier
scenes are replaced by temptations designed with subtler penetration to pierce to the soul. Secret evils in the life of the Church are
cited by the fiends as proof that the institution in which he puts
his trust is rotten and corrupt. A vision of the yawning fires of
Hell is revealed to him in prophecy of the doom that awaits
after death.

It is a matter of interest that the long passage dealing with the
corrupt monasteries[43] has no original in Felix. Unless it rests on
some text of the *Vita* unknown to us, it must be considered an
addition made by the Old English poet, and in some degree reflecting prevailing criticism of the monastic orders. That the conditions described had begun to manifest themselves in the English
Church we know definitely from letters of Alcuin and Bede.

It is always easy to overemphasize the defects of an age, or an
institution. The Church included within its fold both in parochial
office and in the monastic establishments many humble and sin-

42. *Guthlac*, 374-83.
43. *Guthlac*, 412-512.

cere men whose purity of character and earnestness of life left their stamp on all who came within their influence. With this in mind, St. Guthlac repudiates the slurring insinuations of his tempters, and asserts the homely truth that, as years bring wisdom, the follies of youth give place to the discipline and virtue of age:

> You reproach me with condoning the lax rules and un-bridled spirit of young men in God's temples; thus would you disparage the reputation of holy men. The weaker you sought out; the better you judged not according to their deeds. Yet they shall not remain unknown. I will speak the truth. God shaped youth and man's joy, and youth can not bring forth the after-harvest in the first blade. Young men have joy in the delights of the world, until the passing of years disciplines their youth so that the spirit loves the aspect and condition of that maturer mood, by which many throughout the world are governed in their way of life. When the spirit puts aside the follies of youth, then men show the world their wisdom. This you do not bring out; you rehearse the guilt of the sinful, but are unwilling to make known the spirit and conduct of the righteous.[44]

In these lines, if we are to regard the passage on the monasteries as an addition by the Old English poet, we seem to have his reason for the interpolation. What more telling blow could be struck against unjust slander of the monasteries than to introduce it as an element in the trial of St. Guthlac's faith, in order to show by his reply how inaccurate and incomplete an estimate it afforded both of individual and institution?

Silenced by the saint's eloquent defense of the monasteries, the demons subject his faith to a new test. They bear him captive to the doors of hell and there, in sight of all its horrors, prophesy that his soul is doomed to eternal punishment in torment of fire. But Guthlac recites his trust in the power of the Trinity whose

44. ll. 488-507.

decrees uphold earth and heaven, and proclaims the damnation of the fiends: 'It is for you that dark home is prepared. There you shall suffer an everlasting torment.'[45]

St. Bartholomew is sent to rescue Guthlac from his bondage. By his command the fiends are compelled to lift up the saint in their hands, and bear him unharmed back to his hermitage. The return of Guthlac is hailed by all his woodland neighbors of bird and beast in a passage that is unique in Old English poetry for delicacy of nature-painting, and sensitive suggestion of a living sympathy between the spirit of man and the forms of the natural world about him:

> In joy and triumph   the hermit returned
> To his hill-side home,   where many a creature
> Sang Guthlac's praises   in fervent strains.
> The birds of the woodland   made known by their notes
> The saint's home-coming.   He held them out food
> While they flew in hunger   about his hand
> In great desire,   in his succor rejoiced.
> So that kindly spirit,   from man's joys severed,
> Served the Lord   and, forsaking the world,
> Found joy in wild things   and beasts of the wood.
> Sweet were the meadows,   the season new;
> Winsome the bird-calls,   the blossoming earth;
> The cuckoos sang Spring.   Steadfast and blessed,
> Guthlac was gladdened   with joy of his home.
> In God's safe-keeping   the meadows lay green.
> A helper from heaven   had driven out the fiends.[46]

What joy, asks the poet, could be more fair than this victory of Guthlac over the powers of evil, which came to pass 'within the days of our own time'? The final lines of the poem rehearse briefly the latter years of the saint, and his steadfastness in a piety of life wherein he 'lessened little.' His death is mentioned, but is

45. ll. 673-9.
46. ll. 732-48.

not, as in *Guthlac B*, described at length. His soul is borne in the arms of angels before the face of the Eternal Judge. The record of his life is stressed by the poet as a pattern for pious men, who win eternal life in heaven by their words and works on earth.

GUTHLAC B

Guthlac B, or *Guthlac's Death*, begins with a prologue appropriately adapted to introduce the theme of death. The opening lines contain a compressed rehearsal of the Creation and the Fall of Man, by which death first came into the world. Never since that day has there lived a man 'so wise of heart, or eager in the will of God, that he could shun the bitter drink that Eve of old poured out for Adam.' Death, since that tragic Fall, has had inexorable power over men. Now it comes to Guthlac. So runs the sequence of the poet's thought.

This prologue is followed by a very brief résumé of Guthlac's life as a hermit, including a vivid duplicate of the *Guthlac A* description of the forest birds that fluttered about his hands in hunger as he dealt out their daily food. There is brief reference to the saint's ministrations to the sick and wretched, and to the trials which he had endured at the hands of the demons.

After fifteen years of hermit life Guthlac's last illness came upon him, his body burning with disease, his flesh wasted, his limbs heavy with pain. 'The drink was now at hand that Eve brewed for Adam in the beginning of the world.' This renewed allusion to the Fall forms the prelude to a brief inset on the inexorable and inevitable nature of death, which is poetically one of the 'show' passages of *Guthlac B*. The poet, in the course of 12 lines, personifies Death in three quite distinct images: Death, the cupbearer; Death, the keeper of the door which swings suddenly wide; and Death, the lone and relentless warrior who rushes on man with greedy grasp. Briefly as each image is sketched, the whole is superb in its fusion and sharpness of suggestion:

No man ever   of the sons of men,
No mortal on earth,   from the first beginning
Could shun the draught   of the bitter drink
In Death's deep cup.   When the dark hour comes,
Sudden the latch lifts,   and the entrance opens.
No mortal ever,   mantled in flesh,
Lofty or lowly,   has escaped with life,
But Death rushes on him   with greedy grasp.
So the Lone-Stalker   in the shadows of night,
Gauntest of warriors,   greedy for slaughter,
Drew nigh unto Guthlac.[47]

The disease from which the saint suffers runs its swift course. The season is Holy Week. Guthlac prophesies his death in seven days' time, and comforts the tears of his attendant with a description of the willing journey on which he is setting forth to a land where is neither sorrow nor pain, but blessedness and joy forever. When the morning of Easter dawns, Guthlac summons his ebbing strength to join in the services of that holy festival, proclaiming the gospel to his attendant with such wisdom of revelation that 'it seemed rather to be the words of an angel than the teaching of any mortal man.'

When six days have passed, about midday of the seventh, Guthlac's end is at hand. He sends a last greeting to his sister, with prophecy of their union hereafter 'before the face of the Eternal Judge.' Questioned by his attendant concerning an unknown voice which he has often heard in secret converse with Guthlac, the saint reveals that from the first beginning of his hermit-life a heavenly visitant had appeared to him night and morning, bringing spiritual guidance and strength. So pass the last hours of Guthlac's life.

The death-scene is perhaps the finest bit of sustained description in the poem. Form and mood furnish illustration, partly of the conventional imprint of the saint's legend itself, and partly of a

47. ll. 987–99.

vivid simplicity of description which is the poet's own. The mood
is the pervading spirit of religious piety, the flower and fulfilment
of the Christian faith. The passing of a saintly spirit is heralded by
heavenly anthems of triumph and joy as Guthlac's soul finds
everlasting peace:

As in summer season   the flowers are fragrant
Blooming in meadows,   blowing honey-sweet,
So all the long day   to the dropping of evening
The saint's breath rose.   The shining Sun
Sank to its setting,   dusking the northern sky,
Dark under cloud   draping the world in shadow,
Enfolding in darkness;   night fell on the treasures of earth.
Then came a great gleaming   holy from on high,
Shining in splendor   over the cities of men.
Stricken by death-darts   the blessed one bravely
Awaited his life's ending,   and all the night through
Brightly a glory   gleamed round the saint.
Shadows vanished   dissolving under the sky;
A radiance shone,   a heavenly candle,
Round the holy house,   from the evening gloaming
Till dawn from the east   rose over the sea,
The warm sun's gleam.   Then the heir of glory
In spirit courageous   spoke to his thane:
"'Tis time to betake you,   and hasten your errand,
Bearing to my dear one   the message I bade.
Now my soul severs   its ties to the body,
Eager for its journey   to the joys of God.'
Then humbly houseled   with heavenly food,
And lifting his eyes,   the head's holy gems,
His hands to heaven,   in joy of his reward
He sent forth his spirit   in grace of good works
To bliss everlasting   in the glory of God.
Then was Guthlac's soul   blessedly guided
On its upward way.   Angels bore it
To eternal bliss.   But the body lay cold,
Lifeless under heaven.   The beacon shone,
Brightest of beams.   The radiance lay

Round the holy house,   a heavenly splendor,
Filling the air   like a tower of flame
Brighter than sun   ever seen in the sky,
Or beauty of stars.   Then bands of angels
Sang songs of triumph;   the strains resounded
Wide under heaven,   the joy of the saints.
The heavenly bliss   filled the saint's abode
With winsome odors,   and wondrous sound
Of angel voices.   There it was sweeter
Than speech may tell   as the savor and song,
The heavenly harmony   and the holy hymns,
The glory of God,   filled all the firmament,
Strain upon strain.[48]

A reader is tempted to believe that the final lines of *Guthlac B* must have been penned by the Old English poet with the elegiac strains of the *Wanderer* in mind. The association would be in no way an unnatural one, since there are elements in the final scene of *Guthlac* which call to memory the grieving exile whose life has been so bitterly darkened by the death of his lord. The fate and mood of the Wanderer are in this sense similar to the fate and mood of Guthlac's faithful attendant, whose master also is now 'covered over with earth,' and who departs in sorrow to bear the saint's last greetings to his sister. The opening lines of his announcement of Guthlac's death seem to echo unmistakably in phrase and mood the *Wanderer's* stoic lament:

Courage is best   for the heart that must bear
Many bitter evils,   and darkly brood
On the loss of his lord,   when the dread hour nears,
Fixed by Fate's weaving.   That he knows well
Who with grieving heart wanders   knowing his gold-lord
Rests under earth.   Wretchedly he departs
With sorrowful spirit.   All joy is spent
For one who heavy-hearted   endures such hardships.[49]

48. ll. 1273–1325.
49. *Guthlac*, 1348–56.

Both the theme and phraseology of the passage are a compressed duplication of those poignant strains of the *Wanderer*[50] which deal with the tragic state of an exile uprooted and driven with the wind by the death of his lord, who ponders with sad heart the vanished joy of the past.

DREAM OF THE ROOD

In three Old English poems veneration of the Cross receives stressed and memorable expression: the *Elene*, *Christ III*, and *Dream of the Rood*. Of these, *Christ III* and the *Dream* have most in common both in spirit and detail. Cynewulf's *Elene*, as we have seen, is a narrative of the Invention of the Cross, which attains its greatest poetic distinction in two incidental passages, the descriptions of Constantine's battle against the Huns, and Elene's sea-journey. In the lines which deal with the Cross itself, the *Elene* makes little display of that lyric emotion which is so continuously characteristic of the *Dream of the Rood*, and which colors at least two passages in *Christ III*. Of the three poems, it is the *Dream of the Rood* which, among all Old English religious poems, has pre-eminent distinction as a superb lyric presentation of a religious adoration which finds its symbol in the Cross.

The veneration with which Old English poets glorify the Cross as the greatest of all symbols cannot be considered in itself a derivative, solely or even chiefly, of the poetic imagination. Whether or not they were professional churchmen, the religious poets were obviously well versed in doctrine and patristic learning, and reflected in their poems much that was conventional in professional exegesis, and in mystical interpretation of ecclesiastical detail. Cynewulf, in the epilogue to *Elene*, refers to the care with which he had gathered, weighed, and sifted details of the Cross legend, until greater knowledge had brought him deeper understanding. It seems unlikely that this statement refers merely to the

50. *Wanderer*, 15-29.

Crucifixion, or to the Invention of the Cross. His phrasing is suggestive, rather, of a pious concern with the corpus of mystical interpretations by which the medieval mind extended the symbolic significance of the Cross, linking its wood to the tree of life, and its shape to the shining sign of the Son of Man, which at the Judgment shall illumine and transcend the universe.

This adoration of the Cross is revealed both in patristic commentary, and in the hymnology of the medieval Church. It was illustrated in Alcuin's imitation of Fortunatus in the composition of cruciform acrostics and hymns to the Holy Cross. Even beyond the walls of the Church the cross became a frequently recurring symbol, and stone crosses, often skillfully adorned with carving and inscription, served not merely as mortuary monuments but as boundary marks, oratories, and places of public worship.

It is on one such cross, the Ruthwell Cross[51] near Dumfries on the Scottish border, that we find inscribed, as a part of the decoration, brief passages from the *Dream of the Rood*.[52] Through this inscription the *Dream of the Rood*, with little warrant, was for a time associated with the name of Cædmon.

The theory that Cædmon was author of the fragments of the *Dream* inscribed on the Ruthwell Cross rested on two postulates. Daniel Haigh[53] in 1856 dated the Cross as of the seventh century, and suggested that the runic lines on the Cross are fragments of a lost poem of Cædmon of which the *Dream of the Rood* is a later version. Ten years later Stephens[54] supported this theory of Cædmonian authorship by his assertion that an almost obliterated inscription on the upper runic panel included the words, 'Cædmon

51. For a detailed description of the Ruthwell Cross slightly condensed from Anderson, *Scotland in Early Times*, second series, pp. 232 ff., see Cook's edition of the *Dream of the Rood*, Introd. pp. ix–x; and Cook and Tinker, *Translations from Old English Poetry*, p. 100. For an engraving of the Cross see *Archaeologia Scotica*, vol. 4.

52. The inscriptions on the Ruthwell Cross correspond to portions of the following lines of the *Dream of the Rood*: 39–41; 44–5; 48–9; 56–9; 62–4.

53. *Archaeologia Aeliana*, Nov. 1856, p. 173.

54. *Old Northern Runic Monuments*, i, 419–20.

made me.' But repeated and careful examinations of the Cross have rendered these theories untenable. Critical studies of the beasts, flowers, and foliage in the ornamentation suggest a date definitely later than the seventh century, possibly as late as the year 1000.[55] The language of the inscription is regarded by Cook[56] as of equally late date. Victor, after thorough examination of the Cross, was unable in 1895 to find any convincing traces of the name of Cædmon.[57]

It was Dietrich[58] who first called attention to a number of reasons for attributing the poem to Cynewulf. He attempted to connect the *Dream of the Rood* with the *Elene*, since the theme of each was the Cross, and conjectured that the poet was inspired to write of the Invention of the Cross by the influence of the vision which he narrates in the *Dream*. He called attention to a similarity in tone between the personal passages of Cynewulf's signed poems and certain lines of a personal nature which end the *Dream of the Rood*, and found additional support for his theory in correspondence of diction between the *Dream* and the authentic Cynewulfian poems. He concluded that the *Dream* was written by Cynewulf toward the end of his life.[59]

The question of the authorship of the *Dream of the Rood* must be determined in the light of the following facts: that the diction of the *Dream* is, on the whole, Cynewulfian; that Cynewulf had written and signed another poem on the Cross in which he handled the vision of Constantine with evident appreciation of its beauty; and that a somewhat extended passage at the end of the *Dream* is remarkably similar in substance and tone to the personal passages which conclude the *Christ* and *Elene*. These facts, taken

55. Müller, *Dyreornamentiken i Norden*, p. 155, note.
56. *Academy* xxxvii, 153, and 'Notes on the Ruthwell Cross,' *PMLA*, xvii, 367–91.
57. *Die Nordhumbrischen Runensteine*, 1895.
58. *Disputatio de Cruce Ruthwellensi.*
59. Cf. the note of age in lines 122 ff. of the *Dream*.

in conjunction, tend to make probable the theory that Cynewulf wrote this lovely lyric of the Cross.

In its blending of lyric grace and religious adoration, the *Dream of the Rood* is one of the most beautiful of Old English poems. The poet employs the frame of the medieval dream-vision within which to set the glorious image which appeared to him in the midnight when mortal men lay wrapped in slumber. It seemed to him that he beheld the Cross upraised on high, enwreathed with light and adorned with gold and gems. Throughout Creation the angels of God beheld it; holy spirits gazed upon it, and men on earth. Stained as he was by sin, it was granted him to see the Tree shining in radiant splendor. In his dream the Cross flamed with changing color, now decked with gold and precious jewels, now wet with blood:

> Lo! I will tell   the dearest of dreams
> That I dreamed in the midnight   when mortal men
> Were sunk in slumber.   Meseemed that I saw
> A wondrous Tree   towering in air,
> Most shining of crosses   encompassed with light.
> Brightly that beacon   was gilded with gold;
> Jewels adorned it,   fair at the foot,
> Five on the shoulder-beam,   blazing in splendor.
> Through all creation   the angels of God
> Beheld it shining   —   no cross of shame! —
> But holy spirits   gazed on its gleaming,
> Men upon earth,   and all this great creation.
> Wondrous the Tree,   that token of triumph,
> And I a transgressor,   stained with my sins!
> I gazed on the Rood   arrayed in glory,
> Fairly shining   and graced with gold,
> The Cross of the Savior   beset with gems;
> But through the gold-work   outgleamed a token
> Of the ancient evil   of wretched souls,
> Where the Cross on its right side   once sweat blood.
> Saddened and rueful   and smitten with terror

At the wondrous Vision,   I saw the Rood
Swift to vary   in vesture and hue,
Now wet and stained   with the Blood outwelling,
Now fairly gilded   and graced with gold.[60]

The convention of the dream-vision provides the poet with a
device whereby he is able to shape his material to superb advantage. It is characteristic of the convention that his vision should
come vividly to life with endowment of human thought and
feeling, and human speech. The Cross becomes the narrator of
the Crucifixion and Passion of Christ, and the tragic description
by this device takes on elements of dramatic emotion which could
come in no other way. As the poet in dream gazes with rueful
heart upon the Rood, it begins to speak, recalling its tragic history.
Once, long years before, it grew as a forest tree on the edge of a
wood. But impious hands hewed it from its stock and shaped it
into an instrument for the punishment of malefactors. As it stood
on a hilltop outlined against the sky, it became a spectacular
symbol of the world's evil. Then fear and horror fell upon it. For
it beheld the Lord of all the world hasting in heroic mood to
ascend upon it for the redemption of Man. The terror of the
Cross, as it foresaw its destiny to serve as the instrument of the
Passion of Christ, is a superbly imaginative touch rendered in the
simplest terms. Though struck with horror it could not in disobedience reject the fate appointed. When Almighty God clasped
it with willing arms it trembled with terror, yet dared not bend
or break. It must needs stand fast holding the Lord of all creation,
and wet with His blood. A stark vigor of imagination fuses with
lyric emotion to make the description notable:

Natheless, as I lay there   long time I gazed
In rue and sadness   on my Savior's Tree,
Till I heard in dream   how the Cross addressed me,
Of all woods the worthiest,   speaking these words:

60. *Dream of the Rood*, 1–23.

'Long years ago — well yet I remember —
They hewed me down   on the edge of the holt,
Severed my trunk;   strong foemen took me,
To a spectacle shaped me — a felon's cross!
High on their shoulders   they bore me to hilltop,
Fastened me firmly,   foes enough, forsooth.
Then I saw the Ruler   of all mankind
In brave mood hasting   to mount upon me.
Refuse I dared not,   nor bow nor break,
Though I saw earth's confines   shudder in fear;
All foes I might fell,   yet still I stood fast.
Then the Hero young — it was God Almighty —
Put off His raiment,   steadfast and strong;
With lordly mood   in the sight of many
He mounted the Cross   to redeem mankind.
When the Hero clasped me   I trembled in terror,
But I dared not bow me   nor bend to earth;
I must needs stand fast.   Upraised as the Rood
I held the High King,   the Lord of heaven.
I dared not bow!   With black nails driven
Those sinners pierced me;   the prints are clear,
The open wounds.   I dared injure none.
They mocked us both.   I was wet with blood
From the Hero's side   when He sent forth His spirit.
Many a bale   I bore on that hill-side,
Seeing the Lord   in agony outstretched.
Black darkness covered   with clouds God's body,
That radiant splendor;   shadow went forth
Wan under heaven;   then wept all creation,
Bewailing the King's death;   Christ was on the Cross.'[61]

The last few lines of this passage furnish superb illustration of the imaginative realism which underlies the simplicity of the poet's phrasing. The darkness which falls upon the earth at the consummation of the Passion he inherits from Biblical source. But he puts it to striking and reverent use in a contrast between the darkness of obscuring cloud and the radiant splendor of the body of Christ

61. ll. 24-56.

hanging on the Cross. The weeping of all Creation at the Savior's death may well have come into the poet's mind from Gregorian homily, or from memories of the Balder legend and its reference to the mourning of all nature at Balder's death. But the stroke which completes the passage is his own, a brief half-line of pregnant compression in which all the drama and destiny of mankind are gathered up in the symbol of eternal love transcendent over evil: 'Christ was on the Cross.'

There follows, in the speech of the Rood, a description of the Deposition and Burial. The Cross stained with Christ's blood, and wounded with the arrows of the war-wolves who had slain Him, was hewed down and covered over in a deep trench—'a fearful fate.' But later friends and thanes of God recovered it and decked it with silver and gold. The Rood which was once the bitterest of tortures was honored by the Prince of glory above all forest trees, even as He had honored His mother, Mary, over all the race of women. The dreamer is then commanded to reveal his vision to men. The speech of the Cross ends with rehearsal of the Ascension, and prophecy of the Day of Judgment to come.

This vision of the Cross and its narrative of the Crucifixion find closest parallel in mood and detail in *Christ III*, where the more extended description of the Crucifixion and the shining image of the Cross transcendent in the Day of Judgment produce a unique fusion of realism and symbolism. Wherein, then, lies the unique emotional appeal of the *Dream of the Rood*? It springs, in considerable degree, from the inherent value of the poetic device which the poet has adopted, the dream-vision, within the conventions of which the Crucifixion, as told by the Cross, receives uniquely personalized rehearsal. The resultant note of emotional fervor, in which the triumphant and the tragic are so closely blended, is a superlative derivative of the spirit of religious devotion effectively supplemented by elements of literary form.

The lines which follow, and which conclude the poem, unite

highly personal reflection with a prophetic delineation of the joys of the blessed in the life to come. In mood and diction these lines are so suggestive of the personal passages of Cynewulf's signed poems that, even though the runes are lacking, we are tempted to regard the poem as his. If the *Dream of the Rood* is not Cynewulf's, it is the work of a poet who has imitated with singular faithfulness all the characteristics of the personal mood invariably associated with the Cynewulfian signature. Even in *Elene* and *Christ II* there is no more exquisitely sensitive and personalized revelation of religious faith and hope than that which graces the ending of the *Dream*:

> Then in solitude I prayed to the Rood fervently and with joyful heart. My soul was eager to be gone; I had lived through many an hour of longing.   Now have I hope of life, that I may turn to the triumphant Cross, I above all men, and revere it well. Thereto I have great desire, and my hope of succor is set upon the Cross. I have not now in this world many powerful friends. They have departed hence out of the pleasures of this earthly life, and sought the King of glory; they dwell now with the High Father in heaven, and abide in glory. And every day I look forward to the hour when the Cross of my Lord, of which I had vision here on earth, may fetch me out of this fleeting life and bring me where is great joy and rapture in heaven, where God's people are established forever in eternal bliss; and set me where I may hereafter dwell in glory, and with the Saints have joy of joys. May the Lord befriend me, He who on earth once suffered on the Cross for the sins of men.[62]

Whether written by Cynewulf himself, or by some singularly faithful imitator, the intimate biographic appeal of such a passage brings conviction to ear and mind that here is an authentic and extended parallel to the signed revelations of the Cynewulfian poems.

62. ll. 122–46.

IX. THE RELIGIOUS HEROIC TALE

Andreas; Judith

TWO other religious poems deserve separate consideration as illustrations of a special type and method in the handling of religious themes. These are the *Andreas* and *Judith*. Their special poetic quality lies in the attempt of the authors to set forth a religious narrative in the spirit and form of the heroic tale. We see in these poems, as we have also seen in Cynewulf's *Elene*, the familiar epic devices for emphasizing the heroic mood: the stress on courage and endurance, the dramatic dialogue, the martial imagery, the reflections of the *comitatus* bond, the inset passages dealing with landscape, sea, and weather, and the swift-moving action leading to heroic triumph and glory.

ANDREAS

In the *Andreas*, so far as the religious theme permits, the narrative style imitates the structure and heroic mood of the *Beowulf*. Many passages suggest that the poet must have known the *Beowulf* well, and must have intentionally adopted its form and spirit to govern his own narrative of the heroic deeds of St. Andrew. Even a brief comparision of the *Andreas* with other more typical saints' legends, such as *Guthlac* and *Juliana*, will make clear the poet's effort to shape an epic tale out of the materials of saints' legend.

The 1722 lines of the *Andreas* are found in the Vercelli MS.,[1] in conjunction with the immediately following text of the *Fates of the Apostles*. It has been suggested that the *Fates* should be read as an intended epilogue to the *Andreas*, and Cynewulf's runic signature in the *Fates* applied, therefore, to the *Andreas* as well.

1. Fol. 29^b –52^b.

In a previous discussion we have seen that there is little convincing evidence to support this hypothesis.[2] Indeed, the evidence derived from the text of *Andreas* itself as to vocabulary, idiom, and narrative style, runs counter to such a theory.

There are two Old English versions of the legend of St. Andrew, a prose version and the poetic version of the *Andreas*. The ultimate source of the legend seems to have been a Greek text of the *Acts of St. Andrew and St. Matthew*.[3] No existing tradition of the Greek *Acts*, however, can be regarded as the direct source of the *Andreas*. The poet must have worked from some intervening text, in all probability a Latin translation, as is shown by the detailed studies of Bourauel[4] and Krapp.[5] Although no complete Latin text has been discovered, fragments have survived, a study of which led Krapp to consider it 'an extremely probable inference that there once existed a complete Latin translation of the Greek' from which all the Western versions of the legend were derived.

The shaping of the *Andreas* is particularly interesting in certain broad parallels of structure which suggest the *Beowulf*. The poem begins with the characteristic epic formula of appeal to tradition:

> Lo! we have heard   of twelve mighty heroes
> Honored under heaven   in days of old,
> Thanes of God.   Their glory failed not
> In shock of battle   when banners clashed;
> After their parting   each went his way
> As his lot was cast   by the King of heaven.
> Famous those heroes,   foremost on earth,
> Brave-hearted leaders   and bold in strife,
> When hand and buckler   defended the helm
> On the plain of war,   on the field of fate.[6]

2. See pages 232-4.

3. Tischendorf, *Acta Apostolorum Apocrypha*, 132–66.

4. *Bonner Beiträge*, xi, 65ff. Bourauel believes that the poet may have used both Latin and Greek texts.

5. Krapp, *Andreas*, Introd., pp. xxi–xxix.

6. *Andreas*, 1–11.

As the poem progresses, familiar patterns and reminders of *Beowulf* disclose themselves. In each poem the action begins with the description of a wrong to be righted, an evil to be wiped out. In each poem, after this initial material, the poet takes his reader to another land from which rescue is to come, notes the hero's dedication to his task, his preparations for travel, and in vivid detail his sea-journey to the land of distress. In each poem, with divine intervention and aid at critical points, the hero succeeds in his undertaking and overcomes the evil against which he strives. In each poem, when the triumph is won, the story is rounded out by the hero's preparation for departure, the general grief at his going, and the return voyage by which he sails back to the land from which he came. In each poem, the final scenes are laid upon a sea-headland looking out over the ocean.

The shaping of the story of St. Andrew has produced a lively narrative made up of a succession of carefully elaborated episodes memorable for their descriptive, dramatic, or lyric quality. The poem, throughout, gives evidence of a sustained striving for literary effect.

Opening with a reference to the heroic fame of the twelve Apostles, the poem passes quickly to a description of the fate which has befallen St. Matthew, a captive in the country of the Mermedonians. In that land, writes the poet, there is neither food nor water for refreshment, but the inhabitants drink blood and eat human flesh. Any traveler from a foreign country becomes their prey. They blind the eyes of their wretched victims, and brew for them a magic drink which transforms them so that they cease to yearn for human joy, but eat grass and hay like cattle.

On his arrival among that people, St. Matthew had been bound and cast into prison. In his wretchedness he prayed to God for deliverance, and there shone into the prison a glory as of the shining sun. The voice of the Lord spoke from heaven promising in seven and twenty days to send St. Andrew to set him free.

Each dawn the Mermedonians gathered about the prison, eager for the flesh of an appointed victim. 'For they skillfully computed, and set down in runic writing, the end of every man's life, and the hour when they might take him for food.' Thirty days was the span of time allotted to each.

When only three days remained, the scene, as in *Beowulf*, shifts to the land from which deliverance is to come. The Lord appeared to St. Andrew in Achaia, bidding him set sail for Mermedonia to deliver Matthew from bondage. The immediate response of the saint is to question how he can make so extensive a voyage over uncharted seas, or act for Matthew's deliverance in a strange land whose men and their ways are unknown to him.

God rebukes the saint for his hesitation: 'Alas! Andrew, that ever you should be slow to this mission!' If God wished, so runs the speech, He could by His word alone transfer the city of Mermedonia to Achaia where Andrew stood. But let Andrew keep the faith. At daybreak he will find a ship moored at the shore wherein he may set sail for this land of savage men where hardship and danger await.

Strengthened in resolve, St. Andrew accepts the charge laid upon him, and in the morning with his companions betakes himself to the shore:

> Then in the dawn,   at the break of day,
> Over the sand dunes   he tramped to the shore,
> Keen of courage,   his comrades about him
> Treading the shingle.   The ocean roared,
> The combers crashed.   The hero exulted
> When he saw on the sand   a broad-beamed ship.
> Morning sun came,   the brightest of beacons,
> Heaven's candle flaming   over the floods,
> Holy light dawning   out of the dark.[7]

Sitting in the ship are three sailors who have the appearance of experienced ocean-voyagers. Though St. Andrew fails to recog-

7. ll. 235-44.

nize them in their mariner's garb, two of the figures are heavenly angels; the third is God himself. Learning that they are from Mermedonia, Andrew requests passage thither, though he has neither food nor money, land or linked rings, jewels or plated gold, by which to make payment. The Prince of men, 'seated upon the gangplank,' asks how it has come about that the saint is undertaking so extended a voyage without store of provision.

St. Andrew's reply is somewhat loosely based upon the substance of Matthew x. 5-15. Christ's commandment, in sending forth His disciples upon their mission, that they forego all provision of material things, taking 'neither gold nor silver nor brass in your purses, nor scrip for your journey, neither two coats, neither shoes, nor yet staves,' is the original out of which the saint's answer is elaborated. Pleased with words and spirit, the Shipman accepts Andrew and his companions into the ship, bringing forth food to strengthen them against the sea-journey.

The voyage is hardly begun when the seafarers encounter a heavy storm, and the description of it is one of the most spirited bits of sea-verse in Old English poetry:

> The depths were troubled.   The horn-fish darted,
> Gliding through ocean;   the gray gulls wheeled,
> Searching for carrion.   The sun grew dark;
> A gale arose,   and great waves broke;
> The sea was stirred.   Halyards were humming,
> Sails were drenched.   Sea-terror grew
> In the welter of waves.   The thanes were adread,
> Who sailed with Andrew   on the ocean-stream,
> Nor hoped with life   ever to come to land.
> Not yet was it known   Who guided their bark
> Through the breaking seas.[8]

This fine sea-passage is an unmistakable evidence of the poet's creative shaping of his material. There is no description of a storm

8. ll. 369-81.

in the Greek original. We have here to do with an insertion by the Old English poet of an element contributing to the general design and the shaping of structure. The passage is so vivid in its realism that one is tempted to read into the description the authenticity of personal experience. Certainly, the references to the sound of the wind in the rigging, and to the sails drenched by breaking seas, are details which suggest first-hand description rather than the conventional elements of 'literary' borrowing.

So terrified by the storm are Andrew's thanes that the Shipman suggests making for land, and there leaving them to await on shore the saint's return from Mermedonia. In the speech in which this proposal is rejected, the poet seizes the opportunity to color the material of his original with the conventional poetic stress on *comitatus* loyalty. The passage, though briefer, is as dramatically authentic as is Wiglaf's speech in *Beowulf*, or Byrhtwold's in *Maldon*:

> If we desert you, where shall we turn without a lord, sorrowing, and sinful, and empty of good? We shall be loathed in all lands, and despised of all peoples, wherever valiant men debate which of them has best supported his lord in battle, when hand and shield on the field of war, hacked with swords, were hard pressed in the fight.[9]

As the storm continues, Andrew heartens his thanes by telling how he had once sailed with Christ through just such a gale.[10] On that occasion, when the storm broke over them, the disciples were overcome with terror, crying out in their fear. But the Prince of angels rebuked the winds and stilled the waves, so that the stretches of ocean-stream grew calm again. 'Therefore,' comments the saint, 'I tell you for a truth that the Living God will never forsake a man on earth, if his courage holds out'—words which represent a Christianizing of the conventional heroic phras-

9. ll. 405-14.
10. Cf. Mark iv. 35-41.

ing illustrated in *Beowulf* 572-3, and in other passages in the heroic
verse. Thus Andrew strengthens the hearts of his companions
until with the passing of the storm the seas subside, and the weary
men fall asleep beside the mast.

In an ensuing conversation between Andrew and the Shipman
the saint praises the seamanship which has brought them safely
through the storm, and begs for instruction in the skill which has
preserved them:

> Sixteen voyages[11]   early and late
> It has been my lot   to sail in my sea-boat,
> With freezing hands   as I smote the sea,
> The ocean-streams.   Now this is another.
> Never have I known   one like to thee,
> Of the sons of men,   steering over stem.
> The roaring billows   beat on the strand;
> Full swift this bark   and most like a bird
> Foamy-necked faring   over the waves.
> Well I know   that I never have seen
> In any sailor   more wondrous sea-craft.
> Most like it is   as if on land
> The boat stood still,   where wind and storm
> Could stir it not,   nor breaking billows
> Shatter the high prow;   yet it speeds over ocean
> Swift under sail.[12]

To Andrew's request the Shipman responds that all who sail
the seas are in the hands of God. It is clear that Andrew enjoys His
favor and protection, for even the winds and waves have recognized it, and subsided.

The Shipman then turns to other matters, inquiring of the
saint why the Jewish race had failed to believe in the Son of God
though He performed so many miracles openly. The answer of the

11. Brooke and others have interpreted the foregoing reference to sixteen voyages
as a realistic detail reflecting the past experience of the poet himself. However, a
similar mention of sixteen voyages occurs in the Greek.

12. *Andreas*, 489-505.

saint does not meet the question directly, but rehearses a series of miracles including the healing of lepers and cripples, the gift of sight to the blind, hearing to the deaf, and speech to the dumb, the raising of many from the dead, the turning of water to wine, and the multiplication of five loaves and two fishes into food for five thousand.

'So you can see, most dearest youth,' ended the saint, 'what wonders He wrought by His word, though faithless men believed Him not. Many glorious tales I still could tell, but you could not endure or understand them, wise as you are.' Thus Andrew all day long glorified the teachings of the Savior until suddenly on the whale-path sleep came upon him, as he sat there close by the Heavenly King.

St. Andrew is borne in the arms of angels to the outskirts of Mermedonia, and there left sleeping at the roadside. Awaking at dawn he saw before him the tiled roofs and towers of Mermedonia, and round him his companions still deep in slumber. Rousing them he proclaims that now he recognizes it was God himself who ferried them safely over the ocean-stream. Once more the Lord appears to them, this time clearly revealed, bidding St. Andrew go into the city and deliver St. Matthew. There he will suffer bondage and torture but not death, and in the end by his heroic endurance many in Mermedonia will be converted.

St. Andrew enters the city. As he approaches the prison in which St. Matthew is confined the seven prison-wardens are suddenly struck down in death, and 'by a hand-touch of the Holy Spirit' the prison doors are thrown open. From the prison St. Andrew leads out Matthew and a great host of men and women praising and glorifying God.

St. Andrew makes his way to a brazen column in the midst of the city, and there sits awaiting his fate. The Mermedonians, gathering to select a victim from among their prisoners, find the prison-gates open, the wardens dead, and the prison empty. 'Sad of heart with dread of hunger, that pale table-guest,' they cast lots among themselves to determine 'which shall serve the rest as food.' The lot falls upon an aged warrior who buys his own safety by promising the life of his stripling son. As the multitude rush to seize the lad, St. Andrew intervenes. By God's grace the weapons of the Mermedonians 'melt like wax,' and the youth escapes.

'Then,' writes the poet, 'was a wailing lifted up in the cities of men, and a great lamentation. Heralds cried aloud; weary and oppressed by hunger they bewailed the lack of food.' The Devil appears to the multitude, denounces St. Andrew as the cause of their evil plight, and incites the Mermedonians to violence against him. Overcome and made captive, Andrew is roughly dragged through the land until his body is broken and drenched with blood. All day long he endures pain and torture, and with the coming of evening is cast into prison.

There follows in the *Andreas* a description of the bitter cold endured by the saint during this night of imprisonment. The passage consists mainly of material introduced into the narrative by the Old English poet as an expansion and embellishment of the theme of St. Andrew's captivity. In this poetic description of wintry cold we have the same conscious endeavor to adorn the tale with conventional elements of literary tradition which we noted in the earlier description of the storm at sea. In this instance, however, the traditional material is less naturally introduced, since the setting gives little appropriateness to what is actually a typical and extremely vivid depiction of the cold of a Northumbrian winter, weather 'as wild and hard,' writes Brooke, 'as that of which we hear in *Beowulf,* and are told in the *Seafarer.*' The passage is obviously a 'set-piece' of spirited description, arbitrarily inserted into the narrative for the creation of atmosphere:

> Then was the saint   in the shades of darkness,
> The noble hero   through the livelong night,

Bitterly beset.   Snow bound the earth
With winter storms;   the winds grew cold
With fierce hail-showers.   Frost and rime,
Those gray old warriors,   locked the land,
The homes of men.   The earth was hung
With wintry icicles;   water's might
Shrank in the sea-streams.   Ice made a bridge
Over the black ocean.   Blithe-hearted bode
That virtuous man,   of valor mindful,
Bold and enduring   in his bitter need
Through the winter-cold night.[13]

A second day, and a third, St. Andrew is led out to renewed torture, and at nightfall taken back to prison. Each day his wounds are multiplied and his blood flows afresh. Throughout the second night he is engaged in prolonged struggle with the Devil, who appears to him in his prison cell, taunting him with his helplessness, and tempting him to despair.

When for the fourth time he is led back to prison, God appears to Andrew, heals his wounds, and announces the end of his trials. 'Then the man of might, unharmed by the affliction of his grievous tortures, rose up and thanked God; nor was his appearance marred, nor the hem of his garment loosed, nor a hair from his head, nor bone broken, nor body bloodstained by the wounding blows.'

At this point (line 1477) there occurs a brief pause in the narrative. 'For some time,' writes the poet, 'I have been rehearsing in song the story of the saint, a tale famous and beyond my power. There is much still to tell, but it will take a wiser man than I count myself to know the complete record of the trials which the saint endured. Nevertheless, I will continue, and recount brief portions of the story.' This passage has been sometimes interpreted as indicating a break in the poem, or even a possibility that from this point the narrative was continued by another poet. There is no

13. ll. 1253-65.

warrant for these assumptions. By a reasonable reading of the
lines, the author is saying that a poem dealing with all the events
of St. Andrew's life and mission is beyond his power and intent,
but that he will continue his poem with a brief treatment of
selected material. Indeed, this interposed comment of the poet
stresses his already obvious intention to fashion St. Andrew's ex-
periences in Mermedonia into a heroic tale. His purpose is not to
write a complete poetic life of the saint.

As the poem continues, the narrative refers to two stone pillars
which stand in the Mermedonian prison. The lines seem to reflect
a reminiscence of two passages of *Beowulf*, in which the columns
which uphold the dragon's barrow are described.[14]

At the bidding of the saint, there bursts forth from the base of
one of these stone shafts a rushing deluge, which quickly over-
flows the land and sweeps away many of the Mermedonians.
With a characteristically grim touch of Old English irony, the
poet compares the flood to a drinking carnival: 'That was a bitter
beer-drinking! The cupbearers and serving-thanes were not slow;
there was drink enough for every man from the dawn of day!'

Many sought to escape to the safety of mountain-caves. But
an angel of the Lord prevented them, overspreading the city with
fire and flame.

> Then waves waxed great;   the sea resounded;
> Fire-sparks flew;   the flood flowed forth.[15]

The waters rose above the breasts and shoulders of men. Waves of
fire engulfed the city walls. The hearts of the Mermedonians were
terrified, and they turned to St. Andrew for help. Then the saint
bade the streams subside and the floods abate. Miraculously, a
great mountain was cleft asunder, and the yawning gulf sucked
in the flood and with it the most evil of the Mermedonians. With

14. *Beowulf*, 2542–6; 2715–19.
15. *Andreas*, 1545–6.

one accord the multitude began to call upon the Lord, proclaiming the mighty power of the true God who had sent St. Andrew as a help to that people. The saint prayed for those who had perished, and speedily many rose from death, their souls and bodies once more united. A church was built and consecrated on the spot where the deluge burst forth, and a certain Platan was ordained bishop. By the ministry of St. Andrew many of the Mermedonian people were converted and baptized, and their idols destroyed. 'Sore was that for Satan to endure,' writes the poet, 'a great sorrow of spirit, when he beheld the multitude by Andrew's kindly teaching turn away from idol-worship to that fairer joy where no fiend, or hostile spirit, ever has entrance.'

At last the days of St. Andrew's mission in Mermedonia were fulfilled. A vessel was made ready for his return to Achaia. The Mermedonians accompanied their beloved teacher to the sea-headland, and there brought him to the prow of the waiting ship. As he set sail they stood weeping upon the shore as long as their eyes could follow the noble prince over the seal-path. And even in their grief at his departure they glorified God, saying, 'There is one eternal God of all creation. His power and might are revered on earth, and His glory shines in heaven forever, with angels and saints. He is a noble King.'

The *Andreas* has been called the 'Christian *Beowulf.*' The phrase can hardly be considered a happy one. It is doubly unfortunate in blurring analysis of both poems. It seems to suggest that the *Beowulf* is a pagan poem, a suggestion far from precise, for we have seen that the ancient epic tale, though fashioned of varied and pagan material, is consistently Christian in spirit. Again, the phrase seems to suggest that the poet of *Andreas* has succeeded in moulding his religious material into heroic form somewhat comparable in epic structure and dignity to the *Beowulf.* Once more the implication strikes wide of the mark. The *Andreas* is not a *Beowulf*, pagan or Christian. What may be truly said of it is that the *Andreas* poet has consciously and earnestly, perhaps too earnestly, endeavored to set forth the material of saint's legend shaped into epic design, and embellished with the stylistic devices of the heroic mood. In this endeavor he has frequently given evidence of knowledge, and here and there of conscious imitation, of the *Beowulf.*

It must be remembered that the *Andreas* poet followed his source faithfully. Careful study of the poem and its antecedents shows that, so far as action is concerned, there is no incident in *Andreas* that was not suggested by its original.[16] If, therefore, the reader has perception of broad parallelisms of structure and style which link the *Andreas* to the *Beowulf,* these parallelisms are the product not of imitatively invented action, but of a creative re-working of source material by selection and elaboration, subordination or stress, until there emerges from the unshaped substance of saint's legend a unified religious poem, spirited in action and dialogue, and moulded in the conventions of the heroic tale.

The method of the *Andreas* poet can be clearly discerned in three passages already noted which represent extension of source material, or elaboration and embellishment of it. These are: the spirited description of the storm at sea (369-80), the refusal of St. Andrew's companions to leave him (405-14), and the depiction of the nocturnal cold of the saint's prison cell (1253-65). The conscious art of the poet is nowhere more clearly indicated than in these passages. The storm at sea, as we have seen, is obviously Old English in feeling. The passage grew from a suggestion, in the original, of a dread of the sea felt by the saint's followers, but the description, in form, is a conventional 'set-piece' woven by the poet into the Old English narrative for its decorative value. It gives specific and vivid embodiment to what in the original is general and brief, and has literary value as a natural poetic elaboration of source material.

16. Krapp, *Andreas,* Introd., p. li.

The introduction of the *comitatus* stress into a depiction of the loyalty of St. Andrew's comrades is a not unnatural poetic extension. But in this instance also the theme is developed in accord with stereotyped literary convention and, by his borrowing of the stereotype, the poet colors the final lines of the passage with a specific battle imagery that has little appropriateness in its setting.

Finally, in the winter scene we have a poetic addition for which there is no immediate suggestion in the original. It is difficult to accept the dictum that in these lines 'the allusion to the night passes over into a description of the winter, the primitive mythic matter of night and winter being thus fused into one theme.'[17] For it is precisely the lack of any such fusion with which one has here to deal. The passage lends itself much more convincingly to interpretation as an arbitrary borrowing of conventional poetic material, which introduces into the poem elements inadequately fused with the context in which they are set.

Other evidences of this same straining for literary effect are found in passages in which martial imagery is employed in situations where it goes somewhat beyond the bounds of realism. When the Mermedonians capture and imprison St. Andrew, the description is of a weaponed host in armor marching to war:

> Then up rose the valiant;   with din of an army,
> Bold under banners,   the warriors thronged
> To the gates in the wall;   in a war-host mighty
> To strife advancing   with buckler and spear.[18]

Obviously, such a passage is an illustration of an arbitrary employment of heroic mood and martial image where they are not realistically appropriate in a description of the capture and imprisonment of an unarmed man by a hostile crowd.

We shall be doing the poet of *Andreas* less than justice, however, if we overlook the fact that there are passages not a few in which

17. Krapp, *Andreas*, Introd., p. liv.
18. *Andreas*, 1202-5.

he displays an amazingly firm and imaginative control of imagery, and a skill in personification which has left us striking and memorable phrasing. Hatred (768-70) is compared to the 'baleful venom' of dragon or serpent. Hunger (1088) is a 'pale table-companion.' Frost and rime (1258) are 'hoary warriors striding forth to battle' and locking the homeland of heroes in wintry bonds. The flood that overwhelmed the Mermedonians is a 'bitter beer-drinking.'

The outstanding quality of *Andreas* among Old English religious poems, and the element which is chiefly responsible for its characteristic flavor, is its continuous evidence of the poet's effort to shape selected source material, by adopted conventions, to a finished work of art. In no other religious poem, not even the *Elene* or the *Judith*, can we so readily discern a continuous process of moulding and fashioning in obedience to the persistent influence of an adopted model. Something like this process went on in the composition of *Exodus*, where the author struggles valiantly to weld into a perfected unity various symbolic elements from the Church liturgy for Holy Saturday. But the poet of *Exodus* was not, like the poet of *Andreas*, working from a model, and his problem was less a problem of selecting and shaping than of integrating into a poetic whole the concepts of an associated group of religious symbolisms. Each poem, however, reveals in unusual degree a conscious striving for literary form. And each poem is marked by unevenness of achievement, by alternation of passages memorably poetic, with passages of oddity, ineptitude, and strain.

The chief literary merit of the *Andreas* can hardly be said to reside in the poet's handling of structure and general design, ambitious though it was. It is rather in the occasional instances of sharp and dramatic phrasing, and the spirited excellence of descriptive episodes such as the pictures of fire and flood, storm at sea, and winter weather. In these passages we feel the quality of a poetic gift which passes beyond ambitious design.

Judith

The *Judith*, a religious heroic poem of unusual spirit and excellence, is preserved in the final pages of the Cotton MS. immediately following the *Beowulf*. The 350 lines of *Judith* represent only a fraction of the original, the greater portion having been lost. The poem is divided into sections in the manuscript, Roman numerals indicating the beginning of section X after line 14, section XI after line 121, and section XII after line 235. The fragment as we have it, therefore, begins near the end of section IX, and in the middle of a sentence. The poet seems to have based his poem on a Latin version of the Apocryphal Book of Judith, though he used his material somewhat freely. Comparison with the source, and analysis of the narrative method employed in the Old English fragment, reinforce the implications of the section numbering, and indicate that in its original form *Judith* must have been a poem of some 1200 to 1500 lines, developed in the heroic tradition, and with something approaching epic stress. As in the case of the *Waldere*, the quality of the surviving fragment suggests that the missing sections of *Judith* were heroic verse of outstanding excellence.

Although the text of *Judith* was written out in the Cotton MS. by the same scribe who worked on the second part of *Beowulf*, the syntax, vocabulary, and metrics of *Judith* indicate that the poem is much later than *Beowulf*, and is probably to be dated as of the first half of the tenth century. The selection of this warlike and bloody instance of feminine heroism as a theme for poetic elaboration has led to conjecture that the poem may have been inspired by historic event, and written in honor of some queen, or great lady, whose achievements could have been suitably symbolized and memorialized by the Apocryphal legend. The suggestion has been advanced that the poem may have been prompted by the arrival in England in 856 of Judith, the Continental wife of

Æthelwulf, father of King Alfred.[19] But the date is early, and there is nothing except the identity of name to support the conjecture. Certainly, under the circumstances, the selection of such a theme as that of *Judith* to welcome the arrival of a bride would hardly seem a happy choice.

A more tenable theory connects the poem with the 'Queen of the Mercians,' Æthelflaed, daughter of King Alfred, and widow of Æthelred of Mercia,[20] who after her husband's death led the Mercian forces against the invading Danes, winning victories and recovering lost ground. It is suggested that a wave of patriotic feeling might have found fitting symbol for her achievements in the heroic resolution and strength of the Apocryphal Judith. The dates of her successes, late in the second decade of the tenth century, would link well with the conjectured date of the poem.

While this theory is on the whole more plausible than the first, it should be noted that there is actually no external evidence to lend support to either conjecture. Nor is the emergence of the Judith legend in Old English religious poetry so remarkable or strange as to require special explanation. The story of Judith is a religious tale stressing feminine heroism in a righteous cause, as are the legends of Elene and of Juliana. The fact that it is also a fierce and bloody tale would hardly have restricted its acceptability for poetic use in the savage period of the Danish invasions.

The fragment begins with lines which stress the religious faith of Judith and her trust in that Highest Judge by whose mercy she finds protection in her hour of greatest need. Here, as elsewhere, the poet represents Judith less as a Hebrew than as a Christian heroine. Before her slaying of Holofernes, for example, she prays to the 'Savior of all men,' beginning her petition with an invocation of the three persons of the Trinity.[21]

19. Cook, *Judith*, Introd., p. xi.
20. T. G. Foster, *Judith*, Strassburg, 1892.
21. *Judith*, 81-4.

After Judith's prayer the narrative continues with a description of the great feast which Holofernes, leader of the Assyrian army of invasion, gave to the captains and leaders of his troops. There is a brutal realism in this scene of debauchery which is of a piece with the grim and bloody detail of the murder scene, and which elsewhere in the poem marks the prevailing mood of the poet. Compared with this scene of drunkenness and brawl, the banquets of *Beowulf* are notable for their graceful ceremonial and gentle manners. But that there was undoubtedly ample justification in Germanic and Old English life for such a description is indicated by a well-known passage in the *Fates of Men*,[22] which gives so realistic a picture of a drinking bout in the course of which a quarrelsome member of the *comitatus* is killed. In any case, the account of Holofernes' feast is one of a number of passages in *Judith* which furnish evidence of the poet's gift of a stark and brutal realism in descriptive detail:

> Then came to the banquet,   took seat on the benches,
> Proud at the wine-feast,   his comrades in woe,
> Bold warriors in byrnies.   Great bowls were brought,
> Borne along the benches,   flagons and tankards
> Filled for the feasters.   Fierce warriors drank
> Destined for death,   though their chief knew it not,
> The grim lord of men.   Then the gold-friend of heroes,
> Great Holofernes,   had joy of the feast;
> He roared with laughter,   he bellowed and bawled,
> So that men, from afar,   could hear how the fierce one,
> Mead-flushed and frenzied,   shouted and stormed,
> Bidding the benchers   to bear them like men.
> And so, that evil one   all the long day,
> The arrogant overlord,   deluged his vassals,
> Drenched them with wine   till they all lay swooning
> As if struck down in death,   and drained of all good.[23]

22. *Fates of Men*, 48–57.
23. *Judith*, 15–32.

When evening came, Holofernes commanded Judith to be taken to the great pavilion where his bed stood draped with a golden fly-net. The Assyrian leader, heavy with wine, was helped back to the tent by his soldiers, and there, overcome by his long debauch, fell upon the bed in a drunken stupor.

The episode which follows is notable for its dramatic intensity. Judith is portrayed as the righteous avenger of evil, and the liberator of her people. Standing over Holofernes she draws a sharp sword, tempered in many battles, and prays for strength equal to the deed: 'With this sword, grant me to hew down this lord of sin. Avenge now the hot rage that burns in my breast.' The ensuing narrative of the killing of Holofernes is so brutal in its realism, even to the description of Judith's hauling at his inert body to dispose it for her blows, that the moral righteousness which the poet reads into the act barely suffices to save the scene from its revolting and bloody detail:

Then the holy one's mood and her hope were strengthened;
The heathen hero she gripped by the hair;
Undone in his shame dragged him toward her,
Deftly disposed him as best she could deal with
The loathsome man. The maid of woven tresses
Smote the fierce-hearted with bloodstained blade,
Half severed his neck; he lay in a swoon,
Wounded and drunken. Not yet was he dead,
Not wholly lifeless. Then grimly again
The bold maid hacked at the heathen hound,
Till his head rolled out over the floor-boards,
And behind lay lifeless the loathsome trunk.
His soul departed to the bottomless pit
And ever thereafter enslaved and enthralled,
It was racked with torture, enwreathed with serpents,[24]

24. The description of hell as a *wyrmsele* seems obviously suggestive of a snake-pit, a detail which appears also in *Christ and Satan*. The *wyrmum bewunden* of the present passage (l. 115) lends support to the conjectural emendation of *winnaþ ymb wyrmas* to *windaþ ymb wyrmas* in *Christ and Satan*, 134.

Fast bound in torment,   and trammeled in pain,
Deep in hell-fire   after his death.
Nor needed he hope,   hedged in by darkness,
Out of that snake-pit   ever to escape.
But there forever,   world without end,
He must dwell in that dark home,   joyless and hopeless.[25]

After the killing, Judith and her attendant, carrying the bloody head of Holofernes, return to their native city of Bethulia. To the watchmen on the walls Judith proclaims the gracious mercy of God, and the release of her people from the evils they had long endured. As the inhabitants of the city, men and women, old and young, come thronging and crowding by thousands to the city gates, Judith displays the head of Holofernes as the token of her triumph. She bids the Bethulians prepare for victorious battle against the death-doomed Assyrians. The host quickly makes ready. The poet's description of the arming and attack has the color and movement of the conventional Germanic battle scene of heroic poetry, making use of all the traditional detail including the eagle, raven and wolf:

Quickly the brave   were weaponed for war,
Bold men for battle,   kingly of mood,
Comrades in armor,   marching together,
Bearing their banners   forth to the fight.
From the holy city   men under helmets
Advanced to battle   at the break of day.
Loud resounded   the din of shields;
The lean one exulted,   the wolf in the wood,
And the corpse-greedy bird,   the black-coated raven.
Well they both knew   that warriors were minded
To work a slaughter   on fated foes.
Following them flew   the wet-feathered eagle,
Dusky of hue   and horny of nib,
Craving carrion,   shrilling its war-song. . .
Showers of arrows   the archers let fly,

25. *Judith*, 97–121.

Their battle-adders,   from bows of horn,
Their fearsome darts.   The fierce men stormed,
Hurling their spears   on the hostile host.[26]

The Assyrians are roused to their danger, and the captains of the army gather quickly about the tent of Holofernes. But no one of them dares to wake him. 'They all supposed that their lord and the fair maid were still together in the splendid pavilion.' They stand crowding about the entrance, terrified by knowledge of the impending attack, hoping in vain that the noise of their tumult will rouse their leader. At last one of them summons resolution to enter the tent, and there finds the headless body of Holofernes. Tearing his hair and robe, he announces to his comrades the token of their coming doom.

As the news spreads, the Assyrian host throw down their weapons and flee. The Bethulians are swift in pursuit, with their sharp swords hacking a war-path through the press of their flying foes. The land is filled with reeking corpses. But few of the Assyrian host ever return alive to their own country. Thereafter for a month's time, says the poet, the Bethulians were engaged in gathering the spoil of battle, carrying within the city gates gold-adorned weapons and armor and greater treasure than any man can tell. To Judith they gave the great sword and helmet of Holofernes, and his broad byrny decorated with red gold. And Judith, whose courage and resolution had brought about her people's triumph, gave thanks to God for this earthly glory and for the heavenly reward which her faith and steadfastness had earned. 'For all this,' writes the poet, 'glory be to the dear Lord forever, to Him who fashioned the wind and air, the sky and broad earth and raging sea, and at the last the joys of heaven.' So ends the poem.

The Old English *Judith*, though but a fragment of the original, is fortunately a complete section of the story concerned with its

26. *Judith*, 199–225.

most centrally important episodes. It is vividly conceived, and
developed with a guiding sense of dramatic values. The poem is
quite obviously the work of an accomplished poet exercising a
deft control of his material and adopted technique. The verse-
rhythm is unusually well adapted to the varied elements of the
story, swelling out at appropriate points into the weightier
measures of the long line which is used so effectively in *Genesis B.*
Even a brief study of the poet's handling of the alliterative rhythm
reveals the skill with which he parallels the use of the short line
in passages of rapid action by a highly successful employment of
the long line in the prayers of Judith, and in elements of narrative
which involve psychological or dramatic stress.

The poetic talents of the author are of a high order of excellence.
His felicitous control of realistic detail and keen sense of dramatic
value are everywhere visible. His mastery in depiction of crowded
scenes and violent action is equally evident. Perhaps less obvious,
but none the less notable, is a gift of psychological penetration, a
sensitive perception of the subtler currents of character and mood.
Finally, his verse displays an artist's felicity in the choice of
words, especially verbs; a precision and force in the rendering of
fact by symbol which is a noteworthy poetic skill.

The heroic spirit, so appropriate to the material of the poem,
is firmly pervasive throughout. If *Judith* is to be assigned to the
first half of the tenth century, as we have seen is probable, it
furnishes evidence of the survival of the heroic tradition, and of
a highly sophisticated poetic art, into a late period of Old English
verse. These elements of tradition, moreover, are clothed with
the energy and strength which, even at a later date, mark the
battle scenes and *comitatus* passages of *Maldon*. Not only has the
old spirit lived on to be evoked by the challenge of the Danish
invasions, but the literary tradition which expressed that spirit
still has power, in *Judith*, to color and transmute the material of
the Apocryphal legend.

The *Judith* furnishes in this respect an interesting contrast to the *Andreas*. In the treatment of the legend of St. Andrew, the poet strove with painstaking effort to unify and shape the unorganized material of saints' legend within the frame of the heroic pattern. But the task was difficult, and it is not overlooking the merits of *Andreas* to note that here and there the material remains stubbornly unsuited to the poetic technique employed. In *Judith*, on the other hand, the material lends itself easily to this technique, and the result is a firmly wrought re-rendering of Hebrew legend, transformed by the spirit and traditional embellishments of the heroic lay, and colored by the influence of the Christian faith.

X. CHRISTIAN ALLEGORY

Phoenix; Panther; Whale; Partridge

IT IS altogether natural that Old English poetry, in its wide range and variety, should include poems in which the central and shaping influence derives from the element of Christian allegory. The same influence which so often governed iconographic detail in the adornment of Christian buildings, monuments, and sarcophagi, had frequent expression in medieval literature and found its place in Old English religious poetry.

This spirit of allegorical invention created many widely recognized ecclesiastical symbols in which Christian concepts received a conventional embodiment; for example, the representation of Christ by the acrostic fish-symbol. The employment of such allegorical symbolisms in Old English religious poetry is well illustrated in the *Physiologus* and in the *Phoenix*, the latter a poem of exceptional merit.

THE PHOENIX

The 677 lines of the *Phoenix* are found in the Exeter Book, folios 55^b-65^b. The poem is based upon a Latin poem on the Phoenix commonly attributed to Lactantius. Like *Guthlac B* and the *Dream of the Rood*, the Old English *Phoenix*, though unsigned, has been claimed by many for Cynewulf. The only evidence for or against Cynewulfian authorship is such as has resulted from repeated studies of the metrics, vocabulary, and stylistic characteristics of the poem. Such evidence has been by no means conclusive, though the metrical tests, considered alone, disclose such wide variance between the *Phoenix* and the signed poems of Cynewulf that Mather remarks:[1] 'We need have no hesitation in

1. *Mod. Lang. Notes*, VII, 207.

denying the *Phoenix* to Cynewulf. The interesting point of this conclusion is that there must have been, contemporary or nearly so with Cynewulf, another poet of equal or greater skill than he, the author of the *Phoenix*, the most artistic poem in the Anglo-Saxon language.'

It seems at least questionable whether such metrical tests can be considered as conclusive as one might wish. And in this instance it should be noted that both in vocabulary and in general style the *Phoenix* has certain very definite similarities to the signed Cynewulfian poems. In one passage of the *Phoenix*[2] there is a direct parallel to an idea expressed in the runic signature of *Christ II*[3] where Cynewulf, in prophesying the Day of Judgment, contrasts earth's ancient devastation by the waters of the Deluge with its ultimate destruction in the fires of Judgment: 'Long was our portion of life's joys locked in by ocean-floods, our possessions on earth. In that day treasure shall burn in the fiery blast; brightly shall rage the swift, red flame darting in fury throughout the wide world.' The same contrast is briefly set forth in *Christ III* (984-6).' In the *Phoenix* (41-9) the idea is developed at greater length, and in somewhat more specific phrasing: 'As of old the might of the waters, the sea-flood, covered all the world and compass of earth, yet the noble plain stood altogether uninjured, firm held against the watery surges, by God's grace blessed and unhurt by the driving waves; so it shall abide and blossom until the coming of the fire of God's Judgment.' It must be noted, however, that these parallel passages cannot be interpreted as conclusive evidence of a borrowing from one of these poems to the others. The idea underlying all three passages may in each instance have been independently derived from St. Augustine's *De Civitate Dei* xx, 16,[4]

2. *Phoenix*, 41-9.

3. *Christ*, 805–14.

4. 'tunc figura huius mundi mundanorum ignium conflagratione praeteribit, sicut factum est mundanarum aquarum inundatione diluvium.'

or from II Peter iii. 6-7, upon which the *De Civitate* passage seems to rest.

The evidence at hand does not permit dogmatic opinion in regard to Cynewulfian authorship of the *Phoenix*. Cook has pointed out[5] that Cynewulf would undoubtedly have found such a theme congenial, and the Latin poem of Lactantius may well have been known to him, as the name of Lactantius was mentioned by Alcuin among the authors represented in the Library of York.[6] In any case, whether by Cynewulf or another, the Old English *Phoenix* is outstanding in artistry and grace of composition.

The poem begins with a description of the idyllic land in which the Phoenix lives. The description, in certain of its details, reveals a definite influence of the widespread legend of an Earthly Paradise. The legend was probably of Oriental origin, and includes elements which are paralleled in the descriptions of Paradise in the Biblical Genesis (ii.8-10) and in the more allegorical references of Ezekiel (xlvii.7-9, 12) and Revelation (ii.7; xxii.1-2). The tradition found patristic expression in the works of such writers as Ephraem Syrus,[7] Basil,[8] Bede,[9] and other early Christian writers.

The landscape of the *Phoenix*, reflecting the landscape of Lactantius, reproduces the chief elements which Cook points out as central to the tradition:[10] Paradise visualized as a high mountain or tableland, noble groves of trees bearing blossom and fruit in every season, a fountain of sweet water each month overflowing and fructifying the land, an idyllic landscape in which no leaves wither nor fruits decay, and in which nothing is noisome or evil,

5. *The Christ of Cynewulf*, pp. lxiv-lxv.
6. Lactantius' authorship of the *De Ave Phoenice* has been questioned, but, in a review of the matter in 1919, Cook expressed the opinion that 'the arguments in favor of Lactantius' authorship are . . . convincing, if not overwhelming.' (*The Old English Elene, Phoenix and Physiologus*, p. xxxviii.)
7. *Hom. 1 on Paradise*, op. III, 563.
8. *Hom. de Paradiso*, Migne, *Patr. Gr.*, xxx, 64.
9. *Hexameron*, Migne, *Patr. Lat.*, xci, 43.
10. *The Old English Elene, Phoenix, and Physiologus*, p. lii.

all things joyous and pleasant. The Earthly Paradise is removed by vast stretches of sea and land from all regions now inhabited by men. The parallelism of the descriptions in Lactantius and in the Old English *Phoenix* can be particularly noted in the serene and unchanging weather of the Earthly Paradise, the catalogue of noxious and noisome things unknown there, and the location of the Happy Land near the gates of heaven.[11]

The first 84 lines of the *Phoenix* are devoted to a memorable description of this land of joy and delight:

> Lo! I have learned   of the loveliest of lands,
> Far to the eastward,   famous among men.
> But few ever fare   to that far-off realm
> Set apart from the sinful   by the power of God.
> Beauteous that country   and blessed with joys,
> With the fairest odors   of all the earth.
> Goodly the island,   gracious the Maker,
> Matchless and mighty,   who stablished the world.
> There ever stand open   the portals of heaven,
> And songs of rapture   for blessed souls.
> The plain is winsome,   the woods are green,
> Widespread under heaven.   No rain or snow,
> Or breath of frost,   or blast of fire,
> Or freezing hail,   or fall of rime,
> Or blaze of sun,   or bitter-long cold,
> Or scorching summer,   or winter storm
> Work harm a whit,   but the plain endures
> Sound and unscathed.   The lovely land
> Is rich with blossoms.   No mountains rise,
> No lofty hills,   as here with us;
> No high rock-cliffs,   no dales or hollows,
> No mountain gorges,   no caves or crags;
> Naught rough or rugged,   but the pleasant plain
> Basks under heaven,   laden with bloom.

11. For discussion of the influence in medieval romance of traditional descriptions of Paradise, see Patch, 'Medieval Descriptions of the Otherworld,' *PMLA*, xxxiii 601–43.

Twelve cubits higher   is that lovely land,
As learned scholars   in their writings disclose,
Than any of these hills   that here in splendor
Tower on high   under heavenly stars.
Serene that country,   sunny groves gleaming;
Winsome the woodlands;   fruits never fail,
Or shining blossoms.   As God gave bidding,
The groves stand forever   growing and green.
Winter and summer   the woods alike
Are hung with blossoms;   under heaven no leaf
Withers, no fire   shall waste the plain
To the end of the world.   As the waters of old,
The sea-floods, covered   the compass of earth,
And the pleasant plain   stood all uninjured,
By the grace of God   unhurt and unharmed,
So shall it flourish   till the fire of Judgment,
When graves shall open,   the dwellings of death.
Naught hostile lodges   in all that land,
No pain or weeping   or sign of sorrow,
No age or anguish   or narrow death;
No ending of life   or coming of evil,
No feud or vengeance   or fret of care;
No lack of wealth   or pressure of want,
No sorrow or sleeping   or sore disease.
No winter storm   or change of weather,
Fierce under heaven,   or bitter frost
With wintry icicles   smites any man there.
No hail or hoar-frost   descends to earth,
No windy cloud,   no water falls
Driven by storm.   But running streams
And welling waters   wondrously spring
Overflowing earth   from fountains fair.
From the midst of the wood   a winsome water
Each month breaks out   from the turf of earth,
Cold as the sea-stream,   coursing sweetly
Through all the grove.   By the bidding of God
The flood streams forth   through the glorious land
Twelve times yearly.   The trees are hung

With beauteous increase, flowering buds;
Holy under heaven the woodland treasures
Fail not nor wither; the fallow bloom,
The fruits of the wildwood, fall not to earth;
But in every season on all the trees
The boughs bear their burden of fruit anew.
Green are the groves in the grassy meadow,
Gaily garnished by might of God.
No branch is broken, and fragrance fair
Fills all the land. Nor ever comes change
Till He, whose wisdom wrought its beginning,
His ancient creation shall bring to its end.[12]

In this Paradise of wonder and beauty lives the Phoenix, for a thousand years not tasting of death. Each day it watches the rising of the sun. As black night steals away, the beauteous bird turns its gaze eastward to where God's candle, noblest of stars, rises over the ocean waves. Twelve times ere the sun's rising the Phoenix bathes in the waters of Paradise, and after its water-sport wings its way to a lofty tree whence it can behold the course of the sun. As the gem of heaven climbs the sky, the Phoenix soars upward from its forest tree, caroling to heaven with clear voice in varied strains:

> The melody of its hymn is sweeter than all songcraft, fairer and winsomer than any harmony. Neither horn nor trumpet can be likened to that sound, neither music of harp, nor the voice of any man on earth, nor organ, nor melody of song, nor feathered swan, nor any of those pleasant sounds that God created to be a joy to men in this mournful world.[13]

So it carols till the sinking of the sun in the southern sky. Then the song is hushed.

The brilliant hues and varied marking of the Phoenix furnish the Old English poet with subject matter for a remarkable passage

12. *Phoenix*, 1–84.
13. ll. 131–9.

of description, rich in detail and flavored with an obvious delight in the play of color and contrast. We can hardly credit the poet with inventive originality in these lines, for Lactantius contains a similar descriptive passage, and the Old English poet at this point is obviously following his Latin original closely. But the re-rendering is done with spirit, and there is interfused throughout the Old English description a sensitiveness to shades and contrasts and a poetic pleasure in the almost Oriental massing of color which mark the passage as unique in Old English poetry:

> Fair-breasted that fowl, and gleaming with varied colors. The back of the head is green, beautifully mottled and blended with scarlet. The tail feathers are variegated, part brown, part crimson, and cunningly set with lustrous spots. The backs of the wings are white, the neck green under and above, and the nib shining like glass or gem. The beak is comely within and without. The eye is piercing, in hue most like to a stone or sparkling gem when mounted by a cunning smith in a setting of gold. Round about the neck it is like the orb of the sun, most shining of rings woven of feathers. Comely the belly beneath and wondrously fair, shining and bright. Beautifully over the back of the bird the shield is spread. The legs are grown with scales, the feet are yellow. The Phoenix is unique in appearance, most like to a peacock.[14]

When a thousand years have passed, the aged Phoenix flies from the Earthly Paradise to a remote region in the land of Syria. Hosts of birds accompany the flight, acknowledging the sovereignty of the Phoenix over all birds. In Syria it lodges, solitary and concealed from men in a tall tree, brightest blooming of all on earth. In the halcyon days when the wind lies at rest and waters are tranquil, when storms are stilled under heaven and the weather candle shines warm from the south, the Phoenix builds its nest. In the tall tree's leafy shade it fashions its house, surrounding itself

14. ll. 291-312.

with pleasant herbs and the fairest blooms of earth gathered from far and near. As it sits there in the burning sunlight, the nest kindles into flame. 'The herbs grow warm, its lovely home steams with pleasant odors. In the grasp of fire the Phoenix burns with its nest. The funeral flame is kindled.' Bone and flesh are consumed and the spirit goes forth.

But at the appointed time its life is renewed. When the fire is spent, there appears in the cold embers the likeness of an egg, from which springs a wondrous fair worm. The worm grows to a fledgling like an eagle's young, then to a full-grown bird once more beautified with brilliant plumage. Even as from grain, harvested and resown, there springs anew the bounty of earth, so the Phoenix grows young again and once more clothed in flesh. But it tastes no food save the honey-dew that falls at midnight, until once more it comes to its former home.

Gathering in its talons the leavings of the fire, bone and ash, the Phoenix returns to the Earthly Paradise where it buries in the soil of that pleasant island all the remnants of its former body. Men on earth marvel at the beauty of the bird and record in writing, and engrave on marble, the day and hour of its flight. A great retinue of singing birds accompany the Phoenix on its homecoming to the Earthly Paradise, where they leave it, returning sad-hearted to their own domain. The details of this flight of the Phoenix, the exultant song of the feathered hosts, and their grief as they turn away from the borders of Paradise are developed as an allegory of the Ascension of the risen Christ and the sadness of the disciples who remained behind on earth.

In the poet's use of this material, it is interesting to note the recurring association of the Phoenix with the rising sun. It is a detail which reflects the Egyptian origins of the myth, and the early linking of the Phoenix with the worship of Ra, the sun god, and with the sun-rites of Heliopolis. This symbolic association, indeed, was central in the myth. In accord with this general

tradition, and its specific expression in Lactantius, the Old English
poet retains and stresses this element of symbolism:

> When the stars are hid   in the western wave,
> Dimmed at dawn,   and the dusky night
> Steals darkly away,   then strong of wing,
> Proud of pinion,   it looks over sea,
> Eagerly over ocean,   for the rising sun
> When the bright blaze shall burn   in the heavens above,
> Gliding from eastward   over the wide water. . .
> When the sun climbs high   over the salt streams
> The gray bird wings   from its woodland tree
> And, swift of pinion,   soars to the sky
> Singing and caroling   to greet the sun.[15]

The second half of the *Phoenix*, that is, lines 393-677, is devoted
to an elaborate interpretation of the Christian allegory implied in
the narrative of the fiery death and resurrection of the Phoenix.
As the Old English poet develops the allegorical implications of
the theme, the flight of the Phoenix from the Earthly Paradise
typifies the banishment of our first parents from Eden by the Fall
of Man. The lofty tree in a foreign land wherein the bird builds
its nest represents God's mercy and grace to men. The herbs and
fragrant blossoms with which the Phoenix shapes and adorns its
nest are the good deeds of a righteous life. The fire in which the
nest is kindled is the fire of Doomsday. The rebirth of the Phoenix
is the resurrection to eternal life. This interpretation of the legend,
however, is not maintained with uniform consistency throughout
the poem. Whereas in lines 508-14 and 552-61 the rebirth of the
Phoenix is made to symbolize man's resurrection, in a later passage
(642-54) the bird is identified with Christ, as in the Latin *Physiologus*, in which the Phoenix symbolizes Christ, and its two wings,
the Old and New Testaments.

In putting the legend of the Phoenix to this use as Christian
allegory, the Old English poet was writing in a well-established

15. ll. 90-103; 120-24.

tradition. Allegorical use of the Phoenix myth seems to be implicit in a verse of the twenty-ninth chapter of Job,[16] and it is clear that the poet had this passage in mind. He makes specific reference to the Book of Job in line 549, and paraphrases Job xxix.18 and xix.25-6 in lines 552-69 of the *Phoenix*. The paraphrase, moreover, is emphasized by a statement of the poet in the lines which follow: 'Thus the wise prophet of God in days of old sang of his resurrection to eternal life, that we the more clearly might recognize the glorious truth which the radiant bird typifies in its burning.'

As the *Phoenix* draws to its close we have, in the manner so characteristic of Cynewulf and his imitators, a vivid description of the consuming fire of Judgment Day which shall destroy the splendor and wealth of earth. Then shall death be ended. The souls of men shall enter once more into their bodies, and all shall rise to Judgment. In the fire of Doomsday the blessed shall be surrounded by their good works, which are the sweet and fragrant herbs with which the Phoenix builds its nest. 'Let no man think,' writes the poet, 'that I fashion this poem and frame this lay with falsehoods.' The passage from Job is then cited as a foundation for the poet's interpretation of the fable.

There follows a beautiful passage rehearsing the joys of the blessed. Adorned with bright crowns of precious stones, and with halos of light, they dwell in beauty with the Father of angels. They know not sorrow or sin, want or toil, burning hunger or bitter thirst, old age or misery, but round the throne of God lift up their voices in eternal praise. The poet's description of these celestial anthems includes a versified elaboration of the 'Sanctus.'

The poem ends with an unusual passage of macaronic verse in which Old English and Latin are used alternately throughout eleven lines. In each line the first half-line is in Old English, the second in Latin. The normal vowel and consonant alliterations are employed to bind the half-lines into unity. This type of poetic

16. In nidulo meo moriar, et sicut palma multiplicabo dies.

line, while unusual in Old English religious poetry, is not confined to the *Phoenix*. Conybeare in his *Illustrations*[17] reprints from
Wanley other examples of the type. One such passage[18] is of
special interest in the fact that both Latin and Greek phrases are
alternated with Old English in the text.

The *Phoenix* stands out in Old English poetry as a finished and
skillful use of allegory. It has more than a touch of that poetic
magic which shapes a secret world of strangeness and wonder. It
is in this mood that the essential elements of the fable are elaborated: the idyllic landscape, the shining beauty of the Phoenix, the
adoration of the sun, the divine promise hidden in the heart of an
age-old symbol. Even stronger than the poet's pleasure in the
decorative beauty of the legend was his dominant concern with
central doctrines of the Christian faith, the victory over death, the
resurrection to life eternal. Others before him had turned the fable
to this use. In following them, he has left us one of the most
memorable and graceful examples of Old English religious verse.

THE PHYSIOLOGUS

On folios 95[b]-98[b] of the Exeter Book are three other Old English poems which, like the *Phoenix*, employ traits and habits of
animals as allegorical illustration of Christian themes. These are
the *Panther, Whale,* and *Partridge*. As we shall see later, the three
poems are bound into a series, and are undoubtedly in some degree
based upon the early Christian *Physiologus*, or *Naturalist*, the
earliest texts of which were probably Greek. The wide popularity
of the Christian *Physiologus* was attested in the fact that by the
fifth century it was translated into Latin, Ethiopic, Syriac, and
Arabic, and later, in whole or in part, into various European
languages including Old High German, Old French, Old English,
Middle English, and Icelandic.

17. *Illustrations*, pp. viii–x.
18. MS., Coll. Corp. Ch. Cant., K. 12.

The precise relation of the Old English *Panther*, *Whale*, and *Partridge* to the Continental *Physiologus*, and to one another, is not in all respects clear. Three principal and differing theories regarding these poems have been proposed. It has been suggested: first, that the three poems are versifications of three separate and unrelated sections of the *Physiologus*; second, that they are a connected unit, but only a portion of a much longer Old English *Physiologus*, which has been lost; and third, that they constitute a connected and abbreviated Old English *Physiologus*, complete in itself save for a break in the text of the *Partridge*.

The evidence of the text itself renders the first of these theories untenable. The three poems are demonstrably a unit, with indications of formal beginning and formal ending. The first poem of the three, the *Panther*, opens with eight lines of general introduction referring to the variety of birds and beasts on earth, of which one, the Panther, is selected for description. The nature and phrasing of this passage suggest at once that it marks the beginning of a poem, or a series. The third poem, the *Partridge*, ends in the Exeter MS. with the conclusive word *finit*, a device employed nowhere else in the Exeter MS., but which may well have been present in the earlier text from which the scribe was copying. Between these notations of a beginning and an end, the *Panther*, *Whale*, and *Partridge* are bound into a series by the continuative implications of the Old English adverb *gēn* (moreover, further, next), which occurs in the opening lines of the second and third poems.

It seems clear, therefore, that the three poems are intentionally organized into a unity. But the question still remains whether that unity is substantially complete in the poems as we have them, or whether there has been extended loss. The uncertainty arises from the break in the text of the *Partridge* after the word *wundorlīcne* in line 2. Since it is the last word on folio 97^b of the manuscript, it is obvious that the break indicates the loss of one or more leaves between 97 and the present 98.

The theory that the *Panther*, *Whale*, and *Partridge* represent only a fragment of an original Old English *Physiologus* is based on the assumption that after folio 97, instead of a single leaf, a gathering may have been lost containing the material of the missing sections of the Continental *Physiologus*.[19] This theory, of course, necessarily involves also the supposition that the two fragments of the third poem relate to different birds, the first two lines to the Partridge, the material after the break to another bird of the *Physiologus* cycle, the Charadrius. But the evidence of the manuscript itself is quite against this theory, since recent examinations of the Exeter Book indicate that only one leaf has been lost after folio 97.[20]

We may accept, therefore, as the most tenable interpretation of the whole matter, the opinion set forth by Dobbie:[21]

> Assuming the loss of a single leaf (that is, two pages) we have approximately eighty lines as the original length of the *Partridge*, as compared with seventy-four lines for the *Panther*, and eighty-nine lines for the *Whale* — a reasonably close correspondence in length between the three poems. The evidence of the manuscript, then in so far as it applies, favors the conclusion that, except for the gap of two pages in the text of the *Partridge*, we possess the whole of the Anglo-Saxon *Physiologus*. Such a *Physiologus* would be reasonably complete in itself, dealing as it does with the three kinds of animals, — of the land, the water, and the air.

THE PANTHER

The *Panther* is a brief poem of 74 lines, lacking the poetic beauty and grace so notable in the *Phoenix*. As presented in the *Physiologus* and in the Old English poem, the Panther is an animal which wears a medieval air of strangeness and wonder. The traits ascribed to it, like details in the legend of the Unicorn, savor

19. See Sokoll, *Zum Angelsächsischen Physiologus*.
20. Krapp and Dobbie, *The Exeter Book*, pp. xi–xii.
21. Op. cit. p. li.

of quaint and curious lore notably at variance with realism. The
quality first stressed is the last to be expected, the kindly disposition of the beast, his friendliness to all other creatures except the
Dragon. It is the Panther's habit, after eating his fill, to sleep for
three days and then to rouse from slumber crying with a loud
voice. With the voice goes forth a fragrance, and other beasts
lured by this fragrance run to the Panther and follow him.

The description of the beast in the Old English poem, where
these elements are centrally embodied, is naively, and vividly,
presented. The substance of the passage may be freely translated
as follows:

> The beast is named Panther. The writings of learned
> men tell of this solitary rover. He is gentle and kindly to
> all other creatures save only the Dragon, against whom
> he wages unceasing war by every hostile means he can
> muster. Like Joseph's coat of many colors, the coat of the
> Panther is wondrous resplendent, of bright and shining
> hues each more beautiful than the others. His nature is
> unique, amiable and gentle, gracious and kindly. Naught
> of hostile or evil will he do against any save only the
> venomous Dragon, his ancient foe. When fain of feasting
> he eats his fill, after the meal he seeks rest in a secret place
> among mountain caves where overcome by sleep he
> slumbers for three nights' time, and on the third day
> glorified rises straightway from sleep. Then comes a
> melody from the mouth of the beast, most pleasing of
> strains, and a fragrance with the melody, rising in that
> place stronger and more sweet than the sweet smell of
> blossoming spices, or forest fruits, more excellent than
> all the beauties of earth. Then from the cities, from royal
> dwellings and castle halls, men in multitudes throng the
> roads, and animals with them, hasting to that fragrance.[22]

From this fable the Christian poet derives allegorical references
to Christ, Satan, and the Resurrection. The enmity between the

22. *Panther*, 12–54.

Panther and the Dragon is the unceasing spiritual warfare between
God and Satan. The Panther rousing from three days' sleep is the
risen Christ. The fragrance of the Panther's voice is God's grace
to man in the Resurrection. The multitudes who congregate about
the Panther attracted by this fragrance are those who follow their
Redeemer and Lord.

The suggestion for the early identification of the Panther with
Christ was probably found in Hosea v. 14, where the Septuagint
text has 'panther' instead of the 'lion' or 'young lion' of the
Authorized Version. Rooted in this brief suggestion, a sustained
allegory was developed both in the Greek *Physiologus* and in the
Old English poem. This allegory the poet painstakingly unriddles,
point by point:

> So the Lord God, Giver of all joys, is gentle and kindly
> to all creatures save only the Dragon, the Prince of
> Poison. That is the ancient Fiend whom He bound in the
> pit of torment, constrained in fiery chains and fettered in
> durance; and on the third day the Prince of angels and
> Lord of victory arose from the grave after suffering death
> for us for three nights' time. That was a lovely fragrance,
> sweet and delightful over all the world.[23]

The didactic element in the *Panther* stands out. In the descriptive section of the poem the Dragon is twice mentioned. The Old
English poet particularizes these allusions as references to God's
binding of Satan in hell. Whether the reference is to the Hexaemeral tradition, in accordance with which Satan was bound
after the fall of the angels, or to the tradition by which Satan was
bound by Christ during the Harrowing of Hell, is not altogether
clear. In any case, the poet's interest in the allegory and its unriddling is, one feels, primarily didactic. In this respect the poem
is inferior to the *Phoenix*, in which the poetic and didactic elements
are more completely and firmly fused.

23. ll. 55–65.

THE WHALE

The allegory of the Great Whale is more firmly integrated, more dramatic and more convincing than the fable of the Panther. The germ of the legend as set forth in the *Physiologus* is of very early date, in all probability going back to narratives of a voyage which Nearchus, an admiral of Alexander's fleet, made in 325 B.C. past the island of Ashtola, or Sungadeep, off the coast of Beluchistan. Arrian and Strabo both give accounts of this voyage, and of the wondrous nature of the island on which, if a ship moored, both ship and sailors disappeared. Later rationalizing explanations of the myth attempted to trace this legend of disappearing mariners to a fatally unhealthful climate, or to traditions of a pirate rendezvous on the island.[24]

As time passed, the legend altered form, and became a tale of a mysterious island which turned out to be a huge sea-beast. When approached by sailors who mistook it for the land it seemed to be, the huge beast sank into the sea, drawing down with it both ship and sailors.[25]

In many versions of the fable the sea-beast is represented as a huge tortoise, and the sea-monster of the Old English poem apparently had its remote and original source in the tortoise tradition. This seems to be implied by the fact that the poet in line 9 names his sea-beast *Fastitocalon*. The name sounds like a corrupted form of the noun ἀσπιδοχελώνη, which in the Greek *Physiologus* is applied to a species of tortoise known as the 'shield-turtle,' or more properly 'asp-turtle.'

In spite of these implications of the name *Fastitocalon,* the Old English poet repeatedly calls his sea-beast a whale, and the descrip-

24. For extended discussion see Cook, *Old English Elene, Phoenix, and Physiologus,* Introd., pp. lxiii–lxxiii.

25. Milton's well-known description of Leviathan, P.L. I, 201 ff., based apparently on a tale of Olaus Magnus, is probably a variant of the same general tradition.

tion of the monster, as the poet develops it, accords with that concept. The depiction of the huge sea-beast with wide, open jaws, by a marvelous fragrance attracting unwary schools of fish which swim into the cavernous mouth and are lost, is certainly definitely suggestive of the whale rather than of the tortoise. Nor is it in any way extraordinary that the Old English poet should so visualize the great sea-monster, since classical writers such as Pliny and Strabo stressed, and exaggerated, the huge size of the whale, and descriptions by later writers such as Basil and Ambrose compared whales to mountains and islands.

The Old English description of the sea-monster is done with vivacity and feeling, and is marked by imagination and felicity of phrasing, in unusual degree. 'I will compose further,' wrote the poet, 'and fashion a poem of the Great Whale':

> Its appearance is like a rough rock, or a great mass of tossing seaweed surrounded by sand-dunes, at the sea-shore; so that mariners think they gaze on an island, and make fast their high-prowed ships by anchor-ropes to this land which is no land; they fetter their ocean-steeds at the sea's edge and boldly set foot upon the island. Their ships are fast moored by the shore, encompassed by the tide. The sea-weary mariners encamp there and have no thought of peril. On the island they kindle a fire; the flames leap high. Joy returns to dispirited men, eager for rest. When the Whale, crafty in evil, feels that the sailors are well established and encamped there, joying in fair weather, then suddenly with the venturesome band the guest of ocean plunges downward in the salt wave, seeks bottom, and in that hall of death drowns sailors and ships. . . .
>
> The proud Swimmer of Ocean has another trait even more marvelous. When hunger torments him in the sea and the monster is fain of food, then the Sea-warden opens his mouth, his wide jaws; and there comes from within a winsome fragrance so that other kinds of sea-

fish are beguiled thereby. Swiftly they swim to where the sweet odor comes forth. In unwary schools they enter in until the wide mouth is filled; then suddenly he snaps together his grim jaws around his prey.[26]

The poet has hardly completed his description of the vast sea-monster sounding to the bottom with his hapless prey, when he turns eagerly to the unriddling of the allegory. 'This,' he exclaims, 'is the way of devils, and the custom of demons, to deceive men by cunning guile.' The Old English interpretation of the fable is derived from the earlier expositions set forth in the Greek *Physiologus*. In that work interpretation of the myth was grounded on verses in the fifth chapter of Proverbs, which have to do with the luring wiles of the harlot.[27] 'Her feet go down to death; her steps take hold on hell.' But the Greek *Physiologus* adds to this interpretation a much more general warning against the varied and cunning deceptions of Satan. It is this more general solution of the allegory that has interested the Old English poet. His verses contain no reference to Proverbs, or the wiles of 'strange women.' The Great Whale is Satan, endowed with every device of soul-destroying evil. The yawning jaws into which the unwary swim in great schools have a vivid parallelism to the open dragon jaws which were so frequently employed in medieval art as a symbol of Hell-mouth.[28] The false semblance of the great sea-monster, which disguises ultimate destruction by a deceptive appearance of refuge and safety, is to the poet a convincing symbol of Satan's guile. When by secret wiles the Tempter has snared the unwary, and lured them into his power, savagely he plunges them in eternal ruin, dragging them down to the bottomless lake in the gloom of hell.

The sweet fragrance which has betrayed them, and lured them

26. *The Whale*, 8–31; 49–62.

27. Proverbs v. 3–5.

28. Cf. the representations of Hell-mouth in the drawings of the Junius MS.

to their doom, flows from the lusts of the flesh, the temptations of worldly desire. Thus the seductions of the world, combining with a spiritual blindness which mistakes evil for good, danger for safety, betray the soul to ruin. 'And when the Crafty One, cunning in evil, drags down to that surge of flame those who in life hearken to his teaching and cleave to him in their sins, then at death he snaps together over them his grim jaws, the gates of hell.'

The Partridge

As we have already noted, the text of the *Partridge* is seriously impaired by a break in the manuscript. Assuming that one leaf only is missing, and that the original length of the poem was approximately 80 lines, we have in the 16 lines that have survived only a small fraction of the whole. These 16 lines, moreover, are divided by the break in the manuscript into two fragments which represent the beginning and the end of the poem. Practically the entire fable of the *Partridge* was included in the missing lines, and is lost to us. All that remains to identify the subject of the poem is the poet's statement in the first eight words: 'About a certain bird, also, I have heard a wondrous . . .' With the word 'wondrous' comes the break. The text that immediately follows the break obviously has to do with the interpretation of the missing fable.

Although the 'wondrous' bird is nowhere named in the Old English text, there are sound reasons for assuming that it is the Partridge. The Panther, Whale, and Partridge appear in conjunction, and in that order, in many manuscripts of the Continental *Physiologus*. Of all birds, then, it is the Partridge which one would most naturally expect to find in association with the two animals that have preceded it in the Old English *Physiologus*. Perhaps more important, the 14 lines of Old English text devoted to interpretation of the allegory set forth ideas which accord well with the fable of the Partridge as told and interpreted in the Continental tradition.

In the Greek *Physiologus* the author, after citing the reference to the Partridge in Jeremiah xvii. 11, describes the bird as one that broods on and hatches the eggs of other birds. When the bantlings are grown they desert the Partridge, the birds of each species returning to the companionship of their own. 'In like manner,' comments the author, 'the devil gets possession of the foolish in heart. But when they have come to full age, they begin to recognize their heavenly parents, our Lord Jesus Christ and the Church, the apostles and the prophets, and betake themselves to them.'[29] It is against this background of tradition that the fragments of the Old English poem must be interpreted.

In the 7 lines immediately following the break in the text of the *Partridge* we find the following promise addressed by the Prince of Glory to mankind:

> In such time as ye shall turn to me with true faith in your hearts, and cease from your black transgressions, in that same hour will I turn to you in love and mercy for all eternity, and ye shall thereafter be accounted and numbered unto me as glorious, blessed, radiant brothers instead of sons.[30]

Here quite obviously is exegesis in accord with the early tradition. If mankind will turn away from Satan, who strives to include all men in his evil brood, and will recognize that they are children of God, then shall they be received of their Father and numbered among the brethren in Christ.[31]

The evidence available, then, indicates that the two fragments following the *Whale* are brief portions from the beginning and end of a poem on the Partridge. So much has been lost that one

29. Cook, op. cit., pp. lxxxv-lxxxvi.

30. *Partridge*, 5-11.

31. Cook (op. cit. p. 139, note on *Partridge*, 11) points out the reflection in these lines of the doctrine in Hebrews ii. 10, 11: 'For both he that sanctifieth and they who are sanctified are all of one: for which cause he is not ashamed *to call them brethren.*'

can form little judgment concerning the merit of the poem in its original state. But that it could have possessed either the grim realism and vigor of the *Whale*, or the quaint medievalism of the *Panther*, seems unlikely.

Many forces have joined in the shaping and religious use of these medieval descriptions of animal forms. Old tales of travel in uncharted lands provided naive fusions of falsehood with fact. Credulity and superstition added strength to tradition. Imagination and ingenious fancy moulded from these fables the symbols of allegory, and piety and didacticism devoted them to the service of the Christian faith.

Time has dealt variously with these ancient allegories, some retaining life and vigor, some preserved like flies in amber. The fable of the Great Whale is superb in its dramatic strength, its realism, its adaptation to theme. Even the Phoenix, in its remoteness, wears not too unconvincingly the miraculous attributions of the antique myth. But the Panther and the Partridge are not remote, and certain of the realisms associated with them in the minds of men conflict with the ideas of which they are made to serve as symbols. Such fables survive, wearing an air of medieval strangeness. They are illustrations of allegory ingeniously invented to serve as a means of instruction in religious truth.

XI. MINOR RELIGIOUS POEMS

Solomon and Saturn; The Soul to the Body; Pride; Resignation;
Counsels of a Father; Descent into Hell;
Doomsday; The Grave

SCATTERED through the Old English manuscripts are a
number of minor poems, apparently of late date, on various
religious subjects, and of various literary types. Relatively brief
as they are, some of these productions present matters of great
interest either in their structure, or in the nature and derivation of
material. Included in this group are the two poetical dialogues, or
'debates,' of Solomon and Saturn; two 'addresses' of the Soul to
the Body; two homiletic poems on Pride and Resignation; a
Descent into Hell, two poems on the Judgment Day; and certain
minor versifications of homiletic material.

SOLOMON AND SATURN

The two Solomon and Saturn dialogues are of special interest,
presenting as they do Old English examples of the 'debate' or
contest of wit, and displaying, particularly in the second dialogue,
elements of material and structure which are obviously derivative
from the literature of riddles and gnomic verse. The text of these
two poems is found in two manuscripts of the Corpus Christi
College Library in Cambridge.[1] MS. A contains not only a portion of the first poetic dialogue between Solomon and Saturn,
and the whole of the second, but also a prose dialogue between
the same speakers. MS. B preserves 93 lines, written on the
margins of another work, which seem to belong to the first poetic
dialogue. The two poems are in all probability of Anglian origin,

1. MS. CCCC422 (MS. A), and MS. CCCC41 (MS. B).

and to be dated in the latter half of the ninth century, or early in the tenth.[2] Menner suggests that these dialogues 'are dependent on lost Solomonic Christian dialogues in Latin, which in turn were presumably adopted from Greek originals that had their ultimate source in the Hebrew legends of King Solomon.'[3]

Behind the two speakers in these dialogues lie long ages of tradition. The Old Testament story of the wisdom and power of King Solomon developed during the early Christian and medieval periods into two distinct bodies of legend. Christianized tradition made Solomon not only the wise and magnificent ruler of the Old Testament, but a prophetic type of the Christ of the New Testament,[4] a figure well fitted to uphold in the Old English dialogues the supremacy of Christian over pagan learning. By a second tradition Solomon came to be represented not only as the author of such books as Proverbs, Ecclesiastes, the Book of Wisdom, and the Song of Songs, but also as a subduer of demons,[5] and author of books of magic. In the Old English poetic dialogues, in Menner's opinion, 'traces of the magician remain in the curious power of the runic letters of the Pater Noster over the Devil (Poem 1), and in the subduing of the demonic Vasa Mortis (238-72).'[6]

The tradition by which Saturn, in the Old English dialogues, was made the opponent of Solomon and the upholder of pagan wisdom is obscure and difficult to trace. In the later medieval Latin, German, and French dialogues, the opponent of Solomon was a certain Marcolf, or Marcol. This name evidently became connected with the Solomonic tradition prior to the Old English dialogues, since the second dialogue states (180) that Saturn in search of wisdom had visited, among other eastern countries, the

2. For date and origin see Menner, *Solomon and Saturn*, Introd., pp. 12-21.
3. Menner, op. cit. Introd., p. 26.
4. Menner, op. cit. Introd., pp. 47-8.
5. See McCown, *The Testament of Solomon*, Leipzig, 1922.
6. Menner, op. cit. Introd., p. 22.

land of *Marculf*. It has been suggested that in early tradition Saturn
and Marcolf were the same figure, and that the fusion may have
resulted from an identification of the Hebrew Markolis with the
Latin god Mercury, the identification being complicated by a
subsequent confusion of Mercury and Saturn.[7] In any case,
whereas Solomon-Marcolf 'debates' were well known in medieval
literature, it is only in the Old English poetic and prose dialogues
that the opponent of Solomon is Saturn.

The first of the two Old English poems is less clearly than the
second a dialogue or 'debate.' Though it includes three speeches
by Saturn, the greater portion of the poem is devoted to a single
long expository speech of Solomon. Saturn's introductory words
refer to his search for wisdom, and his willingness to give for it
'thirty pounds of pure gold' and his twelve sons. He asks who
most easily can open the doors of heaven, and is told by Solomon
it is the Lord's prayer, or Pater Noster. Saturn then asks how the
prayer is to be used, and Solomon's answer fills 106 lines with
earnest, and in passages eloquent, praise of the Pater Noster. In the
course of this poetic exposition, not only does the author personify
the Pater Noster in its entirety, but he also personifies the individual letters of the prayer visualized as armed warriors fighting
against Satan and the powers of evil. These letters are represented
in the manuscript in runic form, and the shapes of the runes in
some instances suggest to the poet the weapons by which the
Devil is combated and conquered. Thus, the P-rune is described
as a goad to scourge, the T-rune as a dart to stab. Three of the 19
letters which occur in the Pater Noster are omitted from the Old
English poem.

The Pater Noster is referred to in line 39 as 'palm-branched.'
This unusual use of the epithet, and the reference in line 63 to the
adornment of the Pater Noster with gems, may perhaps imply
that the poet was writing of a particular text of the prayer

7. See Menner, op. cit. Introd., pp. 26–35.

wrought in silver and gold, decorated with a scroll of palm branches, and inset with precious stones. On the other hand, the language may be purely figurative. The spirit of mystical reverence in the passage reflects the voice of the medieval Church in its emphasis on the importance of the Pater Noster and the Creed.

God's prayer is golden   and gleaming with gems.
It has leaves of silver;   secretly each
By grace of the Spirit   rehearses the gospel.
It is wisdom to the spirit   and honey to the soul. . .
It saves the soul   from eternal night
Far under earth,   let the Fiend with fetters
Chain it never so deep.   Though He lock and fasten
With fifty bolts,   it will break His strength
And utterly blast   His cunning devices.
It banishes hunger   and ravages Hell;
Hell-fire it scatters,   Heaven's glory it builds.
In all this earth   in mood it is prouder,
More firm of foundation   than the strength of all stones.
To the halt it is healing,   light to the blind,
A door for the deaf,   a tongue for the dumb,
A shield for the sinful,   the seat of the Creator.[8]

The second dialogue of Solomon and Saturn is much more consistent in adherence to the structural pattern of the medieval 'debate.' The first line of the poem announces it as a contest between Saturn, a Chaldean, far-traveled and learned in books, and Solomon, represented as more widely known for his wisdom. Thus the stage is set at the beginning for the final victory of Solomon, and one is not surprised to read in the four lines of the epilogue that 'the wise son of David had mastered and overcome the Chaldean prince.' Most of the questions are asked by Saturn and answered by Solomon. In this sense, the 'debate' is not a balanced contest of wit. But the forms of dialogue are sustained throughout, in marked contrast to the largely expository pattern of the first poem.

8. *Solomon and Saturn, I*, 63–79.

The material which is brought under discussion is blended of Hebrew, Germanic, and Christian elements. The Hebrew elements include references to Chaldean pride and the Tower of Babel; to a certain Wulf, a seafarer and friend of Nimrod, who slew 25 dragons, and perished himself; and to a strange demon, Vasa Mortis, known to the Philistines. Side by side with this material is material derived from Germanic and Christian themes: Fate and Providence; fortune and misfortune; man's appointed span of life and the angelic or demonic spirits that guard or tempt him. Intermingled throughout are snatches of riddle-themes, and fragments of gnomic and elegiac verse. One of the loveliest, and briefest, compressions of the elegiac spirit into a single memorable image is found in lines 305-7:

> A little while   the leaf is green;
> Then it fades,   and falls to earth,
> Molders there,   decays to dust.

In spite of the Christian nature of much of the material in *Solomon and Saturn II*, there is present a pervading sense of Necessity and law. Here and there the poet stresses those universals of human fate in comparison with which variations of experience lose significance. The wicked man may live longer than the good man. It is a matter of no ultimate importance. In the end death comes to all. A mother may bring forth twins to widely differing fortune. Man's destiny is not written in the stars by accident of birth, but is ordained by an all-ruling Fate not to be altered or predicted. Sunshine and riches are not equally distributed in this world. Nevertheless, in the end the unfortunate shall be rewarded according to his deserts. At one point in the dialogue Saturn's words become an echo of the old gnomic stress on certain of those universals of nature and human experience by which man's life is conditioned.

> Night is darkest of weathers;   Need, hardest of fates;
> Sorrow, heaviest of burdens;   Sleep, most like to death.

Throughout the poem, many of the characteristic features of the medieval 'contest of wit' are present. In addition to specific references to the contest in prologue and epilogue, the widely ranging and 'topical' nature of the material treated by question and answer is quite in accord with the conventions of the type. Nowhere is the spirit of the 'debate' more clearly indicated than by the employment here and there of the 'riddle' approach to topics presented for discussion. It is this element in the dialogue which is illustrated in one of the finest passages of the poem. In a section of ten lines Saturn introduces, in the form of a riddle, the theme of Old Age, the solution of which is set forth by Solomon in a passage of equivalent length. The enigmatic spirit of Saturn's references to Old Age is firmly and skillfully sustained throughout the series of suggested attributes. Nowhere is this more true than in the references to the power of the unknown force over stones, stars, gems, and water, a series which provides a keen-witted solver of the riddle with clues by which he could reject Death as a possible solution:

> Quoth Saturn:
> 'What is that Wonder   that fares through the world,
> Stalking inexorable,   shattering foundations,
> Wakening tears,   winning its way hither?
> Neither stone nor star,   nor sparkling gem,
> Wild beast or water   one whit shall escape it.
> Into its hand goes   the hard and the soft,
> The great and the small;   it seizes for food,
> Year after year,   of dwellers on earth,
> Of fliers in air,   of swimmers in ocean,
> Of numbered thousands   thrice thirteen.'
> Quoth Solomon:
> 'OLD AGE on earth   hath power over all;
> With punishing chains   for her battle-captives,
> With long-drawn fetters   she reaches far;
> With stretching cable   restrains what she will.
> The tree she shatters,   breaking its branches,

The standing trunk   she stirs from its place;
Smites it to earth,   consumes it thereafter.
She conquers the wolf,   and masters the wild bird;
She outlasts stones,   outlives steel,
Eats iron with rust;   so doth she to us.'[9]

Another enigma definitely phrased as such, the riddle of the
Book, is found in lines 221-8: 'Who (or what) is the dumb one
who dwells in a dale, very wise, having seven tongues, each
tongue having twenty points, each point having an angel's
wisdom whereby one may behold the gleaming walls of the
golden Jerusalem, and the joy-giving Cross?' The enigma ends
with the conventional riddle-formula: *Saga hwæt ic mæne*, 'tell
my meaning.' The wording of the whole suggests a work of religious learning, though varying interpretations could be made of
the 'seven tongues' and 'twenty points.' These details, however,
seem to have been considered clearly suggestive, for the poet
begins Solomon's answer with the words: 'Books are famous.'

Perhaps the most interesting feature of the Solomon and Saturn
dialogues is the fusion of tradition which they illustrate. Descended
from classical dialogue as reshaped in patristic literature for instructional purposes, the Solomon and Saturn poems, in their
riddles, 'hard' questions, and gnomic replies, include elements
characteristic of the medieval contest in wit and wisdom.

Even with this fusion of elements, and the inclusion in the
second dialogue of much pagan material, both dialogues are
firmly Christian poems. The first deals with the power of the
Pater Noster. The second has extended passages of Christian material, and references to such traditional or doctrinal themes as the
Fall of Lucifer, the Flood, the Last Judgment, and the Heavenly
Jerusalem. Lines 484-96 are devoted to the widespread belief in
a guardian angel that watches over the Christian soul. Indeed, the
poems are governed by religious design. For the dialogues are

9. *Solomon and Saturn II*, 273-92.

symbolic contests between the Christian and pagan ways of life, and the triumph of Christian knowledge is implicit in substance and design.

THE SOUL TO THE BODY

Two other religious poems exemplifying a tradition which continues throughout the medieval period, and which has illustration in Middle English literature, are the two poetical addresses of the Soul to the Body, one found in the Vercelli MS.,[10] the other in the Exeter Book.[11] The Vercelli poem, often referred to as *Soul and Body I*, is a poem of 166 lines in which, first a condemned soul, then a blessed soul, are imagined as addressing the bodies from which they have been separated by death. The text breaks off at the bottom of a page in the manuscript, the ending of the poem being lost as a result of one or more missing folios. The Exeter poem, *Soul and Body II*, is a variant of a portion of the Vercelli text. With the omission of four brief passages, the addition of two lines, and numerous differences in detail and arrangement, the Exeter version corresponds to the first 126 lines of the Vercelli poem, the portion dealing with the body and the damned soul. In the Vercelli text we have also an address of a blessed soul to its body, and, in possessing this, Old English poetry has one of the very few examples of the type in European literature.

In medieval tradition the *Soul and Body* poems fall into two structural types. In the first, the body makes no reply to the soul's denunciation for its sinful life on earth and the eternal misery which that life has visited upon the soul. The second type includes a reply, so that the poem develops not as a continuous 'address' but as a dialogue. Which type is earlier cannot be stated with certainty, but it seems likely that the structurally simpler 'address' may have antedated the dialogue form. Both types continue in

10. Fol. 101b–103b.
11. Fol. 98a–100a.

later medieval literature side by side. The two Old English poems
are 'addresses' in form, and afford early vernacular illustration of
this poetic type.

Thorpe, in editing the Exeter Book, stated categorically of
Soul and Body II that 'the original of the present poem is a prose
homily to be found in most of the MSS. (of which a Latin original,
no doubt, exists).' But it has never been clear what homily, or
what manuscripts, Thorpe had in mind in this reference.

Since the Vercelli poem, though incomplete, contains speeches
of both a damned and a blessed soul, it may serve as illustration of
Old English poetic treatment of this religious theme. The first
16 lines of the poem are introductory and homiletic, urging the
need of every man to think of the fate that will come upon his
soul when death divides it from the body. After death, moaning
in wretchedness, it shall return every seven nights for three
hundred winters to revisit its body, 'unless God shall earlier bring
the world to an end.' Stopford Brooke suggests[12] that this reference to three hundred years as the period during which the soul
shall return to haunt the body may reflect contemporary belief
that the world was to come to an end in the year 1000. On this
basis he is inclined to date the 'address' of the damned soul early
in the eighth century, and to regard the speech of the blessed soul
as a later and inferior addition.

The soul laments that ever it had to dwell in the body. In that
house of sin it seemed like thirty thousand years before death
could bring release. In worldly splendor exalted, the body lived on
earth proudly banqueting, sated with wine, while the soul thirsted
for God's body and the wine of the spirit. Now the body is no
dearer to the living, to father or mother or kin, than the black
raven. Deaf and dumb and joyless it lies. But the soul, tormented
with its sins, night by night must revisit its former home, turning

---

12. *History of Early English Literature*, p. 353.

away at cock-crow. 'In the great day when all things are revealed,' says the soul, 'it is you who must answer for us both. What then will you say to God in the Day of Judgment?' But the clay lies where it lay, and can make no answer, nor any promise of comfort or help!

The poem is notable for an attitude of mind not entirely unique in English poetry, but one seldom given such violent expression—a grim and bitter loathing of the flesh which goes beyond asceticism, and issues in a detailed, exhaustive, sadistic stress upon the processes of physical decay. Elsewhere in English poetry, it is true, the coffin-worm has emerged from darkness and corruption to add grimness to the printed page. For all his wise saws, Polonius lay in the end 'not where he eats, but where he is eaten: a certain convocation of politic worms are e'en at him. Your worm is your only emperor for diet.' But it is difficult to think of another passage in English verse which dwells in such detail upon the processes of physical corruption. Named and personified, the grave-worm, Gifer, captains his burrowing bands in loathsome regimentation:

> The head shall be cloven,   the hands disjointed,
> The jaws distended,   the palate severed,
> The sinews sucked,   the neck gnawed through.
> In bands, fierce worms   shall worry the ribs,
> Athirst for blood   shall banquet on the corpse.
> Into ten pieces   the tongue shall be torn
> To solace the hungry.   No more shall it speak
> In ready words   to the wretched soul.
> The worm's name is Gifer.   Its greedy jaws
> Are sharper than needles.   'Tis the first to descend
> Down into the grave;   it tears at the tongue,
> Bores through the teeth,   eats through the eyes
> Up into the head;   for other worms works a way
> To the banquet where the body   lies cold in the ground.[13]

13. *Soul and Body II*, 102-18.

In an illuminating essay on *Gifer the Worm*,[14] Kurtz has shown
how alien is such a passage to the spirit of classical antiquity, or
Northern paganism, or the writings of the early Christian Fathers.
But in the Book of Job are repeated references to corruption and
the worm,[15] sardonic and bitter, though lacking the detailed
realisms of the Old English poem. From this source, suggests
Kurtz, and perhaps influenced by some strain of Manichean contempt of the flesh, have come the grisly details of the Old English
text. Such, he believes, is the derivation of Gifer, the Worm, 'the
meanest and most grotesque symbol of hatred of the body, and
fear of a future life.'[16]

The speech of the blessed soul to the body is inferior to the
preceding lines. The situation lacks the dramatic elements of terror
and regret, and the verse loses correspondingly in force and
realism. The prevailing mood is one of pious thanksgiving for the
ascetic devotion of the body to the life of the spirit while still on
earth. The poem ends with a prophecy that soul and body will
once more be united in the Day of Judgment.

PRIDE and RESIGNATION

Two brief homiletic poems in the Exeter Book, the first 84
lines in length,[17] the second 118,[18] have to do with the general
themes of Pride, and Resignation. The lines on Pride begin with
an autobiographic passage which is not developed and has little
organic relationship to the body of the poem. In general type, the
poem is most nearly a 'character piece,' in the course of which the
author gives an extended and realistic description of a man in
whose nature Pride has become the effective force and governing
vice. The poet avails himself of the opportunity to trace this

14. *University of California Publications in English*, II, no. 2, pp. 235–61.
15. Job xvii. 14; xviii. 12-14; xix. 26; xxi. 26; xxiv. 20; xxxiii. 22.
16. Kurtz, op. cit. p. 261.
17. Fol. 82a–84b.
18. Fol. 117b–119b.

deadly sin to its origin in the angels who revolted and were cast out of heaven. The verse is consistently homiletic, though the 'character' or 'portrait' quality of certain lines elevates them above the general level of the poem. This 'portrait' passage is some 35 lines in length, but a brief selection will illustrate its quality:

> Proud at the banquet,   emboldened with wine,
> Working discord   with cunning words,
> Puffed up in power   and filled with pride
> He burns with envy   and insolent hate!
> Now you may know,   if you meet such a man,
> By these few intimations,   he's a child of the Fiend
> Appareled in flesh,   living perverted,
> A hell-destined spirit   hostile to God.[19]

No source is known, and it is probable that the poet was developing his theme in accordance with the general tradition of religious denunciation illustrated in Isaiah xxviii. 1-4.

The poem which Dobbie refers to as *Resignation*[20] has been variously entitled, Wülker designating it simply as one in a series of prayers, others calling it 'The Exile's Prayer,' or 'The Exile's Lament.' It is in fact a prayer rather than a lament, but a prayer in which both mood and matter reflect influence of the penitential Psalms. The religious spirit, therefore, is by no means completely suggested in the title, *Resignation*. The poem has throughout a sustained subjectivity, and the simplicity and sincerity of its personal revelations are noteworthy qualities. The author of the prayer is not to be thought of as an actual exile in the sense in which that bitter fate is set forth poignantly and at length in the *Wanderer*. The 'exile' imagery[21] is employed symbolically to represent the sorrow and wretchedness of mortal life and the spiritual isolation of one whose past deeds have spurned the good, and cut

---

19. *Pride*, 40-49.

20. Krapp and Dobbie, *Anglo-Saxon Poetic Records*, iii: *The Exeter Book*, pp. 215-18.

21. *Resignation*, 88 ff.

him off from the love of God. The poem ends with a two-line tag of gnomic stress upon the need and virtue of resignation or en- durance.

HOMILETIC VERSE

The homiletic poem of 102 lines known as *The Order of the World*[22] is a loosely organized and uninspired versification of familiar Christian themes. The opening lines have the intimate, instructional tone generally characteristic of Old English homiletic verse. Idiom and diction throughout are suggestive of the Cyne- wulfian vocabulary, but the lack of structural design and poetic inspiration place it among the inferior productions of those who wrote in Cynewulf's manner. Lines 38-85 present a somewhat unbalanced treatment of the Creation, in which precisely half the passage is devoted to a glorification of light, and accompanying descriptions of the rising and setting of the sun. The concluding lines set forth briefly the joys of the blessed in the heavenly life, admonishing every man to spurn the idle lusts and fleeting delights of this world, that he may come at last into the better kingdom.

The Exeter Book contains an alliterative versification of the Pater Noster; two others are preserved in manuscripts in the Corpus Christi Library,[23] and in the Bodleian.[24] The Exeter Book version is the briefest, and probably the earliest. The prayer occurs side by side in the manuscript with three other brief religious fragments. The nine lines of *Alms-giving*[25] stress the efficacy of alms-giving in healing the wounds of evil and purging the sinful soul. Eight lines of verse dealing with the size of the army with which Pharaoh attacked God's people[26] begin with the formula *Saga mē hwaet*. It is likely, therefore, that these lines are a frag-

22. Exeter Book, fol. 92b–94a.
23. MS. 201.
24. MS. Junius 121.
25. Fol. 121b–122a.
26. Fol. 122a.

mentary survival from some poem of the dialogue or question-and-answer type, of which the *Solomon and Saturn* poems are illustrations. Another religious fragment, 20 lines long,[27] seems obviously incomplete. It reads like an intended beginning of a strongly doctrinal versified homily, stressing as it does one faith, one baptism, one eternal Lord and Creator of mankind, from whom alone come surety and strength in this changeful world.

The *Counsels of a Father*,[28] possibly earlier in date than some of the homiletic material we have been considering, is a versification of ten admonitions in matters of moral conduct and manners, spoken by a father to a son. The instructional purpose of the author is evident and earnest, but the lines have no spark of poetic distinction. These homiletic counsels deal with ten different themes. There is, however, no correspondence with the Decalogue, save for the fact that lines 9 to 14 set forth the substance of the fifth commandment. It is possible that the phrase *fremdre mēowlan*, of line 39, is an echo of the 'strange woman' of Proverbs v. 20, as Ten Brink has suggested, for the *Counsels of a Father* illustrates a type of Christian homiletic verse which could well have been suggested, and influenced, by the Book of Proverbs.

The Descent into Hell

The *Descent into Hell* of the Exeter Book[29] is a poem of 137 lines, perhaps incomplete. In its description of the Harrowing of Hell it offers interesting contrast to the treatment of the subject in the *Christ and Satan* of the Junius MS. Both developments of the theme have ultimate derivation from the Apocryphal Gospel of Nicodemus.

The descent of Christ into hell is described in the heroic manner conventional for the theme in Old English verse. But in spite of

27. Fol. 122a–122b.
28. Exeter Book, fol. 80a–81a.
29. Fol. 119b–121b.

the traditional mood, the narrative begins with an unusually
sensitive passage in which the poet takes occasion to stress the
spiritual nature of the omnipotence by which hell and the powers
of darkness are overwhelmed:

> He needed no helmet-bearers for that battle, and
> wished no mail-clad warriors against those city-gates.
> The locks and barriers fell from the stronghold; the king
> rode into hell. . .
>   And John, in his wretchedness, beheld the Victor-Son
> of God with kingly following coming into hell. He per-
> ceived it was the approach of God himself. He saw the
> doors of hell shining with light which formerly had long
> been locked, and covered with darkness.[30]

The same poetic imagination which in the opening lines rejected physical armor as an inappropriate symbol of spiritual warfare is responsible for the vividly flashing detail which confers
sudden distinction on the final lines of this passage. There are few
more memorable images in Old English religious poetry than the
picture of the doors of hell, so long shrouded in black darkness,
suddenly shining with light at the approach of the Redeeming
God.

There follows a long speech of Adam in which he greets the
Savior. It includes apostrophes in the Cynewulfian manner to
Gabriel, Mary, Jerusalem, and the river Jordan, and glorifies the
significance in the Christian drama of the Annunciation, Nativity,
and Baptism. Ending with this material, the poem contains no
reference to the release of the patriarchs, and in this respect differs
from *Christ* 558-85, and from the Harrowing of Hell in *Christ and
Satan*.

Doomsday

In this group of minor religious poems must be included two
poems on the Last Judgment. The first, a poem of 118 lines, is

30. *Descent into Hell*, 37-40; 50-55.

found in the Exeter Book;[31] the second, 305 lines long, in MS.
201 of Corpus Christi Library, Cambridge. The subject matter of
these poems is in general the traditional material which is presented more elaborately, and with epic development, in the third
part of the *Christ*.[32]

The *Doomsday* of the Exeter Book need not detain us. It deals
briefly with material which in *Christ III* is expanded into a long
poem, and the shaping spirit is homiletic rather than epic or
dramatic. The Exeter *Doomsday* lacks the imaginative energy
which gives brilliance to the Doomsday lines of the *Christ*.

The Corpus Christi *Doomsday* is a much finer poem. It is based
upon a Latin poem, *De Die Judicii*, which has been attributed both
to Bede and to Alcuin,[33] and the reliance of the Old English upon
the Latin text is noted in the comment written at the top of page
161 of the MS.: *Incipiunt versus Bede presbiter de Die Judicii;*

> *Inter florigeras fecundi cespites herbas,*
> *Flamine ventorum resonantibus undique ramis.*

Since the Old English lines follow their original somewhat
closely, the substance and structure of the poem cannot be credited
to the imaginative design of the Old English poet. Nevertheless,
the Corpus Christi *Doomsday* displays a deft and sensitive craftsmanship. The translation of the opening lines of *Inter florigeras* is
done with creative spontaneity and zest. The result is a passage of
nature poetry unique in Old English verse. The borrowed nature
images are reproduced with lyric grace, and express a romantic
joy in nature which is more frequently met in Middle English
than in Old English poetry. There is artistry of a high order in the
poet's rendering of the change in mood, by which delight in the
natural scene is darkened to dread and fear by the wind and tumult

31. Fol. 115b–117b.
32. ll. 867–1664.
33. For the Latin text, see Lumby's 'Be Domes Dæge,' *Publications*, E.E.T.S., No.
65, pp. 22–6.

that herald the approaching storm. Simply as it is versified, the passage catches the full symbolic value of the storm as a prophecy of the destruction of earth's joys in the cataclysmic might of Doomsday.

> Lo! I sat alone   in a leafy bower
> Deep in a wood   and sheltered in shade,
> Where welling waters   murmured and wandered
> Through a lovely meadow,   all as I tell.
> There flowers gay   were budding and blooming
> In a throng together   in that sweet expanse.
> Then trees began tossing   with roaring sound,
> The clouds were driven by dreadful winds,
> And my sad spirit   was sorely troubled.
> Suddenly fearful,   with sorrow of soul
> I began to sing   those doleful verses,
> All as you said;   I remembered my sins,
> The evils of life,   and the long hour
> Of the dark coming   of death in the world.
> Greatly I dread   the Day of doom
> Because of the evil   I have done on earth.[34]

Depending as it does upon the material and structural organiza-tion of the Latin poem, the *Doomsday* differs widely from *Christ III*. The Judgment section of the *Christ* is a descriptive panorama objectively conceived and dramatically rendered. But Doomsday, as set forth in the Corpus Christi text and in the Latin poem on which it is based, is subjectively realized, the poet in each in-stance looking forward to the Judgment with highly personalized emotion. The subjective note is struck at the beginning in the nature prelude we have noted, and continues with the author's reference to the 'doleful verses' to which his troubled spirit gives voice. It is notably present in a passage beginning at line 26 in which the mood of penitence and remorse is expressed in the imagery and with the emotional fervor of the penitential psalms:

34. *Doomsday*, 1–16.

the beating of the breast, the cheeks wet with tears, the prostration in the dust. It has illustration in lines 65-70 where the poet demands of his wretched heart and sinful tongue why they delay in seeking forgiveness while there is still time for repentance. It is dramatically set forth in an address to the sinful flesh which parallels in mood and imagery the arraignment of the body by the damned soul in the *Soul to the Body*.

Central in the poem (ll. 92-150) is a rehearsal of the conventional signs of Doomsday: the quaking of earth, the crumbling of mountains and darkening of sun, moon, and stars, the hurtling flame that fills the universe, the coming of the heavenly hosts and all mankind to the Judgment, with the revelation of every secret and hidden thought, word, and deed.

There follows a description of the torments of hell which is marked by the same grimness of horror that is noteworthy in *Christ and Satan*. The souls of the damned shall burn in the fires of hell with serpents feeding upon their hearts. The eyes of sinners shall weep for the dreadful, torturing heat; their teeth shall chatter in alternating throes of bitter cold. One loathsomely realistic detail not found in other Old English verse-descriptions, though present in the homilies, is the reference to the perpetual stench of foul odors in hell, which add to the torment of the damned.

In contrast, the life of perfect joy in the heavenly kingdom is eloquently described, not only in its positive attributes, but also by the traditional list of afflictions and tribulations which condition mortal existence, and of which the heavenly life is free. Both the material and the rhetorical structure include the conventional elements noted in Lactantius' description of the Earthly Paradise, and illustrated in Old English homiletic and poetic visions of the life of the blessed:

> Black night shall never darken there the brightness of
> the heavenly light, nor shall sorrow come, or pain, or old
> age with its afflictions, or toil, or hunger, or thirst, or

fitful sleep. There shall be no fever or sickness, no sudden pestilence, or burning of fire, or fearful cold. There shall be no sadness or weariness, no decay or grief or savage torment, no lightning or terrible storm, no winter or crashing thunder, no cold or bitter hail-storm mingled with snow. There shall be no poverty or loss, or dread of death, no misery or affliction, nor any mourning, but peace shall rule there with power, justice with eternal goodness, glory and honor, worship and loving concord, and eternal life.[35]

The poem concludes with a vision of the various orders of the heavenly host, the saints and angels, patriarchs and prophets in a garden of roses in the midst of the Holy City. There also is a maiden band of bright damsels adorned with blossoms, round about Mary, the Virgin and Mother of God. The vision is simply told but, perhaps by its very simplicity, attains a strain of lyric adoration. In this realm of holiness and beauty the souls of the blessed find their everlasting home. 'If one tells truth,' so ends the poem, 'what hardship can there be in this life, if thereby we can come to live eternally in light among that host, and in those heavenly mansions have bliss henceforth forever?'

THE GRAVE

Outstanding in this collection of minor verse is a poem commonly known as *The Grave*, and described by Thorpe as 'singularly impressive and almost appalling.' It was first edited by Conybeare in *Archaelogia*[36] in 1814, and later presented in his *Illustrations*. Thorpe included it in the *Analecta Anglo-Saxonica.*[37] The poet Longfellow translated it. A revised text, based on a restudy of the MS., was printed by Schröer in 1882.[38] The poem

35. *Doomsday*, 253-70.
36. xvii, 173-5.
37. Page 153 ff.
38. *Anglia*, v, 289-90.

is preserved on page 170[a] of a Bodleian manuscript of hymns and sermons catalogued as MS. Bodleian 343. It is a very late specimen of Old English verse, displaying many evidences of transition to Middle English linguistic forms. The handwriting is of the twelfth century. The last three lines were subsequently added on the lower margin in a thirteenth-century hand.

The theme of the poem is a description of the grave as the dwelling appointed for man before he is born, a dwelling dark and cold, with low sills and low ceiling, of which Death holds the key. A trenchant brevity of phrase and sustained vigor of imagination combine to give the lines a startling and grim precision of imagery which make them memorable.

It has been somewhat generally assumed that *The Grave* belongs in the 'Soul and Body' tradition. Kleinert[39] pointed out that certain lines are identical with lines in the Worcester 'Fragments,' which set forth speeches addressed by a soul to its body. Estimating *The Grave* as older, he regarded it as the source of the 'Fragments.' Buchholz, in a later study,[40] considered *The Grave* 'a further fragment of the poem preserved in the Worcester Fragments.' Both assumed that *The Grave* is a 'Soul and Body' poem.

A more convincing interpretation of the facts is that set forth by Louise Dudley in 1914.[41] Regarding *The Grave* as a poem of 22 lines complete in itself, she shows that both in tone and substance it displays marked differences from the 'Soul and Body' poems. In the typical 'address' of the soul to the body, 'the power lies in the recognition of the fact that the miserable plight described could have been avoided; it was the result of sin. The power of *The Grave* lies in the fact that it is describing the fate of every one, saint as well as sinner.'[42] In this sense, the *Grave* is

39. *Über den Streit zwischen Leib und Seele*, Halle, 1880.
40. 'Die Fragmente der Reden der Seele an den Leichnam in Zwei Handschriften zu Worcester und Oxford,' *Erlanger Beiträge*, II, Heft VI, 1890.
41. *Modern Philology*, XI, 429–42.
42. Dudley, op. cit. p. 439.

perhaps hardly to be considered a Christian poem. Certainly, its
spirit is stoic. It deals with the great universal of human fate, and
from a contemplation of it derives lines which are probably the
most trenchantly grim in the whole range of Old English verse.
Once read, *The Grave* is not easily forgotten:

> For you was a house built   before you were born,
> Earth marked out   ere you came from your mother.
> But it was not made ready,   nor the depth of it reckoned,
> Nor yet was it measured   how long it must be.
> Now men bring you   where you needs must lie;
> Now men measure you,   and the mold thereafter.
> This house of yours   is not timbered high,
> But low and level,   when you lie therein.
> Low are the sills,   and low the side-walls;
> Close to your breast   the roof is built.
> Full cold shall you lie   in that lodging of mold,
> Dark and dim;   the den decays,
> A house without doors,   and dark within.
> Long you'll be locked there,   and death has the key.
> Loathsome that earth-house   and hateful to live in;
> There you shall bide   and be wasted by worms.
> Thus are you laid,   leaving your dear ones,
> And never a friend   will fare to see you,
> Or ever look   how you like the house,
> Or undo the door,   and descend to join you,
> For soon you'll be loathsome   and hateful to see.
>
> Soon shall your head   be despoiled of hair,
> And all the fairness   of your locks be faded;
> Soft fingers shall stroke it   never again.

XII. THE HISTORIC BATTLE POEMS

Brunanburh; Maldon

THE year 782 may be taken as a convenient date from which to note the decline of the Northumbrian and Mercian culture, and the dwindling of that stream of Northern verse which had been one of its characteristic expressions. It was the year in which Alcuin left the School of York to enter the service of Charlemagne, first as Master of the Palace School at Aachen, and subsequently as Abbot of Tours.

Under the wise administrative guidance of Archbishop Ecgberht of York (732-66) and his learned successor, Æthelberht, the School of York had attained a prestige which attracted not only the youth of England, but eager scholars from the Continent as well. Alcuin's presence there had added lustre to the fame of an institution widely known for its fine collection of books, and for the variety and excellence of its program of studies. References in Alcuin's *De Pontificibus et Sanctis Ecclesiae Eboracensis* indicate the range of that program, which in its stress upon grammar, rhetoric, arithmetic, geometry, astronomy, music, and a knowledge of canon law, constituted a medieval scholarship which blended the liberal arts of classical tradition with a study of the Scriptures and the writings of the early Christian Fathers.

The loss of Alcuin was paralleled in the same year, 782, by the death of Æthelberht, a misfortune of the first magnitude to the School he had so zealously and wisely fostered. Darkest disaster of all for the culture of which York was the center and symbol was the prolonged Danish onslaught, and Scandinavian settlement of the North and East, which set the prevailing trend of the ninth century in England.

An entry in the *Anglo-Saxon Chronicle* for the year 793, eleven years after Alcuin left England, records the first of the Danish raids on the coast monasteries of Northumbria. 'The harrowing inroads of heathen men,' says the *Chronicle*, 'made lamentable havoc in the Church of God at Lindisfarne by rapine and slaughter.' A year later came a similar raid upon Jarrow and Wearmouth. During the next five decades the *Chronicle* continues to record Danish attacks of increasing severity. The change from raids to permanent encampment on English soil is indicated by an entry for 866, which describes the coming of a large heathen army into England who 'fixed their winter quarters in East-Anglia, where they were soon horsed, and the inhabitants made peace with them.' This was the Danish host which in the following year made its fury felt throughout Northumbria, marching 'over the mouth of the Humber to the Northumbrians as far as York. . . Then was there an immense slaughter of the Northumbrians. . . The survivors made peace with the army.'

The ruthless fury of the warfare by which the Danes overran northern and central England, with the attendant destruction of monasteries, is tragically illustrated in the description, in the *Chronicle* for 870, of the ruin of Medhamsted to which the Scandinavian forces came 'burning, and breaking, and slaying abbot and monks and all that there they found. They made such havoc there that a monastery which was before full rich was now reduced to nothing.'

Brief and barren of detail as the entries in the *Chronicle* often are, they amply indicate the storm of bloodshed and ruin which swept over Northumbria and the Midlands. The very silence of the records is often more eloquent than words. The blood-stained years in which priests were slain at their altars, and scholars at their books, were little conducive to the fostering of learning, or the writing of poetry. Even of what had been written much of incalculable worth must have perished in the widespread devastation.

In no record do we have a clearer picture of the havoc wrought by the Danes, and the wholesale destructiveness of its impact upon the learning and culture of England, than is contained in the well-known statement of Alfred the Great in his Preface to the translation of Gregory's *Cura Pastoralis*. In that document Alfred reviews the vanished glory of an age when England had prospered 'in war and in wisdom,' that is, when she had had strength to defend herself against attacks from without, and to foster and maintain the scholarship of which York and other monastic schools were the centers. In those happier days men had come to England to seek learning. 'Now,' writes Alfred, 'we ourselves must go abroad to get it.'

Dark as is the picture, the light of learning had not been wholly extinguished. In the conquest of York in the autumn of 867, some of the precious manuscripts must have escaped destruction. The City eventually became the seat of established Danish rule over all Northumbria, and in the more ordered state of the northern kingdom portions of the ancient literature and learning were preserved. Whatever escaped the wholesale devastation of the Northumbrian monasteries, if it had scholarly or literary value, would naturally have found its way to York for safekeeping, just as the survivals of the burned and pillaged collections of Mercia may have drifted to Worcester. It was perhaps from these two centers chiefly that manuscripts were later carried southward, contributing to the West Saxon Renaissance of learning under Alfred at Winchester.

As one reads of the desperate defense of England throughout the ninth century, and the gradual winning back of occupied territory which characterized the tenth, it seems altogether appropriate that the final strains of Old English poetry should sing of the glory of historic battles. We have inherited from the tenth century two notable poems which celebrate respectively the battle of Brunanburh in 937, and the battle of Maldon in 991.

BRUNANBURH

The *Battle of Brunanburh* is one of a group of short poems or lays in praise of royal personages, or historic events, included among the entries in the Anglo-Saxon Chronicle.[1] Aside from the *Brunanburh* these metrical insertions in the *Chronicle* are of little poetic worth. Such significance as they possess lies rather in their mood of dawning national consciousness than in any literary merit.

In *Brunanburh*, however, patriotic emotion and a sense of national destiny receive distinguished and memorable expression in poetic form. The poem has sometimes been misinterpreted. It has been criticized for its failure to name individual heroes or recount individual exploits in the battle. Its lack of evidence that the author had been in any way personally concerned in the event he describes, as participant or eyewitness, has been adversely contrasted to the detailed and spirited realisms of the *Maldon*.

One reading of *Brunanburh* should be sufficient to reveal the true nature of the poem. It is not, and was not intended to be, a detailed description of a battle scene. It is rather a chant of triumph, a paean of victory, celebrating an engagement which had impressed itself on the English consciousness as one of those decisive military successes that stand as milestones marking the development of national unity and the growth of national strength.

The battle at Brunanburh was the most famous battle of the reign of Æthelstan, the grandson of Alfred the Great.[2] The victory was the more significant in a national sense because of the authority he claimed. In addition to his power as King of the West

1. For the years 937, 942, 973, 975, 1036 and 1065.
2. For various notices of the battle in English and other records see Alistair Campbell, *The Battle of Brunanburh*, Appendices III, IV, and V, pp. 147–62.

Saxons, Æthelstan had extended his rule northward over Mercia and Northumbria. The Welsh and the Anglo-Danes of Northumbria became increasingly jealous of his growing strength. In 937 Anlaf (Olaf), who may have been a son of a former Danish king of Northumbria, returned from Ireland with a fleet, if we can believe Simeon of Durham, of 615 ships and a large army, inciting the Northumbrian Danes to an uprising against their West Saxon ruler. The rebellious Northumbrians were aided by the Britons of Strathclyde, and by a force of Scots under Constantine. Æthelstan and his brother Edmund led their troops northward to meet this challenge to the English power, and battle was joined at Brunanburh.

The precise location of Brunanburh has never been identified with certainty. There have been many theories as to the site,[3] these theories falling into two groups according as they do or do not accept the statement of Florence of Worcester that Olaf began his invasion by sailing into the mouth of the Humber. Of the western sites suggested two perhaps deserve special consideration: Burnswark in Dumfriesshire, and Bromborough in Cheshire about ten miles north of Chester and a mile from the Mersey River. Such evidence as is afforded by the history of place-names seems to point to Bromborough, since it alone of the various place-names suggested has in the early charters, among other variants, the form *Brunaburh*. In a recent study, A. H. Smith remarks: 'The formal identity of Bromborough and Brunnanburh is fairly certain. Apart perhaps from Burnswark (Dumfries), evidenced as *Burnyswarke* from 1542 . . . , it is the only name where the connection has been established, and along with Burnswark it merits close attention as a likely site for the battle of Brunnanburh.'[4] In favor of the site of Bromborough or Burnswark it has

---

3. See Campbell, *The Battle of Brunanburh*, pp. 58–9, note 4.

4. A. H. Smith, 'The Site of the Battle of Brunnanburh,' *London Medieval Studies*, 1, 56–9, 1937, p. 59.

been argued, by those who discount the statement of Florence of Worcester about the Humber, that so large a ship-army from Dublin would have been more likely to land on the west coast than to sail around Scotland, or through the English Channel.

The battle of Brunanburh was stubbornly fought, with great slaughter on both sides. In the end, the huge forces which had been marshaled against the West Saxons were decisively defeated. By his victory Æthelstan firmly established his position as King of all England.

This was the event the glory of which the poet has undertaken to celebrate. The poem reveals a sophisticated style appealing to a courtly audience, and a skillful use of the traditional elements which moulded the spirit of the ancient battle-poetry. The hewing of the shield-wall with the edge of the sword, the fall of doomed men pierced by spears, or shot over shield, the day-long pursuit of the foe with mill-sharpened blades, the scavenging eagle, raven, and wolf, these familiar details are skillfully knit into the texture of the verse. The characteristic Old English irony of understatement conventional in the older poetry is present here. The Mercians 'did not refuse hard handplay to any man.' Constantine 'had no cause to boast of the clash of swords!' The West Saxons turned home in triumph leaving to their feast of carrion the ancient scavengers of the field of war. Never had there been greater slaughter in battle since the Angles and Saxons came to England!

A sense of the epic importance of Brunanburh as a heartening symbol of national power marks the spirit and shapes the structure of the poem. The poet measures the significance of the battle in contrast to all other heart-stirring triumphs since first the Angles and Saxons came to Britain. With the exception of the conventional and appropriate laudation of the leaders, Æthelstan and Edmund, the victory is set forth, not in terms of individual deeds of courage or endurance as in *Maldon*, but as an effective triumph

of the united and, in some sense, national power of the West
Saxon army. To the Old English poet the battle was a never-to-
be-forgotten victory in which the sons of Edward had won eternal
glory in defending their land, their hoard, and their homes:

> Æthelstan King,   lord of earls,
> Ring-bestower,   and also his brother,
> Edmund ætheling,   won with the sword-edge
> Lifelong glory   in battle at Brunanburh.
> They cut their way   through the wall of bucklers,
> Hacked the war shields   with hammered blades.
> Such was the way   of the sons of Edward,
> Ever in battle   with every foe
> Defending their land,   their hoard, and their homes.
> Foemen fell,   the Scottish squadrons,
> The ship-warriors also,   doomed to death.
> The field was wet   with the blood of battle
> From the hour of dawn   when the shining sun,
> God's radiant candle,   rose over earth,
> Till the noble creation   sank to its setting.
> Wounded with spears   lay many a warrior,
> Many a northern man   shot over shield;
> The Scotsmen likewise   sated with war.
> All day long   the West Saxon army
> Followed the track   of the hated foe,
> Pursuing, smote them   with sharp-edged swords.
> To none did the Mercians   refuse hard handplay
> Of those who with Olaf   over the sea
> Sought this land   in their broad-beamed ships,
> Fated in war.   Five young kings
> Fell on the battle field   slain with swords;
> Also seven   of the earls of Olaf
> And a countless number   of shipmen and Scots.
> The prince of the Northmen   was put to flight,
> With a little band   beaten back to his boat.
> The ship was launched;   the king set sail
> On the fallow surges,   and saved his skin.

Likewise also   the aged Constantine
Fled in haste   to his home in the North;
The white-haired warrior   had no need to boast
Of that crossing of swords.   He was shorn of kinsmen,
Stripped of friends   struck down in the fighting
On the field of carnage.   There mid the corpses
He left his son,   a stripling in battle,
Broken with wounds.   The gray-headed warrior,
The crafty old captain,   had no cause to boast
Of the clash of swords,   nor had Olaf any!
With the few that were left   they had no need to laugh,
Or boast they were better   in works of war,
On the field of battle,   mid clash of banners,
The crashing of fighters,   the casting of spears,
In the storm of weapons,   the carnage of war,
When they fought their fight   with the sons of Edward.
Then the Northmen embarked   in their well-nailed boats,
The bloody survivors   of battle-spears,
Over Dinges Water   returning to Dublin,
Back to Ireland,   broken in mood.
Likewise also   the brothers together,
King and prince,   returned to their people,
To the West Saxon country,   proud of the war.
They left behind them,   to feast on the fallen,
The dark raven,   dusky-coated,
With horny beak,   and the ash-feathered eagle
With white tail,   and the war-hawk greedy,
Gorging on carrion,   and that gray beast,
The wolf in the wood.   Nor of greater slaughter
In all this island   was tale ever told
By book or scholar,   or more folk felled
Slain by the sword,   since hither from eastward
The Angles and Saxons   sailed over sea,
Over broad billows   seeking out Britain,
Great-hearted war-smiths   eager for honor
Who harried the Welshmen   and held the land.

MALDON

The *Battle of Maldon* was preserved in a manuscript of the Cotton collection catalogued as MS. Otho A, xii. Fortunately, the text was printed by Hearne in 1726, since five years later, in the Ashburnham House fire which did so much damage to the famous collection, the manuscript was destroyed. As the poem has been transmitted, the beginning and ending are missing, apparently as a result of leaves lost from the manuscript, and it is impossible to say with any certainty how much of the text is gone. The structure of the poem and the treatment of material seem to indicate that perhaps the missing portions were not of great length.

The *Maldon* celebrates a glorious defeat, as *Brunanburh* celebrates a great victory. The heroic stand of Byrhtnoth and his death in the battle are referred to in later chronicles, but as to the battle itself we have little trustworthy information other than the account contained in the poem. The most extended reference to Maldon in the *Anglo-Saxon Chronicle* is given in the Parker MS. under date of 993; briefer notices in the other MSS. are dated 991. The Parker MS. entry is as follows:

> In this year came Olaf[5] with ninety-three ships to Stan, and laid waste the country round about, and from there he went to Sandwich, and so into Ipswich and harried all the country. And then he came to Maldon where the ealdorman Byrhtnoth with his force came to meet him and fought against him. And they slew the ealdorman there and were masters of the field of battle, and afterwards peace was made with them, and the King received him at the Bishop's hands.

A *Life* of Archbishop Oswald of York, written not long after the battle, has a florid account of Byrhtnoth's heroic leadership; and there are somewhat extended references to the battle in the

5. Possibly the Norwegian Olaf Tryggvesson.

twelfth-century *Histories* of Ramsey (Chap. LXXI), and Ely (II, 6).
Both the battle and Byrhtnoth's death are mentioned by Florence
of Worcester.

Byrhtnoth was a wealthy and powerful ealdorman of Essex,
named in the poem as 'son of Byrhtelm.' His family may originally have been Mercian. In any case, he came of a distinguished
line and, both in his own right and by marriage, possessed wealth,
power, and prestige. He was one of the great landholders of his
time, owning estates in at least eight counties. He enjoyed the
favor of King and Church and exercised wide political influence
and leadership. Charters are extant which bear his signature, none
later in date than 990.

Gordon has pointed out that 'Byrhtnoth did not spring into
fame as the hero of Maldon; he was one of the great men of his
generation, one of the most powerful among the ealdormen,
prominent in politics at the time of the anti-monastic reaction;
and famed as a zealous defender of the monks and of his country.'[6]
He is praised in the *Liber Eliensis* for wisdom and courage, and
described as one under whose leadership the foremost men of his
district gladly enrolled 'because of his honorable character, so
that under his protection they might defend themselves the better
against the enemy.' Gordon conjectures that Byrhtnoth was born
about 926, and was therefore not far from sixty-five when he died
at Maldon. This estimate is in accord with the poet's reference to
him in line 169 as *hār hilderinc*.

In the *Liber Eliensis* much is made of his benefactions to the
monks of Ely, and his desire for burial there. When the Abbot
learned that the Danes had been victorious at Maldon, and that
Byrhtnoth had been killed and beheaded, he 'went to the field
with some monks, and seeking out the hero's body bore it back
to the church and buried it honorably, placing a round lump of
wax where the head should have been.' The body was probably

6. E. V. Gordon, *The Battle of Maldon*, p. 15.

later removed to Ely Cathedral. The tradition as to the beheading of Byrhtnoth was apparently confirmed in 1769 by an examination of the bones under his effigy in the Cathedral. According to a report made to the Society of Antiquaries in 1772, no head was found, and 'it was observed that the collar bone had been nearly cut through, as by a battle axe or two handed sword.'[7]

The entry in the Parker MS. of the *Chronicle* implies that the Viking force, which had plundered the coast of Kent, sailed up the Blackwater (Panta) and established a temporary base not far from Maldon. If the Viking leader was indeed the famous Olaf Tryggvesson, King of Norway 995-1000, it is highly probable that the invading force was composed chiefly or entirely of Norwegians.[8]

Until quite recently it has not been possible to identify clearly the field upon which Maldon was fought, or to make a reconstruction of the course of the battle which would harmonize with certain specific details given in the poem. The location suggested by Freeman,[9] and for some time generally accepted, quite clearly does not fit the description of the battle as outlined by the Old English poet. Freeman supposed that the Vikings were south, and Byrhtnoth's forces north, of the river at a point above the estuary and not far from the town of Maldon. An old bridge standing near the church at Heybridge marked the site, he believed, of the *bricg* over which Byrhtnoth permitted the Danish force to cross.

In 1925, E. D. Laborde re-examined this question of site, and suggested a location of the battlefield which accords in all important particulars with the implications of the poem.[10] He supposes that the Vikings sailed up the estuary of the Blackwater as far as Northey Island, a little distance below Maldon, and on the

7. See Gordon, op. cit. p. 21.
8. The Old English poet refers to the invaders as 'Danes,' employing the term according to the convention of the time in the broad sense 'Scandinavian.'
9. *Norman Conquest*, I, 271.
10. *English Historical Review*, XL, 161 ff.

island established a temporary base. The main current of the
Blackwater flows along the northern side of the island, and a
branch of the river, now known as Southey Creek, loops around
the island on the south. From the western point of Northey
Island to the mainland, the bottom ridges up into a ford which is
partly exposed at low tide, but is still today completely covered
at high water. This ford, which in modern times has been built
up into a kind of causeway usable at low tide, is about 8 feet wide,
and stretches some 240 feet to the island, a distance across which
the Viking herald could easily have shouted the Danish demand
for tribute (29-41). This ford Laborde identifies as the *bricg* so
valiantly defended by Wulfstan, Ælfere, and Maccus (74-83), and
over which the Vikings were subsequently permitted to cross
(89-99). Laborde's hypothesis accords well with the text of
Maldon, which clearly refers to some kind of ford or shallow
crossing, since the phrases, *þā bricge* (74), *on þā bricge* (78), *aet
þūm forda* (81), and *ofer ðone ford* (88), are applied by the poet to the
same situation.

The poet states that, in crossing, the Vikings went 'west over
Panta.' This statement of westward movement has no meaning
in terms of Freeman's site, but accords precisely with the topog-
raphy of Laborde's. Another detail of the poem made intelligible
by Laborde's hypothesis is the statement in lines 64-6 that the two
armies were prevented from joining battle by the depth of water,
because with the rising tide 'the currents had locked' (*lucon
lagustrēamas*). This picture of conflicting currents meeting in a
tidal river would have precise application to conditions at the ford
in Southey Creek when the tidal waters push upstream.

The Old English poem on Maldon, as we have it, begins with
a reference to a young English noble, a kinsman of Offa, who at
the time of the Viking attack is engaged in the pastime of falconry.
Quickly convinced that Byrhtnoth will not tolerate cowardice,
or countenance slackness in defending the land, he lets his good

hawk fly off to the wood, and takes his place in the line of battle. This opening reference to hawking fits well with the battle site as identified by Laborde. Gordon points out that 'the muddy, shallow banks of the Blackwater attract numerous water-fowl and would be an ideal hawking-ground. The wood to which the hawk flew when released, and to which Godric and others fled, is not two miles away behind the English position.'[11]

There follows in the poem (17-24) an extremely detailed and realistic description of Byrhtnoth's marshaling of his forces. The old warrior, the poet tells us, rode about among his men, showing them how best to defend the ground, and bidding them grasp their shields firmly and have no fear. When he had mustered his troops, he lighted from his horse and took up position in the line of battle where his trusty hearth-companions would be fighting beside him. Brief as it is, the picture is one of intimate personal leadership swiftly made effective in the face of sudden and perilous challenge.

Before the battle began, a Viking herald 'stood on the river bank,' apparently, that is, on the western point of Northey Island near the end of the 'bricg,' or 'ford,' and arrogantly shouted the Norwegian demand for tribute. If Byrhtnoth will agree to a payment, the Vikings will 'take ship with the tribute, and put to sea, and keep the peace.' Byrhtnoth's reply was a contemptuous spurning of the Norwegian demand, and a spirited and ironic challenge to battle:

> Hear you, sea-rover, what my people say?
> The tribute they'll send you is tribute of spears,
> Ancient sword-edge and poisoned point,
> Weapons that avail you little in war!
> Pirate messenger, publish this answer,
> Proclaim to your people tidings more grim.
> Here stands no ignoble earl with his army

11. Gordon, *The Battle of Maldon*, p. 4.

Guarding my lord Æthelred's   country and coast,
His land and his folk.   The heathen shall fall
In the clash of battle.   Too shameful it seems
That you with our tribute   should take to your ships
Unfought, who thus far   have invaded our land;
You shall not so readily   rifle our treasure.
Sword-edge and spear-point   shall settle our account,
The grim play of battle,   ere tribute is granted.[12]

Byrhtnoth then stationed his forces on the river bank. But the tide was running in, the 'currents locked' across the ford, and neither army could attack the other except by the arrow-flights of the archers.

When at last the ebb-tide uncovered the 'bricg,' Byrhtnoth posted three of his bravest warriors, Wulfstan, Ælfere, and Maccus, to hold the ford. The Vikings found that they were faced by 'bitter bridge-wardens,' and sought permission to pass unopposed to the mainland in order to join battle there. In overconfidence, Byrhtnoth granted the request.

The Norwegians crossed to where the English force, in a 'war-hedge of shields,' stood waiting the attack. Then rose the din of battle. The raven and eagle circled above. Bows were busy, shield received point. There was tumult on earth.

Wulfmær, son of Byrhtnoth's sister, was early cut down in the conflict. Byrhtnoth himself, fighting where the battle was fiercest, slew two of the Norwegians, but was mortally wounded by a spear. As he lay upon the ground and the Vikings closed in about him, Byrhtnoth's last words were a thanksgiving to God for all the joys he had met on earth, and a prayer for the peace and salvation of his soul.

When it was seen that their leader had fallen, Godric, son of Odda, leaped upon Byrhtnoth's horse and galloped off to the wood. With his brothers he fled from the battle and saved his

12. *Maldon*, 45–61.

life. It was to this Godric, the poet says, that Offa had previously remarked in council that many were talking boldly who would not hold out when need came.

There follows, after the fall of Byrhtnoth, the most extended, and the most realistic, depiction of *comitatus* loyalty anywhere set forth in Old English literature. The general mood of the passage, and here and there a detail, seem reminiscent of the *Beowulf* poet's narrative of Wiglaf's loyal stand with his doomed leader. In one instance, indeed, the phrasing of the two texts is so similar that a line in the *Maldon* has been cited to justify an emendation in the *Beowulf*.[13] But the *Maldon* passage goes beyond all previous illustrations of the mood, and becomes the classic expression of the *comitatus* ideal.

It is Ælfwine, son of Ælfric, who after Byrhtnoth's fall reminds the retainers of their boasts on the mead-bench, and spurs them to renewed vows of vengeance or death:

> Then was fallen   the leader of the folk,
> Æthelred's earl;   and his hearth-companions
> All beheld   that their lord lay dead.
> Then forward pressed   the proud retainers;
> Fiercely charged   the fearless thanes.
> Each of them wished   one thing of two,
> To lose his life,   or avenge his lord.
> Ælfric's son   spurred them to battle,
> A warrior young;   in words that were bold
> Ælfwine spoke   with spirit undaunted.
> 'Take thought of the times   when we talked at mead,
> Seated on the benches   making our boasts,
> Warriors in hall,   concerning hard battle.
> Now comes the test   who truly is bold!
> I purpose to prove   my lineage to all men,
> That in Mercia I come   of a mighty clan;
> Ealhelm the name   of my aged father,
> A powerful ealdorman,   wealthy and wise.

13. See *Beowulf*, 2524–5, and *Maldon*, 247–8.

None shall reproach me   among that people
That I was willing   to slink from the strife,
Hastening home   when my lord lies dead,
Slain in the battle.   Of all disasters,
That to me   is the greatest of griefs,
For he was my kinsman;   he was my lord!'[14]

As one man, Byrhtnoth's retainers responded to the defiant appeal, devoting themselves to death. Dunnere shook his ash spear and urged on his comrades. Æscferth, the Northumbrian hostage, fought boldly beside them, dealing many a wound, as long as he could wield weapon. Leofsunu lifted up his linden shield and chanted his boast:

Not a foot of ground   will I ever give,
But I'll fight in the van   and avenge my lord.
Steadfast warriors   by the River Stour
Shall never have need   of words to reproach me,
Now my lord is fallen,   that lordless I fled,
Turned back from the battle   and went to my home;
But weapon shall take me,   sword-edge and spear.[15]

The poet calls the bloody roll of honor. Warrior after warrior is named, and his deeds recounted. Edward the Long fought in the forefront of battle, quick and keen; he broke the shield-wall and avenged his lord before he fell. So did Ætheric, Sibyrht's brother. Offa smote down a Viking, and was himself slain as he struck the blow. But he had made good his promise to his lord that they would ride home together or die together; he lay like a good thane beside his prince. Wigstan, Thurstan's son, slew three before he died. All the while, the two brothers, Oswald and Ealdwold, urged on the fight and heartened their comrades. Fighting shoulder to shoulder with the young and strong, the aged Byrhtwold glorified his last battle with that clarion call to

14. *Maldon*, 202-24.
15. ll. 244-53.

fortitude and heroic death whose echoes will never die while friendship and loyalty are dear, and men defend the things they love:

> Heart must be the hardier,   courage the keener,
> Mood must be the bolder,   as our band lessens!
> Here on the ground   our good lord lies,
> Butchered in battle.   Ever will he rue it
> Who now from this war-play   thinks to turn away.
> I am old in years.   I will never yield;
> But here at the last   beside my lord,
> By the leader I loved,   I look to lie.[16]

Few strains of a dying music have been more memorable than the simple and moving eloquence of these lines. They remain an unforgettable assertion of man's unconquerable courage in the face of adversity and earthly defeat. They embody the spirit of that ultimate choice by which death is eagerly preferred to those capitulations which surrender integrity. They set the mood for all hours of heroic striving in which deep-rooted and unshakable devotion to a moral imperative breeds a contempt for the odds of battle.

The words of Byrhtwold belong to the final measures of Old English poetry. It was a poetry conditioned by the changing standards of the age which produced it. If its range to a modern eye seems narrow, its currents ran deep. The earlier secular verse, rooted in the traditions of pagan centuries, reflected the folklore and legend, the heroic ideals, the tragic and conflicting loyalties, the stern necessities and savage wars of primitive Germanic society. It revealed, sometimes sharply and clearly, sometimes dimly and obscurely, the racial culture from which it grew. It preserved a partly buried treasure-trove of Continental folkway and tradition. It gave vigorous and continuous expression to racial character. Passage after passage stressing the ultimate imperatives

16. ll. 309-19.

of loyalty, courage, and vengeance establish the moral tone of this earlier secular verse.

With the conversion of England to the Christian faith came a new frame of reference for the thoughts and strivings of men, an enlargement of the scale of human values, a sensitizing of men's minds and moods, which swelled the currents of life, and varied and colored the play of poetic invention. To the early epic tales and songs of battle were added versifications of Biblical and Apocryphal themes, of homilies of the Christian Fathers, of lives of the saints, and martyrologies. The poetic mood turned from earlier forms to hymns of adoration, dream-visions, and prophetic verse. In this expansion, the reader is aware of the shaping energy of Christian learning, of the moulding force of Biblical exegesis and the Catholic liturgy, of the influence of hexaemeral and apocalyptic tradition, of early Christian allegory, of ecclesiastical dogma and doctrine.

This religious poetry has many reflections both of the classical and the medieval Christian cultures. It is not to be forgotten that the poetry of the eighth and ninth centuries was written at a time when men of learning read portions, at least, of the works of Aristotle and Cicero, or that Old English poetry contains elements which reflect the influence of Pliny, and Virgil. Alcuin's list of authors available in the Library at York includes their names, and Lucretius is cited, and a line from the Sixth Book of Lucretius quoted, by Isidore of Seville, whose writings influenced the *De Natura Rerum* of Bede.

With this definite classical strain was blended the learning of the medieval Christian tradition. Our survey of the religious poems has made clear the debt which Old English poetry owes to the writings of medieval scholars: to Alcuin and Augustine, to Gregory and Bede, to Boethius and Lactantius, and to many others. With this expression of the medieval Christian culture, strains of the earlier secular verse were blended and fused. Conventional elements of landscape and seascape, characteristic details of weather, a stereotyped imagery of warfare and loyalty and death, not only had these been used to enliven and embellish realistic passages of secular verse, but they survive as decorative elements in the religious poetry. Even in the story of the Temptation and Fall of man, as told in the comparatively late *Genesis B*, the causes and consequences of man's disobedience are set forth conditioned and simplified by ancient pagan concepts of loyalty.

Estimated as a whole, Old English poetry expresses in many ways the changing spirit of the age. It was a period during which the limited perspectives of a pagan world were being gradually widened by the Christian philosophy. The stark and primitive social codes expressive of Germanic folkways were being slowly transformed by the spiritual demands of Christian ethics. As the minds of men were liberalized, the Old English world began to find room for a way of thought which was less concerned with variety of human experience, or vicissitude of human fate, than with a conviction that God's kingdom is not of this world, and that the ultimate tragedies and triumphs are of the soul, and beyond death. It became possible for the poet of the Corpus Christi *Doomsday* to exclaim in all sincerity: 'If one tells truth, what can there be of hardship in this life, if thereby we may come to live eternally in light and in those heavenly mansions have bliss forever?'

If this earliest English poetry failed to achieve a fusion or reconciliation of these contending forces of temporal and eternal, if it did not always perceive that God's kingdom, if not of this world, still must be fought for here, not without blood and tears, what then? Has any age yet made perfect reconciliation of stubborn worldly fact with the dream which is the substance of things unseen?

It will still remain true, I think, for many readers who love this ancient verse, that it stands as a testimonial, even if an imperfect one, of a way of life reborn and reshaped by the life-giving touch of the Christian faith, and the ecclesiastical culture of the medieval Church. As these influences enfranchised the thoughts and moulded the lives of men, their poetry too was transformed. The dark legends and narrow codes of the pagan past died into silence, and poets sang with joy of a new way of life, and of the shining symbols which have served to shape the nature and destiny of the Christian world.

Of this Old English poetry much is excellent, some is timeless and immortal. The heartbreak of the elegies, the stout-spirited fortitude of the battle poems, the antique grace and energy of the Christian allegories, the gentle and lonely accents of Cynewulf, the terror and awe of the Judgment poems, the lyric adoration of the *Dream of the Rood*, such poetry is memorable in any age. Towering over all is the *Beowulf*. It is the greatest poetic achievement of its time, most closely approaching a fusion of Germanic, Classical, and Christian, most nearly achieving a reconciliation of worldly necessity with Christian striving. In it, as in the work of Cynewulf and his school, we find the most adequate poetic symbols of an age which touched life with the light of wider horizons, and shaped new hopes for the hearts of men.

APPENDIX

A. The Manuscripts

EXCEPT for a few scattered poems, the corpus of Old English verse has been preserved in four manuscripts which have come to be known as the *Beowulf* MS., Exeter Book, Junius MS., and Vercelli MS.

For a discussion of the significance of section numbering in Old English poetical manuscripts, see Bradley's article on *Beowulf* in the *Encyclopædia Britannica*, and his paper read before the British Academy, 24 Nov. 1915 (*Proceedings of the British Academy*, vol. VII). Basing his suggestion upon studies of *Beowulf, Genesis A, Genesis B, Exodus*, and *Elene*, Bradley conjectures that the section numberings in these poems indicate 'the separate sheets of the archetypal MSS.'

THE BEOWULF MANUSCRIPT

The manuscript volume which contains the text of *Beowulf* and *Judith* is lodged in the British Museum, and known as Cotton Vitellius, A. XV. A combination of two once separate codices, the manuscript contains nine Old English texts, four in the first codex, five in the second. The *Beowulf* (folios 129^a-198^b) belongs to the second codex, in which it is preceded by three prose texts, and followed by the *Judith*. It represents the work of two scribes of the tenth, or early eleventh, century, who were copying from an older manuscript, the first scribe writing out lines 1-1939; the second, the remainder of the poem, The text is not written as verse, but, as was customary in all the Old English manuscripts, in prose form; punctuation is sparse and uncertain, and there is no uniformity in the marking of long vowels. One gathers that the scribes were unlearned copyists, apparently not always under-standing what they copied.

The *Beowulf* manuscript found its way, in the early seventeenth century, into the library of Sir Robert Cotton. The first recorded mention of the poem was made by Wanley in his famous *Catalogue* in 1705, but the terms he used were such as to suggest that he had not read the poem, for his Latin note misrepresents it as a tale of 'the wars which Beowulf, a certain Dane, sprung from the royal stock of the Scyldings, waged against chieftains of Sweden.'

From 1712 to 1730 the Cotton library was lodged in Essex House in the Strand. The purchase of Ashburnham House, West-minster, by the Government in 1730 provided a new housing for the books and manuscripts of the famous collection. It was here that a disastrous fire broke out in 1731 which consumed almost all the printed books and destroyed or injured about 200 of 958 manuscripts. Unfortunately the *Beowulf* manuscript was among those injured. Its edges, scorched by the fire, were rendered brit-tle and subject to progressive deterioration.

It is a matter of good fortune that in 1787 Thorkelin, a Danish scholar, made a transcript of the text of the *Beowulf*, and later in the year had a second transcript made for him. Upon these tran-scripts he based the first printed edition of the *Beowulf* in 1815. Subsequent collation by Thorpe and Kemble of the text of this edition with the *Beowulf* manuscript showed that in the process of deterioration words and letters, visible when the Thorkelin tran-scripts were made, had become illegible or had disappeared. Ultimately steps were taken to preserve the manuscript from further disintegration, each leaf being separately inlaid, and the whole rebound. In 1882, under the auspices of the Early English Text Society, an autotype edition of the manuscript was pub-lished, with a text by Zupitza based on the manuscript and on Thorkelin's transcripts.

THE EXETER BOOK

The priceless Exeter Book has been since 1072 preserved in the Chapter Library of Exeter Cathedral. It is mentioned in the inventory or list of donations made to the Cathedral by Bishop Leofric, and is described as *ān mycel Englisc bōc be gehwilcum þingum on lēopwīsan geworht,* i.e. 'a large English book on various subjects composed in verse.' This Bishop Leofric, trained on the Continent in Lotharingia, had become in 1044 Chaplain and King's Chancellor to Edward the Confessor, and in 1046, on the death of Bishop Lyfing, was appointed to the combined episcopal sees of Devonshire and Cornwall, with his seat originally at Crediton and subsequently at Exeter.

The manuscript thus described as a 'large English book' at some time suffered serious damage. An uncertain number of leaves at the beginning, and seven leaves at scattered places throughout the codex, have been lost. The opening pages of the manuscript, as it now stands, are stained, apparently by a fluid, which has rendered doubtful a number of words on the first five leaves. The first page is badly scored by knife cuts, and the last fourteen pages have been mutilated, either by an ignited substance which fell upon the final page and burned its way into the book, or possibly by the corroding effect of damp. The signs of unusual wear upon the first and last pages of the manuscript indicate that it must have been some time without a binding. For the past two centuries it has been protected by a binding of leather-covered boards dating from about 1700. This has been recently replaced by a new binding.[1]

How large a portion of the Exeter manuscript is missing at the beginning we cannot know. There has been a somewhat general

1. A collotype edition published in 1933 for the Dean and Chapter of Exeter Cathedral, with descriptive and critical chapters by R. W. Chambers, Max Förster, and Robin Flower, has made readily available a facsimile of the Exeter Manuscript.

misapprehension that only seven leaves have been lost, since the present first page of the MS. is marked eight. This numbering, however, is modern and is explained by the fact that, since the loss of the original opening leaves, seven pages of alien manuscript have been bound into the codex, and the numbering of leaves made consecutive from the first page of this new material. It may be, however, that a very considerable portion of the original manuscript has been lost. Indeed, the fact that the manuscript was described in Leofric's inventory as a 'large book,' and that it now is a volume of moderate thickness, would seem to indicate that the loss may have been no small one.

The manuscript is beautifully written upon rather thin vellum in a late-tenth-century script, which has been described as the 'noblest of Anglo-Saxon hands,' achieving 'a liturgical, almost monumental effect by the stern character of its design, and the exact regularity of its execution.'[2] If it is to be assumed that more than one scribe was engaged upon the text, as has been suggested, this postulate rests upon variation in the quality, rather than upon difference in the character, of the script. The codex contains no illuminations or ornamentation other than a series of some sixty large initial letters, the secondary lines of which in some instances develop ornamental extension.

Among the four manuscripts, the Exeter Book is pre-eminent in the range and variety of the verse it contains. There is a large group of religious poems, two of which, the *Juliana* and *Christ II*, contain the runic signature of Cynewulf. Saints' legends are well represented by the *Guthlac* and the *Juliana*. The *Phoenix* is an excellent example of versified Christian allegory.

Side by side with this body of religious verse, the Exeter Book contains poems (*Widsith* and *Deor*) deeply rooted in Continental tradition, and a collection of *Riddles* which furnish an Old English

2. 'The Script of the Exeter Book,' by Robin Flower, pp. 83–90 of *Chapters on the Exeter Book*, 1933.

illustration in the vernacular of this established literary form. Here also we find the *Gifts of Men* and the *Fates of Men*. In addition, the Exeter Book contains a series of elegies, the *Wanderer, Seafarer Ruin, Wife's Lament,* and *Husband's Message,* which are the outstanding examples of Old English lyric verse.

THE JUNIUS MANUSCRIPT

About 1630 the manuscript that was later to be known as the Junius manuscript came into the possession of Archbishop Ussher of Armagh, and was by him presented to Francis Dujon of Leyden, librarian to Lord Arundel and known in literature as Junius. This manuscript contains four poems, the *Genesis, Exodus, Daniel,* and *Christ and Satan.* The codex is divided, however, into two parts only, *Genesis, Exodus,* and *Daniel* being written out as a single poem of 55 sections, and the 3 fragments of *Christ and Satan* as a single poem of 12 sections.

Because of a slight correspondence between Cædmon's *Hymn* and the opening lines of *Genesis,* and because also of a partial correspondence between the subjects ascribed to Cædmon by Bede and the themes of the poems in the Junius manuscript, the four poems were quickly accredited to Cædmon, and the whole referred to as 'Cædmon's Paraphrase.'

An edition was printed by Junius at Amsterdam in 1655, and the manuscript itself was returned to England. Later, with other manuscripts of Junius, it was lodged in the Bodleian Library at Oxford, where it is known as MS. Junius XI. The handwriting of the codex is apparently of the tenth century. The first three poems are in one handwriting; the *Christ and Satan* shows three other hands at work. The corrections throughout the entire manuscript are in a fifth hand. There are some missing folios.[3]

Of the four manuscripts, the Junius codex is the only one that

3. A facsimile reproduction of the Junius MS., with an Introduction by Gollancz, was published in 1927.

is illustrated. It contains 48 drawings scattered through the first 96 pages of the *Genesis*. Vacant pages throughout the remainder of the manuscript indicate that the series was not finished. The drawings which were completed may be later than the text of the manuscript, and have been dated as of the second quarter of the eleventh century. Two artists were at work, the drawings after the Flood showing more definite influence of the style of the Utrecht Psalter, in figure drawing and drapery.[4]

The *Genesis* drawings are probably of the Winchester school of the early eleventh century. Below the second drawing in the series is a portrait, framed in a medallion, and labelled *Ælfwine*. It may be, Morey suggests, that we have here to do with the patron of the work, and that this Ælfwine is to be identified with the churchman of the same name who became abbot of Newminster, near Winchester, in 1035.

THE VERCELLI MANUSCRIPT

The Vercelli Book, a manuscript of the late tenth or early eleventh century, at some time drifted from England to Italy, where it is lodged in the Cathedral library at Vercelli. Like the Exeter Book, it contains two runic signatures of Cynewulf, those of the *Elene* and *Fates of the Apostles*. Unlike the Exeter Book, which contains only verse, the Vercelli manuscript is a miscellany of poetry and prose homilies. In addition to the two signed Cynewulfian poems, it includes the *Andreas* and *Dream of the Rood* together with the *Soul's Address to the Body*, and a fragment of 27 lines of verse based on Psalm XXVIII.

There has been much speculation and conjecture to explain how this Old English codex could have made its way from England to

4. See 'The Illustrations of Genesis,' by C. R. Morey, in *The Cædmon Poems*, Kennedy, pp. 177–95.

northern Italy. Of various theories advanced, that which connects the manuscript with the name of an Italian Cardinal, Guala Bicchieri, seems the most plausible.[5] This Cardinal Guala was made Papal Legate, and in 1208 sent by Pope Innocent III to France. There, and subsequently in England, he served as agent in the endeavor of the Pope to prevent an attempted conquest of England by Philip, the Fair. In England, Guala supported King John, and on John's death assisted in the establishment of the claims of Henry III. He was honored by the new monarch, receiving as a benefice the Church of St. Andrew at Chesterton in Cambridgeshire. On his return to Italy Cardinal Guala founded in Vercelli a Cathedral church notably English in architecture (though the architect seems to have been French), and dedicated it to St. Andrew.

Cardinal Guala was a scholar and lover of letters. It is stated that among his books were two written in English script.[6] It is especially interesting to note that both his Chesterton benefice and the church which he founded in Vercelli were dedicated to St. Andrew. It may well be that the Vercelli manuscript came into Guala's possession precisely because of the importance which the saint had in Guala's ecclesiastical life, and because the Vercelli Book contained in the *Andreas* a long poem having to do with the mission of St. Andrew to Mermedonia. At his death in 1227 Guala left his library to the church which he had founded. While this explanation of the presence of the Old English manuscript in an Italian church library is conjectural, it is also plausible in its reasonable stress upon a set of circumstances which would make the presence of the codex at Vercelli in no way unnatural.

5. This theory was first propounded in an unsigned article in the *Quarterly Review*, 1845, lxxv, 398-9, written as a critical comment on H. G. Knight's essay, *The Ecclesiastical Architecture of Italy*.

6. See Krapp, *Andreas*, Introd., xiii.

OTHER MANUSCRIPTS

In addition to the body of Old English verse which is preserved in these four well-known codices, there are a few other poems, some of them highly important, which survived in other manuscripts.

Two important manuscripts were lost in the Ashburnham House fire of 1731, in which the Cotton collection suffered so much loss and damage. These were the manuscript of the *Rune Poem*, Cotton Otho B. x, the text of which Hickes had printed in his *Thesaurus* of 1705, and a manuscript containing the *Battle of Maldon*, Cotton Otho A, xii. Fortunately, the text of *Maldon* had been printed by Hearne five years before.

The text of the *Waldere* fragments and the *Finnsburg* fragment, we owe to the fact that the leaves on which they had been written were later used in the binding of volumes of homilies. The manuscript pages containing the *Waldere* fragments were discovered among loose leaves in the National Library at Copenhagen; the *Finnsburg* fragment in the Library of Lambeth Palace.

The so-called *Cotton gnomes*, 66 lines of characteristic gnomic verse, are preserved in the British Museum, Cotton MS. Tiberius B, I, 115a-b.

The *Solomon and Saturn* dialogues, and a fine *Doomsday* poem based on the *De Die Judicii* attributed to Bede, are all preserved in the Corpus Christi College Library at Cambridge. The first *Solomon and Saturn* debate is divided between MSS. 422 and 41. The second *Solomon and Saturn* poem is found in MS. 422. The *Doomsday* is preserved in MS. 201.

In addition to the Exeter version, two other alliterative versions of the Pater Noster have survived, one at Cambridge in the Corp. Chr. Coll. MS. 201; the other at Oxford in the Bodleian MS. Junius 121. At Oxford also is the *Grave* in the Bodleian MS. 343.

The *Brunanburh* and five other short poems on historic events were included among the entries in the *Anglo-Saxon Chronicle* for the years 937, 942, 973, 975, 1036, and 1065.

B. The Cynewulfian Signatures

Four poems, the *Juliana, Elene, Christ II,* and *Fates of the Apostles,* contain Cynewulf's signature in runic characters. These characters, ᚻ ᚱ ᚷ ᛗ ᚹ ᚢ ᛚ ᚠ, are the runic forms of the letters C Y N E W U L F. In two of the signatures, those in the *Christ* and the *Fates of the Apostles,* the letter *E* is omitted.

The ingenious nature of these signatures derives from the fact that each of the letters in the Old English runic alphabet had its name. The rune, therefore, could be employed both as a letter and as the word which is its name. In the *Elene, Christ II,* and *Fates of the Apostles* the runic letters stand out in the text and draw attention to the name they spell. But they are also used as words. When these passages are read aloud, as the name of each runic letter is pronounced, the word which is its name forms part of the text in which the rune is imbedded.

In the *Juliana* the method is different. There the runes seem to be used only as letters in three groups, each group, and the whole, referring to the poet and standing for his name. An alternative explanation of the *Juliana* signature assumes that the first two groups of letters, *CYN* and *EWU,* compose words which form part of the text, *CYN* rendered as 'mankind', and *EWU* as 'sheep'. One difficulty with this interpretation is that it leaves the *LF* runes standing alone as letters, since the word meanings which the poet attaches to these runes in each of the other signatures will not compound into an appropriate meaning in this instance.

For the establishment of the meanings of these runic characters, as used in Cynewulf's signatures, the most important document is the Old English *Rune Poem.*[1] The *Rune Poem* is probably of late date, and may have been based on a Scandinavian original. Its

---

1. Cotton MS. Otho B X, destroyed in the Ashburnham House fire of 1731.

interpretation of the runes, therefore, cannot in all cases be regarded as definitely conclusive with reference to their use in an Old English eighth-century poem.

As set forth in the *Rune Poem*, the meanings of the eight runes which spell Cynewulf's name are as follows: ᚻ (C), cēn-torch; ᚼ (Y), ȳr-bow; ᚾ (N), nȳd-need; ᛗ (E), eoh-horse; ᚹ (W), wynn-joy; ᚢ (U), ūr-bull; ᛚ (L), lagu-water; ᚠ (F), feoh-wealth.[2]

Five of these runes, those which represent *N, E, W, L,* and *F,* can be interpreted in the *Elene, Christ,* and *Fates of the Apostles* in the meanings assigned to them in the *Rune Poem.* The other three, *C, Y,* and *U,* require special attention.

The *C* and *U* runes were employed by Cynewulf as homonyms of the words which were their names. By this use, the *C* rune in the signatures of the *Elene, Christ II,* and *Fates of the Apostles* represents not the noun, cēn (torch), but the adjective, cēne (keen, brave). Similarly the *U* rune represents not the noun, ūr (bull), but the possessive adjective, ūre (our). The device is ingenious. Cynewulf's purpose, announced in the personal passages of *Juliana* and the *Fates*, was the interweaving of his name in the text in such a way that his readers might easily recognize it, and pray for him, as he requests, 'by name.' The word values of the *C* and *U* runes would not easily or naturally fit into the established pattern of the signatures. But the use of these runes as homonyms of their names achieved his purpose.

In the reading of the Cynewulfian signatures, it is the *Y* rune which presents the greatest difficulty. Nothing whatever can be done with the meaning, 'bow', set forth in the *Rune Poem.* Moreover, it would in any case be unsound to force on the *Y* rune a meaning derived from the *Rune Poem*, not only because the *Rune Poem* is of late date and based on Old Norse, but also because the Old English *Y* rune probably did not originally designate a long *Y.*

2. See Chapter I, pp. 11-14.

Of the various substitute meanings proposed for the Y rune, some such interpretation as *yrmþu* (misery), or *yfel* (wretchedness), seems best substantiated by the context. Although the corrupt text of the signature in the *Fates* leaves the point somewhat uncertain, it seems probable that in that passage the Y rune means not misery or wretchedness, but miserable or wretched person.

The following translations of the four signatures indicate the manner in which Cynewulf employed the runes, and the general pattern of the signature passages:

Sorrowfully shall depart

C Y N   C, Y, and N;   the King will be stern,
   The Giver of victories,   when, stained with sins,

E W U   E, W, and U   shall await in terror
   What the Judge may decree,   according to deeds done,

L F   As life's reward.   L, F shall tremble,
   And wretchedly wait;   shall remember the woe,
   The wounds of sin   which early or late
   I wrought in the world.   (*Juliana*, 703-11)

C   Then the BRAVE shall in terror   tremble to hear
   The Ruler of heaven   denouncing in wrath
   All who aforetime   feebly obeyed Him

Y N   In days when AFFLICTION   and NEED might find help.
   Then many in terror   shall trembling await
   His dreadful judgments   according to their deeds.

W   In that day JOY   in earth's jewels shall vanish.
U   Long was OUR portion   of life's delights
L F   Locked in by WATER   the WEALTH of earth.
   In that day treasure   shall burn in the blaze.
(Christ, 797-808)

Till then there was conflict,

C   BRAVE warrior drooping,   burdened with woe,
   Though many a treasure   he gained in the mead-hall,

Y   And appled gold.   He bemoaned his AFFLICTION;
N   Comrade of NEED,   he endured distress,

E   That narrow rune,   while his HORSE before him
           Measured the mile paths,   proudly coursing
W   Adorned with jewels.   JOY is gone
           With passing years;   youth is vanished
           And olden pride.   The gleam of youth
U   Once was OURS.   Now former days
           After their appointed time   have passed.
L   Life's joy is gone   as WATER glides away,
F   The hurrying floods.   WEALTH is fleeting
           For all on earth.   (*Elene*, 1257-71)

           Here can a man   of cunning mind,
           Who has pleasure in poems,   find out for himself
F   Who shaped this lay.   WEALTH stands there at the end;
           Men enjoy it on earth,   but cannot keep it always.
U W   OUR worldly JOY fades,   and the fleeting beauty
L   Of the flesh decays,   as WATER glides away.
C Y   Then BRAVE and AFFLICTED   shall seek for strength
N   In the weary night-watches;   NEED constrains,
           The service of the King.   Now may you know
           Who in these words   was revealed to men.
                          (*Fates of the Apostles*, 96-106)

C. THE 'STORM' RIDDLES

Such evidence as the manuscript affords indicates that the 89 lines traditionally divided into *Riddles* 2 and 3, that is the second and third 'Storm' riddles, were regarded by the scribe as a single riddle. The riddles immediately preceding and immediately following (*Riddles* 1 *and* 4) begin with capitals, and conclude with end marks. In the 89 lines under consideration, however, the situation is different. If according to traditional division the first 15 lines of this passage are regarded as *Riddle* 2, and the succeeding 74 lines as *Riddle* 3, this division runs counter to the indications of the manuscript. The scribe has written these 89 lines as a unit. There is a capital at the beginning of the 89 line passage, and an end mark at its conclusion. But there is no end mark to conclude line

15, which would be the final line of *Riddle* 2, and there is no capital beginning line 16, which would be the first line of *Riddle* 3. Thus, the indications of the manuscript in two important details imply the unity of these 89 lines.[1]

These indications of the manuscript are corroborated by evidence implicit in the subject matter and form of the passage itself. It is noteworthy that these 89 lines conclude with a summarizing reference to the four regions of nature in which the force of the wind makes its influence felt:

> And so at times,   a powerful slave,
> I work under earth;   at times I descend
> Under surges of ocean;   at times from above
> I rouse the sea-streams;   at times I mount up
> And whirl the cloud-drift.   Widely I fare
> Strong and swift.

In these lines the energy of the wind is described as working under earth, under sea, above the surface of the sea, and among the clouds. Here then in the final lines of the passage we have a section summarizing a fourfold location of the wind's influence. But, if we divide the 89 line passage into *Riddles* 2 and 3, we have a situation in which the summarizing section at the end of *Riddle* 3 does not correspond to the subject matter it summarizes, since *Riddle* 3 describes the influence of the wind not in four regions but in three: under the earth, above the sea, and among the clouds. Development of the fourth category mentioned in the summary, the energy of wind working in and under the sea, is lacking. It is significant, then, that it is precisely this region of the wind's influence which is the material of description in *Riddle* 2. Only if we follow the indications of the manuscript and read the mag-

1. No evidence, unfortunately, can be derived from the spacing of lines in the manuscript, since the scribe leaves no spacing between riddles, except in so far as the subject matter of a riddle may not fill out its final line. In this case the final line of *Riddle* 2, so-called, is a complete line, and ends a page.

nificent poetry of these 89 lines not as two riddles, but as a single superb whole, does the text afford us the complete fourfold theme which the poet has summarized in his conclusion.

The unity of the passage is also indicated by the poet's use of a stylistic device of parallelism. In the united *Riddle* each of the four categories of description is concluded with a reference to the divine Power that rules over the stormy might of the wind. A fifth such reference ends the *Riddle*. Of these five references, three are phrased as rhetorical questions. The mistaking of the first of these interrogatives for a solution-formula has led to the traditional division of the 89 lines into *Riddle* 2 and *Riddle* 3.[2] Thus, both the scope of the subject matter and the manner of its development support the evidence of the manuscript that in these 89 lines we are dealing with a single riddle. No convincing reason is apparent for the traditional division of these lines.

The material of this superb 89 line *Riddle* dealing with the *wind* inherits many of its details from classical traditions of meteorology. The theory embodied in its second section that earthquakes are caused by violent winds imprisoned within the earth reflects and elaborates the classical tradition noted in Bede, *De Terrae Motu*, cap. 49, and in Isidore of Seville. It is the same tradition which was set forth in detail by Pliny (ii, 81) and by Lucretius (vi, 577-84). The Lucretian passage gives a vivid and extended exposition of the theory:

> There is also another cause of the same great trembling when wind or a very great force of air, either from without or arising within the earth itself, has thrown itself suddenly into the hollow places of the earth, and there in the great caverns first growls tumultuously and is

2. All the evidence is against Tupper's comment on the concluding lines of *Riddle* 2 (*Riddles of the Exeter Book*, p. 3, note); 'The preceding formula clearly marks the close of a riddle.' The question at the end of *Riddle* 2 is not the interrogative solution-formula, but a rhetorical question intended to suggest to the reader's mind God's mastery of wind and storm.

carried whirling about; afterwards the force thus excited
and driven outwards bursts forth, and at the same time
cleaving the earth asunder makes a great chasm.

That part of the tradition of the four provinces of the wind's influence which is likely to seem most fantastic to the modern mind
is the theory that ocean storms can be caused by the violent force
of the wind *within* and *under* the sea, though it should be noted
that something analogous to this tradition is set forth in Shelley's
Ode to the West Wind, and in the second paragraph of his note on
the poem. As in the case of the subterranean power of wind, this
submarine power was recognized in the classical tradition. Pliny's
Natural History (ii, 48) attributes this submarine violence particularly to the South Wind which, Pliny says, 'causes larger
waves than the Northeast because the former, being below, blows
from the bottom of the sea, but the latter from the top.[3] Lucretius
(vi, 439-41) goes into greater detail in describing the entrance of
the wind into the sea when released from a bursting cloud: 'As
soon as it has thrust down the teeming cloud upon the surface of
the main, the wind suddenly plunges itself in full force into the
water and stirs up the whole sea, compelling it to boil with a
huge noise.'[4] It is this tradition of the submarine power of wind
which is so vividly set forth in the subject matter of the first section
of the Old English *Riddle.*

The cause of thunder is explained in the *Riddle* (lines 54-7) as
the collision of wind-driven clouds, and the manner of their meeting is particularized in line 57 as being 'edge to edge.' This explanation of thunder occurs also in Lucretius (vi, 96-8) and it is
striking that a few lines later in the Latin poem the statement is
made that often clouds do not meet 'exactly front to front but pass
by the side in opposite directions, scraping their bodies as they drag,

3. Pliny, *Natural History,* ed. H. Rackham, Cambridge, Mass., 1938, p. 269.
4. Lucretius, *De Rerum Natura,* ed. W. H. D. Rouse, Cambridge, Mass., 1937, p. 475.

which causes that dry sound to grate upon the ear, long drawn out, until they have emerged from their confined quarters.'[5]

In addition to these general reflections of classical traditions of meteorology the Old English *wind Riddle* contains two brief but striking statements which furnish sharp parallels to passages in Pliny. In the earthquake passage of this *Riddle* (16-31), the description of shaking walls and toppling buildings is immediately followed by the arresting statement that 'the air seems still over the land, and the sea is silent, until I burst my way up out of bondage.' It is noteworthy that Pliny in discussing earthquakes similarly remarks: 'I think it indubitable that their cause is to be attributed to the winds, for tremors of the earth never occur except when the sea is calm and the sky so still that birds are unable to soar because all the breath that carries them has been withdrawn.'[6]

In lines 51-81 of the Old English *Riddle* we have a dramatic description of a violent storm of thunder and lightning in the course of which the 'black vessels of rain' empty themselves upon the earth. At the end of this superbly descriptive passage occurs the statement: 'Then low under heaven I bow to earth, and load on my back the burden I carry.' This striking image is certainly suggestive of the statement of Pliny: 'Empty winds sweep down, and then go back again with their plunder.'[7]

If the Old English 'Storm' *Riddle*, then, is read in the light of these classical analogues, it seems clear that the theme of the *Riddle* is *wind*, and that, whether or not the poet drew material directly from Lucretius and Pliny, his composition was governed by classical traditions of meteorology many of which are set forth in the *De Rerum Natura* and in the *Natural History*.

5. Ibid. p. 453.
6. Pliny, op. cit. ii, 81, pp. 324-5.
7. Pliny, op. cit. ii, 38.

A SELECTED BIBLIOGRAPHY

I. BIBLIOGRAPHIES

Heusinkveld, A. H., and Bashe, E. J.: *A Bibliographical Guide to Old English* (University of Iowa Humanistic Studies, IV, 5, 1931).

Renwick, W. L., and Orten, H.: *The Beginnings of English Literature to Skelton, 1509* (London and New York, 1940), pp. 133-219.

Cambridge Bibliography of English Literature (Cambridge, Eng., and New York, 1941), vol I, pp. 51-98.

Annual Bibliography of English Language and Literature (Cambridge, Eng., 1921-   ), *s.v.* Old English.

The Year's Work in English Studies (London, 1921-   ), *s.v.* Old English.

II. COMPLETE TEXTS

Grein, C. W. M.: *Bibliothek der angelsächsischen Poesie,* revised by R. P. Wülker, 3 vols. (Kassel, 1883-98).

Krapp, G. P. and Dobbie, E. v. K.. *The Anglo-Saxon Poetic Records* (New York, 1931-   ) I. *The Junius Manuscript;* II. *The Vercelli Book;* III. *The Exeter Book;* IV. *The Beowulf Manuscript* (in preparation); V. *The Paris Psalter and the Meters of Boethius;* VI. *The Minor Records.*

III. TEXTS OF INDIVIDUAL POEMS

Andreas and the Fates of the Apostles, ed. G. P. Krapp (Boston, 1906).

Anglo-Saxon and Norse Poems, ed. N. Kershaw (Cambridge, Eng., 1922). Text and translation of *Wanderer, Seafarer, Wife's Complaint, Husband's Message, Ruin, Brunanburh.*

Beowulf nebst dem Finnsburg-Bruchstück, ed. F. Holthausen (Heidelberg, 1905-6). 6th edition of the text (1929) contains also *Waldere, Deor,* and *Widsith.*

Beowulf, with the Finnsburg Fragment, ed. A. J. Wyatt and R. W. Chambers (Cambridge, Eng., 1914; 2nd edition, 1936).

Beowulf and the Fight at Finnsburg, ed. F. Klaeber (Boston, 1922; 3rd edition, 1936).

The Battle of Brunanburh, ed. A. Campbell (London, 1938).

Anglo-Saxon Charms, ed. F. Grendon (New York, 1930).

The Christ of Cynewulf, ed. A. S. Cook (Boston, 1900).

Christ and Satan, ed. M. D. Clubb (New Haven, 1925).

Deor, ed. K. Malone (London, 1933).

The Dream of the Rood, ed. B. Dickins and A. S. C. Ross (London, 1934).

The Old English Elene, Phoenix, and Physiologus, ed. A. S. Cook (New Haven, 1919).

Exodus and Daniel, ed. F. A. Blackburn (Boston, 1907).

Die ältere Genesis, ed. F. Holthausen (Heidelberg, 1914).

The Later Genesis and Other Old English and Old Saxon Texts Relating to the Fall of Man, ed. F. Klaeber (Heidelberg, 1913).

Gnomic Poetry in Anglo-Saxon, ed. B. C. Williams (New York, 1914).

Judith, ed. A. S. Cook (Boston, 1904).

Juliana, ed. W. Strunk (Boston, 1904).

Byrhtnoth and Maldon, ed. E. D. Laborde (London, 1936).

The Battle of Maldon, ed. E. V. Gordon (London, 1937).

The Poetical Dialogues of Solomon and Saturn, ed. R. J. Menner (New York, 1941).

The Riddles of the Exeter Book, ed. F. Tupper (Boston, 1910).

Old English Riddles, ed. A. J. Wyatt (London, 1912).

Runic and Heroic Poems of the Old Teutonic Peoples, ed. B. Dickins (Cambridge, Eng., 1915). Contains the *Rune Poem, Waldere, Finnsburg Fragment,* and *Deor.*

Three Northumbrian Poems: Cædmon's *Hymn,* Bede's *Death Song,* and the Leiden *Riddle,* ed. A. H. Smith (London, 1933).

Waldere, ed. F. Norman (London, 1933).

Widsith: A Study in Old English Heroic Legend, ed. R. W. Chambers (Cambridge, Eng., 1912).

Widsith, ed. K. Malone (London, 1936).

IV. TRANSLATIONS

GENERAL COLLECTIONS

Cook, A. S., and Tinker, C. B.: *Select Translations from Old English Poetry* (revised edition, Cambridge, 1926). In prose and verse. Contains selections from *Beowulf, Brunanburh* (Tennyson's rendering), *Maldon,* the elegies, selected riddles, charms, and gnomic verses, *Dream of the Rood, Judith, Phoenix,* and selections from *Christ, Genesis, Exodus, Andreas,* and *Elene.*

Faust, C. and Thompson, S.: *Old English Poems* (Chicago and New York, 1918). In alliterative verse. Contains *Widsith, Deor, Waldere, Finnsburg;* selected charms, riddles, and gnomic verse; the elegies; Cædmon's *Hymn,* Bede's *Death Song,* selections from *Genesis, Exodus, Elene, Christ.* Also the *Dream of the Rood, Judith, Phoenix, Brunanburh, Maldon, The Grave.*

Gollancz, I.: *The Exeter Book, an Anthology of Anglo-Saxon Poetry,* Part I (London, 1895). Continued by W. S. Mackie: *The Exeter Book,* Part II (London, 1934). A text and verse translation of each of the poems in the Exeter Manuscript.

Gordon, R. K.: *Anglo-Saxon Poetry* (London, 1926). In prose. A comprehensive collection, containing *Beowulf, Widsith,* the elegies, all the Cædmonian and Cynewulfian poems, *Physiologus, Judith, Brunanburh, Maldon,* and selections from the riddles, charms, and gnomic verses.

Hall, J. L.: *Judith, Phoenix, and Other Anglo-Saxon Poems* (New York, 1902). In alliterative verse. Contains, beside the poems named in the title, *Maldon, Brunanburh,* and *Andreas.*

Kemble, J. M.: *The Poetry of the Codex Vercellensis.* With an English translation (London, 1843-56).

Kershaw, N.: *Anglo-Saxon and Norse Poems* (Cambridge, Eng., 1922). Contains text and prose translation of *Wanderer, Seafarer, Wife's Complaint, Husband's Message, Ruin, Brunanburh.*

Malone, K.: *Ten Old English Poems* (Baltimore, 1941). In alliterative verse. Contains *Dream of the Rood, Wanderer, Seafarer, Wife's Lament, Eadwacer, Finnsburg, Brunanburh, Maldon, Widsith, Deor.*

Spaeth, J. D.: *Old English Poetry* (Princeton, 1922). In alliterative verse. Contains *Beowulf, Widsith, Dream of the Rood, Wanderer, Seafarer, Husband's Message, Brunanburh, Maldon;* selections from *Genesis, Exodus, Elene, Guthlac, Christ, Phoenix;* and selected charms, riddles, and gnomic verses.

Thorpe, B.: *Codex Exoniensis.* A collection of Anglo-Saxon poetry from a manuscript in the library of the Dean and Chapter of Exeter. Complete text with translation (London, 1842).

INDIVIDUAL WORKS

Andreas, R. K. Root (New Haven, 1899).

Beowulf and The Fight at Finnsburg, J. R. C. Hall (London, 1901). In prose. New edition (*Beowulf and the Finnsburg Fragment*) revised by C. L. Wrenn and J. R. R. Tolkien (London, 1940).

Beowulf and the Finnesburh Fragment, C. G. Child (Boston, 1904). In prose.

The Oldest English Epic, F. B. Gummere (New York, 1909). In alliterative verse. Contains *Beowulf, Finnsburg, Waldere, Deor, Widsith,* and the German *Hildebrandslied.* Also in Harvard Classics, vol. 49 (1910).

The Song of Beowulf, R. K. Gordon (New York, 1923). In prose. Included in Gordon's *Anglo-Saxon Poetry* (London, 1926).

Beowulf, W. E. Leonard (New York, 1923). In meter imitating the Nibelungen couplet.

Beowulf, A. Strong (London, 1925). In the long rhymed couplets used by William Morris in *Sigurd the Volsung.*

Old English and Medieval Literature, G. H. Gerould (New York, 1933). In alliterative verse. Contains *Beowulf,* excerpts from Cynewulf, and *Wanderer.*

Beowulf, C. W. Kennedy (New York, 1940). In alliterative verse.

Battle of Brunanburh, Tennyson, in *Ballads and Other Poems* (1880).

The Cædmon Poems, C. W. Kennedy (London, 1916). In prose. Contains *Cædmon's Hymn, Genesis, Exodus, Daniel, Christ and Satan.*

Cynewulf's Christ, with a Modern Rendering, I. Gollancz (London, 1892). Text with translation.

The Christ of Cynewulf, C. H. Whitman (Boston, 1900).

The Poems of Cynewulf, C. W. Kennedy (London, 1910). In prose. Contains *Andreas, Christ, Dream of the Rood, Elene, Fates of the Apostles, Guthlac, Juliana, Phoenix.*

Old English Elegies, C. W. Kennedy (Princeton, 1936). In alliterative verse. Contains *Wanderer, Seafarer, Ruin, Deor, Wife's Lament, Husband's Message, Beowulf* 2231-70.

The Elene of Cynewulf, L. H. Holt (New Haven, 1904).

Fight at Finnsburg. See under *Beowulf.*

The Grave, Longfellow, *Poetical Works,* Cambridge edition, p. 618.

Juliana, H. S. Murch, in *Journal of English and Germanic Philology,* v, 303-19 (1904).

The Old English Physiologus, A. S. Cook (New Haven, 1921). Text with translation.

Runic Poem. In B. Dickins: *Runic and Heroic Poems* (Cambridge, Eng., 1915). Text with translation.

Widsith, R. W. Chambers (Cambridge, Eng., 1912). Text with translation.

V. CRITICAL STUDIES

Brandl, A.: *Geschichte der altenglischen Literatur* (Strassburg, 1908).

Brooke, S. A.: *The History of Early English Literature* (New York, 1892).

Brooke, S. A.: *English Literature from the Beginning to the Norman Conquest* (London, 1898).

Cambridge History of English Literature, vol. 1 (Cambridge, Eng., 1907). Chapters I-VII.

Chadwick, H. M.: *The Heroic Age* (Cambridge, Eng., 1912).

Chambers, R. W.: *Beowulf, an Introduction*, revised edition (Cambridge, Eng., 1932).

Chambers, R. W.: 'The Lost Literature of Mediaeval England,' in *The Library*, 4th ser., 5. 293-321 (London, 1925).

Earle, J.: *Anglo-Saxon Literature* (London, 1884).

Gerould, G. H.: *Saints' Legends* (Boston, 1916).

Girvan, R.: *Beowulf and the Seventh Century* (London, 1935).

Hart, W. M.: *Ballad and Epic* (Boston, 1907).

Ker, W. P.: *Epic and Romance* (London, 1896).

Lawrence, W. W.: *Beowulf and Epic Tradition* (Cambridge, 1928).

Mead, W. E.: 'Color in Old English Poetry,' in *Publications of the Modern Language Association*, XIV, 169-206 (1899).

Panzer, F.: *Studien zur germanischen Sagengeschichte. I. Beowulf* (Munich, 1910).

Phillpotts, B.: 'Wyrd and Providence in Anglo-Saxon Thought,' in *Essays and Studies by Members of the English Association* (Oxford, 1928).

Pons, E.: *Le thème et le Sentiment de la Nature dans la Poésie Anglo-Saxonne* (Strasbourg, 1925).

Pope, J. C.: *The Rhythm of Beowulf* (New Haven, 1942).

Ricci, A.: 'The Anglo-Saxon Eleventh-Century Crisis,' in *Review of English Studies*, V, 1-11 (1929).

Ricci, A.: 'The Chronology of Anglo-Saxon Poetry,' in *Review of English Studies*, V, 257-66 (1929).

Sarrazin, G.: *Von Kädmon bis Kynewulf* (Berlin, 1913).

Scholz, H. v.d.M.: *The Kenning in Anglo-Saxon and Old Norse Poetry* (Utrecht and Oxford, 1929).

Smithson, G. A.: *The Old English Christian Epic* (Berkeley, 1910).

ten Brink, B.: *Early English Literature,* translated H. M. Kennedy (London, 1883).

Wardale, E. E.: *Chapters on Old English Literature* (London, 1935).

Williams, M.: *Word-Hoard* (New York, 1940).

Williams, R. A.: *The Finn Episode in Beowulf* (Cambridge, Eng., 1924).

Wyld, H. C.: 'Diction and Imagery in Anglo-Saxon Poetry,' in *Essays and Studies by Members of the English Association* (Oxford, 1925).

VI. History and Culture

Aberg, N.: *The Anglo-Saxons in England during the Early Centuries after the Invasion* (Uppsala, 1926).

Anderson, L. H.: *The Anglo-Saxon Scop* (Toronto, 1903).

Anglo-Saxon Chronicle, translated J. Ingram (London, 1912).

Baugh, A. C.: *History of the English Language* (New York, 1935). Chapters II-IV.

Bede: *Ecclesiastical History of the English People,* translated A. M. Sellar (London, 1907).

Bright, W.: *Early English Church History* (Oxford, 1897).

Brown, G. B.: *The Arts in Early England,* 6 vols. (London, 1903-30).

Chadwick, H. M.: *Studies on Anglo-Saxon Institutions* (Cambridge, Eng., 1905).

Chadwick, H. M.: *The Origin of the English Nation* (Cambridge, Eng., 1907).

Chambers, R. W.: *England before the Norman Conquest* (London, 1926).

Cockayne, T. O.: *Leechdoms, Wort-Cunning, and Starcraft of Early England,* 3 vols. (London, 1864-6).

Dale, E.: *National Life and Character in the Mirror of Early English Literature* (Cambridge, Eng., 1907).

Gummere, F. B.: *Germanic Origins* (New York, 1892), reissued as *Founders of England,* with supplementary notes by F. P. Magoun (New York, 1930).

Hodgkin, R. H.: *A History of the Anglo-Saxons,* 2 vols. (Oxford, 1935). To the death of Alfred.

Jiriczek, O. L.: *Northern Hero Legends,* translated M. B. Smith (London, 1902).

Kendrick, T. D.: *A History of the Vikings* (London, 1930).

Leeds, E. T.: *The Archeology of the Anglo-Saxon Settlements* (Oxford, 1913).

Mawer, A.: *The Vikings* (Cambridge, Eng., 1913).

Olrik, A.: *The Heroic Legends of Denmark*, translated and revised by L. M. Hollander (New York, 1919).

Oman, C.: *England before the Norman Conquest* (London, 1910).

Payne, J. F.: *English Medicine in Anglo-Saxon Times* (Oxford, 1904).

Plummer, C.: *Life and Times of Alfred the Great* (Oxford, 1902).

Pollock, F.: 'English Law before the Norman Conquest,' in A. Bowker: *Alfred the Great*, pp. 209-39 (London, 1899).

Quennell, M. and C. H. B.: *Everyday Life in Anglo-Saxon, Viking, and Norman Times* (London, 1926).

Schütte, G.: *Our Forefathers: The Gothonic Nations*, translated J. Young, 2 vols. (Cambridge, Eng., 1929-33).

Stenton, F. M.: 'The Danes in England,' in *Proceedings of the British Academy*, XIII, 203-46 (1927).

Thompson, A. H., editor: *Bede, his Life, Times, and Writings* (Oxford, 1935).

Vinogradoff, P.: *English Society in the Eleventh Century* (Oxford, 1908).